A FULL AND CORRECT ACCOUNT OF THE MILITARY OCCURRENCES OF THE LATE WAR BETWEEN GREAT BRITAIN AND THE UNITED STATES OF AMERICA;

WITH

AN APPENDIX,

AND

PLATES.

By WILLIAM JAMES,

AUTHOR OF "A FULL AND CORRECT ACCOUNT OF THE CHIEF NAVAL OCCURRENCES, &c."

Alterum alterius auxilio eget.

SALLUST.

IN TWO VOLUMES.

VOL. II.

London:

PRINTED FOR THE AUTHOR:

AND SOLD BY BLACK, KINGSBURY, PARBURY, AND ALLEN, LEADENHALL-STREET; JAMES M. RICHARDSON, CORNHILL; JOHN BOOTH, DUKE-STREET, PORTLAND-PLACE; AND ALL OTHER BOOKSELLERS.

1818.

Printed and bound by Antony Rowe Ltd, Eastbourne

MILITARY OCCURRENCES,

&c. &c.

CHAPTER XI.

British force on the Niagara in October, 1813—Attack upon the piquets—Effects of the surrender of the right division—Major-general Vincent's retreat to Burlington—His orders from the commander-in-chief to retire upon Kingston—Fortunate contravention of those orders—General Harrison's arrival at, and departure from Fort-George—Association of some Upper Canada militia after being disembodied—Their gallant attack upon, and capture of, a band of plundering traitors—General M'Clure's shameful conduct towards the Canadian inhabitants—Colonel Murray's gallant behaviour—Its effect upon general M'Clure—A Canadian winter—Night-conflagration of Newark by the Americans—M'Clure's abandonment of Fort-George, and flight across the river—Arrival of lieutenant-general Drummond—Assault upon, and capture of Fort-Niagara—Canadian prisoners found there—Retaliatory destruction of Lewistown,

Youngstown, Manchester, and Tuscarora—Attack upon Buffaloe and Black Rock, and destruction of those villages—American resentment against general M'Clure—Remarks upon the campaign; also upon the burning of Newark, and the measures pursued in retaliation.

HAVING brought the campaign of 1813 to a close upon the northern, and north-western, Canadian frontiers, the operations along both shores of the Niagara come, next, to be detailed. Major-general Vincent, who again commanded, in the absence of general De Rottenburg, the centre-division, had received, since the middle of September, a reinforcement of the 100th regiment; in order to counter-balance the reduction his force would sustain in the departure of the 49th and 104th regiments, already noticed.* The general's head-quarters were at the Cross Roads; and the piquets of his advanced corps, which was commanded by colonel Murray, occasionally showed themselves in the town of Newark. From the American accounts only we learn, that, on the 6th of October, "about 500 militia-volunteers and about 150 Indians, commanded by colonel Chapin," attacked the piquet-guard of the British; and, "after an hour and a half's hard-fighting," drove it upon the main-body; when "the whole British army,

* See Vol. I. p. 261.

consisting of 1100 men, with the great general Vincent, at their head, fled into the woods." The British are declared to have sustained a loss of 32 in killed only, and the Americans of four killed and wounded.* This is the way the "literary gentlemen" of the United States contrive to fill their "histories." Colonel, or doctor Chapin (for he professes, and is equally mischievous in, both characters) had lately escaped from the British,† and, for that exploit, been promoted; probably by the secretary at war himself, as he was known to have been in the neighbourhood of the Niagara, while the Montreal expedition was preparing.

On the 9th of October intelligence of the disaster that had befallen the right division, reached the head-quarters of the centre-division; and caused general Vincent, after destroying considerable quantities of stores, provisions, and Indian goods, to retreat, with his troops, towards Burlington Heights: where colonel Proctor joined him with the small remnant of his division. As soon as general Vincent and his troops had got well on their way to Burlington, major-general M'Clure, with the whole of his force, numbering 2700 men, besides Indians, marched a few miles along the road, and back. This was not without an object; for we were afterwards told, that

* Hist. of the War, p. 158. † See Vol. I. p. 218.

"general M'Clure, with the New York militia, volunteers, and Indians, succeeded in driving the British army from the vicinity of Fort-George, and pursued them as far as the Twelve-mile Creek."*

Major-general Proctor's discomfiture reached the head quarters of the commander in chief about the middle of October; and orders were instantly forwarded to major-general Vincent, directing him to commence upon his retreat without delay, and to evacuate all the British posts beyond Kingston. Some delay did fortunately take place, owing chiefly to counter-orders, not from head-quarters; and a council of war, summoned at Burlington Heights, came to the noble resolution of not moving a step to the rear, in the present conjuncture of affairs on the peninsula. Fatal, indeed, would have been the retreat. There was still a considerable number of sick, both at Burlington Heights and at York; and, considering the season of the year, and the state of the roads, the whole of them must have been left to the protection of the enemy. Nor, for the same reason, could the ordnance, ordnance-stores, baggage, and provisions, have followed the army; and yet the garrison of Kingston, upon which place the troops were directed to retire, had, at this time, scarcely a week's provision in

* History of the War, p. 158.

store. This abandonment of territory so soon following up the affair at the Moravian village, what would the Indians have thought of us?—In short, it will not bear reflection.

Towards the end of October, among other sacrifices caused by the dread of general Harrison's zeal and promptitude, two companies of the 100th regiment, which had been stationed at Charlotteville, in the London district of Upper Canada, were ordered to evacuate that post, and join the main body of the centre-division of the army at Burlington, distant 60 miles. Orders were at the same time issued, to disembody and disarm the militia. The officer who had this duty to perform, having ascertained that a large body of traitors and Americans had been plundering the houses of the inhabitants, while the latter were away in the service of their country, left a supply of arms and ammunition with some of the militia officers and privates. These, in number 45, immediately formed themselves into an association; and marched, with lieutenant-colonel Bostwick, of the Oxford militia, at their head, against the marauders; whom they fortunately fell in with on the Lake Erie shore, about nine miles from Dover. An engagement ensued; in which several of the gang were killed and wounded, and 18 taken prisoners. These 18 were afterwards tried at Ancaster for high treason; and all, except three, convicted.

Eight of the 15, so convicted, underwent the penalty of the law. The remaining seven were respited, to await the prince regent's final decision; and have since been transported. How highly, and yet how justly, this well-planned and well-executed enterprise was appreciated by the president of Upper Canada, will be seen in the general orders which he caused to be issued upon the occasion.*

About the 1st of November general Harrison arrived at Fort-George, with about 1700 of his troops; who, agreeably to Mr. Secretary Armstrong's orders, were immediately quartered upon the inhabitants of Newark. In the course of November, both general Harrison and colonel Scott, with their respective corps, embarked on board commodore Chauncey's fleet for Sackett's Harbor; leaving general M'Clure, with his 2700 militia, and a few regular troops, in charge of Fort-George. General M'Clure, now having the entire command to himself, and being disappointed, notwithstanding all the intrigues of his friend Wilcocks, in his endeavours "to secure the friendship and co-operation of the inhabitants," began sending the most obstinate of the latter across to the American side, and then set about pillaging and destroying the farm-houses and barns in the neighbourhood of Fort-George.

* App. No. 1.

PAINTED BY WOOD. PUBLISH'D BY JOSEPH DELAPLAINE S.W. CORNER OF CHESNUT & SEVENTH S[TS] PHILAD[A] 1814. ENGRAVED BY W.R. JONES.

MAJOR GENERAL HARRISON.

These atrocities were represented to major-general Vincent, and he was strongly urged to allow a small regular and Indian force to be marched against general M'Clure. Colonel Murray finally gained his point; and, taking with him 379 rank and file of the 100th regiment, about 20 volunteers, and 70 of the western Indians, led by colonel Elliot, moved forward on the road towards the Forty-mile Creek; beyond which point he had been ordered not to proceed. The advance of this small detachment soon reached the ears of general M'Clure, who had taken post at the Twenty-mile Creek, and who now retreated, in haste, to a position somewhat nearer to Fort-George. Colonel Murray obtained fresh permission to extend his march to the Twenty-mile Creek, and subsequently to the Twelve-mile Creek. These movements had driven the American general and his men to Fort-George; and then commenced a scene of devastation and horror, of which no adequate idea can be formed, except by such as had the misery to be spectators. How, then, shall we hope to succeed in describing it?

The winter of 1813, according to general Wilkinson, set in earlier than usual. Lambert, in his account of the climate of Lower Canada, says that Fahrenheit's thermometer is sometimes 36 degrees below 0, and that the mean of the cold in winter is about 0.* The climate of Upper, is certainly not quite so rigorous as that of Lower Canada; but yet the mildest winter of the former, bears no comparison whatever to the severest winter of this country. For several days previous to the 10th of December, the weather in Upper Canada had been unusually severe, and a deep snow lay on the ground. Towards night-fall on that day, general M'Clure gave about half an hour's notice to the inhabitants of Newark, that he should burn down their village. Few of the poor people believed that the wretch was in earnest. Soon, however, came round the merciless firemen. Out of the 150 houses of which Newark had consisted, 149 were levelled to the dust! Such articles of furniture and other valuables as the incendiaries could not, and the inhabitants had neglected or been unable to, carry away, shared the general fate. Of counsellor Dickson's library, which had cost him between 5 and 600*l.* sterling, scarcely a book escaped the ravages of the devouring element. Mr. Dickson was, at this time, a prisoner in the enemy's territory; and his wife lay on a sick bed. The villains—how shall we proceed?—took up the poor lady, bed and all, and placed her upon the snow before her own door; where, shivering with cold, she beheld, if she could see at all,

* Lambert's Travels, Vol. I. p. 107.

her house and all that was in it consumed to ashes. Upwards of 400 helpless women and children, without provisions, and in some instances with scarcely cloaths upon their backs, were thus compelled, after being the mournful spectators of the destruction of their habitations, to seek shelter at a distance; and that in such a night, too!—The reader's imagination must supply the rest.

In what way will the American historian, or will he at all, describe the conflagration of Newark? Not one word about it appears in doctor Smith's book. Mr. Thomson says briefly: "General M'Clure determined on destroying the town of Newark."* It is Mr. O'Connor whom we have to thank, for being explicit upon this point. "As a measure deemed necessary to the safety of the troops, the town of Newark was burned. 'This act,' said general M'Clure, (proceeds Mr. O'Connor) 'however distressing to the inhabitants and my feelings, was *by order of the secretary of war*, and I believe, at the same time, proper.' The inhabitants, (continues Mr. O'Connor,) had 12 hours' notice to remove their effects, and such as chose to cross the river were provided with all the necessaries of life."†

With the knowledge that Mr. Secretary Armstrong had recently been in the neighbourhood of, if not at Fort-George, we can readily sup-

* Sketches of the War, p. 188. † Hist. of the War, p. 158.

pose general M'Clure acted, as he says, by the former's orders. This confers additional atrocity upon the offence; but, on that head, we shall forbear comments. "Distressing to my feelings:"—was not some such language used by captain David Porter, of the American navy, after he and his crew had been massacring the natives of the small island of Nooaheevah, which he had unfortunately visited during his celebrated cruize to the Pacific?* As to the "twelve hours' notice," the liberty to "cross the river," and the promise that the poor people should be "provided with all the necessaries of life," we give Mr. O'Connor himself credit for the whole; and can only attribute his not having come forward with a better excuse, to a sudden qualm of conscience, or perhaps to a momentary torpor in those inventive faculties, on most other occasions so serviceable to him.

The nearer colonel Murray approached to the neigbourhood of Fort-George, the louder were the complaints of the people against the "lawless banditti" by whom they had been oppressed. That active officer immediately wrote to general Vincent; and, anticipating the answer he should receive, dashed forward to Fort-George. General M'Clure's scouts gave him timely intelligence of the approach of the British; and the cowardly wretch, with the whole of his minions,

* Quart. Review, Vol. XIII. p. 364—9.

abandoned Fort George, and fled across the river. Not the slightest opposition did he make; although the fortifications had been so much strengthened, since the capture of the fort in the preceding May, that the American commander, with only half the force he possessed, might have maintained a regular siege. He was in too much haste to destroy the whole of his magazines, or even to remove his tents; of which a sufficiency for 1500 men were left standing. Colonel Murray, in his first letter, states that general M'Clure had passed over his cannon, as well as stores.* But, in a second letter, he mentions that one 18, four 12, and several 9-pounders, together with a large supply of shot, were found in the ditch. Even the destruction of the new barracks, which we had recently erected on the Niagara, was not deemed, by Mr. Armstrong and general M'Clure, so "necessary in the military operations there," as Mr. Munro has since declared the burning of Newark to have been: consequently, the former were allowed to remain untouched. The indignant feelings of the soldiers, as they beheld the smoking ruins of what was once, as acknowledged by all, a beautiful and flourishing village, would have burst with a heavy vengeance upon the heads of the American general and his troops, had they not followed up their atrocious conduct by a precipitate flight.

* App. No. II.

Mr. O'Connor informs us that "a council of war," that fatal damper of American military ardor, decided that Fort-George "was not tenable." Of the guns, or the fortifications, he says nothing. Mr. Thomson concurs in opinion that the post was "untenable;" and gives as a reason, that the British force outside consisted of 1500 regulars, and at least 700 Indians;" calls general M'Clure's troops "the remnant of an army;" and then informs us, that the American general "determined on destroying the batteries;"* leaving to doctor Smith to advance the next step; who, as if to confirm his predecessor's discernment, says roundly: "Fort-George was soon afterwards abandoned, and *blown up*, by general M'Clure."†

Early in November lieutenant-general Drummond and major-general Rial had arrived from England; the former to relieve major-general De Rottenburg, in the military command and presidency of the upper province. These officers had been detained below, to see the end of general Wilkinson's expedition. That business concluded, they moved on to Kingston and York; at which latter place general Drummond was sworn into office; and then, along with major-general Rial, hastened to join the centre division of the army. Both generals arrived at St. David's, major-general Vincent's present

* Sketches of the War, p. 188. † History of the War, p. 265.

head-quarters, soon after the capture of Fort-George; and at a time when colonel Murray's prompt and decisive measures had given a new aspect to affairs.

This officer contemplated a retaliatory attack upon the opposite lines; to which plan general Drummond yielded, not only his approbation, but, rightly judging that the delay of waiting for permission from the commander-in-chief, then at Quebec,* might recover the enemy from his panic, and thus defeat the object,—his immediate sanction. No more than two batteaux were on the Niagara shore, the remainder were in Burlington Bay. Captain Kerby, an active militia-officer, under the orders of captain Elliott, the deputy assistant-quarter-master-general, contrived, notwithstanding the inclemency of the weather, and the badness of the roads, to effect the carriage, by land, of a sufficiency of batteaux for the enterprise.

Every thing being prepared by the evening of the 18th, the troops destined for the assault, consisting of a small detachment of royal artillery, the grenadiers of the royal Scots, the flank companies of the 41st†, and the effective men of the 100th regiment, amounting, altogether, to fewer than 550 rank and file, and commanded by colonel Murray, crossed the river on that night, and landed at the Five-mile Meadows, about

* Distant 530 miles.

† 2d Battalion which had recently arrived from Europe.

three miles above Fort-Niagara. At about four o'clock the troops commenced their march; and the advance, consisting of the grenadiers of the 100th regiment, and a small party of the royal artillery, succeeded in cutting off two of the enemy's piquets; as well as in surprising the sentries on the glacis, and at the gate, by which means the watch-word was obtained, and the entrance into the fort greatly facilitated. While three companies of the 100th, under captain Martin, stormed the eastern demi-bastion, five companies of the same regiment, under colonel Murray in person, assisted by lieutenant-colonel Hamilton of the 100th, entered the fort by the main gate, which had been left open for the return of the guard from relieving sentries. The American main guard now rushed out of the south-east block-house, and fired a volley or two; and some musketry was fired from another stone building within the fort; but the bayonet overpowered all resistance, and the British union, in a few seconds more, waived triumphantly upon the stone-tower of Fort-Niagara.

The number of prisoners taken, including two officers and 12 rank and file wounded, amounted to one captain, nine lieutenants, two ensigns, one surgeon, one commissary, 12 serjeants, and 318 rank and file. Add to this number 65 in killed,* and "about 20 that effected their escape," and we have 429 for the

* Appendix, No. 3.

garrison of Fort-Niagara. Upon the different defences were mounted no fewer than 27 pieces of ordnance; and, among them, some 32-pound carronades. The arsenal contained upwards of 3000 stands of arms, and many rifles. The ordnance and commissariat stores were immense; and so was the quantity of army-clothing and camp-equipage. A portion of the articles consisted, no doubt, of such as general M'Clure, in his flight, had brought across from Fort-George. Had the garrison afforded an opportunity for a greater display of gallantry on the part of the assailants, the capture of Fort-Niagara, a post by far the strongest of any on the inland frontiers, would have been a still more brilliant achievement: it was no slight consolation, however, that we managed the business with the trifling loss of six men killed, and five wounded; including the gallant projector and commander of the enterprize, colonel Murray, severely in the wrist. Nor is it without feelings of exultation, that we compare the number of British sent against Fort-Niagara, with the number of Americans,—covered too by the fire from a fleet of ships, and from that same fort,—sent against Fort-George,* so much its inferior in point of strength and armament.

The deputy incendiary M'Clure, with well-grounded apprehension of British vengeance, had, since the very day of his crossing from Fort-

* See Vol. I. p. 153.

George, ordered the commandant of Fort-Niagara to prepare to defend the post, and be with "a proportion of hand-grenades in the different block-houses."* He did not consider the disaster as "attributable to any want of troops, but to gross neglect in the commanding officer of the fort, captain Leonard, in not preparing, being ready, and looking out for, the expected attack." † General M'Clure describes the British that captured Fort-Niagara, as of "great force," and as consisting of regulars and "Indians;" although not an Indian was at the attack; for even the "Indian chief," Norton, who was present, is a Scotchman. The official letter then states that, on entering the fort, we "commenced a most horrid slaughter." This is utterly false, as respects the implication intended. The piquets and sentries, as in all cases of assault or surprise, were bayonetted; and so were those within the fort who made any resistance. The fort was entered in darkness, and a formidable opposition expected; particularly as general M'Clure had himself been boasting, that the block-houses and defences within-side, aided by the 32-pounder and other carronades, which were so mounted as, if necessary, to be fired inwards, would enable a small garrison to drive out or destroy 1500 British. No musket whatever was discharged by the latter; nor, from the moment that the soldiers could be

* App. No. 5. † Ibid, No. 4.

certain of all resistance having ceased, was a single bayonet employed.

Mr. O'Connor describes the assaulting party as "regulars, militia, and Indians, to the number, by the most probable account, of 1500 men," who, he says, entered the fort while the men were nearly all asleep, "killing, without mercy or discrimination, those who came in their way."* Doctor Smith considers the capture of Fort-Niagara to be a sore subject; therefore merely states that, in the month of *January*, it "was surprised and captured." Mr. Thomson begins his account by stating, that the fort was "garrisoned by 324 sick and effective men"; although we took, as prisoners, 20 more than that number, exclusive of those that had escaped and been killed. He proceeds: "At 4 o'clock on the morning of the 19th, the enemy, 400 in number, crossed the Niagara, under colonel Murray, and approached the principal gate which was then open."—We find no "*Errata*" referred to in Mr. Thomson's book, but must consider that the printer has made "400" of what was intended for "1400."—This editor, caught by the word "Indians" in the official letter, then says: "Accompanied by his Indian warriors, he rushed furiously in upon the garrison." "On entering the garrison," continues Mr. Thomson, "colonel Murray

* History of the War, p. 159.

received a wound in the arm; after which he yielded the command to colonel Hamilton,—under whose superintendance, the women of the garrison were stripped of their clothing, and many of them killed, and the persons of the dead officers treated with shocking indignity."*—Never was so base a falsehood! But who, out of the United States, will believe this pettifogging scribbler's story? and as to those in the United States who may do so, they are too insignificant, we are sure, to give the gallant colonel the slightest uneasiness.

Among the valuables found in Fort-Niagara, were eight respectable Canadian inhabitants; who, in direct violation of civilized warfare, had been taken from their peaceful dwellings to be immured within the walls of a prison. That no doubt may remain of the fact, we here present the reader with the names of six out of the eight individuals, who were thus so happily released from bondage. The names are: Thomas Dickon, Samuel Street, and J. M. Cawdle, esquires; Messrs. John Tompson, John Macfarlane, and Peter M'Micking; the latter 80 years of age.

On the same morning on which Fort-Niagara was carried, major-general Rial, taking with him detachments from the royal Scots and 41st regiments, amounting to about 500 rank and file, crossed over to Lewistown. About 500

* Sketches of the War, p. 189; and *third* edition!

Indian warriors had preceded this force, and had a skirmish with, and completely routed, a detachment of American militia, under a major Bennett; in which affair the latter lost eight men killed. No sooner had the Americans abandoned Lewistown, than the Indians commenced setting fire to it. Major-general Rial, who found no enemy to contend with, took possession of a 12 and 6-pounder gun, with travelling carriages, and every thing complete; also a considerable quantity of small arms, some ammunition, nine barrels of powder, and about 200 barrels of flour. The small villages of Youngstown, Manchester, and the Indian Tuscarora, as soon as the inhabitants had deserted them, shared the fate of Lewistown.

There is no doubt that the Indians committed many enormities; but who could have told Mr. M'Clure,—himself the origin of all that happened,—that the savages were "headed by British officers painted."? Mr. O'Connor is the only one of our three editors who has repeated this story. Major-general Rial and his troops passed on to Fort-Schlosser;* which place they destroyed: they then proceeded as far as Tonewanto Creek,* which is within 10 miles of Buffaloe; but, finding the bridge broken, returned, and crossed over to Queenstown.

The exposed state of the American Niagara-

* See Plate I.

frontier began to excite serious alarm; and general M'Clure, too dastardly to meet in the field the avengers of the conflagration of Newark, had requested major-general Hall to take the command of the regulars and militia, then assembling from all parts, to repel any further encroachments. On the morning of the 23d the major-general fixed his head-quarters at Batavia, a village about 40 miles from Buffaloe. On the morning of the 29th we find him at Buffaloe, reviewing his troops; which then amounted to 2011 men, but were afterwards, it appears, considerably reduced by desertion.*

On the 28th lieutenant-general Drummond took up his head-quarters at Chippeway; and, on the next day, within two miles of Fort-Erie. Having reconnoitred the enemy's position at Black Rock, the lieutenant-general determined to attack him. Accordingly, on the night of the 30th, major-general Rial, having under his command four companies of the 8th, 250 men of the 41st, the light company of the 89th, and the grenadiers of the 100th, regiments, numbering, with 50 volunteer-militia, about 590 rank and file, also a body of Indian warriors, not exceeding 120, crossed the Niagara, and landed, without opposition, about two miles below Black Rock. The light-company of the 89th advanced along the road, and secured an

* Hist. of the War, p. 161.

American piquet, as well as the bridge over the Conjuichity,* or Schojeoquady,† the boards of which had already been loosened, preparatory to their removal. The 250 men of the 41st, and the grenadiers of the 100th, were joined to the light-company of the 89th; and the whole, amounting to about 400 rank and file, in order to secure the passage of the bridge, took up a position, a short distance beyond it, at a place called the Sailor's battery. In the course of the night several attempts were made by general Hall's militia to dislodge the British from their position; but, "owing to the darkness of the night, and the confusion into which the militia were thrown by the enemy's fire,"* every attempt failed.

At day-dawn on the 31st, the royal Scots, about 800 strong, along with a detachment of the 19th dragoons, the whole commanded by lieutenant-colonel Gordon, of the royals, crossed over to land above Black Rock, for the purpose of turning the enemy's position, while major-general Rial's force should attack him from below. Unfortunately, owing to some error in the pilots, several of the boats grounded; and became, in consequence, exposed to a heavy and destructive fire from one 6, one 24, and two 12-pounders, at the Black Rock battery, and from about 600 men‡ drawn up on the beach,

* App. No. 6. † See Plate I. ‡ Hist. of the War, p. 161.

flanked by a number of Indians. The gallant royals, thus sitting in their grounded boats, to be shot at like targets, lost 13 rank and file, killed, and three serjeants, and 29 rank and file wounded. Fortunately, a few well-directed shots from five field-pieces stationed on the opposite shore, and the near approach of major-general Rial's force upon the enemy's right, caused a favorable diversion.

By this time a considerable force of militia, certainly not fewer than 1500, had assembled in the town; but, after a short resistance, the Americans abandoned Black Rock and its batteries, and fled towards Buffaloe, about 2½ miles distant. To this town they were followed, in close pursuit; and, although protected by a field-piece posted on a height that commanded the road, made but a slight resistance, ere they fled in all directions to the neighbouring woods.

The British captured at these two posts eight pieces of ordnance, including a 24 and 18-pounder. For want of adequate means of conveyance the public stores, consisting of considerable quantities of clothing, spirits, and flour, were obliged to be destroyed. All the inhabitants having left Black Rock and Buffaloe, the two villages shared the fate of Newark. The United States' vessels Chippeway, Little Belt, and Trippe, were found aground near Buffaloe Creek; and, along with their stores, were also committed to the flames.

This fact is scarcely noticed by the American editors; although the smallest of these three vessels, when captured from us a short time previous,* was, with the utmost gravity, styled, —"His Britannic majesty's schooner Chippeway."† The British loss on this occasion, including that of the royal Scots already given, amounted to 31 killed, 72 wounded, and nine missing. The American loss does not appear; except where general Hall states, that "many valuables were lost.‡ Owing to the nimbleness of the American militia, and the contiguity of the woods, only 130 prisoners were made; among whom was the notorious colonel, or doctor Chapin. Major-general Hall himself, with nearly 300 of the most pursy of his soldiers, brought up at the Eleven-mile Creek, about three miles from Buffaloe.

The nine *missing* of our troops were some careless fellows who had strayed to the margin of the village, and were captured on the 1st of January, by an American scouting party, headed by a captain Stone. Two officers of this detachment were surprised, while on horseback, by a patrole of the 19th light dragoons, and one, "lieutenant Totman, of the Canadian volunteers," was shot. Mr. Thomson declars, that

* James's Naval Occurrences, p. 286.

† Nav. Hist. of the United States, Vol. II. p. 242.

‡ App. No. 7.

lieutenants Riddle and Totman "would have given themselves up, but for the treatment which other prisoners on the Niagara had recently received."* These American editors are never at a loss. The fact is, Mr. Totman was like his friend Mr. Wilcocks, an Irishman, and an inhabitant of Upper Canada, where he had resided many years. With a halter thus before his eyes, he had a much more powerful inducement than is alleged by Mr. Thomson, for not delivering himself up to the British.

Mr. Thomson is very loud in his complaints against the "timid militia," assembled at Buffaloe and Black Rock. Nor is he so without reason; for, in proof of the numerous population in and around those villages, we find it stated by a writer from Batavia, under date of December the 23d, that 5000 men could be assembled in 24 hours: nay, Mr. O'Connor himself fixes the number of sufferers, by the conflagration, alone, at "12000 persons."† Nor does this number include such as resided even a short distance beyond the narrow slip of land, which was the scene of the British incursion. It was not a week after the pusillanimous behaviour of the American militia upon this frontier, that Mr. Wright, member of congress for Maryland, in a speech which was to prove, that the army of

* Sketches of the War, p. 192.

† Hist. of the War, p. 164.

the United States had "been marvellously successful," said thus: "There was no evidence against the courage or conduct of our army; which had displayed, not Roman but *American* valor: so conspicuous, indeed, had been the courage displayed, by both our army and navy, that he hoped whoever should hereafter speak of Roman valor, on this floor, would be considered as speaking of the second degree, and not of the first."* As far as any thing appears on the minutes of this day's debates, Mr. Wright's language caused no unusual sensation in the house.

After the American Niagara frontier had thus suffered a just retribution for the conduct of the American government along the shores of Upper Canada, the British troops, under major-general Rial, evacuated the whole of the territory of the United States, except Fort-Niagara, at which a small garrison was stationed; and the centre-division of the army of Upper Canada, consisting now of about 2500 rank and file, retired into peaceable winter-quarters at Fort-Niagara, St. David's, Burlington Heights, and York. Mr. O'Connor, after declaring that our proceedings had been marked "with the ferocity of the tiger, and the all-desolating ruin of the locust," adds: "On the 4th of January the robbers retired into their own woods; not daring

* Proceedings of Congress, January 6, 1814.

to wait the chastisement that was preparing for them." He next furnishes us with a piece of useful information. "The enemy," says he, "having declared their conduct on the Niagara frontier to have been committed in retaliation for excesses *said* to have been committed by the American armies in Canada, the censure, or rather indignation, of the suffering inhabitants was turned against general M'Clure, who had the command. The general, previous to retiring from command, published an address to the public, in justification of his own conduct, in which he seems to have been pretty successful."* His *success* did not, at all events, reach to the security of his person; for he was compelled, for a long while, to have a strong guard of regular troops stationed before his door, in order to restrain the justly enraged population from treating him as he deserved.

In the harbor at Erie,† distant 91 miles from Buffaloe, were lying the ships, brigs, and larger schooners of the American fleet; nor could they seek safety upon the lake, on account of the ice that surrounded them. The Americans, having good reason to fear an attack upon, had, by collecting troops and cutting away the ice from the sides of the vessels, made every arrangement for the security of, this important depôt. After the incompetency of the American militia to

* History of the War, p. 164. † See p. 49.

defend the post, had, however, been so well proved, we presume it was the known unbearable state of the ice, and not any special orders from Quebec, that restrained major-general Rial from attempting to carry into effect so desirable an object.

Having now brought to a close the campaign of 1813, against the British provinces; we will borrow an American editor's remarks upon the subject. "Though," says Mr. Thomson, "the American arms had attained a high degree of reputation, no one advantage was obtained, to atone for the blood and treasure which had already been exhausted. The capital of Upper Canada had been taken. It was scarcely captured, before it was abandoned. The bulwark of the province, Fort-George, had been gallantly carried; but an inferior force was suffered to escape, after being beaten; and the conquerors were soon after confined to the works of the garrison, and closely invested upwards of six months. The long contemplated attack upon Montreal was frustrated: Kingston still remained a safe and advantageous harbor, in the hands of the enemy; and a fortress,* which might have been long, and obstinately, and effectually defended, was yielded, with scarcely a struggle, and under circumstances mysterious in the extreme, to the retaliating invaders of the

* Fort-Niagara.

American Niagara frontier. In the course of the summer of 1813, the American army possessed every position between Lake Ontario and Lake Erie, on both sides of the Niagara. In the winter of the same year, after having gradually lost their possessions on the British side of that stream, they were deprived of their possessions on their own."* If we may be allowed to leave out "gallantly"; to substitute "without any" for "with scarcely a"; and to bestow a smile upon the "high degree of reputation which the American arms had attained," we see no objection to Mr. Thomson's recapitulatory observations.

The circumstances that caused the surprising changes which he so naturally deplores, seem to have escaped his notice. "Had "the long contemplated attack upon Montreal" not been attempted, a comparatively large regular army of the United States could still have occupied the peninsula of Upper Canada; and a M'Clure not been wanted, to prove himself the willing tool of Mr. Secretary Armstrong's atrocious purposes. Had not Newark been set on fire, remorse would not have made cowards of M'Clure and his myrmidons; nor would a just indignation have stimulated a small band of British to pursue and punish those guilty wretches; many of whose dwellings happily shared the fate of the

* Sketches of the War, p. 193.

town which they had destroyed. Yet—mark the difference. The destruction along the American frontier was the work of an assaulting foe, glowing with wrath at the commission of injuries, unauthorized by the laws of war. It was an event which the inhabitants themselves had, for the last eight days, been expecting; an event, therefore, which they, by removing their property, and, in many instances, themselves, from the spot, did but partially feel. The burning of Newark, on the other hand, was the deliberate act of an enemy, who had been six months in quiet possession of the country; and who had received no provocation whatever from the inhabitants,—"the innocent, unfortunate, and distressed inhabitants," as M'Clure himself had styled them; and that too in the very proclamation, wherein he pledged himself to protect them. Warning the poor people had none; unless half an hour or so may be called by that name: nor even day-light, to enable them to see to collect their little cloaths and property, and to seek another habitation, in the room of that they had for ever lost. Poor Mrs. Dickson, too!—Who, then, will deny that the wanton conflagration of Newark still remains unatoned for?

CHAPTER XII.

Operations in Chesapeak Bay—Arrival of rear-admiral Cockburn—Preparations for attacking the United States' frigate Constellation in James's River—Her retreat to a safer position—Wanton firing from the shore upon the British boats—Death of two men in consequence—Arrival of admiral Warren—Gallant affair at the mouth of the Rappahannock—Rear-admiral Cockburn's detached command to the head of the bay—Advance upon French-town—Heavy fire upon the boats from a battery—Landing of the British—Flight of the American militia—Destruction of cannon, public stores, and vessels—Admiral Cockburn's system of operations—American misrepresentations corrected—Purchase of stock at Turkey Point and Specucie Island—Display of colours, and firing of cannon, at Havre de Grace—Attack upon this place—Its short but spirited resistance—Disrespect shown to a flag of truce—Consequent proceedings by the British—Destruction of a valuable cannon-foundry—Gross mis-statement of the American editors—Ridiculous behaviour of a prisoner named O'Neil, and ludicrous threat in case of his detention—Advance upon George-town and Frederick-town — Previous warning to the inhabitants—Their violent pro-

ceedings, and destructive fire upon the British —Destruction of houses in consequence—Visit of the British to another town—Civil deportment of the inhabitants, and its salutary effects—Remarks on the American militia-system—Impositions of the American farmers—Capture of the United States' schooner Surveyor—Noble conduct of lieutenant Cririe of the Narcissus—Arrival of troops in the Chesapeake—Affair between H.M.S. Junon and 15 American gun-boats—Open preparations for attacking Craney Island—Correspondent preparations on the part of the Americans—Landing of a division of British at Pig-Point—Advance of another division towards Craney Island—Unexpected grounding of the boats close under the American battery—Impossibility to reach the shore—Destructive fire upon the boats, as well as upon the struggling crews in the water—Remarks upon the attempt to capture Craney Island—Attack upon, and capture of Hampton—Excesses committed there by a part of the British force—American strictures on the occasion—Departure from the coast of the corps that committed the excesses—Landing of the British at Ocracoke and Portsmouth, and capture of two fine letters of marque—American mis-statements corrected.

A THREATENING attitude upon the Atlantic frontier of the United States, in the neighbourhood of the capital especially, being considered likely to weaken the efforts of the American government, now so openly and earnestly directed against our Canadian possessions, rear-admiral Cockburn, in the Marlborough 74, with some frigates and smaller vessels, entered the Chesapeake bay on the 4th of March, 1813.

The United States' frigate Constellation, lying in James's river, near Norfolk, became the first object of attack; but the preparatory movements of the British squadron drove her to a safe position, higher up the river. The rear-admiral afterwards advanced up the bay, sounding and reconnoitring. During the passage of the boats along the shore, in the execution of this service, the Americans frequently fired at them, and, in one instance, killed two men, besides wounding several others; although not a musket had been, on any occasion, discharged from the boats.

About the end of March, admiral Warren, from Bermuda, bringing with him the San Domingo 74, and some other ships, arrived in the Chesapeake. In his way up the bay, the admiral detached a force to attack four armed schooners, lying at the mouth of the Rappahannock river. The breeze failing, the capture of the whole four was effected by five British boats, under the orders of lieutenant (now captain) James Polkinghorne, of the St. Domingo.*

* For the full particulars of this gallant exploit, see James's Naval Occurrences, p. 367.

In a week or two after a junction had been formed between admiral Warren and rear-admiral Cockburn, the latter was directed, with a squadron of small vessels, including two of the captured schooners, to penetrate the rivers at the head of the bay, and endeavour to cut off the enemy's supplies; as well as to destroy his foundries, stores, and public works; particularly a depôt of flour, military and other stores, ascertained, by the information of some Americans, to be at a place called French-town, situate at a considerable distance up the river Elk. Accordingly, the rear-admiral, with H.M. brigs Fantome and Mohawk, and the Dolphin, Racer, and Highflyer, tenders, on the evening of the 28th of April, moved towards the river. Having moored the brigs and schooners as far within the entrance as could be effected after dark, the rear-admiral took with him, in the boats of his little squadron, 150 marines, under captains Wybourn and Carter, and five artillery-men, under lieutenant Robertson, of that corps, and proceeded to execute his orders.*

The boats, owing to ignorance of the way, having entered the Bohemia instead of keeping in the Elk river, did not reach the destined place till late on the following morning. This delay enabled the inhabitants of French-town to

* App. No. 8.

make arrangements for the defence of the stores and town; for the security of which a six-gun battery had lately been directed. As soon as the boats approached within gun-shot of it, a heavy fire was opened upon them. Disregarding this, however, the marines quickly landed; and the American militia fled from the battery to the adjoining woods.

The inhabitants of the town, situate at about a mile distant, having, as far as could be ascertained, taken no part in the contest, were not in the slightest degree molested; but a considerable quantity of flour, of army-clothing, saddles, bridles, and other equipments for cavalry; also various articles of merchandize, and the two stores in which they had been contained; together with five vessels, lying near the place, were entirely consumed. The guns of the battery, being too heavy to be carried away, were disabled; and the boats departed, with no other loss than one seaman wounded in the arm by a grape-shot. The Americans lost one man killed by a rocket, but none wounded.

The rear-admiral's system, and which he had taken care to impart to all the Americans captured by, or voluntarily coming on board, the squadron, was—to land without offering molestation to the unopposing inhabitants, either in their persons or properties; to capture or destroy all articles of merchandize and munitions of war; to be allowed to take off, upon paying the full market price, all such cattle and supplies as the British squadron might require: but, should resistance be offered, or menaces held out, to consider the town as a fortified post, and the male inhabitants as soldiers; the one to be destroyed, the other, with their cattle and stock, to be captured.

Both the editor of the "Sketches of the War" and of the "History of the War" confine the conflagration at French-town, to the two store-houses and their contents; and so does a writer in a respectable American periodical publication, of very recent date, subjoining to his account of the burning of the warehouses,—"but no private dwellings, as has erroneously been stated."* Yet is the editor of the "History of the United States" so totally disregardful of truth, as to accuse the British of having plundered and destroyed the whole village.† Mr. Thomson finds it convenient to describe the contents of the store-houses as goods belonging to merchants of Baltimore and Philadelphia, and to be totally silent about any military stores; but general Wilkinson expressly says: —"By the defective arrangements of the war-department, he (rear-admiral Cockburn)

* North American Review, Vol. V. p. 158.

† Hist. of the United States, Vol. III. p. 283.

succeeded in destroying the military equipments and munitions found there; of which, I apprehend, the public never received any correct account."*

As the boats, in their way down the Elk, were rounding Turkey Point, they came in sight of a large estate, surrounded by cattle. The rear-admiral landed; and directing the bailiff, or overseer, to pick out as many oxen, sheep, and other stock, as were deemed sufficient for the present use of the squadron, paid for them to the full amount of what the bailiff alleged was the market price. Not the slightest injury was done; or, doubtless, one of our industrious historians would have recorded the fact.

Having learnt that cattle and provisions, in considerable quantity, were at Specucie Island, the rear-admiral, with the brigs and tenders, proceeded to that place. In his way thither it became necessary to pass in sight of Havre de Grace, a village of about 60 houses, situate on the west-side of the Susquehanna, a short distance above the confluence of that river with the Chesapeake. Although the British were a long way out of gun-shot, the Americans at Havre de Grace must needs fire at them from a six-gun battery, and display to their view, as a further mark of defiance, a large American

* Wilkinson's Mem. Vol. I. p. 732.

ensign. This determined the rear-admiral to make that battery and town the next object of attack. In the meanwhile, he anchored his squadron off Specucie Island. Here a part of the boats landed, and obtained cattle upon the same terms as before. A complaint having been made, that some of the subordinate officers had destroyed a number of turkies, the rear-admiral paid the value of them out of his own pocket. The Americans, as they were driving the cattle to the boats, jeered the men, saying,—"Why do you come here? Why don't you go to Havre de Grace? There you'll have something to do." About this time a deserter gave the people at Havre de Grace, who had already been in preparation, notice of the intended attack.

After quitting Specucie Island, the rear-admiral bent his course towards Havre de Grace; but the shallowness of the water admitting the passage of boats only, the 150 marines and the five artillery men embarked at midnight on the 2d of May, and proceeded up the river.* The Dolphin and Highflyer tenders attempted to follow in support of the boats, but shoal water compelled them to anchor at the distance of six miles from the point of attack. By daylight, the boats succeeded in getting opposite to the battery; which mounted six guns, 12 and 6-pounders, and opened a smart fire upon

* App. No. 9.

the British. The marines instantly landed to the left; which was a signal to the Americans to withdraw from their battery. Lieutenant G. A. Westphall, having, in the mean time, stationed his rocket-boat close to the battery, now landed with his boat's crew, turned the guns upon the American militia, and drove them to the extremity of the town.

The inhabitants still keeping up a fire from behind the houses, walls, and trees, lieutenant Westphall, by the admiral's orders, held out a flag of truce, and called upon them to desist. Instead of so doing, these "unoffending citizens" fired at the British lieutenant, and actually shot him through the very hand that was bearing the flag of truce. After this, who could wonder if the British seamen and marines turned to the right and left, and demolished every thing in their way?—The townspeople themselves had constructed the battery; and yet not a house in which an inhabitant remained was injured. Several of the inhabitants, principally women, who had fled at first, came again into the town, and got back such articles as had been taken. Some of the women actually proceeded to the boats; and, upon identifying their property, had it restored to them. Many of the inhabitants who had remained peaceably in their houses, as a proof that they were well informed of the principle upon which Sir George

Cockburn acted, frequently exclaimed to him: —"Ah, sir, I told them what would be the consequence of their conduct. It is a great pity so many should suffer for a head-strong few. Those who were the most determined to fire upon you the other day, saying it was impossible you could take the place, were now the first to run away." Several of the houses that were not burnt did, in truth, belong to the chief agents in those violent measures that caused such severity on our part; and the very towns-people themselves pointed out the houses. Lieutenant Westphall, with his remaining hand, pursued and took prisoner an American captain of militia; and others of the party brought in an ensign and several privates, including an old Irishman, named O'Neill. After embarking the six guns from the battery, and taking or destroying about 130 stands of small-arms, the British departed from Havre de Grace.

One division of boats, headed by the rear-admiral, then proceeded to the northward, in search of a cannon-foundry, of which some of the inhabitants of Havre de Grace had given information. This was found, and instantly destroyed; together with five long 24-pounders, stationed in a battery for its protection; 28 long 32-pounders, ready for sending away; and eight long guns, and four carronades, in the boring-house and foundry. Another division of boats was sent up the Susquehanna; and returned, after destroying five vessels and a large store of flour.

No event of the war has been more grossly exaggerated than the proceedings of the British at Havre de Grace. Happily, so much inconsistency and contradiction prevail in the American accounts, that we shall have no great difficulty in exposing the authors to the merited indignation of the disinterested reader. One editor says:—"From Frenchtown they (the British) proceeded down the Elk, ascended the river Susquehanna, and attacked, plundered, and burnt the neat and flourishing, but *unprotected* village of Havre de Grace; for which outrage no provocation had been given, nor could excuse be assigned."* Another says:—"In expectation of an attack from the enemy, the people of Havre de Grace had made preparations for the defence of the place; and a battery had been erected, of two 6-pounders, and one nine."† Six long 12 and 6-pounders, the reader will recollect, were taken by us from that very battery. The same editor admits, that a fire was kept up from the battery till the British commenced their debarkation; "when all," says he, "except O'Neill, an old citizen of Havre de Grace, abandoned their posts; and,

* Hist. of the U. S. Vol. III. p. 283.

† Sketches of the War, p. 209.

following the militia, who had fled with shameful precipitation, left the women and children of the place to the mercy of the invaders."* A third editor says:—" A small party of militia were stationed at Havre de Grace; who, on the approach of the enemy, made a slight resistance, and then retreated. An Irishman," (this is more intelligible than Mr. Thompson's designation,) named O'Neill, with a courage amounting to rashness, and an enthusiasm not confined by cold loyalty, opposed his single arm to the British host, and was taken prisoner and carried on board the fleet, but afterwards released."†

Another American account says:—" The inhabitants of Havre de Grace had, for three weeks previous to this period, been making preparations for defence; and several companies of militia were called in to their aid."—" The militia, amounting to about 250, were kept to their arms all night; patroles were stationed in every place where they could possibly be of any service; the volunteers at the battery were at their guns, and a general determination seemed to prevail of giving the enemy a warm reception."‡ What, then, becomes of doctor Smith's assertion, that Havre de Grace was "unprotected;" or that " no excuse could be

* Sketches of the War, p. 209.

† Hist. of the War, p. 170.

‡ North American Review, Vol. V. p. 160.

assigned" for attacking it?—Perhaps this gentleman grounded his statement upon Mr. Munro's official communication to sir Alexander Cochrane; wherein, as a matter of state-convenience, and in the very teeth of the British official account, announcing the capture of six pieces of cannon, and 130 stands of arms, the American secretary chose to describe the inhabitants of Havre de Grace as "unarmed." In the same spirit of rancor, doctor Smith declares, that "the whole of this little town, house after house, was consigned to the flames."* Mr. Thomson is not explicit upon this point; but Mr. O'Connor expressly says:—"Twenty-four of the best houses in the town were burned;"† and the Boston reviewer says:—"It has been said, in a respectable history of the times," (can this mean doctor Smith's work?) "that one house only escaped the flames; but this is a mistake. Havre de Grace consisted of about 60 houses, and of these not more than 40 were burnt."‡ As, according to the same account, several of the houses were, when the British landed, "already in flames," from the "tremendous discharge of balls, rockets, and shells," we may consider Mr. O'Connor's estimate as alluding exclusively to those destroyed by the British while on shore. It is not a little extra-

* Hist. of the United States, Vol. III. p. 283.

† Hist. of the War, p. 170. ‡ N. Amer. Rev. Vol. V. p. 160.

ordinary, that the same writer who dwells so upon the state of "preparation" in which the inhabitants were, should say: "It is not easy to assign any cause, other than the caprice of its projector, for this violent attack on a defenceless and unoffending village. No reasons of a public nature could have induced it. No public property was deposited there, nor were any of its inhabitants engaged in aiding the prosecution of the war."*

Although it would be idle to question the zeal and industry of any one of our three historians, Mr. Thomson alone has declared that the British "cut open the bedding of the citizens to augment the flames; destroyed the public stages; maimed the horses; cut to pieces the private baggage of the passengers; tore the cloathing of some of the inhabitants from their backs; and left to others those only which they wore; in short, robbing private travellers on the highway of their money and apparel." Mr. Thomson next affirms that, "when several ladies of the first distinction" had taken refuge "in a spacious and elegant private mansion," a British officer "was entreated to suffer this house, at least, to escape the general conflagration; but, as he was obeying the orders of admiral Cockburn, the most he could do was to suspend his purpose, until those unprotected

* North American Review, Vol. V. p. 162.

women could prevail upon the admiral to countermand them."* That the latter part of this statement is utterly false, appears by the testimony of one of the sufferers; one who dates his letter from the spot; who complains that the destruction of Havre de Grace has "ruined" him; and who, therefore, must write with highly irritated feelings against the British. He says: "The inhabitants fled at the approach of the sailors, and the women took shelter in the house of Mr. Mark Pringle; which a party was proceeding to destroy, when Mr. Pringle, with a flag, met them, and they *very readily* desisted."†

One would suppose that the destruction, by an enemy, of 45 pieces of cannon, chiefly long 32 and 24-pounders, would have appeared of sufficient national importance, to engage the attention of such as profess to detail the events of a war. But it was necessary to cast every possible odium upon the British, and therefore highly impolitic to admit that they performed a single act of legitimate warfare. Mr. Thomson is the only editor who deplores the loss "of 50 pieces of elegant cannon;" but he makes amends for his unguarded acknowledgment, by declaring, that the furnace which was battered down, was "private property," and that the

* Sketches of the War, p. 210.

† Philadelphia Gazette, May 4, 1813.

British, "as the last act of atrocity with which this expedition was destined to be marked, tore up a small bridge, constructed over a deep, though narrow creek, and over which travellers of every description were obliged to pass, or venture through a wider channel, at the imminent hazard of their lives."* So that a small party, on shore in an enemy's country, and expecting to be attacked by an enraged population, collecting from all points, are to leave standing a bridge, by which alone, probably, their position can be assailed; because, forsooth, the destruction of that bridge would compel the inhabitants to "venture through a wider channel, at the imminent hazard of their lives." This is such a refinement in warfare, as we did not expect to hear broached by an American. Doctor Smith and Mr. O'Connor, although they have added to the list of enormities committed by the British, that of burning "Mr. Hughes's foundery," have rejected the story of the bridge, as too ridiculous even for them to publish.

Mr. O'Connor, with a fellow-feeling, perhaps, extols highly the courage and enthusiasm of his friend O'Neill. This contemptible old wretch, when taken on board the rear-admiral's ship, cried bitterly; exclaiming every now and then, "God bless king George—I detest the Americans, —will do all I can to save the British," &c. &c.

* Sketches of the War, p. 211.

Next day his daughter, an interesting young woman, came on board, and begged hard for his discharge; urging that he had a large family dependant on him for support. Her tears prevailed, and she carried her father on shore. In a week or ten days afterwards, rear-admiral Cockburn had occasion to go on board the San Domingo, when, to his great surprise, admiral Warren showed him a letter he had just received from the American secretary of state, declaring, if a hair of O'Neil's head was hurt, what his government would do, &c. This ludicrous application was replied to in a proper manner, and the affair ended.

On the night of the 5th of May, the same party of British marines and artillery-men again embarked in the boats, and proceeded up the river Sassafras, separating the counties of Kent and Cecil, towards the villages of George-town and Frederick-town, situate on opposite sides of the river, nearly facing each other. Having intercepted a small boat with two of the inhabitants, rear-admiral Cockburn halted the detachment, about two miles from the town; and then sent forward the two Americans in their boat, to warn their countrymen against acting in the same rash manner as the people of Havre de Grace had done; assuring them that, if they did, their towns would inevitably meet with a similar fate; but that, on the contrary, if they did not attempt resistance, no injury should be done to them or their towns; that vessels and public property only, would be seized; that the strictest discipline would be maintained; and that whatever provision or other property of individuals the rear-admiral might require for the use of the squadron, would be instantly paid for in its fullest value.* The two Americans agreed in the propriety of this; said there was no battery at either of the towns; that they would willingly deliver the message, and had no doubt the inhabitants would be peaceably disposed.

After waiting a considerable time, the rear-admiral advanced higher up; and, when within about a mile from the towns, and between two projecting points of land which compelled the boats to proceed in close order, a heavy fire was opened upon them from one field-piece, and, as conjectured, 3 or 400 militia, divided and entrenched on the opposite sides of the river. The fire was promptly returned, and the rear-admiral pushed on shore with the marines; but, the instant the American militia observed them fix their bayonets, they fled to the woods, and were neither seen nor heard of afterwards. All the houses, excepting those whose owners had continued peaceably in them, and taken no part in the attack, were forthwith destroyed; as were

* App. No. 10.

four vessels lying in the river, together with some stores of sugar, of lumber, of leather, and other merchandize. On this occasion, five of the British were wounded. One of the Americans who entreated to have his property saved, wore military gaiters; and had, no doubt, assisted at the firing upon the British. Agreeably to his request, however, his property was left untouched.

Mr. Thomson says: "The invaders were gallantly ressisted more than half an hour, when they effected a landing; and, marching towards the town, compelled the militia to retire. Colonel Veazy effected his retreat in excellent order."* To prove that this was a gallant affair, Mr. Thomson has made the American force "about 80 militia, and one small cannon," and the British force "18 barges, each carrying one great gun, and manned altogether by 600 men."* Mr. O'Connor contents himself with accusing us of burning the *unprotected* villages of Frederick and George-town.

On his way down the river, the rear-admiral visited a town situated on a branch of it. Here a part of the inhabitants actually pulled off to him; and, requesting to shake hands, declared he should experience no opposition whatever. The rear-admiral accordingly landed, with the officers, and, chiefly out of respect to his rank, a

* Sketches of the War, p. 212.

small personal guard. Among those that came to greet him, on his landing, were observed two inhabitants of George-town. These men, as well as an inhabitant of the place who had been to George-town to see what was going on, had succeeded in persuading the people to adopt, as their best security, a peaceable demeanor. Having ascertained that there were no public property nor warlike stores, and obtained, upon payment of the full value, such articles as were wanted, the rear-admiral and his party re-embarked. Soon afterwards, a deputation was sent from Charlestown, on the north-east river, to assure the rear-admiral, that the place was considered as at his mercy; and, similar assurances coming from other places in the upper part of the Chesapeake, the rear-admiral and his light squadron retired from that quarter.

None of the American historians notice the lenient conduct observed towards the inhabitants of the two last-mentioned towns; unless we are to consider Mr. Thomson as glancing at the subject, when he complains of "the treachery of some citizens of the republic." These editors find relief for their rancorous spirit either way. If the inhabitants preserve their towns by not opposing us, they are "traitors, tories, or British agents:" if they make resistance; and their towns, sharing the fate of other stormed places, are burnt, we are "vile incendiaries, unprincipled marauders."

Much is said by American editors, about robbing the inhabitants of their cattle and live stock; but the truth is, the farmers themselves considered the British squadron in the Chesapeake as their best market. Not contented, however, with getting the highest prices for their stock, small as well as large; their eggs, butter, milk, cheese, garden-stuff, &c. they frequently practised upon their liberal purchasers the grossest impositions.

One writer, doctor Smith, alluding to the proceedings in the Chesapeake, expresses himself thus: "History blushes to recapitulate the depredations and conflagrations which were here perpetrated. The pen of the historian cannot record one solitary exploit of honorable warfare, worthy the arms of an heroic nation. The outrages of their sailors and marines were the last degree shocking and indefensible. They committed indiscriminate havoc upon every species of private property along the shores of the bay, and on the margin of its inlets."*

This is the very language that was used by the "National Intelligencer," "National Advocate," "Democratic Press," and other American newspapers, "known to be friendly

* History of the United States, Vol. III. p. 282.

to the war," for the double purpose of prejudicing the British character in the eyes of the other nations of Europe, and of filling the ranks of the American army from among the western, or Kentucky patriots. American citizens of the first consequence, in Baltimore, Annapolis, and Washington, when they have gone on board the British Chesapeake squadron, as they frequently did, with flags, to obtain passports, or ask other favors, and these inflammatory paragraphs were shown to them, never failed to declare, with apparent shame, that they had been penned without the slightest regard to truth, but merely to instigate their ferocious countrymen in the western states to rally round the American standard. Yet does the sober historian of the United States not "blush" to record as truth these party-serving lies. Such statements soil the historic page; and, by their influence on the passions, may tend, at some future day, to rekindle the flames of war between the two nations.

Fortunately, we have American testimony to aid us in repelling the principal charge advanced against the British by this nest of calumniators. "They (the British) were always," says the writer in the Review, "desirous of making a fair purchase, and of paying the full value of what they received; and, it is no more than justice to the enemy to state that, in some instances, money was left behind, in a conspicuous place, to the full amount of what had been taken away."*

We in England may find it difficult to consider, as soldiers, men neither embodied nor drest in regimentals. That circumstance has not escaped the keen discernment of the American government: hence we are so often charged, in proclamations and other state-papers, with attacking the "inoffensive citizens of the republic." The fact is, every man in the United States, under 45 years of age, is a militia-man; and, during the war, attended in his turn, to be drilled, or "trained." He had always in his possession either a musket or a rifled-barrel piece; knew its use from his infancy; and with it, therefore, could do as much execution in a smock frock or plain coat, as if he wore the most splendid uniform. These soldiers in citizens' dresses were the men whom rear-admiral Cockburn so frequently attacked and routed; and who, when they had really acted up to the character of "non-combatants," were invariably spared, both in their persons and properties. The rear-admiral wished them, for their own sakes only, to remain *neutral;* but general Hull, in his famous proclamation, prepared

* North American Review, Vol. V. p. 158.

with so much care at Washington, invited the Canadian people to become open traitors to their country; and visited upon them that refused, all "the horrors and calamities of war."*

On the 12th of June the boats of the Narcissus 42, containing about 40 men, under the command of lieutenant Cririe, first of that ship, and of lieutenant P. Savage, of the marines, were despatched up York river, in the Chesapeake, to cut out the United States' schooner Surveyor, mounting six 12-pound carronades. Captain S. Travis, her commander, had furnished each of his men with two muskets. They held their fire until the British were within pistol-shot; but the latter pushed on, and finally carried the vessel by boarding, with the loss of three men killed, and six wounded. Captain Travis had five men wounded. His crew amounted to 16;† and so gallant was their conduct, as well as that of their commander, in the opinion of lieutenant Cririe, that that officer returned captain Travers his sword, accompanied by a letter, not less complimentary to him than creditable to the writer.‡ Mr. Thomson has added, "a tender" to the boats of the frigate; and declares that the force of the British was "nine times superior"§ to that on board the Surveyor. Lieutenant Cririe's letter would

* Vol. I. App. No. 4. † American Nav. Mon. p. 219

‡ App. No. 10. § Sketches of the War, p. 213.

have set this matter right, and conferred an honor upon the British commanding officer: either of which reasons would suffice to prevent its appearance in the pages of the "Sketches of the War." None of the other historians have noticed the action.

Admiral Warren, who had left the Chesapeake for Bermuda, returned to his command early in June; bringing with him, according to newspaper-account, a detachment of battalion marines, 1800 strong; 300 of the 102d regiment; 250 of the Independent Foreigners, or Canadian chasseurs; and 300 of the royal marine-artillery: total 2650 men.

On the 18th of June H.M.S. Junon, of 46 guns, anchored in Hampton roads; and captain Sanders despatched his boats to capture or destroy any vessels that might be found at the entrance of James's river. Commodore John Cassin, the naval commanding-officer at Norfolk, observing this, directed the 15 gun-boats at that station to be manned with an additional number of seamen and marines from the Constellation frigate, then moored at the navy-yard, also with 50 infantry from Craney Island; and, under the command of captain Tarbin, to attempt the capture or destruction of the Junon.

It was not till about 4 P.M. on the 20th, that this formidable flotilla, armed with upwards of 30 guns, half of which were long 32 and 24-

pounders, and manned with, at least, 500 men, commenced its attack upon the Junon, then lying becalmed. Captain Sanders warmly returned their fire with his long eighteens; hoping that they would soon venture to approach within reach of his carronades. This the gun-boats carefully avoided; and, between them and the frigate, a distant cannonade, very slightly injurious to either party, was maintained for about three quarters of an hour. A breeze now sprang up; which enabled the Barrosa, of 42, and the Laurestinus, of 28 guns, lying about five miles off, to get under weigh, in the hope to have a share in the amusement. The Junon, also, was at this time under sail, using her best efforts to give a more serious complexion to the contest; but commodore Cassin, who, as he assures us, was in his boat during the whole of the action, considering that the flotilla had done enough to entitle him to display both his fighting, and his literary qualifications, in an official letter, very prudently ordered the 15 gun-boats to make the best of their way back to Norfolk.

Commodore Cassin's letter* will afford a richer treat, when it is known, that the Junon, so "severely handled" as to be placed "upon a deep careen, with a number of boats and stages round her," received only one or two shots in her hull, and sustained no other loss than one

* App. No. 12.

man killed. Three of the gun-boats are stated to have received damage; one man is also acknowledged to have been killed, and two men wounded. The Barrosa, a 42-gun frigate, is under 950, "a razee" from 1640 to 1700 tons;* yet the American commodore could discover no difference between those two classes of ships. Mr. Thomson is the only editor who has recorded this gun-boat exploit. He declares the Junon was "much shattered;" that "the Americans had 15 guns, the British, 150 and upwards;" that "captain Tarbell's conduct, as well as that of lieutenants Gardner, Henly, and others, received the fullest approbation of the surrounding garrisons, and of the citizens of Norfolk."†

The appearance of the two frigates and sloop in Hampton roads soon brought to Norfolk and its vicinity as many as 10000 militia; and the works, recently constructed there, were all manned, ready for defending that important post. At Hampton, also, a militia force had assembled; and batteries were erecting, in case that town should prove the object of attack.

On the 20th of June, 13 sail of British ships, consisting of three 74s, a 64 *armée en flute*, four frigates, and five sloops, transports, and tenders, lay at anchor; the nearest within seven, the furthest off within thirteen, miles

* James's Nav. Occurr. p. 34. † Sketches of the War, p. 214.

of Craney Island. An assemblage of boats at the sterns of several of the ships, on the afternoon of that day, gave no very unequivocal notice to the people on shore, that some expedition was on foot. Accordingly, "Craney Island being rather weakly manned,"* the commanding officer at Norfolk sent 150 of the Constellation's seamen and marines, to a battery of 18-pounders on the north-west, and about 480 Virginia militia,† exclusive of officers, to reinforce a detachment of artillery, stationed with two 24 and four 6-pounders on the west, side of the island. Captain Tarbell's 15 gun-boats were also moored in the best position for contributing to the defence of the post.

After two days' parade of boats and bustle among the British ships, a division of 17 or 18 boats, at day-light on the morning of the 22d, departed with about 800 men, under major-general Beckwith, round the point of Nansemond river, and landed them at a place called Pig's point, near to the narrow inlet separating the main from Craney Island. Owing to some error in the arrangements, unexpected obstacles presented themselves. An attack from that quarter being therefore considered hopeless, and the position itself not tenable, the troops, in the course of the day, re-embarked, and returned to the squadron.

* App. No. 12. † Sketches of the War, p. 213.

A second division of boats, 15 in number, containing a detachment of 500 men, from the 102d regiment, Canadian chasseurs, and battalion-marines, and about 200 seamen, the whole under the command of captain Pechell, of the St. Domingo, arrived, at about 11 o'clock in the forenoon, off the north-west side of the island, directly in front of the battery manned by the Constellation's men. Great difference of opinion prevailed among the officers engaged in the expedition, about the propriety of making the attack at that time of tide, it being then the ebb. Captains Hanchett, Maude, and Romilly of the engineers, were decidedly against it; captain Pechell was for it; and he, being the senior officer, of course carried his point. Captain Hanchett then volunteered to lead the boats to the attack; which he was permitted to do.

Captain Hanchett's boat was the Diadem's launch, carrying a 24-pound carronade, the only boat so armed in the division. He had taken his station about 60 yards a-head of the other boats; and was pulling, under a very heavy and long-continued fire from the batteries, directly in front of them, when his boat unfortunately took the ground, at the distance of about 100 yards from the muzzles of the enemy's guns. Captain Hanchett, who had been previously standing up in his boat, animating his men to hasten forward, now wrapped round his body a union jack, and prepared to wade on shore to storm the American battery. At that instant one of the seamen, having plunged his boat-hook over the side, found three or four feet of slimy mud at the bottom. A check thus effectually given to a daring enterprise, in which all were so ready to join, captain Hanchett waved his hat for the boats a-stern to keep a-float. In the hurry of pulling and ardor of the men, this warning was disregarded; and one or two of the boats grounded. Two others, owing to their having received some shot that had passed through the sails of the Diadem's launch, sank.

In the meanwhile, the Americans at the battery, well aware of the shoal, had anticipated what happened; and, feeling their own security, poured in their grape and canister with destructive effect. A 6-pound shot, which had passed through a launch on the starboard side of captain Hanchett's boat, and killed and wounded several men, struck that officer on the hip, and he instantly fell; but was quickly on his legs again. While he was assisting to save the men that were struggling in the water, in consequence of their boat having been sunk, a langridge shot entered his left thigh. This gallant officer stood as long as he could, and then fainted. A little water, however, restored him; and, after seeing the boats withdrawn from the fire, captain Hanchett went to the rear and reported himself to captain Pechell: that done, the wounded captain ordered himself to be shifted into a lighter boat, which conveyed him to his own ship, the Diadem, then lying at anchor twelve miles off.

While the men from the sunken boats, and who consisted chiefly of the Canadian chasseurs, or Independent Foreigners, were struggling for their lives in the water and mud, the Constellation's marines, and the American infantry, waded a short distance into the water, and deliberately fired at them. When informed of the circumstance, the American authorities, very naturally, declared it untrue: as had been frequently done before, too, "an investigation was ordered;" and which, of course, "resulted in a complete refutation of the allegations."* But, the fact having passed in full view, not only of the officers and men in the other boats, but of sir T. Sidney Beckwith and his party, from their position on the main-land, any attempts at denial could only add to the enormity of the offence.

Huddled together, as the boats were, when they struck the ground; and that within canister-range of a battery, which kept upon them an incessant fire of more than two hours' duration, it required no very expert artillerists to sink three of the boats, and to kill three men and wound sixteen; especially when aided by the muskets of those humane individuals who waded

* History of the United States, Vol. III. p. 285.

into the water to fire at the drowning crews. Including 10 seamen, 62 are reported as missing.* Of these, it appears, 40 gained the shore, and "deserted" to the Americans. As more than that number of missing appear to have belonged to the two foreign companies, this creates no surprise; especially as the only alternative left to the men was to become prisoners of war. Admitting the American statement to be correct, 22 must have perished in the water; the majority of whom, owing to the proximity of the sinking boats to the Diadem's launch, and the strenuous exertions of captain Hanchett and his men to save the drowning crews, must have dropped beneath the merciless bullets of the American troops. The whole loss on our side, which, as we have seen, amounted to 81, has been magnified by the American editors, to 200; and they add, with a degree of exultation, rendered ridiculous by the powerless condition to which accident had reduced the invading party, that "on the side of the invaded, not a man was either killed or wounded."

One American editor makes the British force that arrived in front of the island-battery "about 4000 men," many of whom were French,† and those that landed on the main "upwards of 800 soldiers;" yet, in the very

* App. No. 13. † Sketches of the War, p. 215.

next page, he declares that "3000 British soldiers, sailors, and marines, were opposed to 480 Virginia militia, and 150 sailors and marines."* The batteries were nothing in the account, although Mr. Thomson had just done telling us what destruction they had caused. Another editor, Mr. O'Connor, declares that "1500 men attempted to land in front of the island;† and that the force that landed on the main was "reported, by deserters and others, to exceed 3000 men."‡ The postcript to commodore Cassin's letter states, that "the number of the enemy engaged in the attack was nearly 3000;"‡ implying, of course, that those not engaged were excluded from the estimate. Another writer, whose zeal it would be criminal to question, says:—"An attempt was made against Craney Island, by a force exceeding 1200 men; who were repulsed with disgrace by 700 raw troops, sailors and marines, without the loss of a man."|| We have, in addition to Mr. Thomson's, general Wilkinson's high authority for stating, that a part of the invading force consisted of "a corps designated '*chasseurs Britanniques*,' composed of foreign renegadoes under British officers."||

It is surprising with what facility the American

* Sketches of the War, p. 216.

† Hist. of the War, p. 171.

‡ App. No. 12.

|| Wilkinson's Mem. Vol. I. p. 733.

historian can, by his powers of distortion, convert every event he records to the national advantage. The check which the expedition experienced, when the Diadem's launch and two or three of the foremost boats struck the ground, is represented as "a momentary pause" caused by the "galling fire from the battery;"* and to prove, decidedly, the existence of no other obstacle to the landing of the British, than "this gallant resistance by the naval division on the island," Mr. Thomson follows up his "momentary pause" with,—"Every attempt to approach the shore having heretofore failed, the enemy determined on returning to his shipping with as little delay as possible."* Not one of the other historians mentions a word about the British boats having grounded: all was effected by the "invincible American seamen and marines." We have seen already, and shall see again, as we proceed, that the American editors, in their histories, and the American commanders, in their official letters, can, when the occasion serves, magnify a difficulty, be it ever so slight, into one which no bravery can surmount.

The policy of attacking Craney Island, as a means of getting at Norfolk, has been much questioned; but there can be only one opinion, surely, about the wisdom of sending boats, in broad day-light, to feel their way to the shore,

* Sketches of the War, p. 215. † App. No. 12.

over shoals and mud-banks; and that in the very teeth of a formidable battery. Unlike most other nations, the Americans in particular, the British when engaged in expeditions of this nature, always rest their hopes of success upon valor rather than numbers. But still, had the veil of darkness been allowed to screen the boats from view, and an hour of the night chosen, when the tide had covered the shoals with deep water, the same little party might have carried the batteries; and a defeat, as disgraceful to those that caused, as honorable to those that suffered in it, been converted into a victory. As it was, the affair of Craney Island, dressed up to advantage in the American official account, and properly commented upon by the government-editors, was hailed throughout the union as a glorious triumph, fit for Americans to achieve.

On the night of the 25th of June, the effective men of the 102d regiment, Canadian chasseurs, and battalion-marines; also, three companies of ship's marines, the whole amounting to about 2000 men, commanded by major-general Beckwith, embarked in a division of boats, placed under the orders of rear-admiral Cockburn, and covered by the Mohawk sloop, and the launches of the squadron. About half an hour before day-light on the 26th, the advance, consisting of about 650 men, along with two 6-pounders, under lieutenant-colonel Napier, landed two miles to the westward of Hampton, a town about 18 miles from Norfolk, and separated from it by Hampton-roads. Shortly afterwards, the main body, consisting of the royal marine-battalions under lieutenant-colonel Williams, landed; and the whole moved forward.

A full detail of the little skirmishes that ensued with, certainly, a very inferior body of militia, will be found in Admiral Warren's and sir Sydney Beckwith's despatches.* As might be expected, the town, and its seven pieces of cannon, fell into our hands, after a trifling loss of five killed, 33 wounded, and 10 missing;* or, according to Mr. Thomson, of "90 killed and 120 wounded."† The Americans admit a loss of seven killed, 12 wounded, 11 missing, and one prisoner; total 31.†

Our force, on this occasion, has been, by the American editors, more fairly stated than usual; but they have contrived to make it up, by proportionably diminishing their own. Mr. Thomson tells us that, early in June, from "the suspicious movements and menacing attitudes" of the British squadron lying in Hampton-roads, "the citizens of all the surrounding towns became apprehensive of an attack;" that

* App. Nos. 14 and 15.

† Sketches of the War, p. 240.

"at Norfolk the militia force very soon consisted of 10000 men;" but that "at Hampton, a force of not more than 450 had yet been organized." After the British squadron had practised, during three weeks, "suspicious movements and menacing attitudes," in the very front of Hampton, within 18 miles of which, "10000 men" had already been collected, Mr. Thomson gravely enumerates the force that resisted the British, when they attacked and carried the town of Hampton, at "438 men;"* a smaller number even, than, at the very commencement of these "suspicious movements and menacing attitudes," he admits, had then been organized. Upon the whole, therefore, we shall incur no risk of over-rating the American force at Hampton, by fixing it at 1000 men.

A subject next presents itself for investigation, upon which it is painful to proceed. As soon as the Americans were defeated, and driven from Hampton, the British troops, or rather, "the foreign renegadoes," (for they were the principals), forming part of the advanced force, commenced perpetrating upon the defenceless inhabitants acts of rapine and violence, which unpitying custom has, in some degree, rendered inseparable from places that have been carried by storm; but which are as revolting to human nature, as they are disgraceful to the flag

* Sketches of the War, p. 218.

that would sanction them. The instant these circumstances of atrocity reached the ears of the British commanding officer, orders were given to search for, and bring in, all the Canadian chasseurs distributed through the town; and, when so brought in, a guard was set over them. The officers could do no more: they could not be at every man's elbow, as he roamed through the country in search of plunder;—and plunder the soldier claims as a right, and will have, when the enemy has compelled him to force his way at the point of the bayonet.

No event of the war was so greeted by the government-editors, as the affair at Hampton. All the hireling pens in the United States were put in requisition, till tale followed tale, each out-doing the last in horror. The language of the brothel was exhausted, and that of Billingsgate surpassed, to invent sufferings for the American women, and terms of reproach for their *British* ravishers. Instances were not only magnified, but multiplied, tenfold; till the whole republic rang with peals of execration against the British character and nation. A few of the boldest of the anti-government party stood up to undeceive the public, but the voice of reason was drowned in the general clamour; and it became as dangerous, as it was useless, to attempt to gain a hearing. The "George-town Federal Republican," of July 7, a newspaper published just at the verge of Washington-city, and whose editor has the happy priviledge of remaining untainted amidst a corrupted atmosphere, contains the following account:—"The statement of the women of Hampton being violated by the British, turns out to be false. A correspondence upon that subject and the pillage said to have been committed there, has taken place between general Taylor and admiral Warren. Some plunder appears to have been committed, but it was confined to the French troops employed. Admiral Warren complains, on his part, of the Americans, having continued to fire upon the struggling crews of the barges, after they were sunk."*

It will be scarcely necessary to mention, that, so far from the above statement, or any thing at all resembling it, appearing in the American histories from which we occasionally extract,—the most violent paragraphs out of the most violent journals, have alone that high honor assigned to them. One author, the reverend doctor Smith, has, unfortunately,—heedless how he prostituted his superior talents,—dressed up these calumnies in far more elegant language than either of his contemporaries.

Almost immediately after the affair at Hampton, captain Smith, who commanded the two companies of Canadian chasseurs, waited upon

* See p. 60.

the commander-in-chief, and informed him that, having remonstrated with his men for their behaviour at Hampton, they, one and all, declared, that they would show no quarter to any American whatever, in consequence of their comrades having been so basely fired at, when without arms, in the water, before the batteries at Craney Island. Upon captain Smith's expressing himself convinced that these foreigners would act up to their determination, sir John Warren ordered the two companies away from the American coast; and, although troops were subsequently much wanted in that quarter, the Canadian chasseurs, or Independent foreigners, were never again employed in the British service.

On the 11th of July, sir John Warren detached rear-admiral Cockburn, with the Sceptre 74, (into which ship he had now shifted his flag,) the Romulus, Fox, and Nemesis, all *armée en flute*, the Conflict gun-brig, and Highflyer and Cockchafer tenders; having on board the 103d regiment, of about 500 rank and file,* and a small detachment of artillery, to Ocracoke harbor, situate on the North-Carolina coast; for the purpose of putting an end to the commerce carried on from that port, by means of inland navigation, and of destroying any vessels that might be found there. During the night of the

* Afterwards sent to the Canadas.

12th, the squadron arrived off Ocracoke bar; and, at two o'clock on the following morning, the troops were embarked in their boats; which, accompanied by the Conflict and tenders, pulled in three divisions, towards the shore. Owing to the great distance and heavy swell, the advanced division, commanded by lieutenant Westphall, first of the Sceptre, did not reach the shoal-point of the harbor, behind which two large armed vessels were seen at anchor, till considerably after day-light: consequently, the enemy was fully prepared for resistance. The instant the boats doubled the point, they were fired upon by the two vessels; but lieutenant Westphall, under cover of some rockets, pulled directly for them; and, had just got to the brig's bows, when her crew cut the cables and abandoned her. The schooner's colours were hauled down by the enemy about the same time. The latter vessel proved to be the Atlas, letter of marque, of Philadelphia, mounting 10 guns, and measuring 240 tons: the former, the Anaconda, letter of marque, of New York, mounting 18 long 9-pounders, and measuring 387 tons.

In the course of the morning the troops were landed, and took possession of Ocracoke and the town of Portsmouth, without the slightest opposition. The inhabitants behaved with civility, and their property was, in consequence, not molested; although both Mr. Thompson and Mr. O'Connor have stated differently. One says: — "About 3000 men were landed at Portsmouth; where they destroyed the private property of the inhabitants, and treated the place with no more forbearance than they had shewn at Georgetown and Fredericktown."* Mr. O'Connor makes the attacking party amount to no more than "between 7 and 800;" declares that "the country was pillaged and laid waste by the enemy for several miles;"† and, having found out that some women died, and others were taken ill, in the neighbourhood, about the time of the attack, *supposes* that it all arose from "apprehensions of being treated like the unfortunate females at Hampton."†— After remaining on shore for two days, rear-admiral Cockburn, with his troops and seamen, re-embarked; not, it would appear, because he had performed the service entrusted to him, but—on account of his "not feeling himself competent to the attack on Newburn, now that its citizens were preparing to receive him."* No sooner had the British departed, than the American militia flocked to the post; thus presenting us with a new system of military defence.

* Sketches of the War, p. 224. † History of the War, p. 179.

CHAPTER XIII.

Commencement of the campaign of 1814—Spirited capture, by militia, of a superior detachment of American regulars, on the Thames, U. C.—Unsuccessful assault upon an American log-redoubt—Contemplated re-capture of Fort-Niagara, and attack upon Kingston—Major-general Brown's mistake—His arrival at Buffaloe—General Wilkinson's plan of obstructing the Richelieu—American incursion into Lower Canada—Assemblage of general Wilkinson's army at Champlain—His advance to, and attack upon, La Colle mill—Intrepid behaviour of the garrison—Repulse of the Americans, and their departure from the province—American defensive preparations at Vergennes—British flotilla on Lake Champlain—Ineffectual attack upon an American battery at Otter Creek—Assault upon, and capture of Fort-Oswego—Public property found there—American incursion into the village of Dover, at Long Point; and destruction of all the dwelling-houses and other buildings there—Remarks on that proceeding.

FROM the languid climate of the Chesapeake, we are again suddenly called to the bracing regions of the Canadas, against whose towns and inhabitants the United States' troops were still marching, with augmented numbers and renovated hopes. General Harrison's victory had placed the western district of Upper Canada, at the mercy of every petty detachment which major-general Cass might send from the garrison of Detroit. Early in December the proceedings of a foraging party of 44 of general Cass's regulars, under lieutenant Larwell, reached the ears of Mr. Henry Medcalf, a young man residing near Long Point. Although the depredators were traversing the banks of the river Thames, full 120 miles off, and the Canadian militia at this time disembodied,* lieutenant Medcalf assembled three serjeants and seven rank and file of his own, the Norfolk militia; and, on the 16th of the month, commenced his march, hoping to gain an accession of volunteers on his route. At Fort-Talbot, distant 65 miles, he was joined by one lieutenant, one ensign, one serjeant, and seven rank and file of the Middlesex militia; also, by a serjeant and six rank and file of captain Coleman's provincial dragoons. Thus reinforced, lieutenant Medcalf advanced to Chatham, about 50 miles further; where he was joined by a lieutenant and eight rank and file of the Kent militia; making his total number, including officers, 37. While at Chatham, the commanding officer of this little expedition

* See p. 5.

ascertained, that the objects of his search were at a house belonging to one Macrae, situate on the river-side. Owing to the length and rapidity of the march, eight of the men were quite worn out with fatigue. Leaving these, therefore, as a guard over the dragoon horses, lieutenant Medcalf hastened to Macrae's, with the remaining 28 of his party.

On arriving near the house, the door was found closed, and the 45 American regulars had posted themselves inside; as if intending to make a desperate resistance. Serjeant James M'Queen, of the 2d Norfolk militia, took a very ready method of gaining admittance: he burst open the door with the but-end of his musket. The 29 Canadian militia-men immediately entered; and, after a short scuffle, in which two of the Americans were killed, and three made their escape, took as prisoners lieutenants Larwell, Fisk, and Davies, two serjeants, two corporals and 33 rank and file, of the United States' regular army, total 40; with their arms in their hands. As soon as this affair was made known at the head-quarters of the right division, lieutenant-general Drummond promoted lieutenant Medcalf; and otherwise testified his approbation of the judgment and gallantry which that officer had so successfully displayed. One of the privates, Reuben Alwood, present at the attack, was still in a weak state of health, owing to a severe wound he had received in resisting the attack upon the Red House, in November, 1812.* A sailor's boarding-pike was then thrust into his left eye, and actually passed out at the back of his ear! If 50 American regulars, headed by a captain, succeed in capturing seven or eight Canadian militia, headed by a corporal, the event finds a place in the pages of an American "history." Yet we have searched in vain for any American account of the capture of lieutenant Larwell, and 39 American regulars, by lieutenant Medcalf and 28 Canadian militia.

The re-possession of the Niagara frontier had enabled lieutenant-general Drummond, early in February, to detach a small force of regulars, to check the further inroads of the Americans, along the Detroit and Lake-Erie shores. A part of this force, consisting of the two flank companies of the Royal Scots, the light company of the 89th, and a detachment of rangers and Kent militia, under captain Caldwell, in all 196 rank and file,† was stationed at Delaware-town, an Indian village on the banks of the Thames, about 34 miles above the Moravian village. Late on the night of the 3d of March information arrived, that an American foraging party was at Longwood, about 15 miles along the Moravian-town road. Accordingly at daylight the next morning, captain Basden, of the 89th,

* See Vol. I. p. 111.

† App. No. 16.

moved forward, with the three flank companies and the militia; also about 50 Indians, under colonel Elliot, of the Indian department.

The American party consisted of a detachment of rangers and mounted infantry, of the 24th and 28th regiments, amounting to 160 rank and file, under captain A. H. Holmes, of the 24th;* which detachment had been sent from Detroit, since the 21st of February, by lieutenant-colonel Butler, who, in the absence of major-general Cass, was now the commanding officer. Captain Holmes, having gained intelligence of the approach of the British, fell back five miles, to the Twenty-mile Creek; where there was a wide and deep ravine, bounded on each side by a lofty height. On the western height captain Holmes established an encampment, in the form of a hollow square; covering it on three sides with a redoubt, or breastwork, of felled trees. Here, confiding in the strength of his position, the American commander awaited the attack of the British.

On the morning of the 4th of March, captain Basden, with his detachment, appeared on the height facing that on which the enemy was posted. The snow was, at this time, about 15 inches deep, with a strong crust on the top; thus rendering the approach to the enemy's entrenchment still more difficult. Those pre-

* App. No. 16.

sent, who were well acquainted with the country, offered to lead the troops, by a circuitous route, to the rear of the enemy; but captain Basden preferred a direct attack, not only as more consonant to his own gallant spirit, but, in order to shew a good example to the militia, and make, as he thought, a lasting impression upon the American troops. Captain Basden, having directed the militia to make a flank movement to the right, and the Indians to do the same to the left, dashed, with his regulars, down one height, across the ravine, and up the other height, to within about three yards of the log-entrenchment. Here they were received by a quick succession of heavy and destructive volleys from the sheltered Americans; and, after several vain but gallant efforts to carry the work, were compelled to retire, with the loss of one captain, one lieutenant, and 12 rank and file, killed; and one captain, (captain Basden,) one lieutenant, five serjeants, and 42 rank and file, wounded; also, one volunteer wounded and taken prisoner, and one bugleman missing; total, 65. The loss of the Americans, as a proof how completely they were sheltered, amounted to no more than four killed, and four wounded. The British, however, were allowed to retire without any pursuit; and captain Holmes soon afterwards abandoned his position. Colonel Butler, in his letter, does credit to the gallantry of the British;

but Mr. Thomson, the only editor who appears to have noticed the affair, claims, as usual, the whole for his countrymen.

The Upper Canada peninsula was intended to be the first point of serious attack, in the campaign of 1814. The object, as explained in Mr. Secretary Armstrong's letter, of date the 20th of January, was to compel us to abandon our frontier posts on that line, including Fort-Niagara; and to prevent our sending detachments westward, against Amherstburg and Detroit, or against the American shipping at Erie and Put-in bay.* For this service, 2400 regulars, militia, and Indians, were to be placed under the command of colonel Scott.† The recapture of Fort-Niagara, which was the principal object, was considered to be no difficult task, with 2400 men; because it was known to be "garrisoned with only from 250 to 300 men," and that the British "kept no guards outside the fort."‡ But general Wilkinson, a portion of whose troops was to assist in making up this force, desirous to monopolize all the glory of invading the Canadas, threw obstacles in the way, and defeated the plan.

The Canadian snows were allowed to remain untrodden by hostile steps, except now and then a predatory incursion, for one month longer;

* Wilkinson's Mem. Vol. I. p. 614. † See p. 236.

‡ Ibid. p. 618.

when the American secretary at war, under date of February 21st, says to major-general Brown, at Sackett's harbor:—"You will immediately consult with commodore Chauncey, about the readiness of the fleet for a descent on Kingston, the moment the ice leaves the lake. If he deems it practicable, and you think you have troops enough to carry it, you will attempt the expedition. In such an event, you will use the enclosed as a *ruse de guerre*." The "enclosed" was as follows:—"Public sentiment will no longer tolerate the possession of Fort-Niagara by the enemy. You will, therefore, move the division which you brought from French Mills, and invest that post. Governor Tompkins will co-operate with you with 5000 militia; and colonel Scott, who is to be made a brigadier, will join you. You will receive your instructions at Onondaga Hollow."*—Having to wait two months, at least, ere commodore Chauncey's fleet could move on the lake, general Brown was the more easily led to mistake the fictitious, for the real, point of attack; and accordingly marched, through snow and water, to Onondaga Hollow; a village so named, distant about 70 miles from Sackett's harbor. Immediately on his arrival, a brother-officer pointed out to him his error; and back to Sackett's harbor waded the general and his 2000 men: where we will

* Wilkinson's Memoirs, Vol. I. p. 642.

leave them to recover from their fatigue; while we take a view of operations going on in general Wilkinson's neighbourhood.

Captain Pring's two sloops and gun-boats, or, as Mr. Thomson prefers calling them, "the British fleet destined to operate upon Lake Champlain," had been laid up for the winter at St. John's, situate about 40 miles down the Richelieu. To prevent this "fleet" from practising the same annoyance which it had done in the preceding summer,* general Wilkinson, who, with his army, was still at Plattsburg, sent an officer of engineers, on the 4th of March, to reconnoitre, with the view of fortifying, Rouse's point, on the Richelieu, distant about 26 miles from St. John's; and close to which point is the ship-channel into the lake. Some delay occurred in commencing upon, and the early breaking up of the ice defeated altogether, this most eligible plan.

The uncommon forwardness of the season kept no pace with general Wilkinson's warlike spirit. He longed to be at the Canadians; if only to punish them for treating him so scurvily, on his way down the St. Lawrence. Thus bent on revenge, the general, on the 19th of March, advanced, with his army, from Plattsburg to Chazee, on the road to Champlain, a village, distant about three miles from the boundary-line;

* See Vol. I. p. 242.

and then detached brigadier-general Macomb, with a corps of riflemen, and a brigade of infantry, in sleighs, across the ice, to Isle la Motte; and thence to Swanton, Vermont, near to Missisqui bay, on Lake Champlain. On the 22d this corps crossed the line of separation between the United States and Lower Canada, and took possession of Phillipsburg, a village of 60 or 70 houses, situate on the edge of the bay, about one mile within the lines. On the next day some cannon followed the detachment; but, on the 26th, to the great joy of the suffering inhabitants, the American troops, with their artillery, suddenly re-crossed the lake to Champlain; whither the general had since advanced, with the main body of the army. On the 29th of March, we find the general at the head of "3999," or as, for the reader's ease, we shall say, 4000, "combatants, including 100 cavalry, and 304 artillerists, with 11 pieces of artillery."* Against 1800 British regulars, and 500 militia, which the general assures a council summoned on the occasion, are stationed at La Colle mill, distant eight miles from Champlain, and seven, in an opposite direction, from Isle aux Noix, it is determined that the army shall immediately proceed. The preparatory "general order"† is very full and explicit. It is there fixed, that the troops shall "return victorious;" nor are they to "give ground"

* App. No. 17. † Ibid, No. 18.

against "double the force of the enemy." To provide, also, against any accidental defection; and, by way of operating as an additional stimulus to glory, on the part of the troops, "a tried serjeant will form a supernumerary rank, and instantly put to death any man who goes back."*

The American army commenced its short march at 10 o'clock on the morning of the 30th; and, while the troops are trudging, ancle-deep in snow and water, to effect the fourth invasion of Canada, we will exhibit *our* account of the British force in the vicinity of the lines. At St. John's, distant about 14 miles from Isle aux Noix, and 21 from the mouth of La Colle river, were stationed, under the command of lieutenant-colonel Sir William Williams, of the 13th regiment, six battalion-companies of that regiment, and a battalion of Canadian militia; numbering, altogether, about 750 rank and file. At Isle aux Noix, where lieutenant-colonel Richard Williams, of the royal marines, commanded, were stationed the chief part of a battalion of that corps, and the two flank companies of the 13th regiment; in all about 550 rank and file. The garrison of La Colle mill, at which major Handcock, of the 13th regiment commanded, consisted of about 70 of the marine-corps, one corporal, and three marine-artillerymen, captain Blake's company of the 13th regiment, and a

* App. No. 18.

small detachment of frontier light infantry, under captain Ritter; the whole not exceeding 180 rank and file. At Whitman's, on the left bank of the Richelieu, distant about two miles from the mill, and communicating with Isle aux Noix, was the remaining battalion-company of the 13th. The grenadier-company of the Canadian fencibles, under captain Cartwright, and a battalion-company of voltigeurs, were stationed at Burtonville, distant two miles up La Colle river, and where there had been a bridge, by which the direct road into the province passed. Thus the whole British force stationed within 22 miles of La Colle mill, and 30 of general Wilkinson's head-quarters, amounted, in regulars, to about 1000, and, in militia, to about 430, rank and file. Yet the general's detailed estimate, upon which that presented to the council was founded, places, at Isle aux Noix and La Colle mill, exclusively, 2550 men, and designates the whole, excepting two companies, as regular troops; including, among the "regiments," the voltigeurs, 49th, and De Meuron's,* although not one of these corps, except a company of the first, was stationed to the southward of St. John's.

The mill at La Colle was built of stone, with walls about 18 inches thick, having a wooden, or *shingled* roof, and consisting of two stories. It was in size about 36 feet by 50, and situate on

* Wilkinson's Mem. Vol. III. p. 226.

the south bank of La Colle river; which was frozen over nearly to its mouth, or junction with the Richelieu, from which the mill was about three-quarters of a mile distant. The mill had been placed in a state of defence, by filling up the windows with logs, leaving horizontal intervals to fire through. On the north-bank of the river, a little to the right of the mill, and with which it communicated by a wooden bridge, was a small house, not originally intended for, but, on this occasion, converted into, a block-house, by being surrounded with a breastwork of logs. In the rear of this temporary block-house was a large barn, to which nothing had been done, and which was not even musket-proof. The breadth of the cleared ground, to the southward of the mill, was about 200, and that to the northward, about 100 yards; but, on the flanks, the woods were much nearer. There was, at this time, about a foot of snow on the ground, and that rapidly dissolving.

The American troops, owing to the blunder of their guide, took the road to Burtonville, and did not discover their mistake till they had fired upon, and driven in, a small piquet of captain Cartwright's. They then counter-marched; and, after a second mistake of the road, entered the main road near Odell-town, distant about three miles from the mill. This road had been purposely obstructed by felled trees; which.

before the army could proceed, the American axemen were obliged to cut up or remove. In the course of the march, colonel Bissell's brigade, consisting of the 14th, 20th, and 23d infantry regiments, encountered a piquet, composed of a subaltern and 20 men, sent forward by major Handcock. This piquet was reinforced, and opened a smart fire upon the Americans; in which they killed and wounded one officer and 12 men of colonel Bissell's brigade.* The first intelligence of the enemy's advance reached the garrison at about half-past 10 in the forenoon; but, owing to the delay they had experienced, the American troops did not arrive before the mill, till half-past one o'clock in the afternoon.

The general, in a very masterly manner, now drew up his 4000 Americans, so as completely to invest this great mill-fortress, garrisoned by 180 British. As it was naturally expected, that the latter would soon try to effect their escape, 600 men, under colonel Miller, were detached across the river, to the rear of the mill, in order to cut them off. The firing commenced on the part of the little garrison; and was directed against that part of the enemy's column, which was stationed at the verge of the wood in front of the mill. This continued for about half an hour, when the Americans, after breaking the carriage of an 18, and being compelled to leave on the

* Wilkinson's Mem. Vol. III. p. 244.

road a 12-pounder, succeeded in bringing to a good position, within about 250 yards of the front of the mill, a 12 and 6-pounder, also a 5½ inch howitzer. An incessant cannonade was now kept up from the artillery, and returned by the musketry of the besieged. The firing from the howitzer, was, however, presently discontinued, chiefly on account of the thickness of the wood.* Soon after the attack had commenced, a message from major Handcock, brought to the block-house, from Isle aux Noix, the two flank companies of the 13th, commanded by captains Ellard and Holgate. The sudden rise of water, occasioned by the melting of the snow, had compelled the men to wade nearly up to their waists in mud and water. Major Handcock, not being apprized of the whole amount of the force opposed to him, ordered these two companies to charge the enemy's guns. This was instantly done, in the most resolute manner; but the overpowering numbers of the enemy, and the destruction caused by the flanking fire of his infantry and riflemen stationed in the woods, rendered the efforts of the gallant fellows unavailing, and they retired across the river to their block-house. About this time captain Cartwright's company of the Canadian fencibles, and the company of voltigeurs, eluded the enemy, and came down from Burtonville;

* Wilkinson's Mem. Vol. III. p. 322.

through the woods bordering on the river. The grenadiers of the Canadian fencibles were now joined to the remnant of the two 13th flank-companies, and a second charge was ordered to be made upon the guns. Captain Ellard, of the 13th, having been severely wounded in the first, captain Blake volunteered to head the grenadiers in the second charge. This charge was made and persisted in, with even more gallantry and resolution than the first. The men advanced within a very few yards of the guns; which, in consequence of the vigorous assaults made upon them, were abandoned by the artillerymen, and only rescued from capture by the repeated volleys of the American infantry.

The Americans were, in a manner, astounded at the valor of their opponents on this occasion. Lieutenant-colonel M'Pherson, who commanded the American artillery before the mill, deposed, at general Wilkinson's court-martial, as follows: "The ground was disputed inch by inch, in our advance to the mill; and the conduct of the enemy, that day, was distinguished by desperate bravery. As an instance, one company made a charge on our artillery, and, at the same instant, received its fire, and that of two brigades of infantry."* Lieutenant-colonel Totten, of the American engineers, present in the same action, also deposes thus:—"Judging from the

* Wilkinson's Mem. Vol. III. p. 328.

force of the enemy's charges, it was certainly prudent that a large force should be in the neighbourhood of the artillery, and nothing else saved them."* Brigadier-general Bissell, on the same occasion, says: "There were two desperate sorties made, in which the artillery was left without a man; the piece was regained by the infantry, and the enemy repulsed: men were supplied from my brigade to work the gun."†

Any further attempt at the guns would have been a waste of lives; and therefore major Handcock and his men now acted solely on the defensive. The American artillery still continued the cannonade. Several shots struck the mill, and a 12-pounder passed through the wall near the chimney, where it was weakest. One man of the 13th was killed by a grape-shot, that entered the aperture between the logs in the windows. During the action, captain Pring's sloops, and two or three gun-boats, arrived at the mouth of the creek; which was as near as the ice, had the river been otherwise navigable, would have permitted them to approach. Yet general Wilkinson, by way of augmenting the force he had to contend with, has, in his diagram of the action, actually placed two gun-boats on the river La Colle, directly at the back of the mill; when he ought to have known that, were

* Wilkinson's Mem. Vol. III. p. 238. † Ibid. p. 245.

there no ice at all, the river was not navigable even for canoes.* Lieutenant-colonel Williams was quite misinformed, as to any destruction caused to the enemy by the fire of the gun-boats.† Not an American officer present in the action, who was examined at general Wilkinson's court-martial, states any thing of the kind. On the contrary, lieutenant-colonel Totten swears positively, that "the enemy fired no artillery, except from their gun-boats, which opened a useless fire, 50 or 100 feet above our heads;"‡ the natural consequence, not only of the distance, but of the thick intervening woods.

The spirited and long-continued fire kept up by the British had exhausted their ammunition; and two privates, who had been despatched to Isle aux Noix for a fresh supply, were captured by an American piquet. A third private, belonging to the marines, succeeded in reaching the island. By this time the American artillery had been cannonading the mill, without the slightest apparent effect, for about two hours and a half; and now ceased altogether. The cessation of firing on the part of the besieged occasioned the American troops to advance nearer to the mill; but no attempt was made to carry even the block-house. Just at dusk the American troops

* Bouchette's Top. Desc. of Lower Canada, p. 179.

† Appendix, No. 17.

‡ Wilkinson's Memoirs, Vol. III. p. 235.

retired from the field; and retraced their steps out of the province, to the great joy of the inhabitants of Odell-town, whom they had pillaged unmercifully. They had been slightly annoyed at the first of their retreat, by a small party of Indians. It was natural for major Handcock to consider this retreat of so numerous a force as merely a feint, to draw him away from the mill. He therefore remained at his post during the night; in the course of which two 18-pound carronades had been brought up from the gun-boats, and posted at the block-house; but, as there was now no enemy to be seen, they were not used.

The British loss, in this brilliant affair, could not be otherwise than severe. It amounted, altogether, to 11 rank and file killed; one captain, one subaltern, one serjeant, 43 rank and file, wounded; and four rank and file missing; exclusive of one Indian killed, and one wounded,* in the skirmishing, on the enemy's retreat; total 64. The American loss before La Colle mill, amounted to 13 killed, 128 wounded, and 13 missing:† total 154. Among the wounded were lieutenant-colonel M'Pherson, lieutenants Larrabee, Green, and Parker, of the artillery. So destructive, indeed, was the fire from the mill upon the men at the guns, that out of 18 men

* App. No. 18.

† Burdick's Hist. and Pol. Register, p. 266.

stationed at the 12-pounder, only two remained to work it.

The reader is, no doubt, anxious to see how the American editors have handled a subject which, undoubtedly, gives the finest scope to their well-known talents. Mr. Thomson, after stating that the enemy "was condensing a force of 2500 men at La Colle mill;" that general Wilkinson determined on attacking, and "forced back a part of the enemy" in his approach to it, says: "He then resumed his march to La Colle mill, a large and lofty fortified stone-house, measuring 60 feet by 40, and, at that time, in command of major Hancock, and a strong corps of British regulars,—"* or 180 rank and file. After having nearly committed himself, by enumerating nine regiments as composing the American infantry, Mr. Thomson recovers himself thus: "All these regiments were mere skeletons consolidated."* Nor does he any where divulge the actual force of general Wilkinson's army; although, in the published proceedings of that officer's trial, lieutenant-colonel Totten refers to "the statement made to the council of war,"† for the "*effective* force at La Colle."‡ Consequently, the *whole* force present must have exceeded "3999 combatants."† Doctor Smith gives no numbers on either side; and makes his

* Sketches of the War, p. 257. † App. No. 1.

‡ Wilkinson's Mem. Vol. III. p. 234.

account as brief, as if he were writing a chronological table instead of a "History." Mr. O'Connor it is, to whom general Wilkinson owes such obligations. We must give his account nearly at length:

"The issue of this expedition," says Mr. O'Connor, "was unfortunate, although in its progress, it did honor to the Americans engaged. The enemy claimed a victory, only because he was not vanquished; and pretended to gather laurels, while circumstances concurred to render it nearly impossible to attack or drive him from his cowardly strong holds. General Wilkinson, at the head of his division, marched from Champlain, with the intention of reducing the enemy's fortress at the river La Colle. About 11 o'clock he fell in with the enemy at Odell-town, three miles from La Colle, and six* from St. John's. An attack was commenced by the enemy on the advance of the army under colonel Clerk and major Forsyth. Colonel Bissel came up with spirit, and the enemy was forced to retire with loss. General Wilkinson took part in this action, and bravely advanced into the most dangerous position, declining frequently the advice of his officers, to retire from imminent danger. The enemy having used his Congreve rockets, without producing any effect, retired to La Colle, whither he was pursued. At this

* It ought to be 26

place an action was expected; but the enemy, whose force when increased by a reinforcement from the Isle aux Noix, amounted to at least 2500 men, mostly regulars, declined meeting the American force, although much inferior in numbers and means of warfare."—"Several sorties were made by the enemy, but they were resisted with bravery and success."—"The conduct of every individual attached to the American command, was marked by that patriotism and prowess, which has so often conquered the boasted discipline, long experience, and military tactics of an enemy, who dared not to expose his '*invincibles*' to the disgrace of being defeated by a less numerous force of Yankee woodsmen."*

That general Wilkinson himself does not consider that Mr. O'Connor has, by his remarks, conferred any additional ridicule upon the business of La Colle mill, we gather, not only from the general's official account,† but from his efforts, long subsequently, though vainly made, to save his character from reproach. The glaring impracticability of cramming "2500 men" in a building "60 feet by 40," as well as the positive testimony of one of his own officers, that "400 men" only "could act with

* History of the War. p. 219.

† Not published in this work, but the substance fully given in the last quotation.

effect within the mill,"* induced the general, in his address to the court-martial, to state that the building was "defended by a garrison of,"—not "1800 regulars, and 500 militia,—"† but "600 veteran troops."‡ When, however, lieutenant-colonel M'Pherson, in answer to a question from the court, gave it as his opinion, "that the army should have attempted to force a passage into the mill, and employed the bayonet at every sacrifice; or have renewed the attack with heavier ordnance, at daylight the next morning,"§ general Wilkinson, in a note, adds: "To take such a post, with small-arms, has often been attempted, but never succeeded, from the time of Xenophon, who failed in such an attempt, down to the present day." "Xenophon himself," says the general "was baffled in an attempt against a castle, in the plain of Caycus, and also in his attack of the metropolis of the Drylans, and, in times modern as well as ancient, we have abundant examples of the failure of military enterprises, by the most distinguished chiefs."‖ General James Wilkinson, of the United States' army, then has the effrontery to compare his disgraceful discomfiture before this Canadian grist-mill, with what occurred to—"lord Wellington at Burgos,

* Wilkinson's Mem. Vol. III. p. 328. † App. No. 17.
‡ Ibid. p. 454. § Ibid. 329. ‖ Ibid. 455.

Bonaparte at St. Jean d'Acre, and general Graham at Antwerp." * * * * * *

Presuming that the reader is as sick of this *Bobadil* general as we are ourselves, we shall hasten to place him within that sphere of obscurity, for which his talents have best fitted him. After having, with "4000 combatants,"—men who were "to return victorious, or not at all," and who, against "double force," were not to "give ground,"—been completely repulsed by 340 British, 180 of whom had stationed themselves in a strong stone building, and the remainder in a wooden block-house, general Wilkinson counter-marched his troops of "hardihood and resolution," not only to Champlain, but, for fear the men of the mill should travel after him,—30 miles further, to Plattsburg; and that, while the roads, owing to the prevailing thaw, were in the worst possible condition. How he could console himself, we know not; unless it was by saying, with his brother knight-errant of old, after his equally unsuccessful return from attacking a "fortress," of the same use, and (in part*) denomination, too, as La Colle grist-mill,—

"Prithee, hold thy peace, friend Sancho; the affairs of war are, more than any thing, subject to change."

Soon after this incursion into Lower Canada,

* *Wind* for *water*.

a strong British force assembled at Isle aux Noix and St. John's. This very naturally alarmed commodore Macdonough, at Vergennes, Vermont; where he was superintending the construction of a large ship and brig, destined for Lake Champlain. Vergennes stands upon Otter creek; about eight miles from its mouth, or junction with the lake; and, considering the importance of the object, it required no extraordinary penetration to conclude that a competent British force would, the instant the Richelieu was free from ice, embark on board captain Pring's flotilla, now augmented by a new 16-gun brig and some gallies, and proceed to Otter creek; there disembark, and march up to destroy the naval depôt and the ships at Vergennes. To defeat this conjectural plan, a battery of seven guns was erected on a commanding position at the mouth of the creek; a suitable detachment of regular artillery, sent from general Izard's division at Burlington; a reserve of 500 infantry, ordered up from Plattsburg; and arrangements made with the governor of Vermont, for assembling the militia, the instant the first cannon should be fired.

About the middle of April commodore Macdonough succeeded in launching his vessels; but being unprovided with a sufficiency of guns and stores, was too prudent to venture on the lake. On the 9th of May the breaking up of the ice enabled captain Pring, with his flotilla, on board of which was a detachment of marines, to commence ascending the Richelieu. Contrary winds prevented the vessels from reaching the lake till the 13th. No sooner, however, did the British shew themselves off Burlington, than the inhabitants, fearing an immediate descent, began leaving the town, with their property. On the same evening, a bomb-vessel and eight gallies of the flotilla arrived, and took a station, off Otter creek; and, on the next morning, the bomb-vessel commenced a cannonade upon the battery; and continued it for about two hours, without doing any other injury, it appears, than dismounting one of the guns, and wounding two men. The state of preparation in which the enemy was, and the want of troops wherewith to attack him on shore, compelled the vessels to withdraw, and finally, to return to Isle aux Noix.

A most important object was here overlooked by the commander-in-chief. A corps of 8 or 900 men, so easily to have been spared, would have saved the lives of Downie, and his brave comrades, in the September following; and have averted all those attendant circumstances, still so painful to reflect upon.* When we had scarcely a vessel on the lake, an Everard sailed triumphant

* James's Naval Occurrences, p. 404—25.

over it, and a Murray landed at all the towns upon its shores, undismayed, and unopposed, by the fourfold American force assembled in the neighbourhood.* Here was a reverse!—And yet no blame rested with captain Pring, nor with the officers commanding posts at which the British troops were stationed; and from which they ought to have been supplied.

The active operations going on upon Lake Ontario now claim our attention. Although, about the middle of January, not above 800 troops were at Sackett's Harbor, the reasonable supposition that, with the hourly increasing force of the British, the latter would make some attempt to destroy in the bud the immense naval armament there fitting out, to maintain, during the ensuing summer, the ascendancy on the lake, had, by the end of March, brought to the post 5500 troops, including 1500 to be employed as marines on board commodore Chauncey's squadron. The opportunity of destroying this important depôt a second time lost, sir George Prevost, early in May, was induced to consent to a proposition made by sir Gordon Drummond and sir James Lucas Yeo, to employ the new ships that had been so rapidly equipped, in a combined attack upon the fort and town of Oswego; at which

* See Vol. I. p. 242.

place it was supposed, that a large quantity of naval stores for the new ships at Sackett's Harbor had been deposited.

Oswego is situate on the river of the same name, near its confluence with Lake Ontario; and is distant from Sackett's Harbor about 60 miles. At the mouth of the river there is a safe harbor, with two fathoms water; the channel to which is completely commanded by a well-built fort, although not in the best repair, standing, along with the state-warehouses, barracks, and a few houses, upon the eastern shore of the river; having its front towards the lake. The fort is a three-sided figure, with bastions and ramparts; and contains, within its ditches, upwards of three acres of ground. The site is elevated about 50 feet above the level of the lake; thus rendering the position a very formidable one. On the western bank of the river stands the town, consisting of about 30 houses. This river affords the only water-communication between New York and Sackett's Harbor. The course is up the Hudson and Mohawk rivers; then across a short *portage*, to a small stream leading into Lake-Oneida; thence down the Oswego into (subject to a slight interruption by the Onondaga falls, distant about 13 miles from) Lake-Ontario. This readily accounts for the accumulation of naval stores in the warehouses of Oswego; and gives to that post an importance which it would not otherwise possess.

On the evening of the 3d of May, a detachment of troops, consisting of six companies of De Watteville's regiment, including two newly-raised flank-companies,* the light company of the Glengarry's, the whole of the second battalion of marines, a detachment of artillery, with two field-pieces; also small detachments of rocketeers, and sappers and miners: numbering, altogether, 1080 rank and file, embarked in the vessels of sir James Yeo's fleet, lying at Kingston. Early on the following morning lieutenant-general Drummond went on board the Prince Regent, as commander of the troops. The fleet immediately stood out of the harbor; but, on account of light and variable winds, did not arrive off Oswego till noon on the following day.†

Either suspicion, or direct information, of the attack had led to preparations on the part of the Americans. Since the 30th of April lieutenant-colonel Mitchell had arrived from Sackett's Harbor, with 300 heavy and light artillery, and several engineer and artillery officers. The batteries were repaired and fresh picketed, and new platforms laid for the guns; which were four in number, 24, 12, and 6-pounders; besides

* See Vol. I. p. 261. † App. No. 20, 21, and 23.

a 12-pounder, planted *en barbette* close to the lake-shore. The United States' schooner Growler, of three guns, lieutenant Pierce, was lying in the harbor, preparing, under the superintendance of captain Woolsey, to conduct to Sackett's Harbor a division of batteaux, laden with stores. Arrangements had, also, been made for assembling the militia of the district, and no sooner did the fleet shew itself, at six o'clock on the morning of the 5th, than alarm-guns were fired; which soon brought to the post upwards of 200 militia: thus making a total force of, at least, 540 men. By way, also, of making this force appear treble what it was, in the hope, thereby, to daunt the British, and prevent them from attempting to land, the Americans pitched all their tents upon the opposite, or town-side of the river, while they themselves remained in their barracks.

The exact force in guns, men, and size, of every ship in the rival fleets upon this lake, not only at the attack on Oswego, but at several other important periods, during the continuance of hostilities, will be found clearly exhibited in our naval volume.* At three o'clock in the afternoon, the ships lay-to, within long range of the shore; and the gun-boats, 11 in number, were sent in, under the orders of captain Collier, to induce the enemy to shew the number and position of his guns. At four, by which time

* James's Naval Occurrences, p. 394—401.

the gun-boats had got within point-blank range, the Americans opened their fire; and a mutual cannonade was kept up till about half-past five, when captain Collier, having effected his object, stood back to the fleet. Preparations were now made for disembarking the troops on that evening; but, about sunset, a heavy gale from the north-west compelled the ships to gain an offing; in which effort, four of the boats, their crews being first taken out, were obliged to be cut adrift. As soon as the weather moderated, the fleet cast anchor, about 10 miles to the northward of the fort.

The direction and violence of the wind occasioned one of the four boats to drift on shore. This circumstance, added to the afternoon's cannonade, and the retiring of the British gun-boats, became a fruitful subject in the hands of American historians. They all concur in declaring, that the British, on the afternoon of the 5th, were most gallantly repulsed; and one (Mr. O'Connor says, "some") of their boats captured. Nor did the gun-boats only cannonade the fort: the "enemy's principal ship, and the other *frigates* and smaller vessels," opened a heavy fire upon it; and "15 large boats crowded with troops," approached the shore.* It is fortunate, that we have to oppose to all this the statements contained in an "extract from a letter of a United States' officer," (who

* Sketches of the War, p. 262, and Hist. of the War, p. 220.

was in the action,) "dated Oswego-falls, May 7;" which was published in all the principal American newspapers of the day. This officer witnessed the cutting adrift of the boats, and assigned for it the true cause.

On the morning of the 6th, the ships having returned, and every thing being ready, the two flank-companies of De Watteville's regiment, under captain De Bersey, the light company of the Glengarry's, under captain M'Millan, the battalion of marines, under lieutenant-colonel Malcolm, and 200 seamen, armed with pikes, under captain Mulcaster; the whole under the immediate command of lieutenant-colonel Fischer, of De Watteville's; and amounting to about 770 rank and file, embarked in the boats: leaving the four remaining companies of De Watteville's, and the detachments of artillery, rocketeers, and sappers and miners, as a corps of reserve.

Owing to the shoalness of the water off the harbor, the two largest ships could not approach near enough, to cannonade the battery with any effect. This service was most gallantly performed by the Montreal and Niagara, under a heavy discharge of red-hot shot, which set the former on fire three times. The Magnet took her station in front of the town, on the opposite side of the river; while the Star and Charwell towed in, and covered, the boats, containing the troops. The wind was at this time nearly a-head;

and the consequent tardiness in the approach of the boats exposed the men to a heavy and destructive fire from the enemy's batteries, and from upwards of 500 regulars and militia, drawn up on the brow of the hill. The British, nevertheless, effected their landing, and instantly formed on the beach. Having to ascend a steep and long hill, the troops suffered extremely from the enemy's fire; no sooner, however, had they reached the summit, than the 300 American regulars retired to the rear of the fort, and the 200 American militia fled, helter-skelter, into the woods. In ten minutes from the time that the British had gained the height, the fort was in our possession. Lieutenant James Laurie, of the marines, was the first man who entered it; and lieutenant Hewett, of the same corps, climbed the flag-staff, under a heavy fire, and struck the American colours, which had been nailed to the mast; more, as it would seem, to give trouble to the British, than to evince a determination, on the part of the Americans, of defending the post with any unusual obstinacy.

The British loss in the affair of Oswego was rather severe. It amounted to one captain, (captain Holtoway,) and 14 non-commissioned officers and privates, of the royal marines and De Watteville's regiment, and three seamen, killed; one captain, and one subaltern, (since dead,) of De Watteville's; two captains, one lieutenant, and one master of the navy, 51 non-commissioned officers and privates, of the royal marines and De Watteville's, and seven seamen, wounded; total, 18 killed, and 64 wounded. All three of our American editors, one copying from the other, have declared the British loss to have been, "in killed, 70; in wounded, drowned, and missing, 165; in all, 235."* Their own loss the Americans state, at a lieutenant and five men killed, 38 wounded, and 25 missing. We captured 60 prisoners. Admitting this number to include the wounded, it is no proof that the American commander retired quite so leizurely, or in so "good order," as the American writers would have us believe.

The Americans have pursued their usual exaggerating system, as respects the relative numbers in the attack upon Fort-Oswego. General Brown declares that the British force, "by land and water, exceeded 3000;"† but he is not explicit enough to tell us, what portion of this force came on shore and captured the fort. This we gain from other sources. Mr. Thomson says we landed 1700;* Mr. O'Connor, 2000,‡ and doctor Smith, "between 2 and 3000"§ men; but the American officer, who writes from Oswego, states the number that landed, at 1200; which is but a moderate increase upon 770. In estimating their own force at Oswego, the

* Sketches of the War, p. 263. † App. No. 24.

‡ History of the War, p. 220.

§ History of the United States, Vol. III. p. 308.

American writers, not excepting general Brown himself, pursue quite an opposite course. With us, every man within sight or hearing of the place is to be estimated: with them, it is only such as were bold enough to fight. Therefore, because the American militia thought best to run, without firing a shot, they are not to be reckoned as part of the numerical force, whose duty it was to oppose the landing of the British. The behaviour of the militia is well explained in the American officer's letter:—"The militia, at this time," says he, "thought best to leave us: I do not think they fired a gun." Considering the commanding position of the batteries, the length of time during which, owing to the shoalness of the water and state of the wind, the troops a-float were exposed to hot and cold shot and musket-bullets, and, after they did effect a landing, the difficulty of ascending the hill, under the fire from the cannon, and from a body of troops, well-posted upon its summit, it would not have been extraordinary, if 500 men had succeeded in keeping off an enemy "for nearly two days,"* instead of scarcely as many hours; nor would general Brown's "General Order," in which he thought fit to boast, that the Americans at Oswego had "established for themselves a name in arms, worthy of the gallant nation in whose cause

* App. No. 24.

they fight," have had quite so much the air of a lampoon.

Although the chief part of the stores, for the capture of which the expedition had been undertaken, was removed to Onondago falls, about 13 miles from Oswego, a considerable quantity still remained. Among the captured ordnance and ordnance stores, were three long 32, and four long 24-pounders, besides guns of smaller caliber; and several 42 and 32-pounder round, grape, and canister shots. We also captured, and carried away, upwards of 1000 (one official account says 2400*) barrels of provisions,† 70 coils of rope and cordage, a quantity of blocks, two or three schooners, and several boats. Among the property destroyed by us were, eight barrels of gun-powder, all the shot of small caliber, the platform and works at the fort; also the barracks, both there and in the town. We have no very accurate account of what the Americans themselves destroyed. They mention having scuttled and sunk the Growler, United States' schooner, with three long 32-pounders, and a quantity of ordnance-stores, on board. The federal, or opposition papers of the day, complained much against the government, for concealing the amount of the loss sustained at Oswego. How trifling that loss was made, is clearly shewn, by the statements of our three

* App. No. 22. † App. No. 23.

historians upon the subject. Mr. Thomson says: "The enemy took possession of the fort and barracks, but for the little booty which he obtained, consisting of a few barrels of provisions and whiskey, he paid much more than an equivalent."* Doctor Smith declares, that we captured nothing but "a naked fort."† Mr. O'Connor, however, is candid enough to admit, that "eight pieces of cannon, and some stores, worth about 100 dollars, fell into the enemy's hands."‡ On the other hand, an American writer from Onondago, values the public property, destroyed or taken away by the British, at "about 40000 dollars." It was highly creditable to the troops, marines, and seamen, that, although the loading of the prizes with the ordnance and other captured property, necessarily detained them in the town for one whole night, not a murmur of complaint, that we can find, has been uttered against them. Every thing being accomplished by four o'clock on the morning of the 7th, the ships and other vessels got under weigh, and departed from Oswego.

A serious business, in which a party of British officers and seamen, on the 30th of May, impelled by their usual gallantry, pursued a flotilla of American boats, up a narrow creek,

* Sketches of the War, p. 263.

† History of the United States, Vol. III. p. 308.

‡ History of the War, p. 221.

till they got ambushed and outnumbered, and were, at last, compelled, after sustaining a heavy loss in killed and wounded, to surrender, will be found detailed in our naval volume.*

An occurrence on the shores of Lake-Erie now requires our notice. Long-Point in the district of London is notoriously one of the most fertile spots in Upper Canada. The ample supply of wheat and other bread-corn which it afforded during the war, rendered the preservation of its resources by one party, and their destruction by the other, a matter of equal importance. On another account, also, was Long-Point a post that ought to be guarded. It was only a day's march thence to Burlington, the grand depôt of the British army upon the Niagara line; and the enemy's entire command of Lake-Erie gave him the facility of bringing troops towards, and landing them upon, the Canadian shore, unseen and unopposed. Lieutenant-general Drummond, therefore, did right in detaching to the village of Dover on Long-Point, early in March, a troop of the 19th light dragoons, under major Lisle. There being no barracks or public buildings at the place, major Lisle and his men took possession of some private buildings, and, among them, of the dwelling-house, saw-mill, and distillery, of Robert Nichol, esquire, a lieutenant-colonel and quarter-master-general of the Cana-

* James's Nav. Occur. p. 398.

dian militia, and then absent from home on service.*

The British capture of Buffaloe and Black Rock, and the dreaded attack upon Erie, where the fleet lay, had occasioned, since early in the year, the assemblage of a force of regulars at the latter place. Aware of the small detachment stationed at Long-Point, colonel Campbell, of the 19th United States' infantry, with 500 troops,† landed there from Erie, on the 15th of May. The dragoons and the few militia that happened to be at Dover, retired; and the Americans instantly "destroyed the flour-mills, distilleries, and all the houses occupied by the soldiers, as well as many others belonging to the peaceable inhabitants of the village."† Mr. Thomson proceeds in his account thus: "A squadron of British dragoons, stationed at that place, fled at the approach of colonel Campbell's detachment; and abandoned the women and children, who experienced humane treatment from the Americans. Colonel Campbell undertook the expedition without orders; and, as his conduct was generally reprobated, a court of inquiry was instituted, to examine into his proceedings, of which general Scott was president. This court declared, that the destruction of the mills

* And who proved himself, during the whole of the war, an active, intelligent, and highly useful officer.

† Sketches of the War, p. 268.

and distilleries was according to the usages of war, but that, in burning the houses of the inhabitants, colonel Campbell had greatly erred. This error they attributed to the recollection of the scenes of the Raisin and the Miami, in the western territories, to the army of which colonel Campbell was at that time attached, and of the recent devastation of the Niagara frontier."*

Admitting the destruction of the buildings which had been occupied by the dragoons, to have been a sanctioned military measure, was it only an "error" in the American commander, to have burnt the houses "belonging to the peaceable inhabitants of the village"? The court did not lessen its dignity in allowing itself to be swayed by the fabricated stuff in every newspaper "known to be friendly to the war;" nor in forgetting what it was that had caused "the recent devastation on the Niagara frontier," so painful to the sensitive "recollection" of the American colonel? The date of this indulgent court of inquiry does not appear; but, referring to the public letter, in which Mr. Munroe, at a day long subsequent, reminds us, that colonel Campbell's "conduct was subjected to a military tribunal," we can readily conceive, that the court sat for no other purpose than to excuse him, and to exculpate the American government, for the commission of an act, which,

* Sketches of the War, p. 268.

as Mr. Thomson says, was so "generally reprobated." This editor is not satisfied with having, as he supposes, freed colonel Campbell from blame: in order to enable him to expatiate upon that sickening subject, American humanity, he must reproach us. To high-minded Americans it could not fail to appear as a very dastardly act, for 70 or 80 dragoons to retreat before 500 infantry. The British having, however, "abandoned the women and children," we shall now present a specimen of the "humane treatment," which the latter "experienced from the Americans." Not only did colonel Campbell, and his 500 regulars, lay waste as much of the surrounding country as came within their reach, and pilfer and carry off as much private property as was easily portable, but they set fire to the whole of the little village of Dover, comprizing the following 46 buildings: one saw-mill, one tan-house, three distilleries, six stores, 13 barns, three grist-mills, and 19 dwelling-houses; thus utterly ruining 25 "peaceable" families. Yet was all this no more than an "error" on the part of the American commander by whose orders it had been perpetrated.

CHAPTER XIV.

Serious preparations for the fifth invasion of the Canadas—American force on the Niagara frontier—British force in the same neighbourhood—Disembarkation of major-general Brown's army—Capture of Fort-Erie, together with its small garrison—British force at Chippeway—Advance of the American army—Battle of Chippeway, or Street's creek—Retreat of major-general Riall—Return of the Americans to their camp—Fresh movement against the British at Chippeway—Further retreat of the latter to Fort-George—Advance of the Americans to Queenstown—Spirited behaviour of a British patrolling party—General Brown's plans developed—General Riall's departure from Fort-George to the Twenty, and Fifteen-mile, creeks—American reconnoissance before Fort-George—Wanton conflagration of the village of St. David—Investment of Fort-George—Retreat of the Americans to Queenstown—Destruction of their baggage, and further retreat to Chippeway—Corresponding advance of major-general Riall's light troops—Re-advance of the Americans towards Queenstown—Skirmishing between the adverse piquets—Arrival of lieutenant-general Drummond with a reinforcement—Detachment sent across to Lewistown—General

Drummond's junction with general Riall—Battle of Niagara, or Lundy's lane—Retreat of the Americans to Chippeway and Street's creek—Their destruction of Street's mills, and of their own baggage, camp-equipage and stores—Their further retreat to Fort-Erie—Various American accounts of these operations—Their gross misstatements corrected.

EARLY in April major-general Brown, with a strong force in regulars, marched, a second time, from Sackett's Harbor to Batavia; and thence to Buffaloe, where he fixed his head-quarters. Here he remained drilling his troops, and receiving occasional reinforcements, till the middle of June; when he received orders, "to carry Fort-Erie, and beat up the enemy's quarters at Chippeway; but," adds the American secretary at war, "in case his fleet gets the control of Lake Ontario, you are immediately to re-cross the strait."* This late commencement of the campaign arose, no doubt, from the backwardness of commodore Chauncey to decide the ascendancy upon Lake Ontario; without which the objects of the American government could be only partially fulfilled.

It took major-general Brown from the 15th of June to the 2d of July, to prepare himself for crossing the Niagara; which, according to the "General Order"† issued upon the occasion, he

* Wilkinson's Mem. Vol. I. p. 641. † App. No. 25.

was then about to do, with two brigades of infantry, a corps of artillery, and a body of volunteers. As far as we can gather from the American accounts, one brigade consisted of the 9th, 11th, 22d, and 25th regiments, under brigadier-general Scott; the other, of the 17th, 19th, 21st, and 23d regiments, under brigadier-general Ripley; the two united brigades numbering 2580 rank and file. The corps of artillery consisted of upwards of 400 men, having in charge eight field-pieces, and one or two howitzers; including, among the former, several 18 and 12-pounders. There was, also, a squadron of dragoons, under captain Harris; which we may estimate at 70 men. To this regular force of 3050 rank and file, were added from 8 to 1100 (say 900) New York, Pennsylvania, and "Canadian" (or traitor) volunteers; and about 150 Indians: making a total force of 4100 rank and file. Besides this force, there were, at different posts between Erie and Lewistown, the 1st regiment of infantry, a regular rifle corps, and from 2 to 300 volunteers, under a colonel Swift; making an aggregate of, at least, 5000 men. But even this number does not include the militia of the district, who, in case of invasion, could assemble to the amount of 2 or 3000; nor 3 or 4000 regulars, whom commodore Chauncey, if disposed to be bold, might bring down from Sackett's harbor. So that the command of Lake

Ontario could very speedily augment the American force upon the Niagara to 10000 men.

The British force upon the same frontier was, at this time, under the command of major-general Riall, and consisted of the royal Scots, (1st bat.) 100th, and 103d regiments, a troop of the 19th light dragoons, and a detachment of artillery; numbering, altogether, about 1780 rank and file. But out of this force were garrisoned the forts Erie, George, Mississaga, and Niagara; (the latter on the American side of the strait;) also the post upon Burlington Heights; comprehending an extent of frontier of full 70 miles.

On the morning of the 3d of July, general Brown's army crossed the strait, in two divisions; one division landing about a mile and a half below, the other about the same distance above, Fort-Erie; against which the American troops immediately marched. Having planted a battery of 18-pounders in a good position in front of the fort, and fired, and received in return, a few shots; by which a loss was sustained; on our part, of one man killed, and, on the part of the Americans, of four men of the 25th regiment wounded, major-general Brown summoned the fort to surrender. Fort-Erie was, at this time, garrisoned by two companies of the 8th and 100th regiments, and a small detachment of artillery, under major Buck, of the 8th; and, in respect to armament or means of resistance, was, as an American general says, "in a defenceless condition."* The fort, consequently, surrendered. The prisoners, 170, including officers of all ranks, were taken across the river, to be marched into the interior of New York; and a small detachment of American artillery, under lieutenant Macdonough, placed as a garrison within the captured fort: in front of which, on the lake, were stationed, as a further security, three armed schooners, under the orders of lieutenant-commandant Kennedy, of the United States' navy.

The British force at Chippeway was under the immediate command of lieutenant-colonel Pearson; and consisted of 230 of the royal Scots, 450 of the 100th regiment, a troop of light dragoons, and a small detachment of artillery, amounting, in all, to 760 rank and file; exclusive of 300 sedentary militia, just assembled at the rendezvous, and about the same number of Indians. The first intelligence of the landing of the invading army reached major-general Riall at Chippeway, at about eight o'clock on the same morning; and he immediately ordered that post to be reinforced by five companies of the royal Scots; but even then, his inferiority of force forbad any other movement, than for the purpose of reconnoitring the enemy's position

* Wilkinson's Mem. Vol. I. p. 647.

and numbers. This service was gallantly performed by lieutenant-colonel Pearson, at the head of the flank companies of the 100th regiment, and a few militia and Indians; and the Americans were seen posted on an eminence, near the ferry at Bertie.* Major-general Riall would have commenced the attack on that evening, had he been joined by the 8th regiment, then hourly expected from York.

On the morning of the 4th, general Scott's brigade, with a company of artillery, advanced, by the main road along the margin of the river, towards Chippeway; and was soon afterwards followed by general Ripley's brigade, and the field and park artillery, under major Hindman; also by general Porter and his volunteers.† On its approach to Street's creek, the first brigade encountered the British advance, now consisting of the light companies of the royal Scots and 100th regiments, and a subaltern's detachment of the 19th light dragoons. General Scott immediately detached in front captain Towson's company of artillery, (100 strong,) with three 18-pounders; and, at the same time, directed a flank company of the 9th regiment of infantry to march out to the left of the brigade, and cross the creek above the bridge; so as to assail the right of the British advance. The heavy firing of the enemy's 18-pounders, and

* See Vol. I. p. 50. † Sketches of the War, p. 274.

the close approach of his main body, compelled colonel Pearson and his small party, to retreat; but "not until they had intrepidly destroyed the bridge over which the advancing column would be obliged to pass."* Captain Crooker's company of the 9th regiment came suddenly upon the detachment of dragoons, under lieutenant Horton, while the latter was covering colonel Pearson's retreat. A skirmish ensued, and the American detachment, which had retreated to a house, would have certainly been captured, but for the arrival of a strong reinforcement, under captains Hull and Harrison, and lieutenant Randolph. Out of this skirmish, in which four of the dragoons, and eight of their horses, were wounded, Mr. Thomson has woven a fine story; concluding it with the declaration of one of the American generals, that, "in partizan war, he had witnessed nothing more gallant than the conduct of captain Crooker and his company."* The American pioneers having repaired the bridge, the army crossed; and, at about 11 o'clock on that night, encamped on the right bank of Street's creek; the first brigade facing the creek and the bridge; the second brigade forming the second line; and the volunteers, the third. The park of artillery was stationed on the right of the encampment, resting on some buildings and an orchard, close to the

* Sketches of the War, p. 274.

river Niagara; and the light troops, or riflemen, together with the Indians, were posted within the same space, on the left, resting on the woods.

The American army, thus encamped, will only differ in numbers from that which crossed the strait,* in the absence of the small garrison, say 50 men, left at Fort-Erie, under lieutenant Macdonough. Consequently, major-general Brown had, under his immediate command at Street's creek, 3000 regulars, (including 70 dragoons,) 900 New York, Pennsylvania, and Canadian volunteers, and 150 Indians; total, 4050 men; along with nine field-pieces and howitzers, including some 12, and three 18-pounders.

Major-general Riall had stationed himself on the left bank of the Chippeway, distant about 1¾ miles from the American encampment; and, having been joined, on the morning of the 5th, by 480 rank and file of the 8th regiment, determined to attack the Americans on that afternoon. His force now consisted of 1530 regulars, (including about 70 dragoons,) 300 sedentary militia,† and about the same number of Indians; total, 2130 men; along with two 24-pounders, and a 5½ inch howitzer.

At the appointed hour the British crossed the Chippeway, and marched to the attack; the Indians, and a part of the militia, advancing

* See p. 116.

† Only partially armed.

through the woods on the right, which were skirted by the remainder of the militia, and by the light companies of the royal Scots and 100th regiments, under lieutenant-colonel Pearson. The approach of the Indians being discovered by the Americans, general Porter, with the whole of his volunteers and Indians, supported by a detachment of 80 men from the second brigade, under captain W. Macdonald, was ordered to advance from the rear, and drive them back. About 220 of our Indians, led by Norton, had kept too much to the right, and were wholly out of the action. The remaining 80, consisting chiefly of Wyandots, led by captain Kerr, on being encountered by general Porter's brigade, fell back, first, upon the militia, and then, along with the latter, upon colonel Pearson's detachment of regulars. A spirited action now ensued; but a few well-directed volleys from the British presently reversed the order of things; and general Porter's brigade of volunteers and Indians gave way, and "fled in every direction." So said general Brown.* But general Porter himself says:—"The action of Chippeway, in which the volunteers took so conspicuous a part, will ever be remembered, to the honor of the American arms. It was commenced by 800 Pennsylvania volunteers and Indian warriors, who met about the same number of British

* Wilkinson's Mem. Vol. I. p. 658.

militia and Indians, overthrew and drove them behind the main line of the British army; destroying, at least, 150, and annihilating, it is believed, this description of the enemy's force."*

The reader may well conceive, what a paragraph can be made out of this modest eulogium, by an American editor; and who so able as Mr. Thomson?—Thus, then, says the latter:—"General Porter met, attacked, and, after a short but severe contest, drove, the enemy's right before him. His route to Chippeway was intercepted by the whole British column, arrayed in order of battle; and against this powerful force the volunteers desperately maintained their ground; until they were overpowered by the superiority of discipline and numbers."† Not only does major-general Riall's despatch shew, clearly, that Mr. Thomson's "whole British column" consisted of "the light troops,"‡ under colonel Pearson; but general Wilkinson himself is compelled to admit, that his friend, general Porter, "surprised a body of Indians, who appeared to be in consultation, and immediately gave way; but, keeping up a brisk skirmish, retreated to where they were strongly reinforced by the enemy's troops," (called "irregulars" in the very next paragraph,) "who, in

* Wilkinson's Mem. Vol. I. p. 658.

† Sketches of the War, p. 277. ‡ App. No. 26.

turn, forced Porter to retreat."* In this way do we expose a "general Porter," as completely as, we trust, we formerly did a "commodore" or captain, of the same name,† and, it seems likely, of the same family too.

Colonel Pearson, with his light troops, militia, and Indians, pursued general Porter's brigade of volunteers and Indians, and captain Macdonald's 80 regulars; till the arrival of a strong reinforcement from general Ripley's brigade, including the whole of the 25th regiment, obliged the British advance to fall back, in its turn. While this skirmishing was going on upon the right of the British line, major-general Riall had drawn up his troops before the enemy's position; placing the 8th regiment, and the two light 24-pounders and howitzer, upon the left, and the royal Scots and 100th regiments, directly in front. The enemy had posted his artillery upon the right of his line; which consisted of the 1st, or general Scott's brigade, and a portion of the 2d, or general Ripley's brigade: another portion had been detached in support of the 3d, or general Porter's brigade of volunteers.

The royal Scots and 100th regiments were ordered to charge the enemy's column. The ground over which they had to pass was uneven, and covered with long grass, which greatly impeded their progress. It was not, however,

* Wilkinson's Mem. Vol. I. p. 651.

† James's Nav. Occur. p. 305—20.

till the enemy's musketry, and a flanking fire from four pieces of his artillery, had caused a serious loss of killed and wounded in the ranks of these brave regiments, that the attempt was given up. Any further contest with a force so superior in numbers being considered as unavailing, the British troops were directed to retire upon Chippeway. This they did in the most perfect order; bringing away, among their guns, a piece that had been disabled, and losing in prisoners none but the wounded. So gallantly was the retreat covered by the 8th regiment and colonel Pearson's light detachment, that the Americans were deterred from advancing with sufficient promptitude, to hinder the British from destroying the bridge across the Chippeway; on the left bank of which, major-general Riall again encamped. This the American general calls being "closely pressed."*

The British loss in the battle of Street's creek was very severe. The killed amounted to three captains, three subalterns, seven serjeants, and 135 rank and file; the wounded, to three field-officers, (including the commanding officers of the royal Scots and 100th regiments,) five captains, 18 subalterns, 18 serjeants, and 277 rank and file; and the missing, to one subaltern, one serjeant, and 44 rank and file; total, 148 killed; 321 wounded; and 46 missing: grand total, (including 433 of the two

* App. No. 28.

before-mentioned regiments,) 515.* The royal Scots were now reduced, in effective strength, to 275, the 100th, to 245, and general Riall's whole force, of regulars, militia, and Indians, to under 1520, rank and file. The loss of the Americans, in the same battle, amounted to two serjeants, and 58 rank and file, killed; one colonel, three captains, seven subalterns, 14 serjeants, and 210 rank and file, wounded; and one lieutenant-colonel, one major, one captain, (all of militia,) two serjeants, and 22 rank file, missing; total, 60 killed; 235 wounded; and 27 missing; grand total, 322:* thus leaving general Brown a force of full 3730 men.

Considering that the firing between the main bodies of the two armies did not continue beyond an hour and a half, and that the 8th regiment, from the nature of its position, participated very slightly in the engagement, the loss on both sides is a proof of the spirit with which it was contested. It is rather extraordinary, that not one of our three historians should have thought fit to state numbers on either side; yet do they all concur in declaring, that the numerical superiority was in our favor. Mr. O'Connor's account not less for its conciseness than its gross extravagance, is worthy of insertion. "The American troops," says this writer, "on no occasion behaved with more gallantry than on the present. The British

* App. No. 27. † App. No. 29.

regulars suffered defeat from a number of men, principally volunteers and militia, — inferior in every thing but courage to the vanquished enemy."*—This is the man whose title-page has the words: "Carefully compiled from official documents;" and yet, who pretends to be ignorant, that the "official" returns on his own side, particularize five regiments of regular infantry and a corps of artillery, as having suffered a loss in the action. Even general Wilkinson, so cautious in these matters, states the effective strength of general Scott's brigade, alone, at 1100 regular infantry,† and the force that crossed the strait under general Brown, at about 3500 men,‡ including about 2700 regulars. §

We will readily admit that, in this battle, the Americans fought with more bravery and determination, than they had done since the war commenced. No opportunity, however, occurred, of employing the bayonet to any advantage; and our troops had to resort to musketry; "in which," says general Wilkinson, "the American soldier, from habits of early life, will always excel." || The general adds: "Comparing small with great things, here, as at Minden, the fate of the day was settled by the artillery; and the American Towson may deservedly be ranked with the British Philips,

* Hist. of the War, p. 254.'

† Wilkinson's Mem. Vol. I. p. 654.

‡ Ibid. p. 646. § Ibid. 668. || Ibid. 652

Drummond, and Foy."* Poor general Wilkinson's comparisons are the most amusing part of his book. Without elevating "the American Towson" to quite so lofty a station, we may observe, that the Americans deserve great credit for the attention they pay to their artillery; which is, in general, fully as well served as our own, and, excepting the accidental circumstance of our having two 24-pounders in this action, of much heavier caliber.

The readiness of the Americans to engage, at the battle of Street's creek, appears to have originated in mis-information. From the prisoners taken at Fort-Erie general Brown learned, that major-general Riall's regular force at Chippeway consisted solely of the first battalion of the royal Scots, and the 100th regiment; and consequently, of not more than 11 or 1200 men. The American commander, therefore, with his 3000 "accomplished troops,"† advanced boldly to the attack. This is confirmed by Mr. Thomson; who, not only mentions no other than the above two regiments as present, but states, that lieutenant-general Drummond ordered up "the 8th or king's regiment from York," in consequence of "the defeat of major-general Riall."‡

On the other hand, intelligence reached the British,—probably through emissaries, or

* Wilkinson's Memoirs, Vol. I. p. 652.

† App. No. 28. ‡ Sketches of the War, p. 280.

spies, purposely sent from the American camp, —that general Brown's force exceeded 5000 men; and major-general Riall himself, from the report of the American militia-officers, taken prisoners at the commencement of the action, considered the enemy's force to amount to "6000 men, with a very numerous train of artillery."† We here see a striking difference in the impression respecting his adversary's strength, under which each of the generals led his troops into battle.

During the 6th and 7th of July, general Brown remained quiet at his encampment on the bank of Street's creek; but, on the morning of the 8th, he determined upon an attempt to dislodge major-general Riall, who was still stationed at Chippeway. To effect this object, general Ripley proceeded, with his brigade and the artillery, to a point on the right bank of the Chippeway, three miles above the British camp, in order to open a road of communication, and to construct a bridge across the river, or creek, for the passage of the troops. After the Americans had planted their artillery on the bank, a detachment of general Riall's artillery arrived in front; but the latter, having now in charge two pieces only, was obliged, after a slight cannonade, to withdraw. The bridge was soon afterwards completed; and the whole of the

* App. No. 26.

American force crossed over. In the mean while, major-general Riall had broken up his encampment, and retired towards Queenstown and Fort-George; at which latter place he arrived on that evening. During the same night, general Brown occupied Chippeway; and, on the following morning, advanced to Queenstown; where he again encamped.

On the 12th, while the Americans were at Queenstown, brigadier-general Swift was detached, with 120 (one American account says 200) of general Porter's volunteers,* to reconnoitre general Riall's position at Fort-George. On arriving near the fort, general Swift, with his detachment, came suddenly upon a corporal and five men, belonging to a patrolling party of 32 rank and file from the light company of the 8th, under major Evans of that regiment. One of the five privates levelled his piece at the American general; and, after mortally wounding him, was himself shot dead. His five comrades now fell back upon the remaining 26 men of their detachment; who, on the report of the first musket, had, with major Evans at their head, marched forward to the spot. The 31 British were instantly surrounded by their 120 opponents; but the former, by their skill and promptitude, extricated themselves, without further loss, from their perilous situation. Mr.

* Sketches of the War, p. 281.

Thomson, who is the only editor that notices the affair, magnifies our force to 60 men; and then pretends that the man, after he had surrendered, shot general Swift. The truth is, from the hour that the Americans landed near Fort-Erie, those inhabitants who "behaved peaceably, and followed their private ocupations,"* instead of being, as was promised by general Brown, in his proclamation to the Canadians, "treated as friends," were plundered of their property, and, in many instances, sent as prisoners to the American side. By way, therefore, of palliating the enormities known to have been committed by the American army in its progress through the country, Mr. Thomson prepares this account of general Swift's death; adding:—"The whole volunteer brigade to which the general was attached, solicited an opportunity to avenge the fall of their brave officer; and an opportunity was not long wanted."†

While at his encampment at Queenstown, general Brown writes commodore Chauncey, under date of the 13th July, to the following effect:—"All accounts agree that the force of the enemy in Kingston is very light. Meet me on the lake-shore, north of Fort-George, with your fleet; and we will be able, I have no doubt, to settle a plan of operation that will break the power of the enemy in Upper Canada, and that in the course of a short time. At all events, let

* App. No. 25. † Sketches of the War, p. 282.

me hear from you; I have looked for your fleet with the greatest anxiety, since the 10th. I do not doubt my ability to meet the enemy in the field, and to march in any direction over his country; your fleet carrying for me the necessary supplies. We can threaten forts George and Niagara, and carry Burlington-Heights and York; and proceed direct to Kingston, and carry that place. For God's sake let me see you. Sir James will not fight. Two of his vessels are now in Niagara river. If you conclude to meet me at the head of the lake, and that immediately, have the goodness to bring the guns and troops that I have ordered from Sackett's Harbor.*

Commodore Chauncey, knowing better than that sir James would not fight, was lying at Sackett's Harbor, awaiting the equipment of his second frigate, the Mohawk; "to maintain," says an American editor, "the existing equality;" but, in reality, to acquire that *one-third* superiority, without which it would not be prudent to appear on the lake.†

On the morning of the 9th, major-general Riall, leaving at the forts George and Mississaga, in lieu of the 350 rank and file of the Glengarry regiment, and of the 300 militia,‡ by whom he had

* Wilkinson's Memoirs, Vol. I. p. 666.

† James's Naval Occurrences, p. 399.

‡ Both recently arrived from York.

there been joined, detachments of the royal Scots, and 8th, and the remaining 245 of the 100th, regiments, proceeded, with a force in regulars and militia, amounting to about 1360 rank and file, towards Burlington heights; where he expected to meet the 103d regiment, and the flank companies of the 104th, the latter of which had recently arrived there. This junction was fortunately effected at the Twenty-mile creek; whence the major-general, with his force, now augmented to about 2000 regulars and militia, marched back to, and took post at, the Fifteen-mile creek, distant about 13 miles from the American camp.

Intelligence of this movement on the part of major-general Riall, unaccompanied, however, by any account of his having been joined by the 103d regiment, reached general Brown on the 14th, the day after he had called for commodore Chauncey's co-operation. The British force, thus assembled, was stated to consist of one wing of the royal Scots, the 100th regiment, and the Glengarry light infantry; amounting, in all, to 1250 men, besides 800 incorporated militia and Indians; making a total of 2050 men.* We have here the total, though not the details, of the British force, as accurately stated as need be. Had the junction of the 103d regiment been known, we may well suppose that major-general Riall's force would have been

* Wilkinson's Memoirs, Vol. I. p. 669.

swelled out to 3000 men ; but, although considered to be a third below that amount, no attack was to be made, without the sanction of a council of war. General Brown's force, on this occasion, "was estimated at 2700 regulars, and 1000 volunteers, militia, and Indians ;"* which amounts, within 30 men, to what we stated to have been that officer's force, after the battle of Street's creek. At this council the minority was for attacking major-general Riall ; the majority, for investing Fort-George. Accordingly, on the 15th, general Ripley's brigade of regulars, and general Porter's brigade of volunteers, accompanied by a detachment of regular artillery, with a 6-pounder and a 5½ inch howitzer, the whole numbering about 2200 rank and file, advanced to the neighbourhood of the British fort. While this strong body of American troops was reconnoitring the fortifications, lieutenant-colonel Tucker, with the detachment of the 8th regiment, and two 6-pounder field-pieces, moved out from Fort-Mississaga ; and, being joined by the few royals from Fort-George, and aided by the guns of that fort, compelled the Americans, in spite of their great superiority of numbers, to retire to a more respectable distance. Not a casualty occurred on our part.

Several slight skirmishes afterwards took place between the adverse piquets, in which the Americans were almost the only sufferers. The fur-

* Wilkinson's Memoirs, Vol. I. p. 669.

ther proceedings of the American troops before Fort-George, are tolerably well defined in major M'Farland's letter:—"The militia and Indians, says he, "plundered and burnt every thing. The whole population is against us: not a foraging party, but is fired on, and not unfrequently return with missing numbers. This state was to be anticipated. The Indians were sent off some days since," (letter dated 25th of July,) "as they were found useless, except to plunder. The militia have burnt several private dwelling-houses; and, on the 19th instant, burnt the village of St. David, consisting of about 30 or 40 houses, This was done within three miles of camp; and my battalion was sent to cover the retreat, as they (the militia) had been sent to scour the country of some Indians and rangers, and it was presumed they might be pursued. My God! what a service, I never witnessed such a scene; and, had not the commanding officer of the party, lieutenant-colonel Stone, been disgraced, and sent out of the army, I should have handed in my sheep-skin.*"— The major declares, in the very same letter,—as a proof of his being a staunch American,—that he desires no better fun than to fight the British troops, (whom he politely calls, "European cut-throats,") giving to them one fourth more than his own number. What, then, must have been the "scenes" and sufferings,

* Commission.

that could excite compassion in such a breast as this?

Although none of the American historians bestow a word upon the burning of St. David's, and the pillage of the surrounding country, we now perceive to what Mr. Thomson more particularly alluded, when he told us, that the whole volunteer brigade had solicited leave to avenge general Swift's death, and that "an opportunity was not long wanted." It is true, lieutenant-colonel Stone was declared, by a "General Order," to have "directed" the burning of St. David's, "contrary to the orders of government;" and the same document concluded thus:—"Lieutenant-colonel Stone will retire from the army." But this summary method of discharging officers was, in the American camp, as customary as it proved ineffectual. Among many instances, general Brown, soon after the battle of Street's creek, ordered captain Treat, of the 21st infantry, "on the spot, to retire from the army," for having been guilty of *cowardice*; and yet a court-martial, presently afterwards, re-instated that officer in his command. Why was not lieutenant-colonel Stone tried for his offence, and thereby allowed an opportunity of shewing whether or not he had exceeded his orders? If he set fire to St. David's without orders, was there not a "General Order," issued by general Brown himself, in which it was expressly declared, that—"Any plunderer shall be punished with death"?* But that the Canadians had experienced, both in their persons and properties, so many flagrant violations of that "General Order," as to entitle it to be considered, unless, in its intended operation upon the public mind, as mere blank paper, we might suppose that the gallant colonel had saved himself, by the quibbling excuse, that he was not a "plunderer," but an incendiary. The most extraordinary thing is, however, that the American government, within seven weeks after the burning of St. David's, and when some apology for that, among other atrocities, was thought due to the representations made on our part, should say;—"For the burning of St. David's, committed by stragglers, the officer who commanded in that quarter was dismissed, without a trial, for not preventing it."† Lieutenant-colonel Stone, then, was not "dismissed without a trial," because he "directed," but "for not preventing," the burning of the village; nor was the act committed by the militia sent, under the orders of this very colonel, "to scour the country," but by "stragglers," under the orders of no one; and this, although the American camp was only three miles off.

On the day succeeding the conflagration of St. David's, general Brown abandoned his

* App. No. 25.

† Mr. Munro's letter to sir Alexander Cochrane, dated Sept. 6, 1814.

encampment at Queenstown, and concentrated his whole force in the neighbourhood of Fort-George; stationing a part of it on the shore of Lake Ontario, to keep a sharp look-out for the arrival of commodore Chauncey's fleet, with the anxiously expected "guns and troops from Sackett's Harbor." After waiting in suspense from the 20th to the 23d, general Brown prepared to retrace his steps to Queenstown and Chippeway; in order, as he says, to draw a supply of provisions from Schlosser, and then march directly to Burlington Heights.* American caution was never more conspicuous than in this retrograde movement of general Brown's. The fortifications of Fort-George were not in a better state than when general M'Clure, with a garrison of upwards of 2000, abandoned them to colonel Murray, with fewer than 500 men;† and now that fort was garrisoned by a smaller number than then besieged it, and was beseiged by double the number that then composed its garrison. Yet major M'Farland, in his before-mentioned letter, assigns, as a reason for general Brown's retreat, that it would require "6000 men, with a large train of battering artillery," to make any impression upon Fort-George. The Americans seem determined to remind us, as well of general M'Clure's bloodless surrender of this same fort, as of

* App. No. 32. † See p. 11.

colonel Murray's gallant assault upon, and capture of, their own Fort-Niagara.

General Brown, with his army, entered Queenstown on the evening of the 23d; and, on the next day, this American general, who had scarcely done boasting that he did not doubt his ability "to meet the enemy in the field, and to march in any direction over his country," finding, by accounts from Sackett's Harbor, that the commodore was unable, or, rather, unwilling, to leave port, became so "apprehensive of an attack upon the rear of his army," * that he not only continued his retreat to Chippeway, but, to quicken his movements, disencumbered the army of its baggage.† Having re-crossed the Chippeway, general Brown encamped on the right bank of that river, with the whole of his army, except the 9th regiment, which was posted on the left, or north bank, protected in front by a block-house. It ought not to be omitted, that the Americans, during their retreat to this place, plundered, and made prisoners of, several of the inhabitants.

Intelligence of general Brown's arrival at Chippeway reached general Riall, on the same afternoon; and, at eleven o'clock that night, the British advance, consisting of the Glengarry regiment, under lieutenant-colonel Battersby; 40 men of the 104th, under lieutenant-colonel

* Sketches of the War, p. 283. † App. No. 32.

Drummond; the incorporated militia, under lieutenant-colonel Robinson, and the sedentary militia, under lieutenant-colonel Parry, of the 103d; major Lisle's troop of the 19th light dragoons, and a detachment of artillery, having in charge the two 24-pounders and howitzer employed at Street's creek, and three 6-pounders; the whole numbering about 950 rank and file, and placed under the immediate command of lieutenant-colonel Pearson, moved from the Twelve-mile creek; and, at seven o'clock the next morning, took up a position near Lundy's lane, leading into the main Queenstown, or Niagara road, and distant from the American encampment about $2\frac{3}{4}$ miles.

The American general, having received intelligence that the British had crossed over, in considerable numbers, from Queenstown to Lewistown; and that the force near Lundy's lane was a mere patrolling party, determined, by way of causing a diversion, to re-occupy the former village. Accordingly, at about a quarter past five on the afternoon of the 25th, general Scott, at the head of his own brigade of regular infantry, Towson's artillery, with his two 18-pounders, "and all the dragoons and mounted men,"* numbering, as we gather from the American accounts, fully 1150 rank and file, marched towards Queenstown; with

* App. No. 32.

special orders "to report if the enemy appeared, and to call for assistance, if that was necessary."*

On arriving at the falls, just two miles from camp, the advanced piquets commenced firing; and general Scott immediately despatched two or three officers in succession, to acquaint general Brown, that the enemy was in force, directly in his front; although he confessed that a narrow wood intercepted that force from his view. As the enemy "was in force," it became "necessary" to send "assistance;" therefore general Brown, who had been reinforced by 250 men of the 1st, and 100 men of the 22d regiments, just arrived in three schooners from Erie, taking with him generals Ripley's and Porter's brigades, and major Hindman's corps of artillery, having in charge seven field-pieces, instantly "pressed forward with ardor."* In the mean while, some of the American officers, having heard at Mrs. Wilson's house, near the falls, and reported to general Scott, "that the enemy could not be in force,"† that officer, with the first brigade, the artillery, and dragoons, "pressed forward with ardor," to attack the British advance. General Riall, who happened to be with the latter, considering general Scott's detachment as merely the van of a force nearly four times superior to his own, ordered colonel

* App. No. 32.

† Wilkinson's Mem. Vol. I. his App. No. 9.

Pearson to retire upon Queenstown; and sent similar orders to colonel Scott, who, with the main body, was advancing from the Twelve-mile creek. We must now relate what caused a sudden change in the destination of the retreating British force.

As soon as intelligence of major-general Riall's discomfiture at Street's creek reached lieutenant-general Drummond at Kingston, the latter, leaving orders for De Watteville's regiment to follow, in two columns, marched to York, with the remnant of the 2d battalion of the 89th regiment, about 400 strong, under lieutenant-colonel Morrison. On the evening of the 24th, the lieutenant-general and suite, with the 89th, embarked at York, on board sir James Yeo's vessels, the Netley, Charwell, Star, and Magnet; and arrived at Fort-Niagara at day-light on the morning of the 25th. Having despatched to Queenstown the 89th regiment, and the detachments of the royal Scots and 8th which had been left by general Riall in the forts George and Mississaga, lieutenant-general Drummond ordered lieutenant-colonel Tucker to proceed up the right bank of the Niagara, with 300 of the 41st, about 200 of the royal Scots, and a body of Indians, supported on the river by a party of armed seamen, under captain Dobbs, of the Charwell brig, in order to disperse or capture an American force encamped at Lewistown. Some unavoidable delay occurred in the march of the troops up the right bank; and colonel Swift, with his 200 volunteers, and whatever other troops belonged to the post, had effected their escape towards Schlosser, and crossed over to the American camp at Chippeway. The British arrived in time only to take possession of about 100 tents, a quantity of baggage and provisions; with which, at about four o'clock on the same afternoon, they crossed over to Queenstown, and there met the detachment under lieutenant-colonel Morrison. After the troops had dined, lieutenant-general Drummond sent back, as garrisons to the three forts in the rear, 220 of the 41st, and the whole remaining strength of the 100th regiments, under the orders of lieutenant-colonel Tucker; and hastened forward to the falls, with the 89th regiment, detachments of the royal Scots, and 8th, and the light company of the 41st regiments, numbering, altogether, 815 rank and file.

No sooner had this seasonable reinforcement, after a rapid march of seven miles from Queenstown, and of 14 altogether, arrived within half a mile of Lundy's lane, than information was brought of the retreat of major-general Riall's advanced division; and the troops had scarcely halted, ere they were joined by the militia which had formed part of it, and whose retreat had been ably covered by the Glengarry regiment. General Drummond, first despatching an officer to recall colonel Scott, pushed forward to Lundy's lane; where he arrived a few minutes before six o'clock, and just as the enemy had approached within 600 yards of the top of the hill. The British force was quickly formed;—the 89th regiment, the 320 men of the royal Scots, and the 41st light company, in the rear of the hill, with their left resting on the Queenstown, or Niagara road; the two 24-pounders a little in advance of the centre, on the summit of the hill; the Glengarry regiment, in the woods on the right of the line; and the militia, and the 120 men of the 8th, on the left of the Niagara road, with the light dragoons, on the same road, a little in the rear: constituting a total of 1770 rank and file, supported by two 24-pounders, two 6-pounders, and a 5½-inch howitzer. Scarcely had the different corps taken their stations, than the American troops, under the command of general Scott, commenced the attack. With the exception, however, of partially forcing back the left, the Americans could make no impression upon the British troops; and, after nearly an hour's combat, retired behind a new line, formed by generals Ripley's and Porter's brigades; to the former of which the 1st regiment, under colonel Nicholas,* and to the latter, a fresh

* App. No. 32.

party of volunteers, had been attached: thus making the total force, under general Brown, upwards of 4000 men.

Finding the British guns upon the hill very destructive, the Americans made several desperate efforts to carry them. After being most gallantly resisted by the 89th, the detachments of the royal Scots and 8th regiments, and the sedentary militia under colonel Parry, the great numerical superiority, and, certainly, well-directed fire, of the American infantry and artillery, enabled them to gain their point. They had no leizure, however, to remove, or, at this time, to employ the captured pieces. The battle had now raged for three hours; "the thickest and most impenetrable darkness prevailed;"* and both armies had suspended their fire; one to collect and re-organize its "faultering" regiments; the other to await the reinforcement momentarily expected from the Twelve-mile creek. Just at the hour of nine, colonel Scott, with the 103d regiment, detachments of the royal Scots, 8th, and 104th regiments, and about 300 sedentary militia, few of whom had muskets, accompanied by two 6-pounders, and numbering, altogether, 1230 rank and file, now came upon the ground. It had been intended that colonel Scott's division should march from the Twelve-mile creek, and the men were

* Wilkinson's Mem. Vol. I. his App. No. 9.

actually under arms, at three o'clock in the morning. Unfortunately, however, the order was countermanded, and the troops did not move till past mid-day. At about a quarter before six, and just as they had arrived within three miles of the field of battle, came general Riall's order for them to retire upon Queenstown; and they had actually made a retrogade movement of nearly four miles, before they received general Drummond's order to re-advance. Having thus been nine hours on the march, the men were a good deal blown and fatigued, when they joined the contending division.

Owing to the extreme darkness of the night, the 103d regiment, and the sedentary militia, under colonel Hamilton, with the two field-pieces, passed, by mistake, into the centre of the American army, now posted upon the hill; and, after sustaining a very heavy and destructive fire, fell back in confusion. The 103d, however, by the exertions of its officers, afterwards rallied; and formed in line to the right of general Drummond's front column. Another disaster ensued from the darkness. The detachments of the royal Scots and 8th, forming part of the reinforcement, unfortunately mistook, for the enemy, the Glengarry regiment, stationed in the woods to the right; and kept upon it a severe and destructive fire.

Under all these circumstances, general Drummond derived but a partial benefit from colonel

Scott's reinforcement. In the meanwhile, the conflict, which had been renewed on the part of the Americans, owing to the supposed advantage gained over the British, in the repulse of the 103d regiment and militia, so peculiarly circumstanced, was assuming a more serious aspect than ever. They were now in possession of the crest of the hill, and of seven pieces of captured artillery; which, in conjunction with their own, they turned against the British column.* On the other hand, the British, besides their inferiority of numbers, were without artillery, and had to march up a steep hill, to regain the guns they had lost; or even, as the Americans were too prudent to descend from their position, to give a decisive character to the contest. After a smart struggle, the British, not only regained their seven pieces of cannon, but captured a 6-pounder and a 5½ inch howitzer, which major Hindman, of the American artillery, had brought up against them. Several determined, but vain efforts, were now made by the Americans, to repossess the hill; and, at about half-past 11, they gave up the contest, and retreated to their camp; leaving, upon the field, the whole of their dead, and many of their wounded.

Major-general Riall, having been severely wounded at the early part of the action, was, with some other wounded officers and attendants, retiring to the rear to have his wounds

* Sketches of the War, p. 292.

dressed, when he and his party were captured by the American 25th regiment, under colonel Jessup, and a detachment of cavalry; which, in driving back the British left, had gained a momentary possession of the Niagara-road. At this time, also, captain Loring, one of general Drummond's aides de camp, and who was proceeding to the rear with orders, was also made prisoner.

The British loss in this action was, one captain, three subalterns, one deputy-assistant-adjutant-general, four serjeants, and 75 rank and file, killed; one lieutenant-general, one major-general, one inspecting field-officer, one deputy-assistant-quarter-master-general, two lieutenant-colonels, eight captains, 25 subalterns, 31 serjeants, five drummers, and 482 rank and file, wounded; one captain, three subalterns, two quarter-masters, 11 serjeants, five drummers, and 171 rank and file, missing and prisoners; one aide de camp, four captains, four subalterns, one quarter-master, four serjeants, and 28 rank and file, prisoners. Total, 84 killed; 559 wounded; 193 missing; and 42 prisoners: grand total 878* The great use made by the Americans of buck-shot, while it swelled out the returns, occasioned most of the wounds to be very slight. That musket-cartridges, in the American service, are invariably made up with buck-shot, is acknowledged by general Wilkin-

* App. No. 31.

son; who, referring to the use of rifles in the dark, says:—"The musket and bayonet, with buck-shot, is preferable; because, in nocturnal affairs, nothing decisive can take place, but at close quarters."*—The British returns of loss show, as clearly, that the militia brought up with colonel Scott's division, and who, as already stated, were, for the most part, without arms, did not rally, after their surprise by the enemy, as that those, forming part of the advance, behaved in a distinguished manner. The few Indians present were of no use whatever.

According to the official returns at the foot of general Brown's letter, the American loss amounted to, one major, five captains, one adjutant, four subalterns, 10 serjeants, and 150 rank and file, killed; one major-general, one brigadier-general, two aides de camp, one brigade-major, one colonel, one lieutenant-colonel, four majors, seven captains, one adjutant, one paymaster, three quarter-masters, 32 subalterns, 36 serjeants, three musicians, and 478 rank and file, wounded; and one brigade-major, one captain, six subalterns, nine serjeants, and 93 rank and file, missing.† Total, 171 killed; 572 wounded; and 110 missing: grand total 854. The loss, thus admitted by the Americans, was highly creditable to the skill and gallantry of the inferior numbers opposed to them. But

* Wilkinson's Mem. Vol. I. p. 538.

† App. No. 33.

general Brown's loss has certainly been under-rated; for 210 dead, besides a great many wounded, Americans were counted upon the field of battle, on the following morning; and, upon the subsequent advance of the British to Chippeway, they found a number of fresh graves, in which the bodies had been so slightly covered, that the arms and legs were, in many instances, exposed to view.

As first in order among the American accounts of this action, we will take general Brown's letter. In American official correspondence, this letter forms, in one respect, an anomaly: it no where mentions, that the Americans had superior numbers to contend with. What are we to infer from this, but that the reverse fact was too glaring to be questioned? The letter is certainly well written; and the writer, we should suppose, gave the number of his own troops, at least, in this "memorable battle." Perhaps the paragraph, containing that information, was suppressed, by the order of the government. Such things, we know, have been frequently done; and, did the number agree with what a writer from Buffaloe stated general Brown's force, in the Lundy's lane battle, to have amounted to, namely, "about 4000 men," the probability is encreased. The American commander begins his letter, with telling us of the "gallant men" he had the "good fortune to lead;" and yet freely confesses, that one regiment "faltered," and another "gave way and retreated." Upon the whole, however, the American troops fought bravely; and the conduct of many of the officers, of the artillery corps especially, would have done honor to any service. Had general Brown's wounds allowed him to remain long enough on the field, he would have found that it was not the last British, but the last American "effort," that had been "repulsed;" and that it was after that last effort, "that the victory was complete." How are we to reconcile this confidence of "victory," with the order which colonel Hindman, of the artillery, received from general Brown, as the latter was retiring from the field, on his way to Buffaloe:—"Collect your artillery, as well as you can, and retire immediately; we shall all march to camp" *? This was deposed to at general Ripley's court-martial. If the American troops, who had marched two miles to the field of battle, needed "some refreshment," what must have been the state of the British troops, all of whom, except the advance, had marched 14 miles to the field of battle?

Some parts of Mr. O'Connor's account are worth extracting:—"Wellington's *invincibles,*" says he, "had just arrived from Europe, and Drummond resolved that they should not only maintain their character, but maintain it in a manner that would make the most desponding

* Wilkinson's Mem. Vol. I. his App. No. 14.

impression on the brave, but raw recruits of the republic." "*A fine moon-light night favored, equally, the operations of both armies.*"—This is excellent; when all the American officers examined at general Ripley's court-martial, concur in the fact, that the night was unusually dark. "The Americans," proceeds this accurate gentleman, "could not be driven, nor withstood: determined not to be overthrown, even by superior numbers, they seemed resolved to crush whatever foe opposed them. Had they been conquered, they would yet deserve honor; as victors, they covered themselves with glory."* He attributes the loss of the "howitzer," to the high-spirited horses having run with it "into the ranks of the enemy." On the other hand, it was the "want of horses" that compelled the Americans to leave to us "*most* of the cannon which were taken." Here we discover, that Mr. O'Connor alludes to the British unlimbered 6-pounder, for which an American one had, by mistake, been placed upon a British limber.† The British loss is made to amount to "between 1200 and 1300 men;" and their "force engaged, by their own confession, 4500 men, mostly, or wholly regulars, besides a *host* of Indians: the American force," proceeds Mr. O'Connor, "did not exceed 2800; consisting, in a great proportion, of the militia of Pennsylvania and New York."* Yet, this writer, in the very next line,

* Hist. of th^ ^^ r, p. 257. † App. No. 30.

refers to "general Brown's official letter;" in which the militia-volunteers are stated at less than a third part of the American force in the field. And how came Mr. O'Connor to omit the honorable corps, styled, in the American returns,—"Canadian volunteers,"† and commanded by the "gallant colonel Wilcocks;" whose traitorous acts, as the assistant of M'Clure, fell so heavy upon the inhabitants of Newark?‡

Mr. Thomson devotes 19 pages of his book to the battle of Lundy's lane. He describes the hour's action previous to the arrival of the whole of Ripley's and Porter's brigades, as fought between generals *Riall* and Scott; although general Drummond, with his reinforcement, had been present from the commencement. He evidently mistakes colonel Scott's, for general Drummond's arrival. This misnomer is of some use to us. Mr. Thomson, after stating that general Riall had "despatched messengers to lieutenant-general Drummond at Fort-George, to inform him of the desperate nature of the conflict," says:—"Until this period of the engagement," that is, until, in reality, colonel *Scott*'s arrival, "his force, including the incorporated militia and some Indians, amounted to 1637 men."§ Mr. Thomson has here, by pure accident, stated nearly the amount of general Drummond's force,

* Hist. of the United States, p. 257.

† App. No. 33. ‡ See p. 7.

§ Sketches of the War, p. 288.

during the first three hours of the battle. He attends every regiment in its marches and counter-marches; and makes a fine thing of the charges upon the artillery. Not trusting to language alone, he has given us a copper-plate representation. So far from the American line here resembling the "pot-hook" line, formed by "captain Clodpole's company" of Carolina militia, in Lambert's Travels,* Mr. Thomson's artist has employed his rule for the purpose; and the line he has formed for Mr. O'Connor's "raw recruits," in this night of "impenetrable darkness," close in front of "a *host* of Wellington's invincibles," reminds us rather, of what we sometimes witness upon the parade in St. James's-park, than of the advance of the American troops, to seize the British cannon at Lundy's lane.

Turning over Mr. Thomson's confused pages, we come at last to his numbers. He makes the American force less, and the British force more, than Mr. O'Connor does. One he states at "2417 men;" the other,—to prove how he can make up for a bad beginning, —at "3450 regulars, 1200 incorporated militia, and 480 Indians, making in all 5130 men."† This moderate increase upon the 1637 arose, it appears, out of four several reinforcements;

* Lambert's Travels, Vol. II. p. 198.

† Sketches of the War, p. 300.

along with the last of which came up "four of the British fleet."*—Poor Mr. Thomson! Into what a dilemma he has here fallen. The river, from the falls, close to which the battle was fought, to Queenstown, a distance of eight miles, is, owing to its turbulence and rapidity, not navigable even for boats; and the four vessels to which this *learned* historian alludes, and which were the same that brought general Drummond and his troops from York, were lying peaceably at anchor opposite to Fort-George, 14 miles from the scene of action.

Our third historian, doctor Smith, has, in his usual brief way, extracted none but the most violent and extravagant parts of the accounts before him; excepting that, while he makes our "force engaged, including the Canadian militia, 4500," some one has persuaded him to advance a step nearer to truth, and state "that of the Americans at less than 3000."† An American writer from Buffaloe, speaking of this action, says: "We had in our whole army 4000 men;"‡ and, in the "Buffaloe Gazette Extraordinary," of July 28, we read: "The enemy's forces engaged must have been nearly 5000; ours,"—here is a frank admission,—"short of that number." After this, will it be pretended, that the Ameri-

* Sketches of the War, p. 296.

‡ Hist. of the United States, p. 313.

§ Albany Paper, Aug. 2, 1814.

cans had not 4000 men in the field at the battle of Niagara?

We had almost forgotten, that we have a fourth historian to glean from. General Wilkinson, finding it easier, and, as we infer from his complaints of ill-usage, more profitable, to fight on paper than in the field, drags us through 54 tolerably close octavo pages, (exclusive of 19 much closer pages of *Appendix*,) till he has done descanting upon "true valor," in the performances of the "heroes of Bridgewater," and,—forgetful of his own behaviour in the Montreal expedition, and before La Colle grist-mill,—upon military imbecility, in the proceedings of generals Brown and Scott, on the "memorable 25th of July." As, for almost every important fact, two opposite statements can be found, it would be only misleading the reader to make extracts. We may suppose, however, that the *five* large diagrams, which the general gives of the action, are tolerably correct. On the contrary, our faith in them is destroyed, thus:—"Of course, the diagram," says the general, "founded on colonel Leavenworth's report, is erroneous."* Although not explicit as to numbers, he takes care to adopt a similar stratagem to that which he practised about the gun-boats at La Colle,† and represents the British columns upon his diagrams, to be five times as large as the American. Even

* Wilkinson's Mem. Vol. I. p. 689. † See p. 88.

here he is doomed to contradict the inference he would have us draw. "I have no authority," says general Wilkinson, "to question general Drummond's report of his own order of battle, or his force, except from the information of colonel Leavenworth and other officers."* And yet, alluding to the materials from which he professes to draw up his history of this battle, he asks: "But how shall we reconcile the very opposite accounts, which have been rendered on oath before a tribunal of justice?"† And why the accounts may well be opposite, he immediately afterwards explains, very satisfactorily, thus: "I will answer, from what I have witnessed, that, in warm military combats, an officer at the head of a platoon or battalion, who does his duty, can see very little beyond his immediate command, and that different men see the same object with different optics;"†—more especially, when "it was so dark at the time, that objects could not be distinguished many paces."‡ The capture of general Riall, and of the other prisoners taken with him, the general very properly attributes to "the confusion incident to a night-attack, and the shifting of the action."* Nor does he, like Mr. O'Connor, and most of the other historians, unwittingly lessen the merit of the victors, by styling the

* Wilkinson's Mem. Vol. I. p. 722. † Ibid. 686.
‡ Ibid. 701.

vanquished—" cowards." The general, very considerately, ranks British, next to American valor; thus: " The enemy, whose persevering courage could not be excelled, but by men who sprang from the same stock," &c.* Our last extract shall be from the general's " Preliminary Observations." " I speak not," says he, " of achievements by which cities have been saved, and states protected; of great and sanguinary battles, wherein the life of the soldier has been bartered for the safety of the empire; of Thermopylæ, or—*New Orleans;*——"† Can we proceed?

After the " victorious" American troops had retired to their camp, and obtained the " necessary refreshment," they were again ordered, with general Ripley, upon whom the command had now devolved, at their head, to march to the " battle ground," there to meet and beat the enemy, if he again appeared."‡ General Brown simply and truly says:—" It was not executed;" leaving his commentators to find excuses. Doctor Smith, either not in the vein of fiction, or become suddenly conscientious, prefers leaving a *hiätus* in his " History," to separating the battle of Bridgewater from the next " brilliant exploit" he has to record. Neither Mr. Thomson nor Mr. O'Connor is so easily staggered. The

* Wilkinson's Mem. Vol. I. p. 706. † Ibid. 676.

‡ App. No. 32.

latter, without the slightest hesitation, says:—"On the morning after the battle, the Americans, under generals Ripley and Porter, reconnoitred the enemy, who did not shew any disposition to renew the contest; and then burned the enemy's barracks, and a bridge at Chippeway: after which they returned to Fort-Erie."* Mr. Thomson attempts to qualify and alter the meaning of general Brown's orders; and to prove that the enemy was a *fifth* time "reinforced." "Under such circumstances," he adds, "it would have been highly injudicious to have attacked him." "General Ripley," proceeds Mr. Thomson, "seeing the impossibility of regaining the field of battle, and the probability of his own flanks being compelled to fall back, by the immense superiority of the enemy's numbers, turned his army towards the Chippeway; whence, having first destroyed the bridge over that stream, as well as the platforms which he had previously constructed at the enemy's old works there, he pursued his retreat towards Fort-Erie; and reached it, in good order, on the following day."* General Wilkinson says—"General Ripley, finding the enemy strongly posted, in superior force, judiciously retired; and then a scene ensued, which has been carefully concealed from the public. By the improvidence of general Brown, the deficiency of transport provided for

* Hist. of the War, p. 257.

his baggage, stores, and provisions, had not been remedied; and a great portion of it was now found necessary to the accommodation of his wounded and sick. The necessity of a retreat could be no longer concealed or delayed; and the consequences were, that a considerable quantity of provisions, stores, and camp-equipage, with a number of tents, were thrown into the river, or burnt. I have this fact from an officer left with the command which performed this duty."*

This is what Mr. Thomson calls, retreating "in good order." But for the strong pique which general Wilkinson bears to general Brown, the above fact would not have reached us through an American channel. Mr. O'Connor, by way of giving a daring feature to this *orderly* retreat, declares that the Americans "burnt the enemy's barracks:" why did he not tell us, that they valiantly set fire to Street's mills, the property of a private individual?

* Sketches of the War, p. 302.

† Wilkinson's Mem. Vol. I. p. 722.

CHAPTER XV.

Newly erected works at Fort-Erie, and vigorous preparations of defence on the part of the American garrison—Discharge of the sedentary militia—Arrival of the right and left wings of De Watteville's regiment, and investment of Fort-Erie by general Drummond—Relative force of the besiegers, and besieged—Unsuccessful attack upon Black Rock—State of the defences at Fort-Erie—Affairs of piquets—Carriage of boats over-land to Lake-Erie, and gallant capture of two out of three American armed schooners stationed off the fort—Cannonade between the British and Americans at Fort-Erie—Advance of the British to the assault of that fort—Unprepared state, and consequent repulse, of the right column of attack—Proceedings of the left and centre columns—Intrepid behaviour of the British at one of the bastions—Accidental destruction of that bastion, and heavy loss and repulse of the British—American Accounts—Remarks on sir George Prevost's intercepted letters—Real cause of the failure—American atrocities at Fort-Talbot on Lake Erie—Proposal of an armistice by the British commander-in-chief in the Canadas—Assent of the American government, if extended to the water—Prompt refusal of the British admiral in the Chesapeake—Agreement for exchange of prisoners of war—Immediate discharge of American prisoners—Shameful delay in discharging the British prisoners—Their suffering state in consequence.

NO sooner had the American army got safe to Fort-Erie, than general Ripley, now the commanding officer, directed the lines of defence to be extended, the fort enlarged, and new batteries erected.* With the aid of his engineers, defences of abattis, traverses, intrenchments, and redoubts, were instantly commenced; and, from the 27th of July until the 2d or 3d of August, the troops were employed, night and day, in placing the works in a state to sustain the expected, and almost certain attack.*

After discharging the whole of the sedentary militia, general Drummond, as soon as the engineer had constructed a temporary bridge across the Chippeway, for the carriage of the troops and cannon, pushed forward to invest Fort-Erie; within two miles of which he arrived on the 3d of August. Having been joined by the right and left wings of De Watteville's, under lieutenant-colonel Fischer, from Kingston, and the 41st regiment, under lieutenant-colonel Tucker, from the forts George and Mississaga, now garrisoned by the remains (except the light company) of the 89th, the general's force amounted to,—not as Mr. Thomson, with an artful

* Sketches of the War, p. 303.

attempt at exactness, says, "5352," but 3150 men; partly embodied militia.

The British general, having approached to within about 700 yards of the enemy's fort; and, having got from Fort-George some battering pieces, and a serjeant's party with rockets, commenced digging intrenchments, and erecting batteries, to overcome the powerful defences constructing on the part of the besieged; while the latter, with unceasing alacrity, were rendering their position hourly more formidable. As to the number of troops within the fort, the most studied concealment runs through all the American accounts. Admitting as many as 1000 to have been placed *hors du combat*, in their dear-bought "victory" of the 25th, general Ripley would still have under his command 3000 men; protected by the fort within which they were intrenched; by the batteries at Black Rock; and by the three armed schooners, Porcupine, Tigress, and Ohio.

In order to facilitate the attack upon Fort-Erie, it became necessary to capture or destroy the Black Rock batteries and armed vessels; to whose heavy flanking fire the British troops, in their advance to the assault, would necessarily be exposed. To effect the first of these objects, lieutenant-colonel Tucker, at the head of six companies of the 41st, the light company of the 89th, and two flank companies (very weak) of the 104th, regiments, amounting, in all, to 460 rank and file, crossed the strait, early on the morning of the 3d, and landed a short distance below Conejockeda, or Schojeoquady, creek.* The American force at Black Rock, consisted of 240 men of the 1st rifle regiment, and a small body of volunteers, under the command of major Morgan; who, having, by deserters, or some other means, gained information of the intended attack, had taken a position on the upper, or south side of the creek, cut away the bridge crossing it, and thrown up a breastwork of logs. Colonel Tucker, with his men, advanced to the creek side, with the view of repairing the bridge, under cover of his fire. "Major Morgan," says Mr. Thomson, "did not attempt to retard the enemy's advances, until he was within rifle-distance, when he opened a fire, which proved so destructive, that lieutenant-colonel Tucker fell back to the skirt of a neighbouring wood, and kept up the contest at long shot. In the mean time, general Drummond threw over reinforcements, and the British detachment now amounted to nearly 1200 men."† We have already had several specimens of Mr. Thompson's powers at bringing up "reinforcements." In this instance, not a man crossed over, except the original party; in which statement we are supported by Mr. Thomson's con-

* See Plate I. † Sketches of the War, p. 304.

temporary; and who, much to his credit, has not made the British force amount to more than "about 500 regulars."* The plan being defeated, colonel Tucker re-crossed the strait with the loss of 25 men killed, wounded, and missing. The Americans admit a loss of two privates killed; one captain, two lieutenants, and five privates, wounded.†

On the 4th of August, brigadier-general Gaines arrived, and took the command of the American army, at Fort-Erie. By the 7th, most of the traverses about the fort were completed. Upon a battery, 25 feet high, situate at Snake hill, the southern extremity of the works, five guns were mounted. Between that and the main-works, there were two other batteries, one mounting three, and the other, two guns. The northern point of the fort had been extended to the water; and the Douglass battery, of two guns, erected on the bank. The American dragoons, infantry, riflemen, and volunteers, were encamped between the western ramparts and the water, and the artillery, under major Hindman, stationed within the main-works. After Mr. Thomson has given this description of the new Fort-Erie, and of the garrison within it, he tell us, very gravely, that the British were "strongly posted behind their works." "General Gaines determined," proceeds this writer,

* Sketches of the War, p. 304. † Hist. of the War, p. 259.

"to ascertain their strength, and endeavour, *if possible*, to draw them out. On the 6th, he sent major Morgan, who had previously been transferred from the American shore, to pass through the woods intervening between the British lines and the fort, and with orders to amuse the enemy's light troops, until his columns should indicate an intention to move: in that event, major Morgan was to retire gradually, until his corps should have fallen back, upon a strong line posted in the plane below the fort, to receive the pursuing British troops. The object of this movement failed; major Morgan having encountered and forced the enemy's light troops into the lines, with the loss of 11 killed; and three wounded and made prisoners; but, notwithstanding he maintained his position upwards of two hours, he could not succeed in drawing forth the main body of the British troops. He, therefore, returned to the fort, after losing five men killed, and four wounded."*

Scarcely a shot could have been fired by a patrolling party, but, apparently, reached the ears of Mr. Thomson. He details several little affairs of the sort; and, by duly arranging the words:—"A large body of the enemy;"—"reinforcements;"—"spirited conflict;"—"precipitate retreat" of the British; and "victory," or, if unfortunate, simply "retiring," of the Ameri-

* Sketches of the War, p. 305.

cans; has compiled abundance of entertainment for his American readers. In the only material fact which he advances, he has been misinformed. "The enemy's line," says he, "was protected by several block-houses."* On the contrary, at this time, there was not, among the British works, even an apology for one. Why did he not find room for stating, that commodore Chauncey, having equipped his second frigate,† and ascertained that the British fleet was divided, had been out upon the lake, since the first of the month; or, in the words of an article from "Batavia, August 13th," say:—"A considerable reinforcement of troops from up the lake joined our army at Fort-Erie, a few days since; and eight or ten hundred more are daily expected from that quarter"?—His reasons will be more obvious, as we proceed.

Captain Dobbs, of the Charwell, which vessel, along with the Netley and others, was lying at Fort-George, had come up with a party of seamen and marines, for the purpose of attacking the three American armed schooners, lying at anchor close to Fort-Erie. The strength of the current, and the danger of attempting to pass between the batteries at that fort and Black Rock, were no slight difficulties in the plan of operations. The Charwell's seamen having brought captain Dobbs's gig, upon their shoulders, from Queenstown to Frenchman's creek, a distance of 20 miles; the next point was, to get

* Sketches of the War, p. 306. † James's Nav. Occ. p. 398.

that gig, as well as five batteaux which had been procured for the purpose, into Lake Erie. Lieutenant-colonel Nichol, quarter-master-general of the militia, pointed out, and offered to transport the boats by, an eight miles' route through the woods.* The proposal was acceded to; and, at half past seven on the evening of the 11th of August, the boats were launched into the lake, eight miles above Fort-Erie. In half an hour afterwards, captain Dobbs, with his gig and five batteaux, containing 75 officers, seamen, and marines,—a greater complement of British, by one-third, than manned captain Barclay's fleet of ships, brigs, and schooners, upon this same lake,†—hastened to attack three American armed schooners; whose united complements were known to exceed 100 men, and those of no ordinary class. The gig and two batteaux formed one division, under captain Dobbs; the remaining three batteaux, the other, under lieutenant Radcliffe, of the Netley. The manner in which the schooners Ohio and Somers were boarded, and carried, by captain Dobbs and his gallant ship-mates, is fully expressed in the American official account.‡ Had Mr. Thomson, instead of inventing a story of his own, paid due respect to lieutenant Conkling's letter, he would not have stated, that "the British general furnished captain Dobbs, of the royal navy, with a suffi-

* See Plate I.

† James's Naval Occurr. p. 289.

‡ App. No. 34.

cient number of *troops*, to man *nine large* boats, which were completely fitted to attack the three schooners, the Somers, Porcupine, and Ohio, then lying at anchor off the fort."* Nor would he have told the still more glaring falsehood, that "the Porcupine," against whose commander the American lieutenant so justly complains, "succeeded in beating them off."* Had not the rapidity of the current, driven the two schooners, after their cables had been cut, past, and a considerable distance beyond, the Porcupine, that vessel would have shared the fate of her two companions. The force of the American schooners, in guns, men, and size, and the trifling loss on both sides, will be found in our naval volume.† These two valuable prizes were taken to Frenchman's creek; and as many of the brave fellows surviving, as were not required to remain on board, hastened, with their leader, to general Drummond's camp.

The success of captain Dobbs's daring exploit induced general Drummond, on the morning of the 13th, preparatory to the grand assault upon the works at Fort-Erie, to open his batteries; which consisted of one long iron, and two short brass 24-pounders, one long 18-pounder, one 24-pound carronade, and a 10-inch mortar. Although this cannonade was continued for two days, the American editors acknowledge no other casualties than 45 men killed or wounded.

* Sketches of the War, p. 315. † James's Nav. Occur. p. 391.

Every arrangement having been made, the 8th, and De Watteville's regiments, with the light companies of the 89th and 100th regiments, and a detachment of artillery, the whole column somewhat under 1300 men,* and commanded by lieutenant-colonel Fischer, of De Watteville's, marched, at two o'clock on the morning of the 15th of August, from a position which they had previously occupied, towards the enemy's intrenchments at Snake hill. As soon as the head of the column had approached the abattis, a heavy fire was opened upon it by the American 21st and 23d regiments, and by one 18 and two 6-pounders, and a $5\frac{1}{2}$-inch howitzer, posted in a strong redoubt. The letter of an American gentleman at Buffaloe describes the onset, thus: "The enemy approached, with bayonets charged, and *guns without flints*, nearly surrounded the piquet, and pursued them so closely, as to enter the abattis with them, and got in the rear of the redoubt." "The scaling-ladders were too short, and destruction was dealt on every side among them."† Mr. Thomson says: "With scaling ladders, of no more than 16 feet in length, he could not possibly throw his troops upon a battery of about 25 feet high, and his second attempt, equally furious as the first, met with

* Sketches of the War, p. 309.

† Washington-city Gazette, Extra. Aug. 18.

no better success. Convinced of his inability to get possession of the battery, and feeling the deadly effects of the incessant showers of grape, which were thrown upon him, he determined, in his next effort, to pass the point of the abattis, by wading breast-deep into the lake, to which the works were open. In this attempt, also, he was unsuccessful, nearly 200 of his men being either killed or drowned, and the remainder precipitately falling back."* According to colonel Fischer's report,† it was not intentionally, but in marching too near the lake, that the troops got into the water. The darkness of the morning, added to the ignorance of the way, might well entangle the men among the rocks; and the incessant showers of grape and musketry, which they had no means of returning, threw them into confusion. This alone, without the insufficiency of the scaling-ladders,--a piece of important information, which we gain only from the American accounts,—sufficiently accounts for the entire failure of the attack, made by the right British column upon the southern extremity of the American works.

The centre British column, at the head of which was lieutenant-colonel Drummond, of the 104th, consisted of the flank companies of the 41st, and 104th (the latter reduced to about 80 men) regiments, and a party of seamen and

* Sketches of the War, p. 309. † App. No. 36.

marines, in all,—not as Mr. Thomson says, "700,"* but 190 rank and file. The left column, under the command of lieutenant-colonel Scott, of the 103d regiment, was composed of that regiment, 500 strong, supported by the flank companies of the royal Scots, mustering, altogether, not "800,"* but 650 rank and file. As the proceedings of these two columns are much more fully detailed in the American, than in the British account, we shall transcribe nearly the whole of the former, deferring to the conclusion, our own remarks upon such inaccuracies as it may contain.

"The attack from the centre and left columns," says Mr. Thomson, "was reserved until the contest became very animated between colonel Fischer's column, and the troops upon the left. From the line of defences, between the Douglass battery and the fort, and from those in front of the garrison, lieutenant-general Drummond supposed reinforcements would be drawn to the aid of the southern extremity of the works; and, with this view, had given greater strength to his right, than to his other columns, and intended to avail himself of the consequent weakened state, of the north and south-east angles of the American post. The piquet being driven in, the approach of lieutenant-colonel

* Sketches of the War, p. 310.

Drummond was heard from the ravine, and colonel Scott's column at the same time advanced along the margin of the water. From the salient bastion of the fort, captain Williams immediately opened his fire upon the centre column, whilst the approach of colonel Scott was attempted to be checked by the Douglass battery, and captains Boughton and Harding's New York and Pennsylvania volunteers, on its right; the 9th infantry, under captain Foster, on its left; and a 6-pounder, planted at that point, under the management of colonel M'Ree. At 50 yards distance from the line, the enemy's left column made a momentary pause, and instantly recoiled from the fire of the cannon and musketry. But the centre column, having advanced upon every assailable point of the fort, in defiance of the rapid and heavy discharges of the artillery, and having ascended the parapet, by means of a large number of scaling-ladders, its officers called out to the line, extending to the lake, to desist firing;—an artifice which succeeded so well, that the Douglass battery, and the infantry, supposing the order to proceed from the garrison, suspended their fire, until the deception was discovered. The left column, in the mean time, recovered from its confusion, and was led up to a second charge, from which it was again repulsed, before it had an opportunity of planting the scaling-ladders, and with the loss of its commander, and upwards of one-third of its men.

"Whilst the second attempt was in operation, the centre column was, with great difficulty, thrown back from the salient bastion; and the troops within the fort were quickly reinforced from general Ripley's brigade, and general Porter's volunteers. But, lieutenant-colonel Drummond, actuated by a determination (not to be overcome by a single repulse) to force an entrance into the garrison, and momentarily expecting the reserve to be ordered up by the lieutenant-general, returned to the assault a second and a third time. By the gallant efforts, however, of major Hindman and his artillery, and the infantry detachment of major Trimble, he was, each time, more signally repulsed than before; and colonel Scott's column having withdrawn from the action, upon the fall of its leader, lieutenant Douglass was busily engaged in giving such a direction to the guns of his battery, as to cut off the communication between Drummond's column, and the reserve of lieutenant-colonel Tucker. The new bastions which had been commenced for the enlargement of the old Fort Erie, not being yet completed, the only opposition which could be given to the enemy's approaches upon those points, was by means of small arms. The batteries of captain

Biddle and captain Fanning (formerly Fontaine's) in the works intervening between Towson's battery and the fort, were therefore opened upon the enemy with great vivacity, and his advances from the plane frequently checked by those gallant and meritorious officers.

"After this third repulse, lieutenant-colonel Drummond, taking advantage of the darkness of the morning, and of the heavy columns of smoke, which concealed all objects from the view of the garrison, moved his troops silently round the ditch, repeated his charge, and re-ascended his ladders with such velocity, as to gain footing on the parapet, before any effectual opposition could be made. Being in the very midst of his men, he directed them to charge vigorously with their pikes and bayonets, and to show no quarter to any yielding soldier of the garrison. This order was executed with the utmost rapidity, and the most obstinate previous parts of the engagement, formed no kind of parallel to the violence and desperation of the present conflict. Not all the efforts of major Hindman and his command, nor major Trimble's infantry, nor a detachment of riflemen under captain Birdsall, who had posted himself in the ravelin, opposite the gateway of the fort, could dislodge the determined and intrepid enemy from the bastion; though the deadly effects of their fire prevented his approaches beyond it. It was now in his entire possession. The loss of their leader, colonel Drummond, did not check the impetuosity of the enemy's troops, and they continued the use of their pikes and small arms until the day broke, and repulsed several furious charges made upon them by detachments of the garrison. The approach of day-light enabled both parties to give a more certain direction to their fire. The artillerists had already severely suffered; but, with those that remained, and a reinforcing detachment of infantry, major Hindman renewed his attempts to drive the Britsih 41st and 104th from the bastion. Captain Birdsall, at the same moment, drawing out his riflemen from the ravelin, rushed through the gateway into the fort, and joining in the charge, received an accidental wound from one of his own men, just as the attack failed. Detachments from the 1st brigade, under captain Forster, were then introduced over the interior bastion, to the assistance of major Hindman; these detachments were to charge at a different point of the salient, or exterior bastion, and were handsomely led on by captain Forster, and the assistant inspector-general, major Hall. This charge also failed; the passage up the bastion not being wide enough to admit more than three men abreast. It was frequently, however, repeated; and, though it sometimes occasioned much slaughter among the enemy's infantry, was invariably repulsed. By the operations of the artillery, from a demi-bastion in the fort, and the continual blaze of fire from the small-arms, added to the effects of the repeated charges, the enemy's column, being considerably cut up, and many of its principal officers wounded, began to recoil; which, being observed by the besieged party, and the contest having entirely subsided on the left flank of the works, reinforcements were brought up from that point, and many of the enemy's troops, in a few moments, thrown from the bastion.

"The British reserve was now expected to come up: the guns at the Douglass battery had by this time been turned so as to enfilade that column in its approach; captain Fanning was already playing upon the enemy with great effect; and captain Biddle was ordered to post a piece of artillery, so as to enfilade the salient glacis. This piece was served with uncommon vivacity, notwithstanding captain Biddle had been severely wounded in the shoulder. All these preparations being made for an effectual operation upon the enemy's remaining column, and from the dreadful carnage which had already taken place, it was scarcely supposed that he would continue the assault much longer. But 3 or 400 men of the reserve, were about to rush upon the parapet to the assistance of those recoiling, when a tremendous and dreadful explosion took place, under the platform, which carried away the bastion, and all who happened to be upon it. The enemy's reserve immediately fell back, and in a short time the contest terminated in the entire defeat of the assailants, who returned with the shattered columns to their encampment. On retiring from the assault, according to the report of general Gaines, the British army left upon the field 222 killed, among whom were 14 officers of distinction; 174 wounded; and 186 prisoners, making a total of 582. Others, who were slightly wounded, had been carried to their works. The official account of lieutenant-general Drummond does not acknowledge so large a number in killed, but makes the aggregate loss much greater. His adjutant-general reported, 57 killed; 309 wounded; and 539 missing—in all 905.† The American loss amounted to 17 killed; 56 wounded; and one lieutenant, who was thrown over the parapet, while defending the bastion, and 10 privates, prisoners;—in all 84 men."*

We are certainly much indebted to the writer who furnished Mr. Thomson with this very full account. "The tremendous and dreadful explosion, which carried away the bastion, and all who happened to be upon it," and which, it is believed, was merely accidental, as satisfactorily explains, why the attack failed upon the right and centre, as the want of flints, and the

* Sketches of the War, p. 312. † App. No. 37.

shortness of the scaling-ladders, upon the left, of the American works at Fort-Erie. If the "British 41st and 104th," as whole regiments, could extort a compliment for what they were supposed to have done, what would the Americans have said, had they known, that "the determined and intrepid enemy," who could not be dislodged from the bastion, were the flank-companies *only* of those regiments, assisted by a party of seamen and marines,* the whole numbering but 190 rank and file?

By an unaccountable inadvertency, Mr. Thomson has overlooked the statement he gave of the British force, just previous to the attack. We then had, he says, "5352 men." Let us see how he disposes of this force at the time of the assault. Colonel Fischer's column he states at 1300, colonel Drummond's, at 700, and colonel Scott's, at 800, in all, 2800; leaving 2552 men, for the reserve, which consisted, he says, of "the royals, another part of De Watteville's regiment, the Glengarians, and the incorporated militia, under lieutenant-colonel Tucker."† Taking the outside of all the American estimates of the detailed parts of this reserve, we cannot make it amount to more than 1200 men;—what then become of the remaining 1352? The fact is, the reserve amounted to 1000 men only; and consisted of the battalion-companies of the royal Scots, six

* All wounded, App. No. 35. † Sketches of the War, p. 308.

companies of the 41st, the Glengarry regiment, and the incorporated militia. So that the British force engaged in the assault upon Fort-Erie, did not exceed 2140 men.

In general Gaines's first letter, not a word appears about the "tremendous and dreadful explosion." The bastion, says the American general, "was regained at the point of the bayonet."* We wish, for his sake, that we had his second letter to refer to. At all events, Mr. O'Connor, who professes to compile "carefully from official documents," is equally silent about the explosion; declaring, to the same effect as the general, that "the bastion was re-taken by the greatest display of courage and exertion."† May not such a catastrophe, as the blowing into the air of, according to an American letter-writer, "200 British," have merited the notice, if not have awakened the sympathy, of the reverend Dr. Smith? Here follows his whole account:—"General Drummond, on the 15th of August, attempted to storm the fort, but was repulsed with the loss of 600 men, one-half of whom were slain. The assault, and defence were of the same desperate character with the battles of Chippeway and Niagara; and could not fail to inspire the British officers and soldiers, with high ideas of the discipline and courage of the American army."‡ Yet, when

* App. No. 38. † History of the War, p. 260.

‡ History of the United States, Vol. III. p. 313.

200 Americans, along with general Pike, were blown up at the capture of York, doctor Smith could find room to tell us, that they were "terribly mangled;"* and Mr. O'Connor himself there gave a very circumstantial account of the "tremendous explosion."† Two short extracts from Mr. O'Connor's book will shew, that he was almost as much "gladdened" as general Gaines, at our discomfiture before Fort-Erie. "The assault," says he, "was of that desperate nature, that was calculated to rub away the stains of former defeats, to resuscitate the sinking charms of an assumed invincibility, and save the British general from contempt, and perhaps disgrace." —"The invincibles were, however, destined to experience another defeat; and the Americans added another wreath to the laurels, with which they were already so plentifully blessed."‡

According to some letters from sir George Prevost to lieutenant-general Drummond, which were intercepted by the Americans, and afterwards published in all the journals, both American and British, the lieutenant-general was blamed for making the attack; sir George adding: "It is not in reproach of its failure that I observe to you, that night-attacks made with heavy troops, are, in my opinion, very objectionable." How far this may be the case, we will not pretend to decide; but we think there appears, in both of

* History of the United States, Vol. III. p. 230.

† History of the War, p. 83. ‡ Ibid. p. 260.

sir George's letters, though somewhat obscurely expressed, sufficient to account for the "hesitation" and "consternation" of the right column. In one letter, he says, alluding to De Watteville's regiment: "I am told they were deprived of their flints." In the other, he says: "It is to be inferred, from lieutenant-colonel Fischer's report, and your statement, that the right column was not sufficiently prepared for the obstacles it had to surmount, in attaining the point of attack."—What can this mean, but that the scaling-ladders were too short? And yet neither general Drummond's, nor colonel Fischer's, official report contains a word about scaling-ladders; nor, indeed, in the *present shape* of those letters, any thing from which an inference can be drawn, "that the right column was not sufficiently prepared for the obstacles it had to surmount." Had the British right possessed the means of scaling the works, the enemy's right would not have been so strongly reinforced, nor colonel Drummond's column been delayed at the fatal bastion; and, consequently, the assault upon Fort-Erie, although "performed in the dark," would have been crowned with success.

The Americans will not allow us to give an uninterrupted detail of open and honorable warfare. Among several petty outrages upon private property, one that occurred on Lake Erie is too heinous to pass unnoticed. On the 16th of August, a party of about 100 Americans and Indians landed at Port-Talbot on that lake; and robbed 50 heads of families of all their horses, and of every article of household furniture, and wearing apparel, belonging to them. The number of individuals who were thus thrown naked and destitute upon the world, amounted to 49 men, 37 women,—three of the latter, and two of the former, nearly 70 years of age,—and 148 children. A great many of the more respectable inhabitants were not only robbed, but carried off as prisoners: among them, a member of the house of assembly, Mr. Barnwell, though ill of the fever and ague. An authenticated account of this most atrocious proceeding, delivered in by colonel Talbot, the owner of the settlement, stands upon the records of the "Loyal and Patriotic Society of Upper Canada;" yet not a whisper on the subject has escaped any one American historian.

Early in the spring of 1814, when general Winder left Quebec for the United States, on his parole, he was understood to be the bearer, from sir George Prevost, of *another* proposition for an armistice. The American government very gladly published the fact; if only to show to the world, who was the first to cry out. At the same time, the annoyance felt from the British fleet in the Chesapeake, which was not, like the river St. Lawrence, shut up during the winter months, rendered desirable, a cessation of hostilities by water, as well as land. A flag of truce was, therefore, despatched to the British admiral, to know if he had authority to extend the armistice in the manner required. Sir Alexander Cochrane very readily answered,—that he had been sent out to fight, not to negotiate; and thus the affair ended.

Previous to general Winder's departure from Quebec, a convention was entered into between him and colonel Baynes, the adjutant-general of the Canadas, and, on the 15th of April, confirmed by sir George Prevost; stipulating, that all prisoners of war, except the hostages then in detention, should be mutually exchanged and delivered up, with all convenient expedition, so as to be able to serve, and carry arms, on the 15th of the ensuing May. In immediate fulfilment of our part of the agreement, all American prisoners in Canada and Nova Scotia were released from confinement; and many of the officers were actually engaged in the battles of July and August, upon the Niagara-frontier. This agreement for a mutual exchange was hailed with joy by the British officers and privates, taken on Lake Erie, and at the battle of the Moravian-town; and who were still eking out their days in Frankfort penitentiary,* and other prisons in the western country. So shamefully, however, did the American government behave on the occasion, that these poor fellows, who had been so long and so rigorously confined, were not

* See Vol. I. p. 298.

allowed to march from their respective prisons, till long after the period when they ought to have been again under arms in the service of their country. And even when they did get away, they were not taken to the most contiguous British port, but marched through the state of Ohio, during the sickly season, to Sandusky, by far the most unhealthy spot of any upon the North-American lakes. When there, no vessel was ready to receive them; although the American journalists were still boasting, that they had our fleet, and their own too, upon this very lake. While waiting at Sandusky for a conveyance, nearly all the officers and men became ill of, and many fell victims to, the prevailing disease, or *lake-fever*. At last, towards the end of August, came a small transport; which took on board a portion of the sufferers, and landed them at Long-Point. We are often told how active the Americans are upon the water, and what quick trips they can make betwixt ports on the ocean. Unfortunately, none of this activity was displayed in transporting the British prisoners across Lake Erie; for the last division did not arrive at Long-Point, till the middle of October. The few survivors were but the shadows of what they had been: all had contracted disease; many died after their arrival in Canada; and scarcely a man of the remainder was again fit for active service.

CHAPTER XVI.

Determination of the United States to repossess Fort-Michilimacinac—British reinforcement sent to the garrison—Perils of the voyage across Lake Huron—Arrival of the reinforcement in safety—Expedition from Michilimacinac to Prairie du Chien, on the Mississippi—Its arrival opposite the fort—Repulse of a heavy American gun-boat—Surrender of the post to the British—American expedition to Lake Huron—Shameful proceedings of the Americans at St. Mary's falls—Reduced state of the garrison at Michilimacinac—Attack upon that post by the American fleet and troops—Their repulse and retreat—Destruction by the Americans of a small block-house and vessel at Nattawassaga—Departure of the American commodore to Lake Erie—Boat-expedition against the United States' schooners Scorpion and Tigress, left to blockade Michilimacinac—Capture of both schooners, and obtainment of the command of Lake Huron.

THE recovery of Fort-Michilimacinac* had long been seriously contemplated by the Ame-

* See Vol. I. p. 56.

rican government; and, but for the lateness of the season when the command of Lake Erie, and the expulsion of the British from the shores of the Detroit, had opened the way for an expedition to Lake Huron, the second north-western campaign would not have been allowed to close, till that object had been accomplished. On the other hand, the necessity of retaining a post, so favorably situated, in the hands of an enemy, for annoying the north-western trade, seems early to have pressed itself upon sir George Prevost's mind; and, in the beginning of April, a small reinforcement, placed under the orders of that active and zealous officer, lieutenant-colonel M'Douall, was forwarded, by a back route, to the little garrison at Michilimacinac.

On the 22d of April, this reinforcement, consisting of a company of the royal Newfoundland regiment, with two or three 6 and 3-pounders; a few Canadian volunteers; and a lieutenant, and 22 subordinate officers and seamen, of the Lake Ontario squadron, altogether under 90 men, departed, in 24 batteaux, deeply laden with provisions and military stores, from Nattawassaga creek, on Lake Huron. Not the most experienced navigator of the ocean can form an idea of the storms that rage, and the perils that are to be encountered, upon the larger North-American lakes; especially, in the winter season, when immense fields of ice overspread the surface; and when the intensity of the cold can scarcely be endured by the hardiest frame. On the 18th of May, after a boisterous passage of 25 days, 19 of them a continued struggle with the elements, the little expedition, with the loss of one batteaux only, but not of her crew or lading, arrived in safety at Michilimacinac. The conduct of both officers and men, in this hazardous enterprise, of which the difficulties and dangers were of the most discouraging kind, cannot be sufficiently praised. Their arrival was greeted by the garrison with the liveliest joy; and colonel M'Douall instantly set about strengthening his post, in order to meet the expected attack from the formidable fleet of Lake Erie.

Soon after colonel M'Douall's arrival, a body of western Indians, under Mr. Dixon, joined the garrison; and others kept flocking to the fort, in sufficient numbers by the end of June, to warrant an expedition against the late Indian post of Prairie du Chien, on the Mississippi, distant about 1400 miles from its mouth, and 450 from Michilimacinac; and which had, since the 2d of the month, been taken possession of by an American force, under general Clark, from St. Louis, on the Missouri. A St. Louis newspaper-editor, after declaring the seizure of this defenceless post to have been a "hazardous enterprise," proceeds thus: "Every attention was directed to the erection of a temporary place calculated for defence: 60 rank and file of major Taylor's company of the 7th regiment, under command of lieutenant Perkins, took possession of the house formerly occupied by the old Mackinaw company, and a new fort was progressing, on a most commanding spot, when the governor left the Prairie. The farms of Prairie du Chien are in high cultivation, 2 or 300 barrels of flour may be made this season, besides a quantity of corn. Horses and cattle are in abundance. Two of the largest boats were left under the command of aide de camp Kennely, and captains Sullivan and Vieser, whose force amounts to 135 dauntless young fellows from this country. The regulars, under lieutenant Perkins, are stationed on shore; and are assisted by the volunteers, in the erection of the new fort." All this preparation proves the post of Prairie du Chien to have been of some consequence, and gives proportionate importance to the expedition sent to attempt its reduction. The detachment for that service consisted of Michigan fencibles, Canadian volunteers, and officers of the Indian detachment, numbering, altogether, 150; one serjeant of artillery with a 3-pounder field-piece, and 500 Indians, the whole commanded by lieutenant-colonel M'Kay, of the Michigan fencibles.

The route was down Green bay and Fox river; near to the confluence of which with the Mississippi, the post of Prairie du Chien was situate.

On the 17th of July the barges arrived in front of the village, behind which, on a commanding eminence, was the fort, containing two block-houses, and mounting, besides swivels, one 3 and one 6-pounder. In the middle of the river was stationed a very large gun-boat, of 70 feet keel, named the Governor Clark, mounting 14 pieces of cannon, some 6 and 3-pounders, the remainder cohorns; and manned with 70 or 80 men, fully armed. This floating block-house is described to have been so constructed, as to be rowed in any direction, and to enable the crew to use their own small-arms, while they remain perfectly sheltered from those of an enemy.* Against this formidable gun-boat, colonel M'Kay, on the afternoon of his arrival, having in vain summoned the fort to surrender, directed his 3-pounder; which was so ably served, that, in three hours, the "dauntless fellows" on board the Governor Clark cut her cable, and dropped down the current, out of reach of further annoyance. Colonel M'Kay had now to reduce the fort, with his remaining six round shot, (including three of the enemy's, which had been picked up,) and with such leaden bullets as his party could make. Having pre-

* App. No. 39.

pared every thing, and being about to put the first ball into the 3-pounder, a flag was hung out from the fort; and the American garrison, numbering 61 combatants, each possessed of a stand of arms, surrendered as prisoners of war.* Great credit is due to colonel M'Kay, and the whole of the white persons with him, as well for their proceedings against the enemy, as for their active and successful exertions, in preventing the Indians, although so numerous, from plundering the prisoners, or the inhabitants of the place. Neither the dislodgement of the Americans from Prairie du Chien, nor the affair between the Indians and the American armed barges, ascending the Mississipi, detailed in colonel M'Kay's letter,* is noticed in any American history that we have seen.

Unexpected difficulties in ascending the straits of St. Clair, with large vessels, had delayed, until the 12th of July, the arrival, at Fort Gatroit, near the foot of Lake Huron, of the American expedition against Michilimacinac. The vessels were the Niagara, St. Lawrence, and Caledonia brigs, and the Scorpion and Tigress, schooners, measuring, altogether, 1170 tons; and whose united strength, when employed as part of the force against captain Barclay's fleet, amounted to 46 heavy guns, and 420 men.† The troops that were at present on board, con-

* App. No. 39.

† James's Nav. Occur. p. 286—95.

sisted, as far as we can gather from the American accounts, of 740 rank and file, under the command of lieutenant-colonel Croghan.

On the 20th of July, the American fleet cast anchor off the old, and then abandoned, military post at the island of St. Joseph; the few houses upon which, a party was sent on shore to destroy. That service performed, a detachment of infantry and artillery, numbering about 280 rank and file, and commanded by major Holmes, of the 32d regiment, embarked in the barges of the fleet, under the directions of lieutenant Turner, of the United States' navy; and proceeded up the St. Mary's strait, to the north-west company's settlement at the falls; where, as neither troops nor Indians were present, the Americans landed, on the 23d, without the slightest opposition.

The few inhabitants of the place were, at this time, employed in fishing, or in haymaking, and other husbandry concerns; but their peaceable demeanor and innocent avocations only exposed them the more to the brutal rage of major Holmes and his party. Some of the acts of the Americans at St. Mary's will not bear recital: suffice it, that they not only destroyed the whole of the property belonging to the north-west company which had not been previously removed, including their houses, stores, and vessels; but killed their cattle, carried off, as prisoners, several of the engagees, tore down the defences, destroyed the gardens, pilfered the furniture, and, in some instances, the cloaths from even the childrens' backs.

Mr. Thomson is very brief, and doctor Smith quite silent, upon the business at St. Mary's: not so Mr. O'Connor. He admits the seizure of the north-west company's property, but agrees with major Holmes, in considering, that "it was good prize, by the maritime law of nations, as recognized in the English courts;" as well as because the company's agent, "Johnson, acted the infamous part of a traitor; having been a citizen and magistrate of the Michigan territory, before the war, and at its commencement, and now discharging the functions of magistrate under the British government."* The proprietors of the tobacco, captured by the British in the Chesapeake, will not thank Mr. O'Connor, for thus admitting, that *merchandize*, on shore as well as a-float, is "good prize;" nor will the American government be well pleased with his unqualified avowal, that the "part of a traitor" can be at all "infamous." Lieutenant Turner, in a letter to captain Sinclair, follows up his account of the destruction of the north-west company's goods, "amounting in value to from 50 to 100000 dollars," with:—"All private property was, according to your orders, respected." He thus, cleverly enough, marks

* History of the War. p. 264.

the distinction between the company's, or "Indian goods," and "private property;" and, at the same time, hopes to free the naval part of the expedition to St. Mary's, from any concern in the enormities that were committed there.

The absence of the detachment of militia and Indians under colonel M'Kay, and of lieutenant Worseley and his seamen, who had proceeded to Nattawassaga in the north-west company's schooner Nancy, for a fresh supply of provisions for the garrison, reduced colonel M'Douall's force to 190 regulars, militia, and Indians, with a 3 and 6-pounder, but no artillery-officer to direct the use of them. On the 26th of July, commodore Sinclair's fleet appeared off the island to reconnoitre; but no attempt was made to disembark the troops till the morning of the 4th of August. The vessels then anchored close to the beach, at Dowsman's farm, situate at the back of the island; a spot that had been pointed out by one of the old residents of the place. The ground was cleared in front, and formed a gentle slope, which enabled the vessels, by their grape and canister, to cover the landing of the troops, in the most effectual manner. Colonel M'Douall posted his little force in a very masterly manner, and repulsed every effort of the Americans to approach the fort.* Cap-

* App. No. 40.

tain Sinclair gives the following account of his reception :—" Michilimacinac is, by nature, a perfect Gibraltar, being a high inaccessible rock on every side, except the west; from which, to the heights, you have nearly two miles to pass through a wood, so thick, that our men were shot in every direction, and within a few yards of them, without being able to see the Indians who did it; and a height was scarcely gained, before there was another within 50 or 100 yards commanding it, where breastworks were erected and cannon opened on them. Several of these were charged, and the enemy driven from them; but it was soon found, the further our troops advanced, the stronger the enemy became, and the weaker and more bewildered our force were. Several of the commanding officers were picked out, and killed or wounded by the savages, without seeing any of them. The men were getting lost, and falling into confusion, natural under such circumstances; which demanded an immediate retreat, or a total defeat and general massacre must have ensued. This was conducted in a masterly manner by colonel Croghan, who had lost the aid of that valuable, and ever-to-be lamented officer, major Holmes, who, with captain Van Horn, was killed by the Indians." Mr. O'Connor informs us, that it was the death of major Holmes and captain Desha, that "threw that part of the line into confusion, from which it was found impossible to recover it;" and that lieutenant Morgan brought up a light piece, to relieve the left, which was suffering from a galling fire. The Americans retreated to their shipping, on the same evening, in the utmost haste and confusion;* which, as all that were alive and well got clear off, was certainly "in a masterly manner." Seventeen of their dead were left on the ground; and the loss, on our part, was only one Indian killed. As there were but 50 Indians upon the island; and, as few, if any, could approach from the main, while the American shipping lay off, captain Sinclair paid no very high compliment to the "hero of Sandusky," and his 5 or 600 troops, in ascribing the retreat to the dread of "a general massacre." Mr. Thompson, however, declares that the Indians alone "exceeded the strength of colonel Croghan's detachment;" and that this "intrepid young officer" was compelled to withdraw his forces, after having sustained a loss of 66 killed, wounded, and missing.†

Having obtained intelligence that lieutenant Worseley, with the Nancy schooner, was at Nattawassaga, captain Sinclair, first despatching the St. Lawrence and Caledonia brigs, with a portion of the troops, to co-operate with the

* App. No. 40.

† Sketches of the War, p. 330.

American army at Fort-Erie, proceeded with the remainder, amounting, including the crew of the Niagara, to "450 souls,"* to attack a post deemed far less difficult of reduction, than the "Gibraltar," from which he and colonel Croghan had just been repulsed. The Nancy was lying about two miles up the Nattawassaga, under the protection of a block-house, situate on the south-east side of the river, which here runs parallel to, and forms a narrow peninsula with, the shore of Gloucester bay. This enabled captain Sinclair to anchor his vessels within good battering distance of the block-house. A spirited cannonade was kept up between the latter, where a 6-pounder was mounted, (besides two 24-pound carronades on the ground,) and the three American vessels outside, composed of the Niagara, mounting eighteen 32-pound carronades, and two long 12-pounders, and the Tigress and Scorpion, mounting, between them, one long 12, and two long 24-pounders. In addition to this force, a $5\frac{1}{2}$ inch howitzer, with a suitable detachment of artillery, had been landed on the peninsula. Against these 24 pieces of cannon, and upwards of 500 men, were opposed, one piece of cannon, and 23 officers and seamen. Further resistance was in vain; and, just as lieutenant Worseley had prepared a train, leading to the Nancy from the block-house, one of the enemy's shells burst

* Captain Sinclair's letter, of date, September 3.

in the latter, and both the block-house and the vessel were presently blown up. Lieutenant Worseley and his men escaped in their boat up the river; and, fortunately, the whole of the north-west company's richly laden canoes, bound across the lake, escaped, also, into French river. After having thus led to the destruction of a vessel, which the American commander had the modesty to describe as—"his Britannic majesty's schooner Nancy,"—captain Sinclair departed for Lake Erie; leaving the Tigress and Scorpion to blockade the Nattawassaga, and, as that was the only route by which supplies could be readily forwarded, starve the garrison of Michilimacinac into a surrender.

After remaining at their station for a few days, the two American schooners took a trip to the neighbourhood of St. Joseph's. Here they were discovered, on the 25th of August, by some Indians on their way to Michilimacinac. On the 31st, lieutenant Worseley and his men arrived at the garrison; bringing intelligence that the two schooners were five leagues apart. An immediate attempt to effect their capture was, therefore, resolved upon; and, on the evening of the 1st of September, lieutenant Worseley, and his party, composed of midshipman Dobson, one gunner's mate, and 17 seamen, re-embarked in their boat; and lieutenant Bulger, of the royal Newfoundland regiment, along with two lieutenants, two serjeants, six corporals, and 50 rank and file, of his own corps, one hospital-mate, one bombardier and one gunner of the royal artillery, with a 3 and 6-pounder; major Dickson, superintendent of Indian affairs, four others of the Indian department, and three Indian chiefs, making a total of 92 persons, embarked on board three other boats. It was sun-down on the 2d, before the boats arrived at the Detour, or entrance of St. Mary's strait; and not till the next day, that the exact situation of the enemy's vessels became known. At six o'clock that evening, the boats pulled for the nearest vessel, ascertained to be at anchor about six miles off. A body of Indians, which had accompanied the expedition from Michilimacinac, remained three miles in the rear; and, at nine o'clock, the schooner appeared in sight. The latter, as soon as she discovered the boats, which was not till they had approached within 100 yards of her, opened a smart fire from her long 24-pounder and musketry. The boats, however, advanced rapidly; and, two boarding her on each side, carried, in five minutes, the United States' schooner Tigress, of one long 24-pounder, on a pivot-carriage, and 28 officers and men.* The British loss was, two seamen killed; lieutenant Bulger, and four or five soldiers and seamen, wounded. The American

* National Intelligencer, July 29, 1815.

loss, three men, including one or two officers, wounded.

On the morning of the 4th, the prisoners were sent in one of the boats, under a guard, to Michilimacinac; and preparations were made to attack the other schooner, which was understood to be at anchor 15 miles further down. Lieutenant Bulger, in his letter,* describes the arrangement that was made; and which resulted in the capture of the United States' schooner Scorpion, manned with 30 officers and men;* and carrying one long 24, and, in her hold, one long 12-pounder. Her loss amounted to two killed, and two wounded; ours to one or two soldiers wounded; making the total British loss, in capturing the two vessels, amount to three killed, and eight wounded. It is a singular, and somewhat ludicrous fact, that the account of the loss of these vessels had reached Washington, a week, at least, before Mr. Madison said: "A part of the squadron of Lake Erie has been extended to Lake Huron, and has produced the advantage of displaying our command of that lake also."†

The Scorpion measured 68½ feet upon deck, and 18½ feet extreme breadth; the Tigress 60½ feet upon deck, and 17¼ feet extreme breadth: so that these two American "gun-boats"

* App. No. 41.

† President's Speech, Sept. 20, 1814.

averaged, according to British measurement, 100 tons. They had on board abundance of shot, including some 32-pounders; and in small-arms, between them, 64 muskets, and 104 cutlasses and boarding-pikes. As a proof of the value of these two schooners, now that they were a-float upon Lake Huron, their hulls and stores were appraised, by the proper officers, at upwards of 16000*l.* sterling. In another point of view, they were still more valuable. Commodore Perry's victory left the Americans without an enemy to fear upon the lakes Erie and Huron; and yet do we find, still on board of the four † smallest of his nine vessels, three times as many seamen, as were on board *all* the "very superior British fleet,"‡ which that "illustrious" American commodore, after an obstinate struggle, had succeeded in capturing.

The loss of the schooners Tigress and Scorpion necessarily underwent, as soon as the officers were discharged from imprisonment, the investigation of a court of inquiry. The British force is there made,—"about 300 sailors, soldiers, and Indians;" which, had the latter been present, was no great exaggeration. Mr. Thomson, not wishing to shock his readers with an account so near akin to truth, says: "Lieutenant-colonel M'Dowall supplied lieutenant Worsley, of

† Including the Somers and Ohio; see p. 168.

‡ James's Naval Occurrences, p. 294

the navy, with 250 Indians, and a detachment of the Newfoundland regiment, with whom, and 150 sailors, he attacked the schooners, on the 9th of September. After a severe struggle, in which he lost a very disproportionate number of killed and wounded, he carried the vessels, and proceeded with them to Michilimacinac."* Mr. O'Connor, having a story at hand, which, he thinks, will afford ten times as much gratification as Mr. Thomson's, omits the force on either side, in order to insert the following:—"Captain Arthur Sinclair, commanding the United States' naval force on the upper lakes, states, in a letter to the secretary of the navy, on the authority of sailing-master Champlin, that 'the conduct of the enemy to our prisoners, (the crew of the Tigress,) thus captured, and the inhuman butchery of those who fell into their hands, at the attack of Mackinack, has been barbarous beyond a parallel. The former have been plundered of almost every article of clothing they possessed; the latter had their hearts and livers taken out, which were actually cooked and feasted on by the savages; and that too, in the quarters of the British officers, sanctioned by colonel M'Dougall.'"* Not to keep the reader a moment in suspense, let him be assured, that this "heart and liver" story is not

* Sketches of the War, p. 331.

† History of the War, p. 266.

even hinted at in the proceedings of the court of inquiry, (filling as they do the column of a newspaper,*) that tried the officers and crew of the Tigress; and which court would, most gladly, have published the fact. And would doctor Smith and Mr. Thomson, so ready at catching tales of the sort, have let pass such an opportunity of stigmatizing the British? The most surprising thing is, that it should be a "fourth edition, revised and corrected," wherein we find so disgusting, and so flagitious a paragraph.

* National Intelligencer, July 29, 1815.

CHAPTER XVII.

*Assemblage of troops in Lower Canada—Contemplated attack upon Sackett's Harbor—Arrival there of general Izard—British camp at Chambly—March of the left division towards Plattsburg—Origin of the expedition—Arrival of the left division near the lines, and correspondent retreat of major-general Macomb—Slow advance of the left division—Behaviour of the American militia—Description of Plattsburg—Required co-operation of the Champlain fleet—Comparative force of the two squadrons—Important particulars from the letters of "*VERITAS*"—Remarks on the American official account—Prisoners and deserters—Loss on both sides—American accounts—Painted representation of the action—Subsequent death of sir George Prevost—Remarks upon plans of conquest matured at a distance—Re-encampment of the left division of the British army in Lower Canada—Proceedings of the right division—Improved state of the defences, and augmented force of the garrison, at Fort-Erie—Effect of sickness and loss on the British—Preparations for a sortie—State of the British Works—Distance between them and the*

British encampment—Advance of the American sallying party—State of the weather—Surprise of the British piquets—Skirmish with the guard, and capture of part of the batteries—Advance of the American reserve—Arrival of the support-brigade from the British camp—Repulse of the American troops, and recovery of the captured batteries—Mutual loss—American accounts—Continued exposure and sickness of the right division—Its removal to a healthier contiguous spot, and subsequent retreat to Chippeway—General Izard's departure from Sackett's Harbor — His cautious proceeding, and junction with general Brown—Amount of the united American forces—Further retreat of general Drummond—Skirmish at Lyon's creek—British command of Lake Ontario—A small reinforcement to the right division—Retreat of the American army to Fort-Erie—A second reinforcement to the British—Abandonment and destruction of Fort-Erie, and departure of generals Izard and Brown from Upper Canada—Distribution of both armies, on the Niagara, into winter quarters—State of alarm at Sackett's Harbor — Two successive predatory incursions into the western parts of Upper Canada.

LEAVING Mr. Madison to profit by the "advantage" he has gained upon Lake Huron, we hasten to Lower Canada; where a force of

British regulars was now assembled, sufficient, for the first time during the war, to give serious alarm to the American government. During the months of June and July, the Quebec papers were continually announcing the arrival of transports with troops, and those troops, too, such as, under Wellington, had hitherto carried all before them. When the people of the Canadas began to reflect, how sparingly they had been supplied with troops, in the first two years of the war, a very familiar proverb could not fail to press upon their thoughts. When, again, they saw nothing but petty reinforcements sent to general Drummond on the Niagara, and that the important post of Sackett's Harbor was still a flourishing depôt in the hands of the enemy, what rational man among them could come to any other conclusion, than that the commander-in-chief was determined to wipe away the disgrace he had incurred in the May of the preceding year?* Sir George, did certainly say something, in his intercepted letters to lieutenant-general Drummond, about ordering a brigade of troops, under major-general Kempt, to Kingston, for the purpose of attacking Sackett's Harbor; although, at the same time, he must have known, that our fleet was not in a situation to appear on the lake; nor likely to be so, till the new 100-gun-ship was launched. So satisfied

* See Vol. I. p. 172.

were the Americans, that Sackett's Harbor would be the first point of attack, even if sir George had to cross the St. Lawrence, and march overland, that general Izard, on the 1st of September, broke up his encampment at Plattsburg, and marched there with between 3 and 4000 regulars.

If any any thing could raise British courage beyond its accustomed height, it was, surely, the emulation which existed between the troops that had recently arrived from the Peninsula, and those that had been originally allotted for the defence of the Canadas: the one, highly jealous of the reputation they had already gained; the other, equally so, of their local experience, and of the dressing they had several times given to superior numbers of the very same enemy, against whom the two united bodies were now about to act. Under these circumstances, will any one, except an American, say, that 11000 of such troops would not have beaten, upon any ground where evolutions could be practised, 17000 of the best troops which the United States could have brought into the field? A British army, then, of 11000 men, with a proportionate and most excellent train of artillery, commanded in chief by sir George Prevost, and, under him, by officers of the first distinction in the service, left their camp at Chambly, "with a view," says the American official account, "of conquering the country, as far as Crown Point and Ticonderoga."* We are here bound to acquit sir George Prevost of being the framer of this expedition. It originated in England.†

The approach of sir George's army, by Odell-town, to the line of demarcation, was the signal for major-general Macomb, with the few regulars of general Izard's army left under his command, to retire from the neighbourhood of the lines, to Plattsburg. His abandoned camp was entered by sir George Prevost on the 3d of September. From this position the left division, of about 7000 men, composed of all but the reserve and heavy artillery, moved forward on the 4th, and halted on the 5th, within eight miles of Plattsburg; having advanced 25 miles within the enemy's territory in the course of four days. On the morning of the 6th, the left division proceeded on its march, major-general Power's, or the right column advancing by the Beckman-town road; and major-general Brisbane's column,—except one wing of De Meuron's regiment, left to keep up the communication with the main body,—taking the road that runs parallel to Lake Champlain. At a bridge crossing a creek that intersects this road, the American general had stationed a small force, with two field-pieces, to abattis and obstruct the way. In the meanwhile the right column, meeting with

* App. No. 45. † App. No. 42.

no impediments to its progress, passed rapidly on, 700 American militia,* upon whom "the British troops did not deign to fire, except by their flankers and advanced patroles,"† retreating before it. General Macomb, out of compliment to the regulars, perhaps, states that 250 of them, under major Wool, "disputed the road with great obstinacy;" yet, in almost the next paragraph, admits that, after the detachment of 310 regulars, with two field pieces, had retired from Dead creek, and joined major Wool, and while the riflemen "at rest," were pouring in a destructive fire," and the field-pieces doing "considerable execution," "so undaunted was the enemy, that he never deployed in his whole march, always pressing on in column." The rapid advance of major-general Power secured major-general Brisbane from any further opposition, than what he might experience from the American gun-boats and gallies. Notwithstanding a heavy fire from their long 24 and 12-pounders, the bridge across the creek was presently re-constructed, and the left column moved forward upon Plattsburg.

The village of Plattsburg contains about 70 houses and stores, and is situate on both sides of the river Saranac, close to its confluence with Lake Champlain. The statement in the British official account, that "the column entered Platts-

* Sketches of the War, p. 318. † App. No. 45.

burg,"* must, therefore, be understood to mean, either the *township* of that name, or the small portion of the village which was situate on the north-side of the stream. It was to the south-side that general Macomb, after taking up the planks of the bridge, had retreated; and it was "on the elevated ridge of land" forming its bank, that the Americans erected their works. General Macomb mentions three forts, and "two block-houses strongly fortified." One of the latter, according to a grand panoramic view of the action, mounted three guns. We believe there were from 15 to 20 guns in all; most of them of heavy caliber. There was, also, a large new stone-mill, four stories high, that formed an excellent position for the American riflemen. It was on the evening of the 6th, that the left division arrived on the north-bank of the Saranac. "But," says Mr. Thompson, "not all the gallies, aided by the armament of the whole flotilla, which then lay opposite Plattsburg, under commodore Macdonough, could have prevented the capture of Macomb's army, after its passage of the Saranac, had sir George Prevost pushed his whole force upon the margin of that stream. Like general Drummond, at Erie, he made a pause, in full view of the unfinished works of the Americans, and consumed five days in erecting batteries, and throwing up breast-

* App. No. 42.

works, for the protection of his approaches. Of this interval the American general did not fail to avail himself; and kept his troops constantly employed in finishing his line of redoubts."* The reader need scarcely to be reminded, that this is the same Plattsburg, at which colonel Murray, with 1000 troops, landed; the river on which it stands, the same Saranac, up which the colonel ascended, three miles, to burn the enemy's barracks; and that those barracks were burnt, while an American regular army, more than twice as strong as general Macomb's, lay encamped in the neighbourhood.†

Unfortunately, a service which one brigade of the left division, had it been allowed to make the attempt, would have most promptly and completely executed, was to be deferred, till a ship, which had been launched only 11 days, was armed, manned, and equipped; and, with her puny companions, ready to fight a much superior fleet of the enemy. There is no doubt that orders were sent from home, for this ship to be laid on the stocks, so that she might be ready to co-operate in the Plattsburg expedition. Six days only after the Confiance had been launched, and nine days before a crew arrived to man her, was sir George's army already in the enemy's territory. If sir George's orders were so impe-

* Sketches of the War, p. 319. † See Vol. I. p. 242—5.

rative as to a naval co-operation, why did he not wait quietly at his camp at Chambly, till the new ship was fitted; and then commence his three days' march to Plattsburg?

A gentleman, residing near the scene of action, has, under the signature of "Veritas," so ably descanted upon the merits of the Plattsburg failure, that we cannot do better, than make an extract from his interesting pamphlet;* first, however, calling the reader's attention to our statement of the action fought between the rival fleets; wherein will be seen detailed some of the many difficulties under which poor captain Downie laboured.† So much of that statement as respects the relative force of the British and American squadrons, cannot well be dispensed with; and is therefore here transcribed:

"*Comparative force of the two squadrons.*

		British.	American.
Broadside-metal in pounds	Long guns,	507	588
	Carronades,	258	606
		765	1194
Complements of men and boys,		537	950
Size in tons,		1426	2540."

"In order," says the writer of 'VERITAS,' "to convey an accurate idea upon the subject of the expedition to Plattsburg, by reasoning upon sir George's official letter, I extract from it, that, on the 3d of September, our army seized

* Published at Montreal, Upper Canada.

† James's Nav. Occur. p. 405—35.

the enemy's entrenched camp at Champlain-town (what a feat!) after it was abandoned by them; that, on the 5th, the army halted within 8 miles of Plattsburg; and, on the 6th, entered Plattsburg, after reversing the position of the enemy at Dead creek, which they abandoned and left to be defended by the gun-boats. Sir George then describes the position of the enemy as upon an elevated ridge south of the Saranac, with redoubts, &c. armed with heavy ordnance, with their flotilla, the Saratoga, Surprise, Thunderer, Preble, and 10 gun-boats, (which gun-boats, please to remark, reader, were, a moment before, said to be at Dead creek,) 'at anchor out of gun-shot from the shore.' He adds, that he immediately communicated this circumstance to captain Downie, who had the 'Confiance, Linnet, Broke, and Shannon,' (captain Pring calls the latter the Chub and Finch,) 'and 12 gun-boats,' and requested his co-operation; (mark that;) and, in the mean time, batteries were constructed. On the morning of the 11th our flotilla was seen over the isthmus of land; (it seems he would not trust to his ears, in respect to the scaling of the guns for a signal as agreed upon;) when, immediately, certain brigades were ordered to advance to force the ford of the Saranac, and escalade the enemy's works upon the heights; but, sarcely had the troops forced a passage and ascended those heights, when he heard the shout of victory (here his ears appear to have been pretty sharp) from the enemy's works, in consequence of the flags of the Confiance and Linnet being struck, (they did not strike within 15 minutes of each other,) and the gun-boats flying. Finally, he adds, 'this unlooked for event, depriving me of the co-operation of the fleet,' (but, in the name of honor and good faith, why did you not co-operate before?) 'without which, the further prosecution of the service was become impracticable, I did not hesitate to arrest the course of the troops advancing to the attack, because the most complete success would have been unavailing, and the possession of the enemy's works offered no advantage to compensate for the loss we must have sustained in acquiring possession of them.'

"Now, would it not be supposed, that all this was done in the time that sir George was turning himself round from looking at the fleet, to look at his troops, and *vice versâ?* but, what must the astonishment be, when it is found, that the Confiance resisted two hours and a half, and the Linnet 15 minutes longer! Surely the troops, whose commander was so impatient to see the fleet come up, ought to have been ready to enter the enemy's works the moment they did appear. Had they so entered, it is unquestionable that our fleet would have been victorious; or, had they been permitted to enter, even when recalled, it is almost demonstrable that the enemy's fleet must have surrendered, or ours at least, have been retaken. There may be some truth in sir George's official narrative, but much is concealed. A letter was sent to captain Downie, strongly urging him to come on, as the army had been long waiting for his co-operation, (stating, as a proof of it, that it had been under arms from day-light the day before, in expectation of the fleet,) and closing with a hope, that nothing but the state of the wind, prevented the fleet from coming up. This last insinuation conveyed more meaning than meets the ear, as if hinting that artificial delays were made. The brave Downie replied, that he required no urging to do his duty; that he should be up the first shift of wind, and make the signal of his approach by scaling his guns. He was as good as his word: the guns were scaled when he got under weigh; upon hearing which, sir George issued an order for the troops to *cook*, instead of that of instant co-operation. At length, when *he saw the fleet*, a movement was ordered, but of course too late, as so little previous arrangement had been made for being ready to come into immediate contact with the enemy, that the troops put in motion, had a circuit of miles to make; and then, when at length close in with their object, were recalled the moment that the fleet fell. As to captain Downie's being urged by sir George to go into action, the whole chain of circumstances corroborate the fact, and the indiscretion of major Coore in furnishing living evidence of what the hero, now no more, said, is not more fortunate for the cause of truth than conclusive thereon. Besides this, every professional man knows, that no naval officer, in his senses, would, from choice, (if left to the guidance of his own judgment,) have gone into action with a new ship and raw crew, immediately after her equipment, without a week or ten days to discipline that crew, and accustom them to their stations and quarters. Much stress is laid by sir George and his friends upon the allegation that the enemy's fleet was out of gun-shot from the shore; which is not true. But why not have entered the enemy's works, and given practical proof of the range of shot against their fleet, instead of making conjectural assertions? Had that been done, widely different would have been the issue. So thoroughly did captain Downie depend upon co-operation by land, that he harangued his men when going into action, to this effect:—'My lads, we shall be immediately assisted by the army a-shore—Let us show them, that our part of the duty is well done.' Poor fellow, how he was mistaken! In 10 minutes afterwards he fell; and left sir George to tell his own story. This speech proved to have a pernicious effect upon the crew, when the promises it conveyed, were seen not to be fulfilled on shore.

"It is a fact, that the American commodore was so impressed with the idea that their works on shore would still be carried, that he did not take possession of our vessels for a long time after the action terminated; he being employed in getting his own out of reach from the shore, apprehending that their own batteries would be turned against them. In the evening he expressed an expectation that, next morning, the British colours would be seen flying upon the American works; and, when genenal Macomb came off at day-light, to say that our army had retreated in the night of the 11th, leaving their sick and wounded behind, and destroying quantities of stores and provisions, commodore Macdonough would not credit the fact; but, when it was persisted in, cautioned Macomb to beware of a *ruse de guerre*, as the British army would either return next night, or was then proceeding by forced marches to Sackett's Harbor. It is known that Macomb, notwithstanding all his puffs about our defeat, was actually sitting in gloomy despair upon a gun, whilst our troops were advancing on the 11th; and was ready to surrender, the moment that the first British soldier appeared upon the parapet. And when he was notified, that they had suddenly halted, and were then on the retreat, he started up, almost frantic with joy, and could hardly believe the evidence of his senses. He had only with him about 1500 of the refuse of the American troops on the Plattsburg duty, the effectives having previously marched off for Sackett's Harbor, under general Izard. To this may be added, perhaps, 3000 militia, chiefly collected after sir George halted on the 6th, at Plattsburg, and on which day he might have entered their works, almost without opposition, had our troops not been kept back for a grand coup, and behold its finale!

"As to saving of men by the retreat, after the loss of our fleet, it is well known that twice the number were lost by desertion, which an assault would have cost us; and this sir George knew at the time he wrote, 'that the possession of the enemy's works offered no advantage to compensate for the loss we must have sustained in acquiring possession of them.' Did sir George really believe, that we had lost the use of our reasoning faculties? Was the ground upon which the men, artillery, and stores at Saranac stood, the object of capture? or was it not (assuredly it was) the men, artillery, and stores, standing upon that ground; and if so, why were they suffered to escape? Surely the military character of the gallant army committed to his charge, and the manes of the gallant Downie, who perished under such circumstances, required some sacrifices. I wonder in what school sir George learnt the humiliating doctrine, that a British soldier's life is more valuable to him than his military honor; and yet to justify such a retreat, that principle must be assumed. Did not the loss of our fleet require a military set-off? and did not that loss absolutely impose it upon sir George, as an imperious duty, to furnish that set-off, by capturing the enemy's army, to prevent the effect which a retreat, under such circumstances, must produce, ornamented, as he well knew it would be, by American gasconade? The mischievous moral effect of the Plattsburg business, has been, and will be, incalculable, both in America and in Europe; for that will be heard of in many countries and places, where it will not be known, that the commander alone was to blame, and the army under him indignant on the occasion. Were the events of sir George's command, and especially the expeditions to Sackett's Harbor and Plattsburg to become examples for the British army to follow; from possessing the hearts of lions, they would soon be reduced to the timidity of lambs; and the future inquiries of military men would be, not who had nobly done his duty, but who had avoided a battle, or who had contrived to escape unhurt.

"It has been said, that his General Orders and official letters were often composed with a view to deceive at a distance; and his Plattsburg letter furnishes direct proof of this accusation's being correct. It is dated there, the 11th of September, 1814, as if written on the spot, immediately after the naval battle, and before the degrading retreat commenced; whereas, it is well known, that the letter did not go from Canada until it was carried by Mr. Secretary Brenton, who sailed from Brandy Pots on the 9th of October; consequently, it was written in Montreal long after the date it bears. In proof of this, read the following paragraph of that letter, 'As the troops concentrated and approached the line of separation between this province,' (is Plattsburgh then in Canada?) 'and the United States, the American army, &c.' What a sad slip of the pen, or memory, is here! But if for 'Plattsburg, 11th September,' be substituted 'Montreal, 21st September,' or any subsequent day, then the blunder will be explained. It is true, such was the celerity of his personal retreat, that on the 13th, he issued an order, dated at Odell-town; but I strongly suspect that, on the 11th, after the action, he was not in a state to write letters any where. Another proof of the official letter's having been written at Montreal, and not at Plattsburg, is, that in the first General Order issued afterwards, the gun-boats were, in a manner, commended for effecting their retreat in safety; (probably from a sympathetic feeling of the moment;) whereas, in the revision of that order, they are left out, although they had been mentioned in this false dated letter as flying; because, upon reflection, their not having done their duty, might lead people aside from the consideration, that he had not done his own. But why was the letter dated at

Plattsburg? Truly, just to deceive JOHN BULL, and prevent the necessity of then letting him know, how many men were lost by desertion in that memorable retreat, and what quantity of provisions and stores were destroyed in it, or during the expedition."

In addition to sir George's, we have copied into the Appendix sir James Yeo's letter.* Captain Pring's, which details the naval battle, will be found in its proper place.† Some parts of the American official account require an explanation. It is by that intended to be understood, that the whole British army was, on the morning of the 11th, drawn up on the banks of the Saranac: whereas, but four battalions were there stationed; the remainder of the troops being at some distance in the rear. Where did general Macomb learn, that our troops were three times "repulsed," in their efforts to cross the river? The fact is, major-general Brisbane, with a portion of his brigade, not only crossed the Saranac, but brought away some prisoners. This was accomplished to shew the practicability of the thing, and not as any part of the general attack *about* to be commenced. Had general Brisbane been permitted to advance, he would soon have made the "brave volunteers and militia" skip along as nimbly as, according

* App. No. 43.

† James's Naval Occurrences, his Appendix, No. 90.

to general Macomb himself, they had already done upon the Beckman-town road. "The gallant conduct of captain M'Glassin," who, on the night of the 9th, "with 50 men, drove off a working-party, consisting of 150, and defeated a covering-party of the same number, killing one officer and six men in the charge, and wounding many,"* was a feat worthy to be performed by Americans. Let us take a view of it, in its unadorned state. The battery mounted two guns, and had suffered so much from the enemy's fire, as to need considerable repairs. These were best performed at night; and the men had actually their coats and accoutrements off, when this "gallant" party surprised them. Such as were not instantly disabled or made prisoners soon picked up their muskets, and drove the Americans back to their works, with the utmost precipitancy. General Macomb, well knowing that captain M'Glassin had not time even to spike the two guns, leaves that to be inferred. Mr. Thomson, while, in stating the routed foe as only *one* "guard of 150 men," he appears to consider general Macomb's "covering party" as the same men *covered* with their cloaths, understands what is expected from him, as to the other part of the account; and therefore unblushingly says: "Being now in possession of a work, which would have incalculably

* App. No. 44.

annoyed the batteries at Fort-Brown, captain M'Glassin destroyed it with all possible haste, and returned to the American works with the loss of three men missing."*

The only prisoners taken by the Americans, near the river, were some of the light infantry company of the 76th regiment, and a few stragglers from other corps, who, having, when the order came for a general retreat, lost their way in the woods, got cut off from general Brisbane's brigade. General Macomb assigns a better reason for the discontinuance of the bombardment by the British, thus: "Every battery of the enemy being silenced by the superiority of our fire."† So wide is this from the truth, that general Brisbane silenced, and drove away the men from, every one of the American guns on the banks of the river, preparatory to the lodgment which he had intended to have made with his brigade, had not the attack been countermanded.

The rear-guard was commanded by this officer, who waited till the bridge at Dead creek was completely destroyed, and left nothing behind, except what the badness of the roads prevented being removed. One of these articles was the broken carriage of a 24-pounder, which a Burlington journalist immediately magnified into "90 pieces of cannon." General Macomb, in his first letter, says: "The light troops and

* Sketches of the War, p. 321. † App. No. 44.

militia are in full pursuit of the enemy, and making prisoners in all directions.". In his second letter, he baulks the expectations he had raised in the minds of his countrymen, by enumerating only "five dragoons of the 19th regiment, and several others of the rear-guard." This "pursuing" enemy, however, knew better than even to shew himself to "the rear-guard." The "prisoners" consisted chiefly of deserters; of whom there were, from first to last,—such an effect had the retreat upon the minds of the men,—more than 800.

In killed and wounded our loss was comparatively small; amounting to two captains, one ensign, four serjeants, 30 rank and file, of the former; and of the latter, one general staff, one captain, six lieutenants, seven serjeants, and 135 rank and file. The missing amounted to four lieutenants, two serjeants, one drummer, and 48 rank and file; making a total of 37 killed; 150 wounded; and 55 missing: grand total, 235.* As this trifling loss would show, at once, what a small portion of the British troops came into action; and that it could not have been the prowess of their opponents that compelled them to retire, general Macomb, to whose numerical accuracy we are no strangers,† says: "The loss of the enemy, in killed, wounded, prisoners, and deserters, since his first appearance, cannot fall short of 2500."‡ This number

* App. No. 42. † See Vol. I. p. 318. ‡ App. No. 44.

satisfies Mr. O'Connor, but not doctor Smith; the latter, therefore, with his ready pen, makes it "3050."* Mr. Thomson pretends to more accuracy. He states the number of deserters that surrendered on the first day, at 400; adding:—"Besides these, sir George lost 75 prisoners; and, as nearly as could be ascertained, about 1500 killed and wounded; among them several officers of rank."† The Americans state their own loss, in regulars, at one subaltern, one serjeant, one musician, and 34 privates, killed; two subalterns, one serjeant-major, four serjeants, two corporals, four musicians, and 49 privates wounded; total, 37 killed, and 62 wounded: grand total 119.† The number of missing among the regulars, or the general return of loss among the volunteers and militia, no where appears.

None of the American editors have magnified the British force beyond 14000 men; and Mr. O'Connor states general Macomb's force at 1500 regulars, and 2500 militia and volunteers; total 4000 men.‡ This is exclusive of 3000 militia that joined during the night of the 11th; and there were, besides, according to an American editor, "many thousands more on the road in full and willing march." The reader is, no doubt, prepared for a budget of boasting, on the

* History of the United States, Vol. III. p. 319.

† Sketches of the War, p. 324.

‡ History of the War, p. 273.

part of the Americans; and, without characterizing it as a "splendid engagement,"* had they not reason? We shall only notice a large "Painting;" of which we have the "Key," now before us. Among the British officers represented as close to the bank, are major-generals De Rottenburg, Robinson, Brisbane, and Baynes; and a horseman, in full speed from one of the contiguous houses, is styled,—"Aide de camp from general Prevost." The British encampment is, by the painter's magic, brought full into view. We are not a little surprised to see—"Colonel Wellington, (Willington,) of the Buffs, encouraging and giving an example to his men;" when Mr. Thomson had, with more accuracy than usual, "killed" that officer, at the head of these same "Buffs," while marching to Plattsburg, on the 6th.† By way of shewing that the "State-dragoons of New York," with their "red coats," had ceased to "give alarm to the militia,"‡ some of the former appear among the fierce groupe on the south-side of the Saranac. As the picture, by all accounts, gave, at "25 cents§ each," every satisfaction to the citizens, two important objects were attained: the proprietor filled his pockets, and the national vanity became raised to the highest pitch.

In all cases where the troops of the United

* Sketches of the War, p. 324. † Ibid, p. 318.
‡ App. No. 44. § About 1s. 1½d.

States have traversed the Canadian territory, their progress has, to borrow an American phrase, been "marked with the all-desolating ruin of the locust." Quite opposite, in its effects, was the retreat of the British along the shores of Champlain; they may be said to have 'shed manna' as they went. Not an inhabitant of the place but was fed and enriched by the Plattsburg expedition; which is all that remains to console us for its unsuccessful result. In the remarks which it has been our duty to make, in order to illustrate this memorable historical event, we hope the reader will understand, that the two services were as willing to co-operate, as, for the glory of their country, they ought always to be. That the fleet did all that could rationally be expected from its means, our naval volume will shew: that the army, had it been allowed to act, would have done the same, with less trouble, and not many more casualties, than usually attend one of its field-days, has, we trust, already appeared in these pages. The individual, who, undoubtedly, caused all this, has since paid the debt of nature.* While, against him and his memory, we disclaim all feelings of a personal nature, we as firmly deny, that the principle—'*De mortuis nil nisi bonum*' can be extended to a public character.

The indiscreet impatience of the Quebec

* James's Nav. Occur. p. 425.

journalists led them to announce, in a pompous and boastful manner, every movement of the left division, after its departure from Odell-town. Unfortunately, just as they had done favoring the public with "the highly gratifying intelligence, that our brave troops entered Plattsburg, with little opposition," the mail closed for England. So that, in one month after our discomfiture, the whole United Kingdom rang with the "INVASION OF NEW YORK, AND TAKING OF PLATTSBURG." The same wind that conveyed home, so quickly, this cheering piece of news, brought accounts, also, of the capture of Penobscot. The editor of a London evening journal, ofter announcing, first, that the "district of Maine" had been captured, and then, that "Plattsburg had been victoriously entered by our troops," says:—"By a glance at the map, it will be seen that, by this invasion, our army had already advanced in the interior to about 50 miles further south than the Penobscot, where the coast-operations were carrying on; leaving, of course, the whole intermediate country between Lake Champlain and the sea, as it were cut off from the United States." Much of the ridicule incurred from hundreds of paragraphs like these, would have been saved, had the troops from Europe been accompanied by a commander-in-chief, competent to lead them; and he directed to govern his movements by circumstances as they might exist at the time of his arrival, and not peremptorily to obey orders, issued at 4000 miles distance; orders, which could not be put in execution, till a six month's fluctuation of events had, in all probability, destroyed their expediency.

After the British army, on its return from Plattsburg, had re-encamped at Champlain, the road to Sackett's Harbor lay open to sir George. Instead of directing his views that way, he marched, with the army, across the lines, to Odell-town; and then set off for Montreal. After his departure, the principal part of the troops were distributed between Isle aux Noix, St. John's, Chambly, and La Prarie; where we will leave them, and attend to the operations of the right division.

No sooner had the British retired to their encampment, after their unsuccessful assault upon Fort-Erie,* than the Americans set about to repair the bastion which had been injured by the explosion; as well as to complete the new works that were constructing, when the attack commenced. In a little while, the defences were all entire, and "garnished with heavy cannon;" numbering, according to Mr. Thomson's plan of the fort, 27 pieces.

On the 2d of September, general Brown, having recovered from his wounds, resumed the

* See p. 178.

command of the garrison; which had, in the mean time, been reinforced by new levies of militia.* On the 3d, came about 320 regulars, in the St. Lawrence brig, from Lake Huron, and a company of riflemen, 80 strong, from Sandusky. Small detachments of regulars, whose numbers cannot be ascertained, also crossed the strait, from Batavia and Sackett's Harbor. Notwithstanding, therefore, the loss sustained on the 15th of August, and by repeated desertions since, the American army still mustered about 3400 men, who, instead of the two captured schooners to protect their flanks, had now, the St. Lawrence, Niagara, Lady Prevost, and Caledonia brigs, and Porcupine schooner; mounting, between them, 58 guns. Well might Mr. Thomson boast that Fort-Erie was rendered "impregnable to the attacks of any other than a vastly superior force."†

The British right division, although it had been reinforced by the 6th and 82d regiments, of, united, about 1040 rank and file, was, on account of its recent loss, and the departure of six companies of the 41st for Fort-George, and of the small remnant of the 103d for Burlington, no stronger in numbers than previously to the assault: but, in effective strength, it was much weaker; for the heavy and constant rains, operating upon the swampy nature of the ground

* Sketches of the War, p. 328. † Ibid, p. 325.

upon which the troops were obliged to be encamped, and the severe privations, for want of provisions and other necessaries, under which they laboured, spread sickness among them. A supply, either of provisions or of men, could not well be forwarded, while the American squadron retained the command of the lake.

Several immaterial affairs of piquets occurred, till general Brown, enspirited by the business at Plattsburg, and encouraged by information of general Drummond's intention to retreat to a healthier position, resolved, by a sortie, to gain the credit of having compelled this movement. To render the enterprise less hazardous, he invited across a reinforcement of 'seven-day men,' or men hired to act for that term only. Of this fact there is no doubt; but we are willing to concede every advantage, in point of numbers, that was derived from it, and to estimate general Brown's force at no more than 3400 men, of whom upwards of two-thirds were regulars. The British had commenced upon a new battery, intended to enfilade the western ramparts of the American works; but, being on the eve of retreating, and having as yet got up no additional guns,* the work had not been persevered in. Two small wooden buildings, denominated, though not worthy the name of, block-houses, one upon the right flank, the

* See p. 168.

other near the centre, of the British lines, had recently been constructed. The British encampment was distant a mile and a half from the works, which were situate in the midst of a thick wood.

Until it is admitted that the mere throwing of a red coat upon a man's back can endow him with all the well-known qualities of the British soldier, no one can be surprised that general Brown should have deferred his sortie till he had ascertained, that De Watteville's regiment, (which, without disparagement to the brave officers in it, was composed of foreigners of all nations and principles,) joined by the few numbers of the 8th, was doing duty at the batteries. It was at about two o'clock on the afternoon of the 17th of September, when the rain was pouring in torrents, that the Americans sallied from the fort. "Lieutenants Riddle and Frazer, of the 15th infantry," says Mr. Thomson, "had already opened a road from the southern angle of the garrison, to a point within pistol-shot of the enemy's right wing, and with such secrecy, that it was not discovered till the actual assault commenced."* We here gain a piece of important information; and, it is our duty to add, that part of De Watteville's regiment composed that "right wing." The Americans, at about three o'clock in the after-

* Sketches of the War, p. 325.

noon, advanced, in two columns, under a heavy fire from their batteries; one column passing through the woods, so as to flank the outer British battery, or No. 3; the piquets belonging to which were completely surprised. The other, emerging from a deep ravine, in which it had been concealed, penetrated the British lines, in front, a little to the right of No. 2, or the centre battery; then, turning short to the left, surrounded the British right, and got almost immediate possession of No. 3 battery, its magazine, and, but not without a struggle, the block-house upon its right, garrisoned by a few men of the 8th regiment.

While a party was securing the prisoners, destroying the three 24-pounders at No. 3 battery, and blowing up the magazine, a strong column turned to the right; and, after meeting with a gallant resistance from the piquets, composed of a part of the 8th, and De Watteville's regiments, succeeded in gaining possession of the remaining block-house and of No. 2 battery. General Miller, at the head of the 9th, 11th, and 19th infantry regiments, joined by the 21st regiment, forming the reserve under general Ripley, inclined towards the river, in order to assail the British battery, No. 1. By this time, the remnants of the first battalion of the royal Scots, of the second battalion of the 89th, and the Glengarry light infantry; also three companies of the 6th, and seven companies of the 82d regiment, had arrived from the British camp. The royal Scots, and 89th, under lieutenant-colonel Gordon, of the former regiment, advanced by the road leading to the block-house, upon the right; and soon drove general Porter and his volunteers, in number 1000,* along with the regulars supporting them, from the block-house, and the battery, No. 3. The recovery of No. 2, and the defence of No. 1 batteries, were entrusted to the three companies of the 6th, under major Taylor, and the seven companies of the 82d, under major Proctor; amounting, together, to about 560 rank and file. These detachments, after a free use of the bayonet, drove the 9th, 11th, 21st, and part of the 19th, United States' regiments, numbering, at the very lowest estimate, 1000 rank and file, from the battery No. 2, before they had effected its entire destruction, or that of the two guns in it, and then across the British entrenchments, nearly to the glacis of Fort-Erie; making several prisoners in the pursuit. In the mean while, the Glengarry light infantry, under the immediate command of lieutenant-colonel Battersby, and accompanied by lieutenant-colonel Pearson, had recovered the possession of the new intrenchment, or

* Hist. of the War, p. 263.

"unfinished battery No. 4."* By five o'clock the works were all re-occupied, and the line of piquets re-established.†

The British loss was very severe. It amounted to 115 killed, 178 wounded, and 316 missing; total, 609: ‡ a very large proportion, when we reflect, that the reserve, composed of major Lisle's troop of the 19th light dragoons, the seven remaining companies of the 6th, and the two flank companies of the 41st regiments, along with a small body of incorporated militia, was not at all in the action. What a contrast, in reference to the numbers of the respective armies, between the returns of casualties at the foot of major-general De Watteville's, and sir George Prevost's, official letters! § The Americans acknowledge a loss of 10 officers and 70 men, killed; 24 officers and 190 men, wounded; and 10 officers and 206 men, missing; total, 510:* nor does this return appear to include the militia or volunteers.

We are only favored with the sight of a short extract from general Brown's official report. It is, however, quite enough to satisfy us of the spirit of the whole. "Within 30 minutes after the first gun was fired," says the general, "batteries, Nos. 3 and 2, the enemy's line of entrench-

* Sketches of the War, p. 326. † App. No. 46.
‡ App. No. 47. § Ibid, No. 43.

ments, and his two block-houses, were in our possession. Soon after, battery No. 1, *was abandoned by the British*. The guns in *each* were spiked by us, or otherwise destroyed."* With this falsehood set abroad, one cannot be surprised that general Brown's sortie should have been proclaimed throughout the republic a "splendid achievement," as he himself, in a private letter to general Gaines, has the modesty to call it; nor at all the bombast to be found in the different American histories. The reader has had enough of this already; we will, therefore, endeavour to be brief. General Brown we dismiss, with a very short extract from a letter written by the American "general Varnum," and dated "Buffaloe, September 18." "Our gallant little army," says this general "has again signalized itself, by gaining a splendid victory over a part of the enemy's forces, near Fort-Erie. Two of the enemy's batteries were carried, the guns spiked, trunnions broken off, and their magazines blown up." Mr. Thomson, after he has done stating, that the Americans had captured the two British block-houses, and all four of the batteries, and had succeeded in spiking the guns, (represented, upon his diagram as 12 in number,) and demolishing the captured works, very naturally tells us, that "the operations ceased, with the accomplishment of all

* History of the War, p. 262.

the objects of the sortie."* There is one part of Mr. Thomson's account, however, that we do not rightly understand. He declares that the impediments,—describing them fully,—which the American regulars, under general Miller, experienced in their approaches to No. 1 battery, " produced some confusion in the column, and made constant appeals to the bayonet necessary."† An enemy's " bayonet," in such a case, would, one might suppose, produce still greater " confusion in the column." To what else, then, can Mr. Thomson allude, as so "necessary," but the " constant appeals to the bayonet," made by one of general Wilkinson's " tried serjeants,"‡

" Just in the place where honor's lodg'd" ?

And, no sooner had the troops, thus doubly beset, faced about, than a still more forcible " appeal" *au derriére*, acting by sympathy upon their heels, continued its potent stimulus, till the Americans reached the very walls of their " impregnable" fortress.

The still unfavorable state of the weather, the increasing sickness of the troops, the loss of three out of six of the battering cannon, and the now very much reduced numbers of general Drummond's army, caused him, at eight o'clock on the evening of the 21st, to

* Sketches of the War, p. 327. † Ibid. 326.

‡ See p. 82.

remove his remaining guns and stores; and retire to the neighbourhood of Black creek, about a mile and a half distant. Here the men bivouacked for the night, under torrents of rain. On the morning of the 22d, the Americans discovered this movement, but offered no molestation; although general Drummond waited till two o'clock on that day, ere he proceeded further downwards. On the 24th, after destroying the bridge across Frenchman's creek, and placing there a small cavalry piquet, the right division arrived, and encamped, in comparatively comfortable quarters, at Chippeway.

As the naval ascendancy of the Americans upon Lake Ontario dismissed any present fears of an attack upon Sackett's Harbor, general Izard's army would, it was considered, be more profitably employed in strengthening the left division, at the head of the lake. Instead, however, of being carried to the British Twelve-mile creek, where a landing would have effectually cut off general Drummond's much inferior force, or to the neighbourhood of Fort-Niagara, so as to have assaulted and tried to recover that fortress, general Izard suffered himself and his army to be disembarked on the south side of the lake; and then stole, by a back route, to Lewistown; where he arrived about the 8th of October, with, according to American accounts, 2400 infantry, artillery, and dragoons, of the regular army.

Why did he not, then, cross instantly to Queenstown, and place general Drummond between two fires?—No;—he preferred keeping on the safe side of the river till, arriving at Black Rock, on the 10th, he crossed over to Fort-Erie, and superseded general Brown; who, on the 6th, had received a reinforcement of 700 regulars from Detroit and Erie. As a proof that we have such authority as an American cannot dispute, for stating the American force upon this frontier at a much higher amount than we have hitherto fixed it, we here subjoin an article taken from the "Ontario Repository, of October 11," an American newspaper published on the spot.—"From Buffaloe, October 11th, we learn, that general Izard's army crossed at Black Rock only on that morning, and was to move down the Canada shore on the following day, with 8000 regular troops." May we, then, be allowed to say, that general Izard's army at Fort-Erie consisted of 6000 regular troops?

Against such a force the British right division, reduced as it now was in numbers, had no chance of success. General Drummond, therefore, broke up his cantonments at Chippeway, and retired upon Fort-George and Burlington. On the morning of the 19th, a skirmish took place near Cook's mills, at Lyon's creek, between a brigade of American regulars, under general Bissell and detachments from the 82d, 100th, and Glengarry regiments, amounting to about 650 rank and file, under colonel Murray. The thickness of the woods gave great advantage to the American riflemen; and, although, with the addition of the reserve, we find the 5th, 14th, 15th, and 16th regiments named, besides a company of riflemen, under captain Irvine, making a total force of at least 1500 rank and file, the American "*corps d'elite*," as Mr. Thomson boastfully calls it, would not risk an encounter, with evidently inferior numbers, upon the open ground. After what may be termed, a drawn battle, each party retired; the British, with the loss of 19 killed and wounded; the Americans, according to Mr. Thomson, of 67 killed, wounded, and missing.* This editor has magnified our force to 1200 men; and made the "marquis of Tweedale," in spite of the severe wound he was still labouring under at Kingston, the commander of the British party.

The British ship St. Lawrence having been launched on the 2d of October, commodore Chauncey, on the 11th, when he had ascertained that sir James would be on the lake in a few days, retired to Sackett's Harbor, and began mooring his ships head and stern, to prepare for an attack. Sir James sailed on the 17th, and, on the 19th, landed at the head of the lake, five companies of the 90th regiment, and a quantity

* Sketches of the War, p. 329.

of provisions; of which the right division was in great need. The fleet returned to Kingston on the 23d; and, on the 1st of November, sailed again to the head of the lake, with the 37th, and recruits for the 6th, and 82d regiments, and a brigade of artillery; all of which, on the evening of the 2d, disembarked near Fort-George. The arrival of the first reinforcement, trifling as it was, and although it would not have augmented general Drummond's force much beyond half the amount of general Izard's, was made an excuse for the retreat of the latter to Fort-Erie. On the 22d of October the American volunteers crossed the strait, to be discharged; and general Brown, with 2000 regulars, pushed forward to the relief of Sackett's Harbor. The arrival of the second Britith reinforcement produced a correspondent effect upon the remnant of the American force. Having, by the aid of their fleet, removed the guns, and completely destroyed the fortifications, the invaders, on the 5th of November, crossed from Fort-Erie to their own shore; "after," says Mr. Thomson,—forgetting in whose possession Fort-Niagara was,—"a vigorous and brilliant campaign."* The greater part of the American troops were distributed into quarters at Black Rook, Buffaloe and Batavia; the remainder, marched to Sackett's Harbor, to assist in repelling an attack

* Sketches of the War, p. 330.

which no one could doubt would be made. The fighting being over upon the Niagara, lieutenant-general Drummond and suite, along with the 41st regiment, and a number of convalescents, departed from the head of the lake, on board the St. Lawrence, and arrived at Kingston on the 10th of November; having left the right division, distributed along the Niagara-frontier, in comfortable winter quarters.

The still defenceless state of the western district of Upper Canada, had exposed the inhabitants to all the horrors of a second American visitation* On the 20th of September a band of depredators issued from the garrison of Detroit; and, crossing the stream, spread fire and pillage through a whole settlement; thereby reducing to misery no fewer than 27 Canadian families. The plunder obtained in this excursion, and the impunity with which the actors in it had got back to their homes, stimulated a more numerous, and better organized body of Americans, having, as their chief, " brigadier-general M'Arthur, of the United States' army." The proceedings of this military officer and his detachment having been thought worthy of a place in one of the American histories, we cannot do better than transcribe the account. " On the 22d of the following month, (October,) brigadier-general M'Arthur, having collected

* See p. 73.

720 effective regulars and militia, proceeded on a secret expedition, along the western shore of Lake St. Clair, and passed into the Canadian territory, at the mouth of that water. He penetrated 200 miles in the enemy's country; destroyed more than that number of muskets; attacked a large body of militia and Indians, encamped on favorable ground; made about 150 prisoners; and dispersed all the detachments to be found at the Thames, Oxford, or Grand River. During the march, he principally subsisted on the enemy, and fired several of the mills, from which the British troops in Upper Canada were supplied with food. Having gained intelligence of the evacuation of Fort-Erie, he abandoned his intention of proceeding to Burlington Heights, and returned to Detroit on the 17th of November. By this rapid expedition, the enemy's hostile intentions were diverted from another quarter, and his means of attacking Detroit entirely crippled; the destruction of his supplies rendering such an attempt altogether impracticable."*

Mr. Thomson has here, by the usual arts of his trade, attempted to convert into a military exploit, what much more resembled the inroad of banditti. That general M'Arthur got possession of *some* muskets, is very probable; because, as the reader recollects, a few had

* Sketches of the War, p. 331.

been left in the hands of some of the inhabitants, by the commanding officer of the district.* No militia were, at this time, embodied; therefore, none could have been "encamped." The "150 prisoners" consisted of peaceable inhabitants, both old and young, and drunken Indians and their squaws. Had there been any "detachments" within even a day's march of the scene of general M'Arthur's exploits, he would not have been so bold. The instant it was ascertained that a detachment of the 103d regiment, numbering less than half "720 effective regulars and militia," had moved from Burlington Heights, the general and his gang "dispersed;" and so "rapid" was their flight, that the British regulars did not get within eight miles of them. If Mr. Thomson can acknowledge, that the American troops "subsisted on the enemy, and fired several of the mills," we may well conceive, what must have been the devastation and ruin that marked the track of general M'Arthur and his mounted Kentuckians.

* See p. 5.

CHAPTER XVIII.

Capture of Moose Island, in Passamaquoddy Bay —Expedition against Penobscot and Castine— Its success—Destruction of the United States' ship Adams — Capture and Destruction of several other vessels, also of a great quantity of ordnance —American militia—Chesapeake Bay—Commodore Barney's flotilla—Its progress against a part of the British force, commanded by captain Barrie, of the Dragon—Landing of the British at Benedict, on the Patuxent—Loss of five straggling marines from the St. Lawrence schooner—American account of the behaviour and death of the serjeant, commanding the party—Barbarous circumstances under which his life was taken—Landing of the British at Lower Marlborough—Intention of the American government to destroy commodore Barney's flotilla, in St. Leonard's Creek—Its prevention by a military enterprise—Repulse of the force blockading the flotilla—Letters of commodore Barney and one of his officers—Arrival in the Potomac of rear-admiral Cockburn—His operations upon the shores of that, and other rivers in the Chesapeake—Reception on board the British ships of American refugee-slaves—American misrepresentation on the subject—Bounty to British deserters.

THE first military event we have to notice, after quitting the Canadas, is the occupation, on the 11th of July, 1814, by lieutenant-colonel Pilkington and captain sir Thomas Hardy, with a detachment of troops from Nova Scotia, of Moose island, near the mouth of Kobbeskook river, opposite to the province of New Brunswick, and on the western side of Passamaquoddy bay. The whole of this bay, as well as the island of Grand Manan in the bay of Fundy, was adjudged to be within the boundary of the British North-American provinces. The ceremony of taking possession of the town of Eastport, and of Fort-Sullivan, on Moose island; and every other particular connected with the expedition, will be found amply detailed in the British official accounts.* The American accounts offer nothing worthy notice; except that they make the British force 2000, instead of about 600 troops.

As connected with the capture of Passamaquoddy, we pass, at once, to an expedition fitted out at Halifax, Nova Scotia, against that part of the district of Maine, in the United States,

* App. Nos. 48. 49. 50. 51. and 52.

lying to the eastward of the Penobscot river; and which contains about 40 villages, and upwards of 30000 inhabitants. As to the probable object of taking possession of this tract of country, we cannot better instruct the reader, than by referring him to a work published by Mr. Nathaniel Atcheson, in 1808, entitled:— "American Encroachments on British Rights." Our business is merely with the conduct of the expedition; which, consisting of a 74, bearing the flag of rear-admiral Griffith, two frigates, a sloop of war, and 10 transports, having on board a company of royal artillery, two rifle-companies of the 60th, and the 29th, 62d, and 98th regiments, in all, about 1750 rank and file, under the command of lieutenant-general sir John Coape Sherbrooke, governor of Nova Scotia, sailed from Halifax on the 26th of August. The arrival of the expedition off the point of destination, its junction with other ships of war, and its further proceedings, resulting in the capture of Castine, Belfast, and Machias, the capture or destruction of 22 ships, brigs, and schooners, including the United States' frigate Adams; also of (including those at Machias) 52 pieces of ordnance, will be found most fully detailed in the several official documents sent home upon the occasion.*

The Adams had been a 32-gun frigate, but

* App. Nos. 53. 54. 55. 56. 57. 58. 59. 60. and 61.

was afterwards lengthened, so as to rate a 36; and then, on account of some defect in her construction, cut down to a corvette: in which latter state she measured 725 tons American, or 783 English. She sailed upon her last cruize, with an armament of four long 18-pounders, 20 *Columbiad*, or short long-guns,* of the same caliber, and two long 12-pounders; total 26 guns; and with a complement, according to a prisoner who was some weeks on board of her, of 248 picked seamen; chiefly masters and mates of merchantmen. The Adams was, therefore, one of the most formidable corvettes that cruized on the ocean. While in the Irish channel, towards the end of July, she was chased by the Tigris, of 42 guns, captain Henderson; and would probably have been caught, had not captain Morris thrown overboard his "quarter-guns." As the Adams was not to fight a frigate, and was an over-match for the heaviest sloop of war in the British navy, we cannot conceive what "glory" the American government expected to derive, from sending such a ship to sea? Although the entire destruction of this fine ship, and the capture of 23 of her guns, were effected by the combined forces detached up the river for that purpose, yet Mr. Thomson concludes his account of our "blowing her up," with stating, that the British were "disappointed in

* James's Nav. Occur. p. 5.

the object of their expedition."* He does not, however, attempt to conceal the behaviour of the American militia; who, he says, notwithstanding captain Morris's judicious arrangements, could not be brought to oppose an "inferior number of British regulars," and fled precipitately.* Captain Barrie's account of the very people who had stood up, though for a few minutes only, as militia, at Hamden, appearing (with, it may be supposed, scarcely breath to speak, after their well-run race) "as magistrates, select men, &c."† at Bangor, affords a tolerable specimen of the real character of Mr. Munro's "unarmed inhabitants."‡

The operations in the Chesapeake, during the summer of 1814, now claim our attention. The American editors have, as usual, by their happy talent for amplification, given importance to many events that occurred in the rivers and creeks of that capacious bay, which we should otherwise have deemed too insignificant to notice. The chief of these consist of the daring exploits and hair-breadth escapes of commodore Barney, (an Irishman), and his flotilla of gunboats. The commodore himself, we must do him the justice to say, is a truly brave man; and, no doubt, feels highly indignant at the numerous ridiculous tales that have been told of him,

* Sketches of the War, p. 235.

† App. No. 59. ‡ App. No. 69.

by even the most moderate of the American editors. Previous to our entering upon any of the operations of the flotilla, it becomes us to apprize the reader of what its force consisted.

The first account we have of the flotilla is, that " a number of boats, carrying heavy metal, were constructed in March, 1814, on the eastern shore of Maryland, for the protection of the bay; and the command of them was given to that intrepid officer, commodore Barney."* Doctor Smith tells us that " a flotilla of small schooners and barges, was fitted out at Baltimore, to scour the bay, and protect its shores, numerous creeks and inlets, from the enemy."† Mr. Thomson says:—" At that period," (end of May, 1814,) " a flotilla, consisting of a cutter, two gun-boats, a galley, and nine large barges, sailed from Baltimore."‡ Another American account numbers the barges, when subsequently blown up, at 13; and a Boston newspaper augments commodore Barney's flotilla, when it left Baltimore, to " 36 gun-boats, and 10 or 15 barges." The commodore's cutter or sloop was the Scorpion, mounting eight carronades, and a heavy long-gun upon a traversing carriage; and two of the gun-boats, we find, were Nos. 137 and 138.*

Whether commodore Barney's flotilla con-

* Hist. of the War, p. 224.

† Hist. of the United States, Vol. III. p. 286.

‡ Sketches of the War, p. 332.

sisted of gun-boats, gallies, "small schooners," or "large barges," it indisputably carried "heavy metal;" as, indeed, it well might, considering that it was expressly fitted out "to scour the bay and protect its shores from the enemy." Rear-admiral Cockburn says, each vessel had a long-gun in the bow, and a carronade in the stern; the calibers of the guns, and the number of the crew, in each, varying, in proportion to the size of the boat, from 32-pounders and 60 men, to 18-pounders and 40 men.* It appears, also, from the American accounts, that most, if not all, of the vessels had on board furnaces for heating shot. In his estimate of the crews the rear-admiral cannot be much out of the way; for, although he mentions having taken some of the flotilla-men as prisoners, an American work states the number of seamen and marines that accompanied commodore Barney to the field at Bladensburg, after the loss of his flotilla, at 600.† Upon adding to this number, such as may not have chosen to follow the commodore, and such as were taken prisoners by lieutenant Scott,* the Americans surely will not charge us with over-rating, if we estimate commodore Barney's original command at 700 men. A flotilla, so armed, manned, and equipped, cruizing in waters known only to itself, and able,

* James's Nav. Occurr. his App. No. 81.

† Hist. of the United States, Vol. III. p. 297.

almost at any time, to seek protection under batteries and formidable positions on shore, within gun-shot of which nothing larger than a boat could approach, was able to cope with any force that two 74-gun ships, or four 46-gun frigates, could send against it.

The first sight gained of this flotilla, by the British, was on the 1st of June, when it was proceeding from Baltimore, past the mouth of the river Patuxent, "to scour the bay." The British vessels consisted of the St. Lawrence schooner, of 13 guns, and 55 men, and the boats, in number seven, of the Albion and Dragon 74s, under the command of captain Barrie of the latter ship. The Americans had the honor of seeing this trifling force retreat before them to the Dragon, then at anchor off Smith's-point. That ship got under weigh, and, along with the schooner and the boats, proceeded in chase; but the shallowness of the water shortly compelled her again to anchor. In the meantime, the flotilla had run for shelter into the Patuxent. Captain Barrie, by way of inducing commodore Barney to separate his force, detached two boats to cut off a schooner under Cove-point; but the commodore, not considering that his orders to give "protection" warranted such a risk, allowed her to be burnt in his sight.

One American account of this affair says: "The commodore discovered two schooners, one of which carried 18 guns, and he immediately gave chase."* Here, evidently, Mr. Thomson has, by mistake, included the American schooner burnt under Cove-point. Mr. O'Connor has fallen into the same error; or rather, he declares there were "three schooners." Not a word appears any where about the schooner that was burnt. One editor says:—"Barney was obliged to take refuge in the mouth of the Patuxent."† Another says:—"This bold exploit did great honor to Barney and his crews:"‡ and all agree, that he fired "hot shot at the enemy."

On the 6th the flotilla retreated higher up the Patuxent; and captain Barrie, being joined on the day following by the Loire 46, and Jasseur brig, proceeded up the river with those two vessels, the St. Lawrence, and the boats of the Albion and Dragon. The flotilla retreated about two miles up St. Leonard's creek, where it could be reached by boats only; but the force of the latter was not equal to the attack. Captain Barrie endeavoured, however, by a discharge of rockets and carronades from the boats, to provoke the American vessels, which were moored in a line a-breast, across the channel, to come down within reach of the guns of the ship, brig,

* Sketches of the War, p. 332.

† Hist. of the United States, Vol. III. p. 287.

‡ Hist. of the War, p. 225.

and schooner, at anchor near the mouth of the creek. At one time the flotilla, or, as Mr. O'Connor says, "the 13 barges" got under weigh, and chased the boats to a short distance, and then returned to their moorings. With a view to force the flotilla to quit its station, detachments of seamen and marines were landed on both sides of the river, and the American militia, estimated at 3 or 400, retreated before them to the woods. The marines destroyed two tobacco-stores, and several houses that formed military posts; but still the flotilla remained at its moorings.

Fear is certainly a great magnifier of objects. To that may we ascribe the frequent appearance of *razees*, in nearly all the rivers of the Chesapeake. The name, once received as applicable to a ship of extraordinary size and force, is in the mouth of every terrified inhabitant of the coast, the moment he descries an enemy's vessel with three masts. The reader may perhaps know, that a razee is a cut-down 74. Three British ships only were fitted in this way; and, although all were sent upon the North American station, only one of the three entered the Chesapeake, and that not till the 25th of August, 1814. The very editors who have just done telling us that the British cannot send their 74s up the rivers, because of their heavy draught of water, make no scruple in placing a cut-down 74 at the mouth of every creek near to which a British frigate had cast anchor. These are the gentlemen, too, who boast that their "authentic" accounts have passed through so many editions.

As another proof of Mr. Thomson's love of the "authentic," he concludes his account of the affair in St. Leonard's creek thus: "The commodore immediately moved upon them," (the British boats,) "and after a smart fire, drove the barges down to the 18-gun vessel, which, in attempting to beat out, was so severely handled, that her crew ran her a-ground, and abandoned her."* This is the very vessel, the St. Lawrence, whose capture by the Chasseur, the Americans so joyfully announced, seven months after she was thus "run a-ground and abandoned." In justice to Mr. Thomson's contemporaries, we must say, that he is the only editor who has favored the public with this "authentic" piece of information.

On the 15th of June, the Narcissus, of 42 guns, joined the little squadron; and captain Barrie, taking with him 12 boats, containing 180 marines, and 30 of the black colonial corps, proceeded up the river to Benedict.† Here the men disembarked, and drove into the woods, without a struggle, a number of militia, who left behind a part of their muskets and camp-equipage, as well as a 6-pounder field-piece.

* Sketches of the War, p. 333.

† See Plate V.

After spiking the latter, and destroying a store containing tobacco, the British again took to their boats, except five or six men who had probably strayed too far into the woods.

The circumstances attending the capture of these men have been fully detailed in an Alexandria newspaper, of the 25th of June, and are too interesting in their nature not to be given entire to the reader. The party, it appears, consisted of a portion of the St. Lawrence's marines, commanded by serjeant Mayeaux, a Frenchman, who had been seventeen years in the British service, and who bore a most excellent character. The Alexandria paper, first assigning as a reason for giving so particular an account of the "late affair at Benedict," that some of the citizens "bore a distinguished part in it," proceeds as follows:—"The cavalry of the district arrived on Tuesday evening, about five o'clock, and at the moment general Stewart was preparing to attack the enemy, who were in possession of Benedict. At this moment a small detachment of the enemy presented themselves at the foot of the hill, not far distant from the place where the cavalry were posted. The order was immediately given to charge, and intercept their retreat, which was done with so much haste and impetuosity, as to break the ranks, which, considering the nature of the ground, was not injudicious. Five of the enemy were taken prisoners. The serjeant of the guard, having been separated from his men, and endeavouring to make his escape, was pursued.—Among the first who overtook him, was Mr. Alexander Wise, of the Alexandria dragoons, who made a bold but unsuccessful assault upon him, and being unable to check his horse, passed ten or fifteen paces beyond him. On turning his horse, he received the fire of the serjeant, and fell dead. At this moment Mr. Alexander Hunter, a young gentleman of this town, (who had volunteered his services for the occasion with the cavalry, and whose conduct has already been the subject of much and well-merited commendation,) came up, when the serjeant faced upon him and received the fire of his pistol, which seemed to take effect. Mr. Hunter's horse being alarmed at the report, ran some distance from the spot. When Mr. Hunter returned, he found general Stewart engaged with this intrepid soldier. He immediately advanced to the general's relief; upon which the serjeant having had his bayonet unshipped, dropped his musket, and, mounting an adjoining fence, fell upon the other side, upon his back. Mr. Hunter dismounted, and, unarmed, immediately followed and engaged him, demanding of several horsemen who advanced, to aid in securing him. Two of whom presented their pistols, and, after calling upon Mr. Hunter to disengage himself from his antagonist, discharged their pistols without effect. This brave marine then retreated, unpursued, to an adjoining swamp. His escape appearing certain, unless immediately pursued, Mr. Hunter begged the loan of a sword, which was presented to him by the general; and with which he alone pursued, and soon overtook him, when a conflict ensued between them, the brave enemy endeavouring by many and vigorous efforts to get possession of the sword, and refusing, though repeatedly urged, to surrender, except with his life, which a fortunate stroke soon after terminated."

As the writer of this article,—which, be it remembered, is extracted from an American newspaper,—alludes to some "erroneous impressions" caused by "the variety of verbal accounts received," we have a right to conclude, that the account he has published is as much mollified as circumstances would admit; particularly, as the gallant Frenchman had not been permitted to live to tell his own story. When we reflect, too, upon the notorious partiality of the southern Americans towards the French, and their equally notorious hatred towards the British, the very fact (the knowledge of which the same account admits) that the poor sufferer was a Fenchman, may have contributed to alter the features of this, even in its present shape, heart-rending story.

After this wounded marine had "dropped his

musket," and, in climbing the fence, fallen (from weakness, no doubt) "upon his back," was it manly in the two American horsemen to "discharge their pistols" at him? or did Mr. Hunter's conduct in stepping aside to allow them to do so, entitle him to "much and well-merited commendation"? Was it not a cowardly act in Mr. Hunter to borrow, and in general Stewart to lend, a sword to attack an unarmed, already wounded man?—And then, "a fortunate stroke" terminated the poor wretch's existence!—We envy not the feelings of the "young gentleman" who committed, or of the general and his party of cavalry and volunteers who abetted, this foul murder:—for, what else can we call it? No truly brave man but would have set a higher value upon the gallant serjeant's life, for the determination he evinced not to surrender. Why not have permitted him to remain in the swamp to which he had fled: what dire mischief could have happened to the republic by the presence of this unarmed individual? A day or two's residence in the woods might have lowered his lofty spirit; and he would then, perhaps, have freely surrendered to a tenth part of those whom he so long kept at bay; and from whom he would, no doubt, have ultimately escaped, had he possessed another musket, or perhaps another load, even, for that which he had. Acquitting the American commanding officer of those accordant feelings which would have prompted him to grant so brave a man his liberty, no alternative remains to account for the general's hot pursuit of him, but that he must have felt piqued, because Mayeaux's conduct was so opposite to that of the American captain of militia, who, in the same neighbourhood, and about a twelvemonth previous, suffered himself to be taken prisoner by a one-handed British lieutenant of the navy.* In vain do we search through the different American works for any account of the capture of serjeant Mayeaux and his party; although the capture of a single individual has, on other occasions, been exultingly recorded by the whole of our three obsequious historians. It must be the wish of every staunch American, that the editor of the Alexandria newspaper had not been so officious: be it our task to give a yet more permanent form to the account of the intrepid behaviour, and the dastardly murder, of serjeant Mayeaux.

After quitting Benedict, captain Barrie ascended the river to Lower Marlborough, a town about 28 miles from the capital of the United States.† The party landed, and took possession of the place; the militia, as well as the inhabitants, flying into the woods. A schooner, belonging to a captain David, was captured, and loaded with tobacco: after which, having burnt,

* See p. 39. † See Plate V.

at Lower Marlborough, and at Magruders,* on the opposite side of the river, tobacco-stores, containing 2800 hogsheads, and loaded the boats with stock, the detachment re-embarked. The Americans collected a force, estimated at about 350 regulars, besides militia, on Holland's clifts;* but some marines, being landed, traversed the skirts of the heights, and re-embarked without molestation; the American troops not again shewing themselves, till the boats were out of gun-shot.

The blockade of commodore Barney's flotilla, and the depredations on the coasts of the Patuxent, by captain Barrie's squadron, caused great inquietude at Washington. At length, an order reached the American commodore, directing him to destroy the flotilla; in the hopes that the British, having no longer such a temptation in their way, would retire from a position so contiguous to the capital. The order was suspended, owing to a proposal of colonel Wadsworth, of the engineers; who, with two 18-pounders, upon travelling-carriages, protected by a detachment of marines and regular troops, engaged to drive away the two frigates from the mouth of the creek. The colonel established his battery behind an elevated ridge, which sheltered him and his men; and, on the morning of the 26th of June, a simultaneous attack of the gun-boats

* See Plate 5.

and battery was made upon the two frigates, Loire and Narcissus.* What with hot shot, the position chosen by the colonel not being commanded by the fire from either frigate, and captain Brown, the commanding officer's, having no force which he could land to carry the battery,† the Loire and Narcissus retired to a station near Point Patience; and the American flotilla, with the exception of one barge, which put back, apparently disabled by the shot from the frigates, moved out of the creek, and ascended the Patuxent. The frigates sustained no loss on this occasion; but commodore Barney admits a loss of a midshipman and three men killed, and seven men wounded.

We have here a fine opportunity of contrasting the difference in style, between a letter written by an adopted, and one written by a native American, upon the same subject. Commodore Barney writes: "This morning, at 4 A.M. a combined attack of the artillery, marine corps, and flotilla, was made upon the enemy's two frigates, at the mouth of the creek. After two hours' engagement, they got under weigh, and made sail down the river. They are now warping round Point Patience, and I am moving up the Patuxent with my flotilla." ‡

An officer on board the flotilla, writes thus:

* Wilkinson's Mem. Vol. I. p. 730. † Ibid, p. 740.

‡ Hist. of the War, p. 226.

"We moved down with the flotilla, and joined in the chorus with the artillery. Our fire was terrible. At six o'clock they began to move, and made sail down the river, leaving us masters of the field. Thus we have again beat them and their rockets, which they did not spare. First, we beat off a few boats; then, they increased the number; then, they added schooners; and now, behold the two frigates: all have shared the same fate. We next expect ships of the line. No matter, we will do our duty." *

On the 4th of July, the Severn, of 50 guns, having joined the Loire and Narcissus, captain Nourse, of the first-named ship, despatched captain Brown, with the marines of the three ships, (150 in number,) up St. Leonard's creek. Here two of commodore Barney's barges were found scuttled, owing to the damage they had received in the action with the frigates. The barges, and several other vessels, were burnt, and a large tobacco-store destroyed. Soon after this, the British quitted the Patuxent.

On the 19th of July, rear-admiral Cockburn, in the Marlborough 74, having been joined by a battalion of marines, and a detachment of marine artillery, proceeded up the river Potomac, for the purpose of attacking Leonard's-town, the capital of St. Mary's county, where the 36th

* Naval Monument, p. 240.

United States' regiment was stationed. The marines, under major Lewis, were landed, whilst the boats pulled up in front of the town; but, on discovering the marines, the enemy's armed force quitted the place, and suffered the British to take quiet possession. A quantity of stores, belonging to the 36th regiment, and a number of arms of different descriptions, were found there, and destroyed; a quantity of tobacco, flour, provisions, and other articles, were brought away in the boats, and in a schooner, which was lying off the town. Not a musket being fired, nor an armed enemy seen, the town was spared.

The Americans having collected some Virginia militia, at a place called Nominy-ferry, in Virginia, a considerable way up Nominy-river, rear-admiral Cockburn, on the 21st, proceeded thither, with the boats and marines; the latter commanded by captain Robyns, during the illness of major Lewis. The enemy's position was on a very commanding eminence, projecting into the water; but some marines having been landed on its flank, and they being seen getting up the craggy side of the mountain, while the main body landed at the ferry, the enemy fell back, and, though pursued several miles, till the approach of night, escaped with the loss of a few prisoners. They had withdrawn their field-artillery, and hid it in the woods; fearing that, if they kept it to use against the British, they would not be able to retreat with it quick enough to save it from capture. After taking on board all the tobacco, and other stores found in the place, with a quantity of cattle, and destroying all the storehouses and buildings, the rear-admiral re-embarked; and, dropping down to another point of the Nominy river, observed some movements on shore, upon which he again landed with the marines. The Americans fired a volley, but, on the advance of the marines, fled into the woods. Every thing in the neighbourhood was therefore destroyed or brought off; and, after visiting the country in several other directions, covering the escape of the negroes who were anxious to join him, the rear-admiral quitted the river, and returned to the ships with 135 refugee negroes, two captured schooners, a large quantity of tobacco, dry goods, and cattle, and a few prisoners. Far from considering tobacco, packed up in hogsheads, ready for shipping, as "good prize, by the maritime law of nations," as he did the north-west company's goods,* Mr. O'Conner calls it "plundered property," and the seizure or destruction of it the "'petty and wanton act of an unprincipled and mean enemy."†

On the 24th of July, the rear-admiral went up St. Clement's creek, in St. Mary's county, with the boats and marines, to examine the

* See p. 193. † Hist. of the War, p. 227.

country. The militia shewed themselves occasionally, but always retreated when pursued; and the boats returned to the ships without any casualty, having captured four schooners, and destroyed one. The inhabitants remaining peaceably in their houses, the rear-admiral did not suffer any injury to be done to them, excepting at one farm, from which two musket-shots had been fired at the admiral's gig, and where the property was, therefore, destroyed.

On the 26th of July, the rear-admiral proceeded to the head of the Machodic river, in Virginia, where he burnt six schooners, whilst the marines marched, without opposition, over the country on the banks of that river; and, there not remaining any other place on the Virginia or St. Mary's side of his last anchorage, that the rear-admiral had not visited, he, on the 28th, caused the ships to move above Blackstone's Island; and, on the 29th, proceeded, with the boats and marines, up the Wicomoco river. He landed at Hamburgh and Chaptico; from which latter place he shipped a considerable quantity of tobacco, and visited several houses in different parts of the country; the owners of which living quietly with their families, and seeming to consider themselves and the neighbourhood to be at his disposal, he caused no farther inconvenience to them, than obliging them to furnish supplies of cattle and stock for the use of his forces; for which they were liberally paid.

On the 2d of August, the squadron dropped down the Potomac, near to the entrance of the Yocomoco river, which the rear-admiral entered on the following day, with the boats and marines, and landed with the latter. The enemy had here collected in great force, and made more resistance than usual, but the ardor and determination of the rear-admiral's gallant little band, carried all before it; and, after forcing the enemy to give way, the marines followed him 10 miles up the country, captured a field-piece, and burnt several houses, which had been converted into dépôts for militia-arms, &c. Learning, afterwards, that general Hungerford had rallied his men at Kinsale, the rear-admiral proceeded thither; and, though the enemy's position was extremely strong, he had only time to give the British an ineffectual volley before the latter gained the height, when he again retired with precipitation; and did not re-appear. The stores found at Kinsale were then shipped without molestation; and, having burnt the store-houses and other places, with two old schooners, and destroyed two batteries, the rear-admiral re-embarked, bringing away five prize-schooners, a large quantity of tobacco, flour, &c. a field-piece, and a few prisoners. The American general Taylor was wounded and unhorsed, and escaped only through the thickness of the wood and bushes, into which he ran. The British had three men killed, and as many wounded. Thus 500 British marines penetrated 10 miles into the enemy's country, and skirmished, on their way back, surrounded by woods, in the face of the whole collected militia of Virginia, under generals Hungerford and Taylor; and yet, after this long march, carried the heights of Kinsale in the most gallant manner.

Coan river, a few miles below Yocomoco, being the only inlet on the Virginia side of the Potomac, that the rear-admiral had not visited, he proceeded on the 7th to attack it, with the boats and marines. After a tolerably quick fire on the boats, the enemy went off precipitately, with the guns: the battery was destroyed, and the river ascended, in which three schooners were captured, and some tobacco brought off.

On the 12th, the rear-admiral proceeded up St. Mary's creek, and landed in various parts of the country about that extensive inlet; but without seeing a single armed person, though militia had formerly been stationed at St. Mary's factory for its defence; the inhabitants of the state appearing to consider it wiser to submit, than to attempt opposition. On the 15th of August, the rear-admiral again landed within

St. Mary's creek; but found, in the different parts of the country, the same quiet and submissive conduct on the part of the inhabitants, as in the places visited on the 12th. The account of the preceding operations on the coasts of the Chesapeake, with a battalion of marines, a detachment of marine-artillery and of seamen, in all, under 700 men, is extracted exclusively, from rear-admiral Cockburn's official report of his proceedings: the truth of which is tacitly admitted by the silence of the American historians on the subject; although the British accounts had long previously come to their hands.

While the British men-of-war were lying in the rivers of the Chesapeake, the negroes from the neighbouring plantations were continually flocking to the banks; entreating, by the most piteous signs, to be rescued from a life of slavery. Could such appeals be made in vain?—They *were* taken off, by hundreds; and obtained from an enemy that liberty, which their own *free* country denied to them. It was in vain that the American government, by asserting, through the medium of the prints "known to be friendly to the war," that the British, after receiving the negroes, "shipped the wretches to the West Indies, where they were sold as slaves, for the benefit of British officers,"* attempted to check

* History of the War. p. 183.

the flow of slave-emigration. This plan failing, the editor of the "Norfolk Herald" was instructed or induced to say:—"To take cattle or other stock, would be consistent with the usage of civilized warfare; but to take negroes, who are human beings; to tear them for ever from their kindred and connexions, is what we should never expect from a Christian nation, especially one that has done so much to abolish the slave-trade. There are negroes in Virginia, and, we believe, in all the southern states, who have their interests and affections as strongly engrafted in their hearts, as the whites, and who feel the sacred ties of filial, parental, and conjugal affection, equally strong, and who are warmly attached to their owners, and the scenes of their nativity. To those, no inducement which the enemy could offer, would be sufficient to tempt them away. To drag them away, then, by force, would be the greatest cruelty. Yet, it is reserved for England, who boats of her religion and love of humanity, to practice this piece of cruelty, so repugnant to the dictates of Christianity and civilization."*

Whether this article was penned at Washington, or on board of one of the British ships in the bay, it is the happiest piece of satire, that has appeared in an American newspaper. It commences with an unqualified admission, that,

* History of the War, p. 185.

"to take cattle or other stock" is "consistent with the usage of civilized warfare;" whereas, in all the American histories, not excepting that even from which the extract is made, the British are accused of "plundering large quantities of cattle." As, however, the British commanders, whenever the owners could be found, invariably paid for what they did take, the admission is of little use. But are not those "human beings, who have their interests and affections as strongly engrafted in their hearts as the whites," part, and a valuable part too, of the "stock" of an American planter?—The reader has only to take up a Charlestown, a Washington, a Richmond, or even a "Norfolk" newspaper, and a whole side of advertisements, will presently assure him of the degrading fact. Let it not be concealed either, that the treatment of the slaves in, and who form so great a portion of the southern population of, the United States, is ten-times more horrid and disgusting than any thing that occurs among a similar class of "human beings" in the British West Indies. In addition to the accounts published in the American newspapers, and the description given, and marks shown by, the refugee-slaves themselves, it is only necessary, in order to substantiate the fact, to refer to the code of laws by which the American, in comparison with that by which the British, negroes are governed. We freely admit that, "to drag away, by force," those slaves who (if any such are to be found in the United States) are "warmly attached to their owners and to the place of their nativity," would be "the greatest cruelty." But who has done so? The British in the Chesapeake, as the Americans themselves inform us, were frequently straitened for provisions; how ridiculous, then, is the charge, that the captains of ships, by way of encreasing the consumption on board, and without any corresponding benefit, should send parties on shore, first to catch,—in which they must have been tolerably active,—and then to "drag away," the slaves of the American planters. If, for receiving on board such as voluntarily offered themselves, the British officers required any other sanction than "the dictates of Christianity and civilization," they might find it in the following resolution, submitted to the consideration of the house of representatives of the United States, by Mr. Fisk, of Vermont:—"Resolved, that the committee on public lands be instructed to enquire into the expediency of giving to each deserter from the British army, during the present war, 100 acres of the public lands, such deserter actually settling the same."* We have here a fine specimen of the "national honor" of the United States, about which so much has been said and written!

* National Intelligencer, Sept. 28th, 1814.

CHAPTER XIX.

Early intimation of the attack upon Washington—Defensive preparations in consequence—Arrival at Bermuda of troops from France—Departure of general Ross in the Tonnant for the Chesapeake—Reconnoissance on shore by the latter and rear-admiral Cockburn—Meditated attack upon Washington—Arrival of the troops from Bermuda—Different routes to Washington—Captain Gordon's affair in the Potomac—Disembarcation of the troops at Benedict in the Patuxent—Pursuit, by the combined forces, of commodore Barney's flotilla—Its destruction—March of the British troops—Their arrival at Upper Marlborough—Rear-admiral Cockburn's junction with them—Advance of the British towards Washington—Correct American account of their number—Retreat of the American army by Bladensburg to Washington—Further advance of the British—American account of general Winder's force—Re-advance to Bladensburg—Appearance on the field of the president of the United States—American account of the battle of Bladensburg—Flight of the Americans—Mutual loss—Behaviour of Mr. Madison—His narrow escape from capture—American plans of their towns and cities; of New York in particular —Brief description of Washington—Advance of part of the British force from Bladensburg——Its encampment near Washington—Reconnoissance of general Ross and other officers—Fire opened upon them—Advance of the light companies—Destruction of the capitol and two houses whence the fire proceeded—Explosion at the navy-yard—Arrival at the encampment of remainder of British forces—Entry into Washington of 200 British—Destruction of the president's house; also of the treasury and war offices—Ancedote of a British centinel—Amount of American force in the vicinity—Accident at Greenleaf's-point—Destruction of the secretary's of state's office, rope-walks, ordnance, bridge, navy-yard, &c. —Amount of public property destroyed—Acknowledged respect paid to private property—Departure of the British from Washington—Their unmolested arrival, and disembarkation, at Benedict—American accounts—Erroneous impression respecting rear-admiral Cockburn's conduct at Washington—Sir Alexander Cochrane's letter to Mr. Munro, and its reply—Mr. Madison's proclamation—British accounts—Annual Register —Parliamentary speech.

SOME hints thrown out by the British commissioners at the conference at Ghent, coupled with the rumoured destination of British troops shipping in the ports of France, induced the American commissioners to intimate to their government, that an attack upon the federal city would probably be made in the course of the summer of 1814. This notice reached Mr. Madison on the 26th of June; and, on the 1st of July, he submitted to his council a plan for immediately calling 2 or 3000 men into the field, and holding 10 or 12000 militia and volunteers, of the neighbouring states, in readiness to reinforce that corps. On the next day, he created into a military district, the whole state of Maryland, the district of Columbia, and that part of Virginia north of the Rappahannock river, embracing an exposed coast of nearly 1000 miles; vulnerable at every point, and intersected by many large rivers, and by Chesapeake bay. On the 4th of July, as a further defensive preparation, the president made a requisition to the several states of the union, for 93500 militia, as authorized by law; designating their respective quota, and requesting the executive magistrates of each state, to detach and hold them in readiness for immediate service. Of these 93500 militia, 15000 were to be drawn from the tenth military district, or that surrounding the metropolis; for whose defence they were intended.

On the 2d of June sailed from Verdun roads, the Royal Oak, rear-admiral Malcolm, accompanied by three frigates, three sloops, two bomb-vessels, five ships *armées en flûte*, and three transports, having on board the 4th, 21st, 44th, and 85th, regiments, with a proportion of royal artillery, and sappers and miners, under the command of major-general Ross. On the 24th of July the squadron arrived at Bermuda, and there joined vice-admiral Cochrane, in the Tonnant. On the 2d of August, vice-admiral Cochrane, having received on board the Tonnant major-general Ross and his staff, sailed, in company with the Euryalus, for Chesapeake bay; and, on the 14th of August, arrived, and joined the Albion, vice-admiral Cockburn, off the mouth of the Potomac. On the next day, major-general Ross, accompanied by rear-admiral Cockburn, went on shore to reconnoitre. The rear-admiral's knowledge of the country, as well as the excellent plan he adopted to prevent surprise, enabled the two officers to penetrate further, than would otherwise have been prudent. The thick woods that skirt, and the numerous ravines that intersect, the different roads around Washington, offer important advantages to an ambushing enemy. Rear-admiral Cockburn, therefore, in his frequent walks through the country, invariably moved forward between two parties of marines, occupying, in open order, the woods by the road-side. Each marine carried a bugle, to be used as a signal, in case of casual separation, or the appearance of an enemy. It was during the excursion with general Ross, that rear-admiral Cockburn suggested the facility of an attack upon the city of Washington; and general Ross determined, as soon as the troops should arrive from Bermuda, to make the attempt.

On the 17th of August, rear-admiral Malcolm, with the troops, arrived, and joined vice-admiral Cochrane, off the mouth of the Potomac; and the whole proceeded to the Patuxent, about 20 miles further up the bay. In the meantime, captain Gordon, with some vessels of the squadron, had been detached up the Potomac, to bombard Fort-Warburton, situate on the left bank of that river, about 14 miles below the federal city; and captain Parker, with the Menelaus frigate, up the Chesapeake, above Baltimore, to create a diversion in that quarter. The successful proceedings of captain Gordon, in the destruction of the fort; and,—a measure entirely his own,—the capture of the populous town of Alexandria, will be found fully detailed in our naval volume.* The direct route to Washington, from the mouth of the Potomac, was up that river, about 50 miles, to Fort-Tobacco; thence, over land, by the village of Piscataway, 32 miles, to the lower bridge across the eastern branch of the Potomac; but, as no doubt could be entertained that this bridge,

* James's Nav. Occur. p. 381—6.

which was half a mile long, and had a draw at the west-end, would be defended, as well by a body of troops, as by a heavy sloop of war and a armed schooner, known to be in the river, the route up the Patuxent, and by Bladensburg, where the eastern branch, in case of the bridge at that spot being destroyed, could be easily forded, was preferred.

Commodore Barney's gun-boats were still lying in the Patuxent, up which they had been driven.* An immediate attempt against this "much-vaunted flotilla" offered two advantages; one, in its capture or destruction, the other, as a pretext for ascending the Patuxent, with the troops, destined for the attack of the city. Part of the ships, having advanced as high up the river as the depth of water would allow, disembarked the troops, on the 19th and 20th of August, at Benedict,† a small town, about 50 miles south-east of Washington. On the evening of the 20th, rear-admiral Cockburn, taking with him the armed boats and tenders of the fleet, proceeded up the river, to attack commodore Barney's flotilla; and to supply with provisions, and, if necessary, afford protection to, the army, as it ascended the right bank. For the full details of the successful enterprise against the American flotilla, we must refer to our naval volume.‡ In

* See 252 p. † See Plate V.

‡ James's Nav. Occur. p. 375.

justice to commodore Barney, we shall here introduce general Wilkinson's statement upon the subject. "Cockburn," says the general, "with his barges, pursued Barney's flotilla, which had, by order of president Madison, been unfortunately abandoned, and was, without resistance, blown up; when it will be apparent to every competent judge, that, from the narrowness of the channel, the commodore could have defended himself, and repulsed any floating force the enemy could have brought against him; and his flanks were well secured, by the extent of the marches on both sides of the river." *

Mr. Thomson has found out, that general Ross, while on his march, avoided an engagement with an inferior number of American troops. Having previously stated the British force at "about 6000 regulars, seamen, and marines," being 1000 more than Mr. O'Connor, and 2000 more than doctor Smith makes them, Mr. Thomson says:—"The enemy approached the wood-yard, a position 12 miles only from the city, and at which general Winder's forces were drawn up. These consisted of about 5000 men, and offered battle to the British troops. But general Ross, upon reaching the neighbourhood of Nottingham, turned to his right, and took the road to Marlborough, upon which general Winder fell back to Battalion Old Fields, about eight miles

* Wilkinson's Mem. Vol. I. p. 766.

from the city."* To make it appear, also, that the British were actually pursued, he, in the very next paragraph, declares, that "several prisoners" were taken. As general Ross, after stating the landing of the army, says merely:— "On the 21st it reached Nottingham," we should have only the improbability of the thing to oppose to Mr. Thomson's gasconade, had not general Wilkinson touched upon the subject. "On the morning of the 22d," says the general, "the cavalry of Laval and Tilghman, say 200 men, with the regular troops, under lieutenant-colonel Scott, about 400 strong, were ordered to advance towards Nottingham, and reached Oden's house, where they were soon followed by major Peter, with six 6-pounders, flying artillery, and a detachment of about 250 select men. General Ross marched from Nottingham, the same morning, by the chapel road leading to Marlborough; and, on discovering the American troops, made a detachment to his left to meet them, which advanced to the foot of the hill near Oden's house, when the American troops fell back, and the enemy resumed their march."†

On the afternoon of the 22d, general Ross, with the troops, arrived, and encamped, at the town of Upper Marlborough, situate about four

* Sketches of the War, p. 334.

† Wilkinson's Mem. Vol. I. p. 765.

miles up the western branch of the Patuxent. The men, therefore, after having been nearly three months on board ship, had, in less than three days, marched 40 miles; and that in the month of August, when the sultriness of the climate could scarcely be tolerated. We may form some idea of the military obstacles that *might* have presented themselves during the march, by the observations of general Wilkinson. "Not a single bridge," says he, "was broken, not a causeway destroyed, not an inundation attempted, not a tree fallen, not a rood of the road obstructed, nor a gun fired at the enemy, in a march of near 40 miles, from Benedict to Upper Marlborough, by a route on which there are 10 or a dozen difficult defiles; which, with a few hour's labour, six pieces of light artillery, 300 infantry, 200 riflemen, and 60 dragoons, might have been defended against any force that could approach them: such is the narrowness of the road, the profundity of the ravines, the steepness of the acclivities, and the sharpness of the ridges."* While general Ross and his men were resting themselves at Upper Marlborough, generel Winder and his army, now joined by commodore Barney and the men of his flotilla, were lying at their encampment at the long Old Fields, only eight miles distant. With the full knowledge of what a fatiguing march the British

* Wilkinson's Mem. Vol. I. p. 759.

had made, the hero of La Colle mill declares, that general Ross, with his "4 or 5000 veteran troops, ought to have marched upon and routed" general Winder.* The latter, however, "rashly kept his position during the night;" and, on the next morning, the American troops were reviewed by Mr. Madison, "their commander-in-chief, whose martial appearance gladdened every countenance and encouraged every heart."* Soon after the review, a detachment from the American army advanced along the road to Upper Marlborough; and, after exchanging a few shots with the British skirmishers, fell back to the main body.

On the morning of the 23d, rear-admiral Cockburn, having left at Pig-point, directly opposite to the western branch,† the marines of the ships, under captain Robyns, and two divisions of the boats, crossed over, with the third division, to Mount Calvert; and proceeded, by land, to the British encampment at Upper Marlborough. The little opposition experienced by the army in its march from Benedict, and the complete success that had attended the expedition against commodore Barney's flotilla, determined major-general Ross to make an immediate attempt upon the city of Washington, distant from Upper Marlborough not more than 16 miles.

At the desire of the major-general, the marine

* Wilkinson's Mem. Vol. I. p. 766. † See Plate V.

and naval forces at Pig-point were moved over to Mount Calvert; and the ship-marines, marine-artillery, and a proportion of seamen, joined the army at Upper Marlborough. It is now time to give the numbers of the British, so fearlessly approaching the metropolis of the United States. Fortunately, the only American account which pretends to any accuracy upon that point, supplies us with the necessary information.

"Those," says Dr. Smith, "who had the best opportunities of counting them, (the British,) calculated that their whole number was about 4000; and this calculation is warranted by the incidents in the field."* He then states, that the British army, under major-general Ross, was distributed into three brigades; the first brigade, commanded by colonel Brooke, of the 44th, and composed of the 4th and 44th regiments; the second brigade, commanded by colonel Patterson, of the 21st regiment, and composed of that regiment, the second battalion of marines, and the ship-marines under captain Robyns; the third brigade, commanded by colonel Thornton, of the 85th light infantry, and composed of that regiment, the light companies of the 4th, 21st, and 44th regiments, one company of marine skirmishers, a detachment of colonial marines, also of royal artillery, with two 3-pounders and a howitzer, and a party of

* History of the United States, Vol. III. p. 298.

seamen and engineers, with rockets.* Leaving captain Robyns, with the marines of the ships, in possession of Upper Marlborough, major-general Ross and rear-admiral Cockburn, with the troops, marines, and seamen, whose number, notwithstanding the absence of captain Robyns and his party, we will still state at 4000, moved forward, on the evening of the 23d; and, before dark, arrived, and bivouacked for the night, at a spot five miles nearer to Washington.†

As if by concert, the American army retired from the long Old Fields, about the same time that the British army advanced from Upper Marlborough; the patroles of the latter actually occupying, before midnight, the ground which the former had abandoned. The American army did not stop till it reached Washington; where it encamped, for the night, near the navy-yard."‡ On the same evening, upwards of 2000 troops arrived at Bladensburg from Baltimore. At day-light on the morning of the 24th, general Ross put his troops in motion for Bladensburg, 12 miles from his camp; and, having halted by the way, arrived at the heights facing the village about half-past 11 o'clock.§ While the British troops are resting themselves, and preparing for the attack, we will endeavour

* Hist. of the United States, Vol. III. p. 298.

† See Plate V. ‡ Wilkinson's Mem. Vol. I. p. 767.

§ See Plate VI. *d d.*

to place before the reader, the force which they had to overcome, before they could enter the metropolis of the United States.

"The army under general Winder," says doctor Smith, "consisted of:—

"United States' dragoons - - - - -	140	
Maryland ditto - - - - -	240	
District of Columbia ditto - - -	50	
Virginia ditto - - - - -	100	
		530
Regular infantry - - - - -	500	
Seamen and marines - - - -	600	
		1100
Stansbury's brigade of militia - -	1353	
Sterrett's regiment, ditto - - -	500	
Baltimore artillery, ditto - - -	150	
Pinkney's battalion, ditto - - -	150	
		2153
Smith's brigade, ditto - - - -	1070	
Cramer's battalion, ditto - - -	240	
Waring's detachment, ditto - - -	150	
Maynard's ditto ditto - - - -	150	
		1610
Beall's and Hood's regiment of ditto -	800	
Volunteer corps - - - - -	350	
		1150
Total at Bladensburg -		6543

At hand,

Young's brigade of militia - - -	450	
Minor's Virginia corps - - - -	600	
		1050
Grand Total -		7593*

* Hist. of the U. S. Vol. III. p. 297.

According to general Armstrong's letter to the editor of the "Baltimore Patriot," of September 3, general Winder had, under his command, exclusive of the 15000 militia he was directed to call out, as many regular troops and seamen, as would make his total force, when assembled, "16300 men." "General Winder," proceeds doctor Smith, "after the battle, reported his forces at about 5000 men;* nearly 2600 less than appears from the preceding detail."† Nor has the general given any account of his artillery; although we find that "the American army had, on the field, not fewer than 23 pieces, varying from 6 to 18 pounders." † This army was drawn up, in two lines, upon very commanding heights, on the north of the turnpike-road leading from Bladensburg to Washington; and, as an additional incitement to glory on the part of the American troops, their president was on the field. "Every eye," says general Wilkinson, "was immediately turned upon the chief; every bosom throbbed with confidence; and every nerve was strung with valor. No doubts remained with the troops that, in their chief magistrate they beheld their commander-in-chief, who, like another Maurice, having, by his irresolution in council, exposed the country to the chances and accidents of a general engage-

* App: No. 66. † Hist. of the U. S. Vol. III. p. 297.

ment, had now come forward to repair the error, by his activity in the field; determined to throw himself into the gap of danger, and not to survive the honor of his country, especially entrusted to his guardianship."*

The affair,—for it hardly deserves the name of battle,—of Bladensburg, may be given in the words of general Wilkinson; assisted by a reference to his own diagram.† "The enemy," says the general, "made the attack with their light brigade; the right wing, led by colonel Brooke, of the 44th regiment, and the left by colonel Thornton, of the 85th. They crossed the bridge in disorder, and the skirmishers advanced in loose order, and forced the battery and riflemen in *h*, *i*. The right wing formed in *u*, *u*, and followed the skirmishers through the corn-field, *p*, *p*, and the orchard, *q*, *q*, and over the field, forward of the tobacco-house, *k*. Captain Doughty," (with a corps of riflemen,) "formed in *l*, gave a few fires, and retired with the rest of the troops; and the enemy pursued to the fence 14, 14; while our troops generally retreated," proceeds the general, "by R, R, R." Before we proceed to detail the operations of colonel Thornton's wing, a little explanation, as to numbers, may be necessary. The American force, thus routed by about 750 rank and file of the 4th and 44th regiments, including a

* Wilkinson's Mem. Vol. I. p. 781. † See Plate VI.

rocket-party, consisted of, regular and militia dragoons, 530; major Pinkney's battalion of militia-riflemen, 150; Doughty's riflemen, number not stated; Stansbury's militia-brigade, 1353; Sterret's militia-regiment, 500; Baltimore artillery, with six pieces,* 150; major Peters, with six pieces of artillery, and lieutenant-colonel Scott, with the 36th United States' regiment, together, 500;† Burch's artillery, with four pieces,‡ number of men not given; Smith's militia brigade, 1070: total 4000 men, and 16 pieces of artillery. It is fortunate that we have American testimony for the extraordinary account here given.

Requesting the reader again to turn to the diagram, we will, with general Wilkinson's assistance, narrate the proceedings of the remainder of the British and American forces. "Colonel Thornton," says he, "with the left wing, pushed up the turnpike-road, and was about to attack the 5th regiment, in flank, when it gave way. There were a great many commanders this day, and, among them, not the least discerning, colonel Wadsworth; who, to avoid interference with others, and render what service he could, had prepared, and, with a few hands, brought forward, two field-pieces to *t*, *t*, on the turnpike, with intention to open and

* See Plate VI. *h*. † Ibid. 9 and 10.

‡ Ibid. O.

maintain a retreating fire upon the column of the enemy as it advanced; which, while his flanks were secure, would undoubtedly have retarded, galled, and cut them sensibly; but, after the first shot, which will be found in the under-work of the bridge, his men introduced the wrong end of the cartridge, and, instead of drawing it to get it out, depressed the muzzle of the piece until the trail and wheels overturned, and, by this time, the enemy was so near as to oblige them to flee for safety. Seeing the troops on his right give way, colonel Thornton advanced, crossed the conduit, and ascended the opposite side of the ravine; but was so warmly received by commodore Barney's battery of three 18 pounders at 4,* that, after some pause and fluctuation, he turned to his left, and displayed in a field in 2, 2, where he, for a few rounds, combated a valorous little band of the marine corps, commanded by captain Miller, with three 12-pounders, in 3, and the flotilla-men of commodore Barney, in 5, 5; which forced him to incline to his left, and endeavour to turn the American right, by a wood, in 2, 2, 2, 2, where he was met by colonel Beall, who was formed under the summit of a conical hill, in 6, 6." General Wilkinson then introduces a long letter from colonel Beall; from which we gather, that, after firing a few rounds, the latter and his

* See Plate VI.

regiment, took to their heels. After a resistance, which, compared to the behaviour of the American troops in general, may be termed gallant, the flotilla-men and marines retreated; leaving upon the field, their commanders, commodore Barney and captain Miller, severely wounded; and who, along with their guns, fell into the hands of the British. Without considering that the American right was reinforced by its retreating left, or the British left by its advancing right, we may state the relative numbers, at this end of the field, as 750 British and 2500 Americans. Ten pieces of cannon were taken; but not above 120 prisoners;* "owing," says rear-admiral Cockburn, "to the swiftness with which the enemy went off, and the fatigue our army had previously undergone."† The retreating American troops proceeded, with all haste, towards Washington; and the British troops, including the rear-division, which had, just at the close of the short scuffle, arrived upon the ground, halted, to take some refreshment.

Had it not been for the American artillery, the loss of the British would have been very trifling. We find 24 pieces marked upon general Wilkinson's diagram.‡ Those at *h* completely enfiladed the bridge, and were very destructive to the advancing column. Under

* App. No. 66. † App. No. 62.

‡ See Plate VI. *h*, *o*, 10, 4, 3, *t t*.

these circumstances, the British loss amounted to, one captain, two lieutenants, five serjeants, and 56 rank and file, killed; two lieutenant-colonels, one major, one captain, 14 lieutenants, two ensigns, 10 serjeants, and 155 rank and file, wounded; total, 64 killed, 185 wounded: grand total, 249. Of the American loss we have no very accurate account. Mr. Thomson, in the single instance of the Bladensburg battle, does not say a word on the subject. Doctor Smith says:—" General Winder supposed that the loss of his army was from 30 to 40 killed, and from 50 to 60 wounded.* It is believed, however, that this is a large computation; for doctor Catlet, the attending surgeon, stated the killed at 10 or 12; and the wounded, some of whom died, at 30."† As the British two 3-pounders and howitzer, being stationed near to *e*, in Bladensburg village, were of little service; and, as the Americans did not stay to receive many rounds of musketry, nor one thrust of the bayonet, their trifling loss is by no means extraordinary. Without wishing to exult over a fallen foe, we may express our surprise, that the classical ground,‡ in the neighbourhood of which " the meritorious conquerors of Tecumseh,"§ among other American troops, were drawn up, should have failed to inspire them

*App. No. 66. † Hist. of the U. States, Vol. III. p. 298.

‡ Thermopylæ, Tiber, &c.

§ Wilkinson's Mem. Vol. I. p. 770; and our Vol. I. p. 294.

with a portion of that "Roman," or, in reference to "American," "*second degree* valor," spoken of by an American congress-man.*

What became of Mr. Madison? is a question the reader is, no doubt, anxious to have solved. We shall here quote, and let it be understood that we are quoting, the words of an American writer:—"Not all the allurements of fame, not all the obligations of duty, nor the solemn invocations of honor, could excite a spark of courage: the love of a life which had become useless to mankind, and served but to embarrass the public councils, and prejudice the public cause, stifled the voice of patriotism, and prevailed over the love of glory; and, at the very first shot, the trembling coward, with a faltering voice, exclaimed:—'Come, general Armstrong; come, colonel Munro; let us go, and leave it to the commanding general.'"† According to the testimony of Mr. William Simmons, one of the witnesses examined by the American committee of investigation, assembled in consequence of the capture of Washington, the American president, the attorney-general, and secretaries of war and state, were indebted to his information, for not having fallen into the hands of major-general Ross, rear-admiral Cockburn, colonel Thornton, and a number of staff-officers, who, in their undress coats, had entered Bla-

* See p. 25. † Wilkinson's Memoirs, Vol. I. p. 783.

densburg, by a circuitous route, unobserved by any but Mr. Simmons. A delay of five minutes would, it appears, have placed the commander-in-chief of the armies of the United States, and the whole executive corps, in the hands of the British.

Europeans, often to their cost, read accounts of the fine rich land to be met with, in almost all parts of the United States. It is a matter of equal policy, to show the existence of markets capable of carrying off the abundant produce of so fruitful a soil: therefore, most plans of towns or cities sent to Europe from the United States, have their sites ready covered with all the streets, which even a century may not see built. We have now before us a large folding map of the city of New York, with all its squares filled up in black, resembling a map of London, rather than of Liverpool, which it scarcely reaches in population. It will not, then, surprise the reader, that the city of Washington, or, as the bard of Lalla Rookh once sang,—

> "This famed metropolis, where Fancy sees
> Squares in morasses, obelisks in trees;
> Which travelling fools and gazetteers adorn,
> With shrines unbuilt, and heroes yet unborn;"

covering, as it does, about eight square miles of ground, should contain no more than 400 houses;

less, than is to be found in a single street of London.*

As soon as the troops were refreshed, general Ross and rear-admiral Cockburn, "with 1000 men,"† moved forward from Bladensburg; and, at about eight o'clock in the evening, arrived at an open piece of ground, two miles ‡ from the federal city. The troops were here drawn up, while major-general Ross, rear-admiral Cockburn, and several other officers, accompanied by a small guard, rode forward to reconnoitre. On arriving opposite to some houses, the party halted; and, just as the officers had closed each other, in order to consult whether or not it would be prudent to enter the heart of the city that night, a volley was fired from the windows of one of two adjoining houses, and from the capitol; § which volley killed one soldier, and general Ross's horse from under him, and wounded three soldiers. || Rear-admiral Cockburn instantly rode back to the detachment, stationed in advance; and soon returned with the light companies. The house was then surrounded; and, after some prisoners had been taken from it, || set on fire; the adjoining house fell with it. The capitol, which was contiguous to these

* Strand. † History of the United States, Vol. III. p. 294.
‡ Wilkinson's Memoirs, Vol. I. p. 791. § App. No. 62.
|| Poulson's Philadelphia paper, of August 29, 1814.

houses, and which was "capable of being made an impregnable citadel against an enemy, with little artillery, and that of the lighter class,"* was also set on fire. The "capitol containing the senate-chamber, representative-hall, supreme court-room, congressional library, and legislative archives;"† these rooms, "or public buildings," as many of our London journalists have called them, could not otherwise than share the fate of the building of which they formed part.

Scarcely had the flames burst out from the capitol and the two contiguous houses, than an awful explosion announced, that the Americans were employed upon the same business in the lower part of the city. By this time the remainder of the British forces from Bladensburg had arrived at the encampment. At about half-past 10, after a party had been sent to destroy the fort and public works at Greenleaf's point, major-general Ross, and rear-admiral Cockburn, each at the head of a small detachment of men, numbering, together, not more than 200,‡ proceeded down the hill towards the president's palace. Finding it utterly abandoned, and hearing, probably, that a guard of soldiers, with "two pieces of cannon, well-mounted on travel-

* History of the United States, Vol. III. p. 296. † Ibid. 294.

‡ Wilkinson's Mem. Vol. I. p. 791.

ling carriages;"* had been stationed at, and but recently fled from, this the American "commander-in-chief's" head-quarters, the British caused it to be set on fire. A log-hut, under similar circumstances, would have shared the same fate, and the justice of the measure not been disputed. Why, then, in a country where "equality of rights" is daily preached up, should the palace be held more sacred than the cottage? The loss of the one falls, where it ought, upon the nation at large; the loss of the other,—a lamentable case, at all times,—solely upon the individual proprietor. Had generals Armstrong and M'Clure consulted this principle, the village of Newark would have remained undestroyed; and the feelings of humanity not have been so outraged as they still are, at the bare recital of that atrocious proceeding.

To the building, containing the treasury and war offices, the torches of the conquerors were next applied. On arriving opposite to the office of the "National Intelligencer," the American government-paper,—whose editor, Mr. Gales, a British subject, had been giving currency to the grossest falsehoods against the British commanders in the Chesapeake, and against the British character in general,—rear-admiral Cockburn observed to the inhabitants near him, that he

* Testimony of Mr. Wm. Simmons, before the American committee of investigation.

must destroy it. On being told, however, that the adjoining buildings would be likely to take fire, he desisted. The rear-admiral, then, wishing the inhabitants 'good night', and assuring them that private property and persons should be respected, departed to his quarters on the capitol-hill. Early on the next morning the rear-admiral was seen walking about the city, accompanied by three soldiers only. Indeed, general Wilkinson says :—" A single centinel, who had been accidentally left on post near the office of the National Intelligencer, kept undisturbed possession of the central part of the metropolis, until the next morning; of which there are several living witnesses."* At this time, too, it appears, an American " force of more than 4000 combatants" was posted upon the heights of Georgetown,* which is a continuation of the city to the westward.

During the morning of the 25th, the secretary of state's office was burnt, and the types and printing materials of the government-paper were destroyed. A serious accident had happened to the party sent to Greenleaf's-point. Some powder, concealed in a well, accidentally took fire, killing 12, and wounding 30, officers and men. Three extensive rope-walks, at some distance from the city, were, by the British, entirely consumed; and so was an immense quantity of

* Wilkinson's Mem. Vol. I. p. 791.

small-arms and heavy ordnance;* as well as the great bridge across the Potomac:† a very prudent military measure, especially as the Americans had themselves destroyed the two bridges crossing the eastern branch:† A party, under captain Wainwright, of the Tonnant; destroyed the few stores and buildings in the navy-yard, which had escaped the flames of the preceding night. As the British were in haste to be gone, and as the vessels, even could they have been floated in safety down the Potomac, were not wanted by us, it was very considerate in the American government to order the destruction of the frigate, of 1600 tons, that was nearly ready to be launched, and of the fine sloop of war, Argus, ready for sea; and whose 20 32-pounders would have assisted so powerfully in defending the entrance to the city by the lower bridge. According to the official estimate of "the public property destroyed,"‡ the value has been much over-rated. It appears not to have exceeded 1624280 dollars, or £365463 sterling.

With respect to private property, we have only to quote passages from American prints, to show how that was treated. One newspaper says:— "The British officers pay inviolable respect to private property, and no peaceable citizen is molested."§ A writer from Baltimore, under

* App. No. 65. † See Plate V. ‡ App. No. 67.
§ Columbian Centinel, August 31st.

the date of "August 27th," says:—"The enemy, I learn, treated the inhabitants of Washington well."* But what says Mr. Gales, the mouth-piece of the government, he whose presses had been destroyed and whose "types had been so shamefully dispersed."?—"When we remarked," says he, "in our paper of yesterday, that private property had, in general, been scrupulously respected by the enemy during his late incursion, we spoke what we believed, from a hasty survey, and perhaps without sufficient inquiry. Greater respect was certainly paid to private property than has usually been exhibited by the enemy in his marauding parties. No houses were half as much plundered by the enemy, as by the knavish wretches about the town, who profited by the general distress. There were, however, several private buildings wantonly destroyed, and some of those persons who remained in the city were scandalously maltreated."† We are to consider that this charge contains the utmost that has been alleged against the British during their 20 hours' occupation of the metropolis of the United States. The "several private buildings," besides "the dwelling-house owned and occupied by Mr. Robert Sewall, from behind which a gun was fired at general Ross," consisted of "a commodious dwelling, belong-

* Boston paper, September 1st.

† National Intelligencer, August 31st.

ing to the estate of general Washington, and Carroll's hotel:"* the former suffered, from its contiguity to, or absolute junction with, the house from which the firing had been directed; the latter, not unlikely, from the act of some of "the knavish wretches about the town, who profited by the general distress." That the British officers did all they could to secure the inhabitants from injury, both in their persons and properties, may be gathered from Mr. Thomson's acknowledgment, that,—"the plunder of individual property was prohibited, and soldiers, transgressing the order, were severely punished."†

We shall dismiss this subject with an American statement, which, we trust, will set at rest all remaining doubts. "The list of plunder and destruction, copied from a vile and libellous print of that city, into several federal papers, is a gross and abominable fabrication, known to be such by every inhabitant. Most of the plunder was committed by rabble of the place, fostered among the citizens; and from whose villainy no place is free, in times of peril, and relaxation of the law. The British army, it is no more than justice to say, preserved a moderation and discipline, with respect to private

* History of the United States, Vol. III. p. 295.

† Sketches of the War, p. 336.

persons and property, unexampled in the annals of war."*

At eight o'clock on the evening of the 25th, the British left Washington, by the way of Bladensburg. Here such of the wounded as could ride, or be transported in carriages, were provided with 30 or 40 horses, 12 carts and waggons, one coachee, and several gigs. With these, preceded by a drove of 60 or 70 cattle, the army moved leisurely along. On the evening of the 29th it reached Benedict,† 50 miles from Washington, without a single musket having been fired;‡ and, on the following day, re-embarked in the vessels of the fleet. No complaints, that we can discover, have been made against the British, during their retreat across the country; although, as an American writer has been pleased to say, "general Ross scarcely kept up his order, sufficiently to identify the body of his army."§ The Americans are very difficult to please. If the British decline fighting double the number of Americans, shiness is alleged against them; if, on the other hand, they not only fight, but conquer, as at Bladensburg, more than double their number of Americans, they are denied all credit. In this spirit doctor Smith says:—"The success of general Ross, in

* Georgetown paper, September 8th.

† See Plate V. ‡ App. No. 62.

§ Hist. of the United States, Vol. III. p. 299.

this expedition, cannot be ascribed to the display of superior military skill. It was not due to his force, or the deportment of his troops in the field. The resolution to march an army, 50 miles into the interior of a country thickly inhabited, and in the face of another, of superior numbers, affords strong proof of his temerity, but none of his prudence. He succeeded against every rational calculation."*—How could this writer touch upon "deportment of troops"?—We rather think, that major-general Ross and rear-admiral Cockburn made their "calculation," upon what they conjectured would be the "deportment" of the American troops; although they certainly did not expect quite so great a contrast to "temerity," as they found upon the field at Bladensburg.

All the American writers who have had occasion to deplore the fate of Washington-city, have levelled their abuse against rear-admiral Cockburn; "on whom," says one of them, "if the safety of the citizens' dwellings had alone depended, they would have rested on a slender guarantee."† How will this writer; how will all the other American writers; how will the British public in general, receive the assertion, that rear-admiral Cockburn got blamed by his commanding officer, for not having acted more

* Hist. of the United States, Vol. III. p. 299.

† Sketches of the War, p. 326.

in the spirit of "retaliation" than he did? This brings us to sir Alexander Cochrane's letter,* in which that harsh word appears. It was an ill-advised letter; serving only to convict us of a seeming intention to do what we never did do. What "towns and districts" upon the American coast, did the British "destroy and lay waste"? Was Washington destroyed and laid waste?—Was Alexandria destroyed and laid waste?—We deny that there was any thing done at either of those places, unless it was the behaviour of an American naval commander at Alexandria,† that was at all "contrary to the usages of civilized warfare." This letter was just what Mr. Munro‡ wanted. It enabled him to declaim, at length, about "the established and known humanity of the American nation."§ The chief of Mr. Munro's unsupported assertions have already been replied to, in different parts of this work: we have, at present, only to do with the paragraph in which he tells us, that "in the course of ten years past, the capitals of the principal powers of the continent of Europe have been conquered and occupied, alternately, by the victorious armies of each other; and no instance of such wanton and unjustifiable destruction has been seen;" and refers us to distant ages for a "parallel" to our

* App. No. 68. † James's Naval Occurrences, p. 383.
‡ Now president of the United States. § App. No. 69.

behaviour. We will dismiss Mr. Munro with this question,—Did any one of the "sovereigns" to whom he alludes, fly "in panic terror" * from one end of his city, while an enemy entered the other? In his search for a "parallel," too, where will he find, even if he goes back to "distant and barbarous ages," that a sovereign behaved, as we have American testimony for asserting, that Mr. Madison, "the commander-in-chief of the armies of the United States," did behave, at, or rather *before*, the battle of Bladensburg?

But Mr. Madison himself must issue his "Proclamation;"† dated from "Washington," too, the "seat of empire," which he, only six days before, had abandoned, to seek "an asylum among the hills, west of the great falls."* The five day's march of our troops, including the battle in which he set so bright an example, he calls a "sudden incursion." He then ventures to state the American troops at Bladensburg, as "less numerous" than their British opponents. This is excellent. Admitting that the British were in possession of Washington "for a single day (and night) only," were the 4000 American troops, drawn up in full view of the destruction of "the costly monuments of state," led forth by Mr. Madison, or led forth at all, to drive the British away? "We destroyed," he says, "the

* Wilkinson's Mem. Vol. I. p. 789. † App. No. 70.

public edifices, having no relation in their structure to operations of war, nor used at the time for military annoyance." Was it no "military annoyance," to kill one soldier and wound three, and, by mere accident, not to kill the British commanding general? Where was the war declared, but in the "senate-chamber and representative-hall," contained within the capitol? What enforced "military annoyance," or gave life to the "operations of war," but the dollars in the "treasury-office"? On the other hand, "the patent-office," in which were collected the rarest specimens of the arts of the country, having no relation to the "operations of war," was not, in the slightest degree, injured.* Who, when colonel Campbell, of the United States' army, destroyed the dwelling-house and other buildings of a Canadian inhabitant, declared the act to have been "according to the usages of war,"† because a troop of British dragoons had just fled from them? Why then was not the destruction of the president's palace, from which a company of American artillery, with two field-pieces, had just fled, equally "according to the usages of war"? The only surprise is, that the American government should have so well succeeded in hood-winking the people of Europe. One British editor rates his

* Sketches of the War, p. 336.

† See p. 111.

ferocious countrymen, for "having levelled with the dust the splendid palaces and sumptuous edifices, by which the city of Washington was so liberally embellished." This can but raise a smile; especially upon a reference to the estimated value of these "splendid palaces."* We shall forbear to notice the long account of "the extent of devastation practised by the victors" at Washington, which has found its way into that faithful record of frays, murders, births, marriages, and deaths, but certainly not of historical events, the "Annual Register for 1814;" and thence, of course, into most of the prints of the United States. But what was there done by the British at Washington, that could provoke an eminent parliamentary orator to describe their proceedings as "so abhorrent, so inconsistent with the habits of a free and generous people;—so to be hated and detested, condemned and abjured"?† "In burning Washington," says this same speaker, "we had acted worse than the Goths, when they were before the walls of Rome." In another place he talks of "the pillage of private property."† What a pity this gentleman did not read even the whole of the *American* accounts, before he ventured to sanction, with his respectable name

* App. No. 67.

† Parliamentary Proceedings, November 8, 1814.

statements so palpably untrue. If he were alive we could show him an American publication, that has devoted 13 of its pages to an account of our proceedings at Washington, and yet contains not one word of comment upon our destruction of the public buildings. When we mention the work as the "History of the United States," and the author as the reverend doctor Smith; the same who said, "No one need question the conduct of the British troops at Hampton;" the same who, in every page of his book, evinces the strongest antipathy against the British; and who, as the reader knows, is not over scrupulous as to the truth of the charges he prefers against them, "no one need question" that doctor Smith was thus lenient, because, in the extraordinary fact, that the British, with only 200 troops, entered and fully possessed, the "seat of empire" of the United States of America, he could find, on their part, at least, nothing but "temerity" to find fault with.

CHAPTER XX.

Skirmish at Moor's fields—Death of sir Peter Parker—Brief description of Baltimore—Alarm of the inhabitants--Exertions of the military—Defensive preparations—Strong inducement for an attack by the British—Accidental cause of its being made—Advance of the fleet to the Patapsco—Landing of the troops—Amount of the British force—Advance of major-general Ross and rear-admiral Cockburn, with a small guard—Skirmish and retreat of the Americans—Death of general Ross—American accounts—Advance of the British main body—Amount of the American force—Details of the battle—Retreat of the Americans—American accounts—British and American loss—Further advance of the British—Reinforcement to the Americans at their entrenched camp—Arrival of British ships near the forts in the Patapsco—Mutual cannonade between the latter and the bomb-vessels and rocket-ship—Boat-expedition up the Ferry branch—American accounts—Reasons given for retiring from Baltimore—Unmolested retreat of the British—American accounts—Remarks upon the Baltimore expedition—Character of general Ross—Departure, on separate destinations, of admirals Cochrane and Cockburn—Boat-expe-

dition up Coan river—Departure of rear-admiral Malcolm — Boat-expedition up the Rappahannock—Return of rear-admiral Cockburn—His departure for the Georgia coast—Capture of St. Mary's—Boat-expedition up the river—Intended attack upon Savannah—Impolitic measures that lead to its frustration.

PREVIOUSLY to our entering upon the proceedings of the combined British forces, after their departure from Washington, we have to notice the untimely fate of sir Peter Parker, baronet, commanding the Menelaus frigate; which, as the reader knows, had been detached on service up the bay.* Having but recently arrived upon the North American station, sir Peter was not aware of the ambushing tricks to which a small invading force would be exposed, in a country so filled with woods, ravines, and defiles; and where local knowledge, and skill with the rifle, were an overmatch for all the valor, much as it was, that he could bring against them. Information having reached the ship, then at anchor off Moor's fields, that 200 American militia were encamped behind a wood, distant about a mile from the beach, captain Parker, at 11 o'clock on the night of the 30th of August, was induced to land with,—not, as the American editors say, "230

* See p. 276.

men,"* but,—104 marines and 20 seamen. It appears that colonel Read, the commander of the American force, stated at 170 Maryland volunteers,* having been apprized of the intended attack, had retired to a small open space, surrounded by woods, distant four or five miles from his first encampment. Thither, having captured a small cavalry piquet, the heedless seamen and marines, headed by their undaunted chief, proceeded. The enemy, with some pieces of artillery, was found drawn up in line in front of his camp. The British commenced the fire; and, charging, drove the Americans, through their camp, into the woods. It was about this time that sir Peter received a mortal wound. Secure behind the trees, the Americans levelled their pieces with unerring aim; while the British, deceived by the apparent flight of their wary foe, rushed on through the woods, till, bewildered and embarrassed, the survivors of this adventurous band were compelled to retreat to their ship; bringing away the body of their lamented commander, and all their wounded but three. The British sustained a loss of 14 killed and 27 wounded: the Americans, as a proof how little they exposed themselves, of not more than three men slightly wounded.*

At the head of a narrow bay or inlet of the

* Sketches of the War, p. 339.

Patapsco river, and distant from its confluence with the Chesapeake about 16 miles, stands the city of Baltimore, containing about 20000 inhabitants. It is nearly surrounded by detached hills; one of which, Clinkapin hill, situated on its eastern side, commands the city itself, as well as the approach to it by land, from the Chesapeake. Its water-approach is defended by a strong fortification, named Fort-Henry, situated at the distance of about two miles from the city, upon the point of the peninsula that forms the south-side of the bay or harbor; which, at its entrance, is scarcely half a mile in width. As an additional security, the Patapsco is not navigable for vessels drawing more than 18 feet water; and, just within the harbor, is a 14 or 15 feet bar.

The arrival of troops in the Chesapeake, and the subsequent operations of the British in the Patuxent and Potomac rivers, could not do otherwise than cause serious alarm at Baltimore, distant from Washington but 35 miles. The panic-struck inhabitants believed, that the British troops would march across the country, and attack them in the rear, while the squadron was bombarding them in front. Our numbers on shore were too small to warrant such an enterprise; but, had it been risked, and had the fleet made a simultaneous movement up the bay, there is little doubt that Baltimore would have capitulated. Fortunately for the city, the military and naval forces within it were becoming hourly more powerful; and, far from desponding, the generals and commodores used their utmost exertions in strengthening the defences, and improving the natural advantages, of the position. Upon the hills to the eastward and northward of the city, a chain of pallisadoed redoubts, connected by breast-works, with ditches in front, and well supplied with artillery, was constructed; and works were thrown up, and guns mounted at every spot from which an invading force, either by land or water, could meet with annoyance. The Java frigate, of 60 guns, and two new sloops of war, of 22 guns each, were equipping at Baltimore. There were also, in the harbor, several gun-boats, each armed with a long French 36-pounder, besides a carronade; as well as several private-armed vessels: so that the Americans had, including their field and regular battery-guns, an immense train of artillery to put in operation against an enemy. As to troops, exclusive of the 16,300 militia, regulars, and flotilla-men, which general Winder had been authorized to call out, for the defence of the 10th military district, volunteers were flocking in from Pennsylvania; and the seamen and marines of commodores Rodgers, Perry, and Porter, had just arrived from the banks of the Potomac, where they had been "distinguishing" themselves so greatly.

If any southern town or city of the United States was an object of immediate attack, it certainly was Baltimore. The destruction of the new frigate and sloops, and of the immense quantities of naval stores, at that depôt, would have been seriously felt by the American government. Yet were the British ships, having on board the troops, waiting in the Patuxent, till the passing of the " approaching equinoctial new moon" should enable them to proceed, with safety, upon the unfortunate " plans which had been concerted previous to the departure of the Iphigenia."* On the 6th of September came a flag of truce from Baltimore; and instantly all was bustle and alacrity on board the British squadron. The Royal Oak and troop-ships stood out of the Patuxent; and vice-admiral Cochrane quitting his anchorage off Tangier island, proceeded with the remainder of the fleet, up the bay to North-point, near the entrance of the Patapsco river. On the 10th and 11th, the fleet anchored; and, by 12 o'clock at noon on the 12th, the whole of the troops and seamen had disembarked at North-point, in order to proceed to the immediate attack upon Baltimore, by land; while some frigates and sloops, the Erebus, rocket-ship, and five bombs, ascended the Patapsco, to threaten and bombard Fort-M'Henry, and the other contiguous batteries.

* App. No. 73.

The amount of the British force that landed has been variously, and, in every instance, erroneously, stated by the American historians. None of these gentlemen estimated the British loss at Bladensburg and Washington, below 400 men; Mr. Thomson, indeed, declared it amounted to "1000:"* nor is it pretended, that any reinforcement of British troops subsequently arrived in the Chesapeake. Yet every one of our three historians, instead of deducting his own estimate of our loss, adds 2 or 3000 men to his own estimate of our force, at Bladensburg and Washington. For instance, doctor Smith, who stated our force at Bladensburg at "4000,"‡ states, without assigning any reason for the augmentation, that we brought to Baltimore "5000 land troops."|| Mr. Thomson, in like manner, makes his "6000 regulars, sailors, and marines,"|| 8000 soldiers, sailors and marines;"† and Mr. O'Connor, his "5000,"|| "between 8 and 9000 men."¶ The British troops that landed, under the command of major-general Ross, at North-point, consisted of detachments of royal and marine-artillery, the remnants of the 1st battalions of the 4th, 21st, and 44th regiments, and the

* Sketches of the War, p. 388. † Ibid. p. 339.

‡ See p. 282.

§ Hist. of the United States, Vol. III. p. 302.

|| See p. 278. ¶ Hist. of the War, p. 232.

85th regiment, the 1st and 2d (or Colonial) battalions of marines, detachments of marines from the ships, and a body of 600 seamen, under captain Edward Crofton; the whole numbering about 3270 rank and file.

Immediately after landing, the British moved forward to the city. On arriving at a line of intrenchments and abattis, thrown up between Black river and Humphries's creek on the Patapsco, and distant about three miles from the point of landing, some opposition was expected; but the American dragoons and riflemen, stationed there, fled without firing a shot. At this time major-general Ross and rear-admiral Cockburn, along with a guard of 50 or 60 men, were walking together, considerably a-head of the advanced or light companies; in order to reconnoitre the enemy. At about 10 o'clock, after having proceeded about two miles from the intrenchment, and some distance along a road flanked by thick woods, they encountered a division of the enemy, consisting, as we may gather from Mr. Thomson, of "two companies from the 5th infantry, 150 in number, under captains Levering and Howard, about 70 riflemen, under captain Aisquith, the cavalry," under colonel Biays, the amount of which not being stated, we shall fix at 140, "and 10 artillerists, with a 4-pounder commanded by lieutenant Stiles;"* in all 370 men. A short skirmish ensued, and the Americans fell back; most of them taking to the woods. Major-general Ross, after saying to rear-admiral Cockburn,—"I'll return and order up the light-companies,"—proceeded to execute his purpose. In his way back, alone, by the same road along which he and his party had just passed, the major-general received a musket-bullet through his right arm into his breast, and fell, mortally wounded. The firing had, at this time, wholly ceased; and the expiring general lay on the road, unheeded, because unseen, either by friend or foe, till the arrival at the spot of the light-companies, who had hastened forward upon hearing the musketry. Leaving some attendants in charge of the lamented chief, the officer commanding rushed on; and it was then that admiral Cockburn learned the loss which the army and the country had sustained. In a few minutes he was by the side of his friend: what passed on that trying occasion, is best given in the words of the rear-admiral himself.†

The death of major-general Ross was a fatal blow to the expedition against Baltimore. Previously to our relating the succeeding events of that day, we are called aside to correct American misrepresentation. Doctor Smith says:—

* Sketches of the War, p. 341. † App. No. 74.

"General Ross put himself at the head of his troops to force general Stricker out of the road to the city." In attempting which he states him to have been shot.* Mr. Thomson, after having given the details of the American advanced force, as already extracted, says:—"This detachment, having proceeded half a mile, was met by, and instantly engaged, the enemy's"—not "advanced guard," but—"main body. The situation of the ground would not admit of the co-operation of the artillery and cavalry; and the infantry and riflemen sustained the whole action, with great gallantry; pouring in a rapid and effective fire upon the British column, killing major-general Ross, and several other officers, and impeding the advance of the British army. Having performed the duty required of them by general Stricker, the whole detachment with a trifling loss, fell back, in excellent order, upon the American line."† This false and highly bombastical account is best answered by a short extract from the American official account, as quoted in another American work; and that work the scrupulous Mr. O'Connor's. After stating that general Stricker had sent forward "an advanced corps, under the command of major Heath, of the 5th regiment;"‡ Mr.

* Hist. of the United States, Vol. III. p. 302.

† Sketches of the War, p. 341. ‡ Hist. of the War, p. 233.

O'Connor, taking the words of general Smyth's official letter, says :—" 'This advance met the enemy, and, after some skirmishing, returned to the line; the main body of the enemy being at a short distance in the rear of their advance.' "* This, as we have seen, was the fact; except that the nearest British force was not the "main body," but the advance or light-companies. Mr. O'Connor does not state, when or how general Ross met his death, merely, when he comes to the enumeration of our loss, saying :—"General Ross, the destroyer of Washington, was killed." The truth is, the citizens of Baltimore were not aware, till our accounts reached them, what a benefit they had derived from the chance-shot of one of their skirmishers.

As soon as the British main body, now under the command of colonel Brooke, of the 44th regiment, closed upon the advance, the whole moved forward; and, at about two miles further, and about five from the city, came in sight of the American army, drawn up, with six pieces of artillery, and a body of cavalry. The exact amount of this force we have no means of ascertaining. Mr. Thomson, referring to the "detachment" sent forward, on the night of the 11th, under general Stricker, designates it as composed of "part of his brigade, a light corps of riflemen, and artillery, from general Stansbury's

* App. No. 77.

brigade, under major Randal, and several companies of the Pennsylvania volunteers; amounting to 3185 effective men."* This is exclusive of "1000 men stationed at the forts and batteries;" and "along the breast-works, about four times that number;"* or, upwards of 8000 men, in the whole. The prisoners estimated their own force drawn up, under general Stricker, at 6000 men;† and Mr. Thomson, by his extracts from the British official accounts, has evidently seen, although he has not contradicted, these statements. We may, therefore, safely estimate the American force, now close in front of a British force of 3270 infantry, with two light field-pieces and a howitzer, at 4500 infantry and cavalry, with six pieces of artillery; backed as they were, in case of a retreat, by at least 8000 troops, and those hourly augmenting; and by heavy batteries in all directions.

The details of the short battle that ensued are fully given in colonel Brooke's and rear-admiral Cockburn's letters. A few extracts from Mr. Thomson's, will tend to corroborate the British account. "The 51st," says he, "which was ordered to open upon the enemy in his attempt to turn the rest of the line, delivered a loose fire, immediately broke, fled precipitately from its ground, and in such confusion, that

* Sketches of the War, p. 340.

† App. Nos. 71. 73. 74. and 75.

every effort to rally it proved ineffectual. The 2d battalion of the 39th, was thrown into disorder, by the flight of the 51st, and some of its companies also gave way. The remainder and the 1st battalion stood firm. Thus abandoned by the retreat of the 51st, general Stricker made new arrangements for the reception of the enemy, and opened a general fire upon him, from the right, left, and centre. The artillery sent forth a destructive torrent of canister against the British left column, then attempting to gain the cover of a small log-house, in front of the 5th regiment. Captain Sadtler, with his yagers from that regiment, who were posted in the house when the British 4th regiment was advancing, had, however, taken the precaution to set fire to it, and the intention of the enemy was, therefore, defeated. The 6th regiment then opened its fire, and the whole line entered into an animated contest, which continued, with a severe loss to the enemy, until 15 minutes before 4 o'clock. At that hour, general Stricker, having inflicted as much injury upon the invaders as could possibly be expected, from a line now about 1400 strong, against a force amounting, notwithstanding its losses, to at least 7000 men, ordered his brigade to retire upon the reserve regiment; an order which was well executed by the whole line, which in a few minutes rallied upon lieutenant-colonel M'Donald. From the point occupied by this regiment, general Stricker, in order to refresh his troops, and prepare them for a second movement of the enemy, retired to a position half a mile in advance of the left of major-general Smith's entrenchments. Here he was joined by general Winder, who, with general Douglass's Virginia brigade, and the United States' dragoons, under captain Bird, took post upon his left." *

This editor is famous for spinning out a battle; nor, is he ever staggered by improbabilities, how gross soever they may be. After stating that his gallant countrymen ran away by whole regiments, he has the impudence to contrast the remaining number, or the "line, now but 1400 strong," with "at least 7000" British. By his own account, the American troops retired four miles and a half, or, "to a position half a mile in advance,"—and, consequently, within full range,—"of the left of major-general Smith's intrenchments," before they could be brought to a stand, or had any stomach to "refresh" themselves, against "a second movement of the enemy." Not a word is there of any charge by the bayonet, which settled the business so quickly; nor of the loss of any pieces of artillery or prisoners.

The British occupied the ground of which the Americans had been dispossessed; but were too

* Sketches of the War, p. 342.

much fatigued to follow up their victory on that evening. The British loss amounted to one general-staff, one subaltern, two serjeants, and 35 rank and file, killed; seven captains, four subalterns, 11 serjeants, and 229 rank and file, wounded; of the army.* The navy lost one petty-officer, three seamen, and three marines, killed; one officer, six petty-officers, 22 seamen, and 15 marines, wounded.† Thus, the total British loss on shore, was 46 killed, and 273 wounded. The great disproportion of wounded arose from the employment, by the enemy, of buck-shot;‡ and the magnitude of the loss, altogether, to the enemy's sheltered position. The loss of the Americans upon the field, Mr. Thomson estimates at 150; which is particularized, by Mr. O'Connor, as "20 killed, 90 wounded, and 47 missing."§ The last item is evidently erroneous; as colonel Brooke carried away with him "about 200 prisoners, being persons of the best families in the city;"‖ and which number might have been considerably augmented, did not the immense inferiority of numbers render the effectiveness of the men for action a paramount consideration.

Early on the morning of the 13th, colonel Brooke, leaving a small guard at a meeting-house, from which the enemy had been driven,

* App. No. 72. † Ibid. p. 76. ‡ See p. 147.

§ History of the War, p. 237. ‖ App. No. 71.

to protect the wounded, moved forward with the army; and, at 10 o'clock, occupied a favorable position, to the eastward of, and distant about two miles from, Baltimore. From this point, the strong defences in and around the city were plainly to be seen; and arrangements were made for storming, during the ensuing night, with the co-operation of the fleet, the American entrenched camp; at which lay general Stricker and his army, now reinforced by Douglas's brigade of Virginia militia, under general Winder, and the United States' dragoons, under captain Bird.*

In their way up the Patapsco, several of the frigates and other vessels grounded; and one or two of the former did not get off till the next day. At about nine o'clock on the morning of the 13th, the Meteor, Ætna, Terror, Volcano, and Devastation, bombs, and the Erebus, rocket-ship, came to anchor in a position, from which they could act upon the enemy's fort and batteries; the frigates having already taken their stations, outside of all. At day-light on the morning of the 13th, the bombardment commenced upon, and was returned by, Fort-M'Henry, the Star-Fort, and the water-batteries on both sides of the entrance. At about three o'clock in the afternoon, the four bomb-vessels and rocket-ship weighed, and stood further in; the latter, to give effect to her rockets, much

* App. No. 77.

nearer than the others. The forts, which had discontinued their fire on account of the vessels being out of range, now re-commenced a brisk cannonade; but which, although persevered in for some hours, did not injure a man on board any of the vessels: two of the bombs only were slightly struck. The close position of the Erebus led the commander-in-chief, whose ship, the Surprise, was, with the other frigates, at anchor in the river, to imagine that captain Bartholomew could not maintain his position. He therefore sent a division of boats to tow out the Erebus. On seeing the rocket-ship and bombs withdraw to a greater distance, the Americans in the batteries were perfectly justified in supposing, that they had "compelled" the British to retire. "This noisy play," as Mr. O'Connor calls it, continued, with short intervals, till day-light the next morning.

The American official account states, that two or three rocket-vessels, and barges, succeeded in getting up the Ferry branch, but that they were soon compelled to retire, by the forts in that quarter; commanded by lieutenant Newcomb, of the navy, and lieutenant Webster, of the flotilla. "These forts also destroyed," says the general, "one of the barges, with all on board."* Mr. Thomson says:—"Under cover of the night, the British commanders despatched a

* App. No. 77.

a fleet of barges to attack and storm Fort-Covington. The attempt was repulsed, however, and the assailants retired, with an immense loss to their bomb-vessels."* Mr. O'Connor tells the story thus:—"Favored by a dark night, one or two of the enemy's bomb-vessels, and several barges, with 1200 chosen men, passed the fort at about one o'clock in the morning of the 14th, and proceeded up the Patapsco, to attack the town in the rear, and, probably, with a view to effect a landing. From their new station they commenced a very warm throwing of bombs and rockets, but were repaid with such vigor and effect, that the screams of their wounded could be heard in the midst of a roar of arms, that made the houses in the city shake for nearly an hour and a half."†

Let us now see how this story will read in our way of relating it. In the middle of the night of the 13th, a division of 20 boats was detached up the Ferry branch, to cause a diversion favorable to the intended assault upon the enemy's entrenched camp, at the opposite side of the city. The rain poured in torrents, and the night was so extremely dark, that 11 of the boats pulled, by mistake, directly for the harbor. Fortunately, the lights of the city disco-

* Sketches of the War, p. 344.

† Hist. of the War, p. 236.

vered to the crews their perilous situation, time enough for them to get back in safety to their ships. The remaining nine boats, consisting of one rocket-boat, five launches, two pinnaces, and one gig, containing, not "1200," but—128 officers, seamen, and marines, under the command of captain Napier, passed up the Ferry branch, to a considerable distance above Fort-M'Henry, and opened a heavy fire of rockets and shot upon the shore; at several parts of which they could have landed, with ease, had the whole of their force been together. After having, by drawing down a considerable number of troops to the beach, effected their object, the British stood back with their boats. When just opposite to Fort-M'Henry, one of the officers caused a rocket to be fired: the consequence was, an immediate discharge of round, grape, and canister, from the fort and water-batteries below; by which one of the boats was slightly struck, and a man mortally wounded. Not another casualty occurred.

It appears that, on the evening of the 13th, after the boats had been ordered upon this service, vice-admiral Cochrane sent a messenger to acquaint colonel Brooke, that, as the entrance to Baltimore by sea was entirely obstructed by a barrier of vessels, sunk at the mouth of the harbor, defended inside by gun-boats,* a

* App. No. 73.

naval co-operation against the city and entrenched camp, was found impracticable. The heavy rain at this time falling greatly increased the difficulty of ascending the steep hill, upon which the camp was situated; and both commanders concurred in the propriety of immediately withdrawing the troops and ships. At about half-past one on the morning of the 14th, the British troops commenced retiring, and halted at three miles distance. In the course of the evening they retired three miles further, and encamped for the night. Late on the morning of the 15th, they moved down to North-point; and, in the course of that day, re-embarked, without having experienced, during their slow and deliberate retreat, the slightest molestation from the enemy. At seven o'clock on the morning of the 14th, the rocket-ship and bomb-vessels were called off from the American batteries; which are stated to have lost, by the long continued bombardment, only four men killed and 24 wounded. In the course of the day, the ships stood down the river, and joined the remainder of the squadron at anchor off North-point.

The American official account is moderate enough; except in the statement respecting the barges, and which statement general Smith could only have obtained from the commanding officer of the forts on the Patapsco. Not a word is said about any pursuit of the British. That would be encroaching upon the duties, and, seemingly, pleasing ones, too, of the American historian. "The excessive fatigue of the troops, all of whom had been three days and nights under arms, in the most inclement weather, prevented their annoying the enemy's rear with much effect, and they made prisoners of none but stragglers from his army."* If, as sir George Cockburn says, the Americans "did not venture to look at" the British upon their retreat,† the former did not certainly annoy their rear "with much effect." Colonel Brooke declares, that not a man was left behind.‡ So much, then, for the "stragglers" taken. Mr. Thomson's account has vastly improved, by passing through the hands of the 'inventor and sole patentee' of the screaming story. For instance:—"It was impossible for veterans, or the most experienced troops, to act with more firm discipline or cool courage, than the citizens of Baltimore, and the troops engaged, did, on this occasion, with the exception already mentioned. A pursuit of the enemy was attempted, without, however, doing him much injury. The troops were so exhausted, with three days and nights' fatigue, that they could do little more than pick up a few stragglers. A line of defences thrown up by the

* Sketches of the War, p. 343. † App. No. 74.
‡ App. No. 71.

Americans from Black river to Humphries's creek, on the Patapsco, were used by the enemy to protect their embarkation."* These are the stories that carry off so many editions among the people of the United States.

Having done with the American accounts of the celebrated Baltimore "demonstration," we have yet to offer upon it a few remarks of our own. No Briton but must regret, that any plan of "ulterior operations" should have obtruded itself, to check the progress of the attack. With respect to naval co-operation, it is well known, that the gallant commanders of the Severn, Euryalus, Havannah, and Hebrus, frigates, volunteered to lighten their ships, and lay them close alongside Fort-M'Henry. The possession of this fort would have enabled us to silence the batteries on the opposite side of the bay; and, indeed, have placed the city completely at our mercy. The very advance of the British frigates to their stations would, probably, have led to the destruction of the Java frigate, and the Erie and Ontario sloops; and then we might have retired, "holding in view the ulterior operations of the troops," with something more to boast of than, not merely an empty, but, considering what we lost by it, a highly disastrous "demonstration." The troops on shore might, and, no doubt, would, have succeeded in carrying the enemy's

* Hist. of the War, p. 235.

intrenched camp; but they could not expect to succeed further, without a simultaneous attack by the fleet. Even the nine boats, and their 128 men, caused a considerable diversion of the enemy's forces: we may well conceive, then, what might have been effected, had no "ulterior" plan been allowed to interfere.

We cannot dismiss the business at Baltimore, without bestowing a few words upon an officer, whose untimely fate has been so universally deplored. His public services are thus briefly enumerated, by the mover, in the house of commons, for a monument to his memory. "General Ross, when major Ross, served in the expedition to Holland, in 1799. He was then in the 28th regiment, and signalized himself in repulsing the attacks made on the lines of sir Ralph Abercromby. Here, displaying the greatest gallantry, he received a severe wound, which deprived his country of his services for a time. In the autumn of 1800, having recovered from the effects of his wound, he accompanied his regiment to the Mediterranean, and, shortly afterwards, served in the expedition to Calabria: here, in the memorable battle of Maida, which so greatly raised the fame of the British arms, and particularly by the use made of the bayonet, major Ross made himself conspicuous; and, by wheeling on the enemy's line, contributed, perhaps, more than any other circumstance, to the route of the enemy on that day. Nothing more occurred to bring him into notice, till he served in the army led by general sir John Moore, in 1807; and, under that gallant and lamented commander at the battle of Corunna, he again shone with no common lustre. In 1812, sailing from Ireland, he joined the army in the peninsula, and, under the command of lord Wellington, so distinguished himself in the battle of Vittoria, that his lordship gave him the command of a separate brigade. Now that a more extended field of service lay before him, in the first great battle of the Pyrennees, where the firmness of the English was most conspicuously displayed, where the French fought with the most determined obstinacy, his valor contributed so much to the glory of that day, that lord Wellington, in his despatch, stated his brigade 'to have distinguished themselves beyond all former precedent; they made four separate charges with the bayonet, and general Ross had three horses killed under him.' At the passage of the Nieve, and the battle of Orthes, he displayed the same undaunted bravery." Another member, who had been intimate with him, said: —"He possessed the happy skill of conciliating by his disposition, and instructing by his example: he possessed, indeed, all those private and distinguished qualifications, by which alone a commander could acquire the full confidence of his men. His military knowledge was great and complete: for it had been the result of practice and constant experience; while his foresight and example in the field were such as to excite the enthusiasm and reverence of those whom he led to victory." General Ross, it appears, was but 40 when he fell. Comparing the *advantages* we derived from the "victory" at Baltimore, with the loss of such a general, we cannot but regret, that the attack was undertaken at all; if not meant to be persevered in, till either the ostensible object was gained, or the British troops had been fairly beaten out of it.

On the 19th of September, sir Alexander Cochrane, with the Tonnant and Surprise, sailed for Halifax, to hasten the construction of the flat-bottomed boats, intended to be employed in the great expedition on foot; and on the same day, the Albion, rear-admiral Cockburn, sailed for Bermuda, leaving the Royal Oak, rear-admiral Malcolm, with some frigates and smaller vessels, and the ships containing the troops, at anchor in the river Patuxent. On the 27th the rear-admiral removed to the Potomac; where, on the 3d of October, the troops were placed into boats, and sent up Coan river. In their way up, two soldiers were wounded, and captain Kenah, of the Ætna bomb, killed, by musketry from the shore. Against so powerful a force, when once landed, the few militia could not be expected to stand: they fired a volley and fled; and the troops advanced, past Northumberland court-house, five miles into the interior. After taking and scuttling two or three worthless schooners; and, according to the American editors, plundering the inhabitants, the troops re-embarked, and stood down the river to their ships. The latter, soon afterwards, descended the Potomac; and, on the 14th, rear-admiral Malcolm, taking with him, the Royal Oak, Asia, and Ramillies 74s, one or two frigates, and all the troop-ships and bombs, quitted the Chesapeake, for the rendezvous at Negril bay, Jamaica.

The officer now left in command at the Chesapeake, was captain Barrie, of the Dragon 74, recently from Penobscot. He had with him the Hebrus and Havannah frigates, two *armées en flûte*, and the Dauntless and Dotterel sloops. The land-troops, if worthy the name, at his disposal, consisted of about 200 colonial marines, or refugee-slaves, in barracks, upon the small island of Tangier, lying off the mouth of the Potomac; and which had, since early in the summer, been taken possession of by sir George Cockburn, as a depôt for receiving and organizing the refugees. The unhealthiness of Tangier, and the badness of its harbor, induced captain Barrie to seize Tilghman's island, a much more eligible spot, and distant only 60 miles from Baltimore. On the 30th of November, a boat-expedition, with about 500 seamen and marines, ascended the river Rappahannock, as high as the town of Tappahannock, which they entered without much opposition, although three times their number of militia were in the neighbourhood. The editor of the American "National Intelligencer," of December 9, after having magnified captain Barrie's force to "2500 troops," says: "The purpose of the enemy seems to be, as heretofore, to steal negroes, stock, tobacco, &c. plunder the houses within their reach, and burn what they cannot carry off." Charges of this description we have already fully answered. We need only repeat here, that the "negroes" come off voluntarily; the "stock" is amply paid for; and the "tobacco" "good prize, by the maritime law of nations."† As much of the latter, as the British could not "carry off," it was right for them to "burn:" the charge of "plunder" we can only hope is groundless. Had that active and enterprising officer, captain Barrie, really had "2500 troops," he would have compelled Mr. Gales to fill his columns with matter fifty times more important than the capture of Tappahannock.

Early in December, rear-admiral Cockburn, in the Albion, from Bermuda, bringing with him the Orlando frigate, and some smaller ves-

* See p. 192.

sels, arrived in the Chesapeake, but merely to carry away the colonial marines; with whom, on the 14th, he proceeded towards Amelia Island, in East Florida: having left orders for captain Barrie to follow, with the Dragon, Hebrus, and Regulus. Accordingly, captain Barrie departed soon afterwards, leaving a few frigates and sloops in the Chesapeake; and, on the 10th of January, arrived off Cumberland Island, the southern-most of the chain along the coast of Georgia, and separated by Cumberland Sound from Amelia Island. Rear-admiral Cockburn not having yet arrived, captain Somerville of the Rota, as the senior officer, determined upon employing the two companies of the 2d West India regiment, and the detachments of royal marines which had recently arrived on that coast, in a combined attack upon the frontier-town of the state of Georgia, St. Mary's, situated a few miles up the river of that name, dividing the United States and East Florida. On the 13th an attack, with about 700 troops, marines, and seamen, under the command of captain Barrie, was made on the fort, or key to the entrance of the river, at Point Petre. This fort mounted two 24, two 18, one 9, and two brass 6-pounders; from which, however, scarcely a single discharge was made, ere the garrison abandoned the post, and fled to the woods in the rear. On the 14th, the combined forces, accompanied by the Terror and Devastation bombs, ascended the river to St. Mary's. Contrary to expectation, here, also, no resistance was made; and the town, the shipping in the harbor, and the merchandize in the stores, were taken quiet possession of. Soon afterwards an expedition of boats, went a considerable distance further up the river, and brought down the Countess of Harcourt East Indiaman, which had been captured and carried in there by a Charlestown privateer; also a beautiful gun-boat, named the Scorpion, a present from the town of St. Mary's to the United States.

On the 15th of January, rear-admiral Cockburn, who had been blown off the coast by strong north-west gales, arrived and took the command; and on the 22d, the British, after removing the guns, and destroying the fort and barracks, at Point Petre, descended the river to Cumberland Island; of which immediate possession was taken. The troops and marines were encamped; and the rear-admiral established his head-quarters at a very large house, built of *tabby;** surrounding it with the ordnance brought from Point Petre. On the 22d of February, eight launches, two pinnaces, and one gig, containing 186 officers, seamen, and marines, under the command of captain Phillott, of the Primrose brig, ascended the St. Mary's river, without

* Oyster-shells, and their cement.

opposition, 120 miles; when a heavy fire of musketry, opening upon them from each side, compelled a retreat. While day-light lasted, a spirited fire was kept up by the boats; but, unfortunately, after dark, the men could not be restrained from firing, by which they exposed themselves to the view of their enemy. The river was, in some parts, so narrow, that a couple of stout trees, many of which were on the banks, felled and thrown across, would have completely cut off the retreat of the boats. That not having been done, the boats got back to the island, with four killed, and 25 wounded.

One of the objects in assembling troops upon this part of the coast was, to assist in a combined attack upon the town of Savannah, in Georgia; a naval station of no mean importance. The town stands upon a flat sandy cliff, elevated about 50 feet above the level of the Savannah river; is distant from the sea about 17 miles; and from St. Mary's, 95 miles. The number of its inhabitants is about 7000; and the quota of militia which, by the secretary of war's order of July the 4th,* the state of Georgia was required to hold in readiness, amounted to 350 artillery, and 3150 infantry; total, 3500 men. The British, since their first arrival at Cumberland island, had been waiting for a reinforcement, under general Power; but whose

* See p. 274.

destination, unknown to them, had been altered. Without this additional force, it would have been imprudent to make the attack. Some other operations, in which a body of Indians and Negroes from the interior of West Florida, was to co-operate, had also been in agitation. But the intended junction had been prevented by the machinations of some of those crafty Americans, who, as "British subjects," living under our own government, were so actively employed against us, during the whole of the late war. Consequently 7 or 800 British troops, and 12 ships of war, including two 74s and three or four frigates, were allowed to remain, for several weeks, in a state of perfect inactivity; at a time, too, when an important, well-struck blow would have produced so *healing* an effect. Had it not been for a communication, opened, through the Spaniards on Amelia Island, with East Florida, both army and navy would have had their idle hours still further embittered by a want of subsistence.

CHAPTER XXI.

Expedition to New Orleans—British at Pensacola and Barataria—Trick played by the Baratarian commandant—Secret act of the American congress to take possession of West Florida—Possession taken of Mobile—Erection of Fort-Bowyer—Attack upon it by four British sloops of war—Loss of the Hermes—Brief description of Louisiana and New Orleans—Arrival of the British fleet off Chandeleur island—Capture of five American gun-boats near Lake Borgne—Proclamation of martial law by general Jackson—Scheming flag of truce—Its object defeated—Disembarkation of the first division of British troops—Description of the ground of operations—Arrival of British advance at Villeré's—General Wilkinson's strictures upon the route chosen by the British—Deception as to the strength of Petite Coquille fort—Accidental low estimate of the British force at Villeré's—Prompt advance of major-general Jackson—U. S. schooner Carolina—Battle of the 23d of December—Destruction of the Carolina by hot shot—Escape of the U. S. ship Louisiana—Arrival of sir Edward Pakenham—Strength of the British forces—Proposed attack in the rear of New Orleans — Its non-adoption—Description of general Jackson's lines of defence—Demonstration of the 28th of December—Destructive fire of the Louisiana—American batteries on the opposite side of the river—Arrival of ship-guns, and erection of battery by the British—Continued cannonade—Mutual rein-

forcements--General Morgan's lines on the opposite bank—British and American forces—Battle of the 8th of January—Fatal neglect to bring up the fascines and ladders—Death of major-generals Pakenham and Gibbs—Misbehaviour of two regiments—Gallant behaviour of a division of the left brigade—Repulse of the British—Strictures upon the attack, by American officers—Launching of the boats into the Mississippi—Successful attack upon the American intrenchments on the right bank—Fatal difference of opinion respecting the possibility of holding that position—Its immediate evacuation—Short suspension of hostilities—Bombardment of Fort St. Philip—Retreat of the British from before New Orleans—The total loss on both sides—American bombast—French general Humbert—Some particulars relative to general Jackson—His honorable conduct—Departure of the British fleet—Surrender of Fort-Bowyer without a shot's being fired at it—Treaty of peace—Canadian preparations for the ensuing campaign—Brief remarks on the treaty, and on the advantages which the Americans have gained by the war.

FROM the paragraphs that appeared in several of the London prints of May and June, 1814, there is no doubt that the conquest of Louisiana had been submitted to the British government, as a measure of no difficult attainment. It was thought, perhaps, that the Louisianians, consisting chiefly of French and Spaniards, were disaffected towards the government of the

United States, and would rather aid, than oppose the landing of a British army. This hazardous, and, as it proved, fallacious conjecture, was suffered to over-balance all apprehension of danger from the thousands of armed inhabitants of the west and north-western territories, that could descend the Mississippi, and prevent any thing like a permanent occupation of the capital of Louisiana. There were not, it is true, any American 74s, or 60-gun frigates, building or lying blockaded at New Orleans; but those who suggested the expedition well knew that, as the cotton crops of Louisiana, and of the Mississippi territory, had been for some years in accumulation, the city-warehouses contained merchandize to an immense amount. Indeed, considering that New Orleans was the emporium of the annually increasing productions of a great portion of the western states, the enormous sum of 3000000*l*. was, perhaps, not an over-estimate of what, in the event of even a temporary possession of that city, would have been shared by the captors.

Scarcely had the people of New Orleans read, in the pages of their newspapers, admiral Cochrane's threatening letter and its reply, and been assured by their governor, that the British had expressed a determination "of wresting Louisiana from the hands of the United States, and restoring it to Spain," than accounts arrived, that the British were exciting the Indians, and, by proclamations dated from Pensacola, in West Florida, endeavouring to persuade the inhabitants of Louisiana and Kentucky, to shake off their allegiance, and join the British standard. Almost at the same instant they received accounts that some British officers had been trying to gain over the Baratarian freebooters, upwards of 200 in number; not only as pilots for that intricate coast, but as active allies in the contemplated invasion. Mr. Laffite, the commandant, played a deep game with the British officers. He received, with seeming acquiescence, all their communications on the subject, and then forwarded them to the governor of Louisiana. He had, at that time, in the gaol of New Orleans, loaded with irons, a brother; whose liberation he, no doubt, hoped to effect. In short, Mr. Laffite not only betrayed the British, but offered the services of himself and his hardy band, in defending the important point of the state of which they had taken possession. These men fulfilled the pledge given by their commandant to governor Claiborne; and, along with Mr. Laffite's brother, received, in the end, a full pardon from the president of the United States.

It is necessary now to mention, that a *secret* law passed the congress of the United States, as early as the 12th of February, 1813, authorizing the president "to occupy and hold all that tract of country, called West Florida, which lies west of the Perdido, not now in the possession of the United States." * On the 14th of March, the order to take possession reached major-general Wilkinson, then the commanding officer of the United States' troops within the territories of New Orleans and the Mississippi; and, on the 15th of April, taking with him a strong naval and military force, the general possessed himself, without opposition, but not without remonstrance, of Fort-Charlotte, near the town of Mobile. General Wilkinsoon, soon afterwards, constructed a fort upon Mobile-point, forming the extremity of a peninsula, which is joined to the continent by an isthmus, four miles wide, dividing the river and bay of Bonsecours from the bay of Perdido.

This fort, named Fort-Bowyer, mounted, in September, 1814, says an American editor, two 24, six 12, eight 9, and four 4-pounders; and contained a garrison of only 130 men;† yet, when we took possession of Fort-Bowyer, in February, 1815, up to which date no reinforcement of guns appears to have been sent to it, the fort mounted, exclusive of one long 24, and two 9-pounders outside, three 32, eight 24, six 12, five 9, and one 4-pounder; also one 8-inch mortar, and one $5\frac{1}{2}$-inch howitzer; total

* Wilkinson's Mem. Vol. III. p. 340.

† Latour's War in Louisiana, p. 34.

28 guns. Its garrison, under the same commander too, consisted, at this time, of 375 officers and soldiers.*

On the morning of the 12th, M.M.S. Hermes, of 22, Carron, of 20, and Sophie and Childers, of 18 guns each, under the orders of captain W. H. Percy, of the first-named ship, anchored on the coast, about six miles to the eastward of Fort-Bowyer; which this officer had unadvisedly determined to attack. The ships, with great difficulty, owing to the narrowness of the channel, and the numerous shoals, arrived, on the afternoon of the 15th, in the neighbourhood of the fort. The Hermes, at last, gained a station within musket-shot distance; the Sophie, Carron, and Childers, anchoring in a line a-stern of her. Previously to this, a detachment of, not "120"† but 60 marines, and not "600"† but 120 Indians, with a $5\frac{1}{2}$-inch howitzer, but no "12-pounder," under the orders of major Nicolls, of the marines, had disembarked on the peninsula. Sixty of the Indians, under lieutenant Castle, had been detached to secure the pass of Bonsecours, 27 miles to the eastward of the fort; so that major Nicolls had, under his command, not 730,† but 120 marines and Indians.

The great distance at which the Carron and Childers had unavoidably anchored, confined the effective cannonade, on the part of the British, to

* Appendix, No. 112.

† Latour's War in Louisiana, p. 40.

the Hermes and Sophie; nor was the latter's fire of much use, as, owing to the rottenness of her timbers, and her defective equipment, her carronades drew or turned over at every fire. The Hermes, before she had fired many broadsides, "having her cable cut, was carried away by the current, and presented her head to the fort. In that position she remained from 15 to 20 minutes, whilst the raking fire from the fort swept, fore and aft, almost every thing on deck."* Soon afterwards the Hermes grounded, directly in front of the fort. Every means to get her off having failed, captain Percy, taking out of her the whole of his wounded, set her on fire. He had but one boat left, and that with only three oars. As a proof of the American captain Lawrence's "characteristic humanity," the fort, on this "memorable day for the garrison," fired round and grape at the boat, till she got out of gun-shot. The Hermes and Sophie were the only vessels that sustained any injury. The loss of the one was 25 men killed, and 24 wounded; of the other, six killed, and 16 wounded; total, with one marine killed on shore, 32 killed, and 40 wounded: while the American editors, major Latour inclusive, have made the British loss before Fort-Bowyer, 162 killed, and 70 wounded.† The Americans acknowledge a loss of four killed, and four wounded.† No event of the war has been

* Latour's War in Louisiana, p. 38. † Ibid. p. 40.

made more of than the indiscreet attack upon Fort-Bowyer. Major Latour, misnaming one vessel, and converting into frigate-built ships the corvettes Hermes and Carron, gives each of the latter "twenty eight 32-pound carronades,"* and crews in proportion. He, then, states the whole "effective British force at 92 guns, and 1330 men;"* which he modestly opposes to eight guns, (all that he says would bear,) and 130 men. Where did this writer learn, that both broadsides of a ship can act together, upon a single object? Major Latour, palpably ridiculous as his statements are, has, however, no criticism to dread in the United States of America.

The attack upon Fort-Bowyer unmasking, at once, the designs of the British upon Louisiana, major-general Jackson, of the United States' army, who, having superseded general Wilkinson, was at this time at Mobile, began making defensive arrangements; and, among them, adopted the extraordinary resolution of taking possession, "without waiting for the authority of his government,"† of the Spanish post of Pensacola, and the contiguous forts. Having assembled 4000 troops, he was enabled, through the treachery of the Spanish governor, to effect his object, on the 7th and 8th of November, without bloodshed. Leaving garrisons in the captured forts, the major-general, with the

* Latour's War in Louis. p. 40. † Sketches of the War, p. 346.

remainder of his troops, departed for New Orleans; where he arrived on the 2d of December. Since the 10th of the preceding month, the governor of Louisiana had informed the legislature, that the British were about to attack the state, with from 12 to 15000 men; and that he was in daily expectation of considerable re-inforcements from Kentucky and Tennessee.

Without a brief description of Louisiana, and particularly of the line of maritime invasion to which New Orleans is exposed, the important operations about to be detailed, will not be so readily understood. The boundaries of Louisiana may be seen upon any map of the North American continent: it is only necessary here to state, that this great expanse of territory has a frontier, with the Spanish internal provinces of 1900 miles; a line of sea-coast, on the Pacific Ocean, of 500 miles; a frontier with the British dominions of 1700 miles; thence, following the Mississippi, by comparative course, 1400 miles; and along the gulf of Mexico 700 miles: from the mouth of the Perdido to the 31° N. latitude, 40 miles; along the latter parallel, 240 miles; having an outline of 6480 miles, and 1352860 square miles of surface.* The parish of New Orleans is bounded north by Lake Pontchartrain and the Rigolets, east by lake Borgne and the parish of Plaquemines, south-east by the gulf

* Darby's Louisiana, p. 12.

of Mexico, and west by the parishes of St. Bernard and the interior of Lefourche; possessing an area of 1300 square miles. The city of New Orleans, the capital of the parish, and of the state of Louisiana, stands upon the left bank of the Mississippi, 105 miles, following the stream, and 90 miles, in a direct line, from its mouth. The present population of the city is estimated at 23242 persons.* The line of maritime invasion extends from Lake Pontchartrain, on the east, to the river Tesche, on the west, intersected by several bays, inlets, and rivers, which furnish avenues of approach to the metropolis. But the flatness of the coast is every where unfavorable for the debarkation of troops; and the bays and inlets being all obstructed by shoals or bars, no landing can be effected, but by boats, except up the Mississippi; and that has a bar at its mouth, which shoals to 13 or 14 feet water.

On the 7th of December, commodore Patterson, the naval commander at New Orleans, received a letter from Pensacola, dated on the 5th, stating that a British fleet of 60 sail, having on board a large body of troops, had arrived off the bar, and were destined for New Orleans. The commodore immediately ordered the gun-boats at the station to proceed to the passes Mariana and Christiana, leading into lake Borgne; by which, and lake Pontchartrain, it was thought

* Darby's Louisiana, p. 18[illegible].

the British would make their approaches. As an additional protection, the Rigolets, forming the communication between lakes Borgne and Pontchartrain, were defended by a small work, named Petite Coquille fort. Detachments of troops had also been sent out, to fell timber across every small bayou or creek, leading from the lakes; and through which a passage for boats could be afforded. The precaution was even taken, in some of the bayous, to sink large frames, and then fill them with earth. To prevent any approach by the Mississippi, general Jackson went himself to superintend the direction of the defences at Fort St. Philip, situated on the left bank of the river, about 40 miles from the Balize. Besides increasing the strength of this fort, the general ordered the immediate construction of two batteries on the opposite side of the river. It is now time to attend to the progress of the expedition.

On the 8th of December, vice-admiral Cochrane, in the Tonnant, along with several other ships, arrived and anchored off the Chandeleur islands. On the same day, two of the American gun-boats fired at the Armide as she, along with the Seahorse and Sophie, was passing down, within the chain of small islands that runs parallel to the shore, from Mobile towards Lake Borgne. Three other gun-boats were presently discovered cruizing in the lake. On the 10th,

11th, and 12th, the remainder of the men-of-war and troop-ships arrived; the 74s anchoring off Chandeleur island; the frigates and smaller vessels between Cat island and the main, not far from the entrance to Lake Borgne. The commander of the American gun-boats, fearing an attack, had, since the 11th, put his boats in the best possible condition.* The bayou Catalan, or Bienvenu, at the head of Lake Borgne being the contemplated point of disembarkation, the distance from the anchorage at Cat island to the bayou 62 miles, and the principal means of transport open boats, it became impossible that any movement of the troops could take place, until these gun-boats were destroyed. It was also an object to get possession of them in a serviceable state, that they might assist, as well in transporting the troops, as in the attack of any of the enemy's forts in the route; therefore, 42 launches, armed with 24, 18, and 12-pound carronades, and three unarmed gigs, carrying, altogether, about 980 seamen and marines, placed under the orders of captain Lockyer, of the Sophie, left the ships on the night of the 12th. For the details of the short battle, ending in the capture of five gun-boats, and an armed sloop, the reader is referred to the British and American official accounts;† upon the latter of which we shall proceed to make a few observations.

* Latour's War in Louisiana, p 59.

† App. Nos. 78. 79. 80. 81. and 82.

It does not appear, by captain Lockyer's letter, than any attack was made upon the Seahorse. Her destruction, therefore, by her commander, could only have been from a dread that she would be attacked; or, if she was attacked, no difficulty, and no casualties beyond her destruction, occurred on either side. This is confirmed, as well by the American return of loss, as by the proceedings of the court of inquiry, held upon captain Jones and his officers; in which neither the Seahorse nor Mr. Johnson, her commander, is at all named. Captain Jones seems to have mistaken the hour at which captain Roberts was detached to take the Alligator, for the time of her capture: from which service the division of boats did not return, till the capture of gun-boat No. 156 had been effected. The "deliberate fire" from one long 32, and four long 24s, did, owing to the tardy approach of the boats against "the force of the current," produce "much effect;" and, till the latter came within range of their carronades, could not be returned. It is singular that a writer, who gives captain Jones's letter in his Appendix, should describe the latter's "objects of so small a size," as "barges almost as large as the gun-boats themselves."* Captain Jones says, "two boats sank." We can assure him, that no other boat sank than the Tonnant's launch; and

* Latour's War in Louisiana, p. 61.

every man in her was saved. The court of inquiry has preferred "several barges"* to "two boats." Major Latour himself thinks "a great number of barges and launches"† better than either. Captain Jones's account of the duration of the action must include the time during which, for the reasons already given, he had the firing all to himself. In less than 20 minutes after the British got alongside of the flag gun-boat, the whole five vessels were in their possession. The defence of the commodore's gun-boat did credit to all on board; nor could the others, when she was captured, have possibly withstood the force operating against them. It is captain Jones's commentators with whom we have more particularly to do. This officer must excuse us for remarking, that his "correct statement" would better have deserved the name, had he contrasted the nature and caliber, as well as the number, of his own, with the number and caliber of his enemy's guns. Why omit to notice the 12 swivels, or half-pounders, or the two 5½ inch howitzers, which were captured among his guns? We will not dispute the numbers of his "effective" crews; yet, according to major Latour, the *effective* crew of gun-boat No. 65, which had been left to assist in guarding the Mississippi, amounted to 40 men.‡ This gentleman's zeal

* Latour's War in Louisiana, p. cxxxiii. † Ibid. 61.
‡ Ibid. p. 191.

has carried him rather too far. Out of the statement in captain Jones's letter, that his vessels, at 2 P.M. on the 13th, "were in 12 or 18 inches less water than their draught," the major has made out that, in the action on the 14th, "it was impossible for the gun-boats to manœuvre," because "several of them were sunk 18 inches in the mud;"* and this, in spite of captain Jones's statement:" At 3, 30, (on the 13th,) the flood-tide had commenced; got under weigh, making the best of my way towards the Petite Coquille."§ Captain Jones, in his estimate of our loss, rather over-rated the prowess of his men, as will be seen by the British returns.‡ Major Latour, as a proof how much he is influenced by "the duty of impartiality" and a "due regard to truth," scruples not to account for nearly two-thirds of this loss, by, what he calls, the "plain fact,"—that "180 men went down in one of the barges which were sunk."† After having already stated that no barge was sunk, nor men drowned, we have only to add, that the largest number of men in any one of the barges was 31. If we seem to pass over our old friends Messieurs Thomson, O'Connor, and Smith, it is not because their statements are less extravagant than those of our two new acquaintances, but because the latter enter more largely into the events of

* Latour's War in Louisiana, p. 61. † Ibid p. 235.

‡ App. No. 79. § App. No. 80.

the Louisiana war. Mr. John Henry Eaton, the biographist of general Jackson, taking the hint from major Latour, about the American gun-boats and British barges being nearly of the same size, presents his readers with the following statement:—

	Boats.	Men.	Guns.
" The British had	43	1200	43
The Americans,	5	182	23
	38	1018	20"*

Nothing could happen better; because it gives us an opportunity of exhibiting a statement also. Supposing Mr. Eaton not to have known, that the smallest of his " boats" was 75 tons burthen, the History of the Tripolitan War would have informed him, that two or three of them had crossed the Atlantic and back in safety. Now for our statement:—

		United States' " boat" No. 23.		" His Britannic Majesty's brig Hunter." †	
Broadside-metal in pounds,	long guns,	50		16	
	carronades,	9		12	
			59		28
Complement,			41		39
Size in tons,			112		74

And did not the American commodore Macdonough, in an official letter, designate two British vessels, the largest of which was two tons smaller than Mr. Eaton's " boat," as " two sloops of war"?‡ We need only add to what has already appeared respecting the state of

* Eaton's Life of Jackson, p. 261.

† Nav. Hist. of the United States, Vol. I. p. 249

‡ James's Nav. Occur. p. 420.

equipment of American gun-boats,* that those taken by captain Lockyer had polished mahogany traversing gun-carriages, and were lavishly supplied with ordnance-stores of every description.

The capture of the gun-boats having thus left open the entrance by the lakes, great consternation prevailed at New Orleans. General Jackson, with a promptitude highly to his credit, redoubled his exertions; and, with what, in our *despotic* country, would be considered a stretch of power, proclaimed martial law. By way of sounding the British as to the route they meant to take, commodore Patterson, on the 15th of December, sent a purser and doctor of the navy, with a flag, under pretence "of obtaining correct information as to the situation of the officers and crews made prisoners on board the gun-boats, and of endeavouring to obtain their being suffered to return to town on parole."† Admiral Cochrane very properly told them, "that their visit was unseasonable, and that he could not permit them to return, until the intended attack was made, and the fate of New Orleans decided."† This was construed into a "wanton outrage on propriety," and all sorts of abuse lavished upon the British character.

On the 16th the first division of troops, consisting of the 85th regiment, landed at Isle aux Poix, a small swampy spot, at the mouth of

* See p. 200. † Latour's War in Louisiana, p. 75.

the Pearl river; about 30 miles from the anchorage, and nearly the same distance from the bayou Catalan, or Bienvenu, intended as the point of disembarkation. Various causes, as detailed in admiral Cochrane's letter,* delayed the arrival of the boats at the fishermen's village, near the entrance of the bayou, till midnight on the 22d; when, immediately, the advance, consisting of 760 rank and file of the 4th, 402 rank and file of the 85th, and 396 rank and file of the 95th regiments, also 100 sappers, miners, and artillery men, with two 3-pounders, and 30 rocketeers, in all 1688 men, under the command of colonel Thornton of the 85th, commenced ascending the bayou Mazant, or principal branch of the Bienvenu; and, at four o'clock on the following morning, landed at the extremity of Villeré's canal, running from the bayou Mazant, towards the Mississippi.

As the country around New Orleans possesses very peculiar features, a slight digression may be necessary. The bayou Bienvenu is the creek through which all the waters of a large basin, or swamp, about 80 miles in extent, bounded on the north by the Mississippi, on the west by New Orleans, on the north-west, by bayou Sauvage, or Chef-menteur, and on the east by Lake Borgne, into which it empties. It receives the streams of several other bayous, formed by the

* App. No. 99.

waters of the surrounding cypress swamps and prairies, as well as of innumerable little streams from the low grounds along the river. It is navigable for vessels of 100 tons, 12 miles from its mouth. Its breadth is from 110 to 150 yards, and it has six feet water on the bar, at common tides, and nine feet at spring tides. Its principal branch is that which is called bayou Mazant, which runs towards the south-west, and receives the waters of the canals of the plantations of Villeré, Lacoste, and Laronde, upon which the British afterwards established their principal encampment. The level of the great basin, on the bank of the principal bayou, is usually 12 feet below the banks of the Mississippi. The overflowing of the waters of all those bayous and canals, occasioned by the tide of the sea, or by the winds raising the waters in the lake, forms, on all their banks, deposits of slime, which are continually raising them above the rest of the soil; so that the interval between two bayous is below the level of their banks, and the soil is generally covered with water and mud, in which aquatic plants, or large reeds, of the height of from six to eight feet, grow in abundance. It sometimes happens that the rains, or the filtrated waters, collected in these intervals, or basins, not finding a vent, form what are called *trembling prairies;* which are at all times impassable to men and domestic animals. The land in Lower Louisiana slopes in the inverse direction of the soil of other countries, being most elevated on the sides of the rivers, and sinking as it recedes from them. The Mississippi, at New Orleans, periodically swells 14 or 15 feet; and is then from three to four feet above the level of its banks. To confine its waters within its bed, dikes or ramparts, called in Louisiana *levées*, have been raised on its banks, from the highlands towards its mouth, a little above the level of the highest swells; without which precaution, the lands would be entirely overflowed, from four to five months in the year. The reader will now be better able to appreciate the difficulties our troops and seamen had to encounter, in transporting themselves, their baggage, provisions, and artillery, to the scene of operations on the left bank of the Mississippi.

The spot at which the British advance had landed, was about a mile from a cypress wood, or swamp, of nearly a mile and a half in depth, running parallel to the Mississippi; between which and the border of the wood, is a slip of land, from 15 to 1700 yards wide, intersected by strong horizontal railings, and several wet ditches, or canals, and principally planted with sugar canes. Several large houses, with their out-offices and negro-huts, are scattered, at irregular distances, over this tract; along which passes, near to the levée, or bank of the river, the high road to New Orleans.

At about noon on the 23d, the piquets of the British advanced division arrived at M. Villeré's house, standing upon the road-side, at the distance of about six miles from the city. Here a company of the 3d regiment of militia was surprised and captured. Soon afterwards, colonel Thornton, with the remainder of his division, arrived, and bivouacked upon the higher ground of the plantation, or that nearest to the river. This point had been reconnoitered, since the night of the 18th, by the honorable captain Spencer, of the Carron, and lieutenant Peddie, of the quarter-master-general's department. These officers, with a smuggler as their guide, had pulled up the bayou in a canoe, and advanced to the high road, without seeing any persons, or preparations.

After general Wilkinson, whose local knowledge in this quarter no one will dispute, has stated, that lieutenant Jones, of the late American flotilla, in answer to the particular enquiries put to him respecting the strength of Fort-Coquille, defending the entrance to Lake Pontchartraine, reported it to mount, instead of eight, —"40 pieces of artilley," and to be garrisoned by, not 50,—but "500 men," and that, in consequence of the supposed strength of that position, the British determined to advance by the bayou Bienvenu, he says:—"To this direction of the invaders, and their halt after they had reached the bank of the Mississippi, may, under God, be ascribed the salvation of New Orleans, and general Jackson's merited fame. By this approach, the enemy placed the American army in their front, leaving its rear open to every species of resource, and its flanks perfectly secured by the river and the cypress swamps; a situation the most desirable to a military chief, because it enables him to condense his force, and disembarrass his mind of every care and every concern, but that of marshalling his men and preparing for battle. Yet, as the enemy had, unperceived, got within two hours' march of the city, if they had proceeded directly forward, the advantages of general Jackson's position, which afterwards became all important, could not have availed him; because the enemy would have carried surprise with them, would have found the American corps dispersed,* without concert, and unprepared for combat; and, making the attack with a superior numerical force of disciplined troops, against a body composed chiefly of irregulars: under such circumstances, no soldier of experience will pause for a conclusion. The most heroic bravery would have proved unavailing, and the capital of Louisiana, with its millions of property, would have been lost. But, blinded by confidence, beguiled by calculations injurious to

* App. No. 85.

the honor of the high-mettled patriot-sons of Louisiana, and considering the game safe, they gave themselves up to security, took repose, and waited for reinforcements." *

Why the British did not approach by the way of Lake Pontchartrain, and take the city of New Orleans in the rear, the general has himself, partly explained, in the *ruse de guerre* of lieutenant Jones, or, rather, of Mr. Shields, commodore Patterson's purser. We say, *partly* explained, because we know this route was suggested by several experienced British officers. Had general Wilkinson been aware that, instead of "4980,†" major-general Keane, even when his reinforcement came up at 10 o'clock on the night of the 23d, had only 2050 men; and had the general reflected, what labour and fatigue these men had undergone since their departure from Isle aux Poix, on the morning of the preceding day, he would not have condemned the British for taking repose on their arrival at Villeré's; more especially, when, instead of "3000," or, as major Letour says, "5000," the British had been informed by Mr. Ducros, and several other prisoners, (who, the night previous, had settled their plans,) that there were from "13 to 14000" troops in the city, and from "3 to 4000" at a fort at the "English turn," ‡ a bend of the

* Wilkinson's Mem. Vol. I. p. 537.

† Latour's War in Louisiana, p. 104. ‡ Ibid. p. 86.

river, about 10 miles below the British encampment.

General Jackson received intelligence of the arrival of the British at Villeré's farm, at about two o'clock P.M. on the 23d; and major Letour, who was the reconnoitring officer, "judged that their number must amount to 16 or 1800."* Not satisfied with this account, major-general Jackson sent forward "colonel Haynes, inspector general of the division;" but, says major Latour, "he had no opportunity to form a correct estimate of their number, which he made to amount to no more than 200 men." Here we have an important fact; accounting for general Jackson's ready advance to the attack; and affording an answer to the loads of bombastical stuff, so characteristic of American accounts. Major Latour gives a detailed estimate of general Jackson's force, on this occasion, making it amount to "2131 men."† The Carolina schooner, which combined in the attack, mounted twelve 12-pound carronades, and two long guns of the same caliber, with a crew of about 90 men. When she opened her fire, several British soldiers, taking her to be an unarmed vessel, were actually standing upon the levée, looking at her. The Caroline had not, at this time, any other vessel in company.‡

The reinforcement that reached colonel Thorn-

* Latour's War in Louis. p. 88. † Ib. p. 105. ‡ App. No. 83.

ton on the night of the attack amounted, not to "2900 men," but to only 230 rank and file of the 21st, and 140 rank and file of the 93d regiments; total 370 men: making the aggregate British force, just at the close of the attack, 2050 men. With these explanatory particulars before him, the reader can take the details of the battle from the official accounts on both sides.* The American commentators, particularly our two new historians, have indulged themselves in such a rhapsody of falsehoods and contradictions, that we shall leave their "faithful histories" to work their own effect. On the morning of the 24th, the United States' ship Louisiana, of sixteen long 12-pounders, and a crew of upwards of 130 men, joined the Carolina. The loss of the British, on the 23d and 24th, the details of which are given in the official return,† amounted to 46 killed, 167 wounded, and 62 missing: total 275. The Americans, who, as the British 3-pounders were not brought into use, had only musketry to contend with, sustained a loss, on the 23d, as particularized in their return,‡ of 24 killed, 115 wounded, and 74 missing; total 213.

The enemy's ship and schooner continuing a heavy and destructive cannonade upon the British troops, a battery of, not as major Latour says, "several 12 and 18-pounders," but of five

* App. No. 83, 85, and 87. † App. No. 84. ‡ App. No. 86.

9 and 6-pounders, the heaviest artillery which had then been got up, was, by day-light on the morning of the 27th, in readiness to act. The second hot shot lodged in the schooner's main-hold, under her cables, and presently set her on fire. Soon afterwards, her crew, with the loss of one killed and six wounded, took to their boats, and reached the shore. By some gross mismanagement on our part, the artillery, instead of being, immediately that the Carolina was seen to be on fire, directed against the powerful ship Louisiana, whose "powder-magazine was above water,"* continued to play upon the flaming wreck. When the latter exploded, which was not till an hour after the commencement of the firing, the British guns were directed against the ship; but her commander, aware of the danger to which the situation of his magazine exposed him, had wisely employed "100 men of his crew,"* in towing the Louisiana out of gun-shot.

Since the evening of the 25th, major-general sir Edward Pakenham, and major-general Gibbs, had arrived at head-quarters; the former to take command of the army, now augmented, by fresh arrivals from the anchorage, to about,—not, as major Latour says, "9 or 10000,"† but—5040 rank and file. The prevailing frosts had greatly improved the road from the landing place; and

* Latour's War in Louisiana, p. 118. † Ibid. p. 125.

rendered a passage across the swamps, in most directions, less difficult than usual. At this time the real strength of Fort-Coquille was generally known in camp; and some one proposed for the army to be moved back, by a route pointed out, to Lake Pontchartrain; and thence, after taking the forts Coquille and St. John, (in which there would be no difficulty,) to proceed down bayou St. John, to the rear of New Orleans. The attack in front, with such an army, was, however, thought to be the readiest, as it certainly was the boldest mode.

There is no means of judging of the strength of the American position, but by a full description. Fortunately, we are enabled to give that in the very words of the engineer who superintended the construction of the lines. By way of still further elucidation, we have made use of major Latour's plan or sketch;* which, although it has reference to the operations of a subsequent day, represents, except as to some of the guns, the same lines which were now about to be attacked. —"Jackson's lines, within five miles of the city of New Orleans, and running along the limits of Rodriguez's and Chalmette's plantations, were but one of those antient mill-races so common in Louisiana, extending from the bank of the river to the cypress swamp. It has already been seen, from my description of the form of the soil

* See Plate VII.

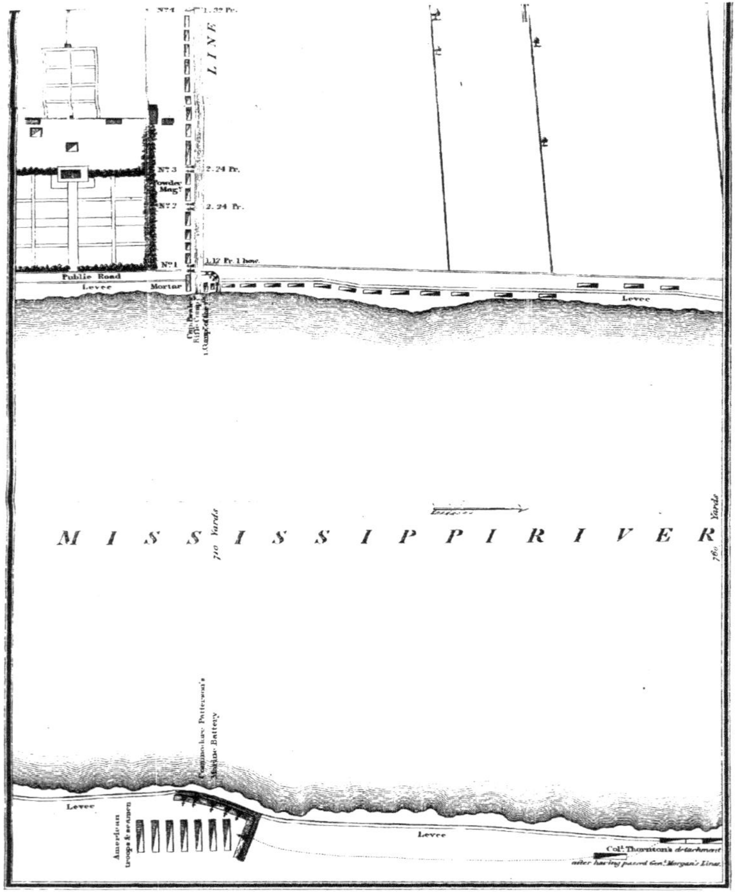

Published as the Act directs, by William James, May 11th 1818.

Mutlow Sculp.

To face p. 364. Vol. 2.

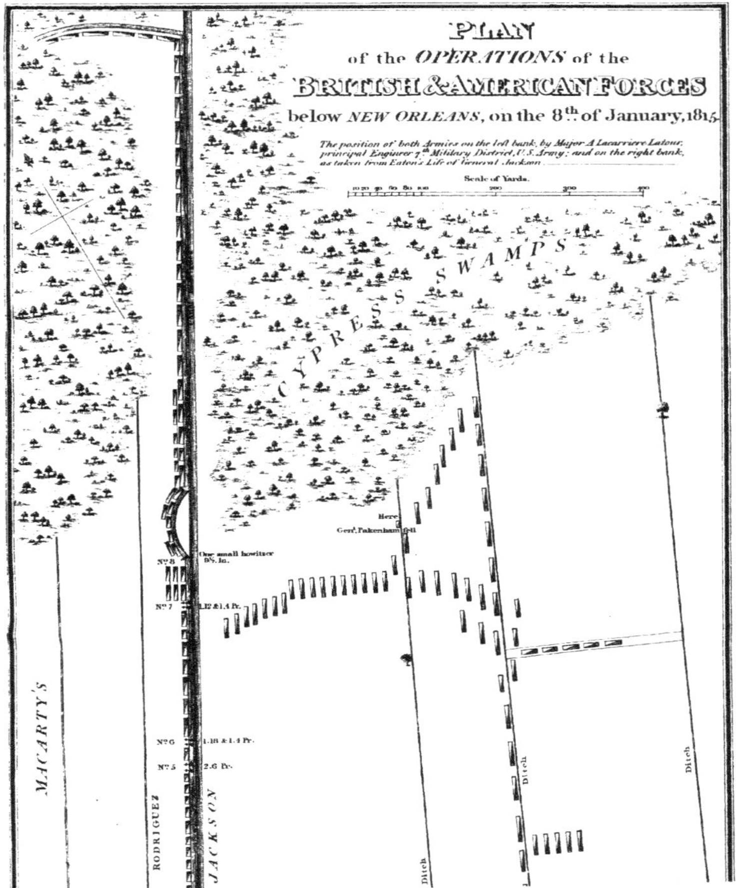

in Lower Louisiana, and from its shelving from the river towards the swamps, that, when the Mississippi is swelled to its greatest height, the level of the surface of its waters is some feet above that of the contiguous soil, and from 12 to 15 feet above that of the praries and bayous, which, at those periods, receive the waters flowing from the Mississippi. To add to the mass and the force of the water, the planters dig canals a few feet deep, throwing the earth on both sides, so as to afford a mass of water from eight to eleven feet deep; and, at the head of these canals, which are commonly 25 feet wide, are constructed saw-mills. The canal on which Jackson's lines were formed, had long been abandoned, having no longer any mill to turn; so that its banks had fallen in, and raised its bottom, which was covered with grass, presenting, rather, the appearance of an old draining ditch, than of a canal. On the 24th of December, general Jackson had taken this position; and, that it was well chosen, will sufficiently appear, on an inspection of the map. I will only observe, that those lines leave the least possible space between the river and the wood, and that from the lines to Villeré's canal, the depth of the high land continually increases, and is at Laronde's plantation nearly three times as great as at the lines. As soon as this position was chosen, the troops began to raise a parapet, leaving the ditch as it was, except that, by cutting the road, it was laid under water, as there was then a temporary rise of the river. Earth was fetched from the rear of the line, and thrown carelessly on the left (or inner) bank; where the earth had been thrown when the bank was originally dug. The bank on the right (or outer) side, being but little elevated above the soil, formed a kind of glacis. All the pales of the fences in the vicinity were taken to line the parapet, and prevent the earth from falling into the canal. All this was done at various intervals, and by different corps, owing to the frequent mutations in the disposition of the troops. This circumstance, added to the cold, and to incessant rain, rendered it impossible to observe any regularity as to the thickness and height of the parapet; which, in some places, was as much as 20 feet thick at the top, though hardly five feet high; whilst, in other places, the enemy's balls went through it at the base. On the 1st of January, there was but a very small proportion of the line able to withstand the balls; but, on the 8th of January, the whole extent, as far as the wood, was proof against the enemy's cannon. The length of the line was about a mile, somewhat more than half of which ran from the river to the wood, the remainder extending into the wood, where the line took a direction towards the left, which rested on a cypress swamp almost impassable. Enormous holes in the soil, made impassable by their being full of water from the canal, rendered a bend in the line* unavoidable."†

The manner in which the artillery was afterwards distributed, and the number and caliber of the pieces, appear on the plan. It is only necessary to state here, that they consisted of one 32, three 24, one 18, three 12, and two 6-pounder long-guns, and one $9\frac{1}{2}$ and one 6-inch howitzer; total 12 guns: but not above half of them were mounted on the 28th of December. In case of being driven from this strong line, general Jackson had caused to be constructed two other lines in his rear; the nearest, or Dupré's line, at the distance of a mile and a half, and the third, or Montreuil line, at the distance of two miles and a quarter, from his outer, or main line. Nor had the opposite, or right bank of the river, which even exceeded the left in capability of defence, been neglected. Boisgervais' canal, at the distance of three miles from the city, had been selected; and the labour of 150 negroes, for six days, completed the parapet along the whole length of the canal, and levelled the earth to form a glacis on the opposite side. There was, also, opposite to the city, on the bank of the river, a strong redoubt, formed by a brick-kiln; surrounded by a ditch, 25 feet wide, with a glacis and parapet. A palisade extended along its whole length on the

* See Plate VII. † Latour's War in Louisiana, p. 149.

inside. The redoubt was furnished with a powder-magazine, and mounted with two 24-pounders; which commanded both the road and the river. *

The British commander determined to make a demonstation upon the enemy's fortified line on the left bank. Accordingly, at day-light on the morning of the 28th, the troops moved forward in two columns; driving in the whole of the enemy's line of out-posts. During the advance of the British, the ship which had been so unfortunately spared, opened a heavy enfilading fire upon them; and continued it during the whole of the forenoon.† Her fire, and that from the enemy's heavy pieces at his works, did considerable execution. On the 30th commodore Patterson planted behind the levée on the right bank a 24-pounder, and on the next day, two 12-pounders; with which he threw shot quite into the British camp. Our loss between the 25th and 31st, as detailed in the return, amounted to 16 killed, 38 wounded, and two missing; total 56.‡ The Americans acknowledge a loss of nine killed; and eight wounded,§ on shore, and of one wounded on board the ship; total 18.

By the evening of the 31st, after considerable difficulty, ten ship 18-pounders, and four 24-pound carronades were brought up the canal, in boats, and four of the former were placed in

* Latour's War in Louisiana, p. 125.

† App. Nos. 89 and 90. ‡ App. No. 94. § App. No. 91.

a battery, formed with hogsheads of sugar, on the main road, to fire upon the ship, if she dropped down the river. Some other batteries were, in the mean time, constructed. The first of January was ushered in with a very thick fog, which did not begin to disperse till towards eight o'clock. As soon as the horizon cleared up, the British opened their batteries upon the American line. "Our batteries," says major Latour, "were the principal objects against which the enemy's fire was directed; but we were not less intent in demolishing his; for, in about an hour's time, our balls dismounted several of his guns; and, when the firing ceased, the greater part of his artillery was unfit for service. Justice obliges us to acknowledge, that the fire of the British was, for a long time, vigorously kept up, and well-directed."* All this while, commodore Patterson's guns, on the opposite bank, shared in the engagement.† A sudden change now took place in the weather; and, so deep was the soil, that it required the greatest exertions of the whole army, aided by the seamen, at this time serving with it, to retire the remaining guns a short distance, before daylight the next morning.

Failing to make any impression upon the enemy's parapet, and unable to approach his flanks; on his right, owing to the river, and on

* Latour's War in Louisiana, p. 133. † App. No. 92.

his left, owing to the impassable swamp by which it was so well secured, the British commander-in-chief determined to wait for the expected reinforcements, under major-general Lambert. We may observe, in this place, what great advantage would have been derived from the 2 or 3000 Choctaw Indians and Negroes, who were ready, and *might* have been brought from West Florida. During the 2d and 3d of January commodore Patterson, having landed four more 12-pounders, and erected a furnace for heating shot, caused, till the evening of the 5th, considerable destruction in the British camp. Our loss, as detailed in the returns,* amounted to 32 killed, 44 wounded, and two missing; total 78: that of the Americans, on the 1st of January, 11 killed, and 23 wounded; total 34.† On the four succeeding days, the cannonade, owing to the ruinous state of the British batteries, was wholly on the side of the Americans. "Our artillery," says major Latour, "continued to fire on the enemy; and, whenever a group of four or five men shewed themselves, they were instantly dispersed by our balls or shells. The advantage we derived from that almost incessant cannonading, on both banks of the Mississippi, was, that we exercised our gunners, annoyed the enemy to such a degree, that he could not work at any fortifica-

* App. No. 95. † App. No. 93.

tion; nor, indeed, come within the reach of our cannon by day, and was deprived of all repose during the night."*

On the 4th of January general Jackson received the long-expected reinforcement of 2250 Kentuckians;† and, on the 6th, the British received their expected reinforcement of the 7th and 43d regiments. On that very day a deserter informed general Jackson of the intended attack; as well as that the British were digging out Villeré's canal, and extending it, in order to get their boats into the river, ready for a simultaneous attack on the opposite side. In the meanwhile major-general Morgan had thrown up two fresh lines, in advance of his works at Boisgervais' canal. Upon these, and commodore Patterson's battery on the river-side,‡ were mounted 16 guns. The last-named officer actually saw, and reported, contrary to the belief of sir Alexander Cochrane,§ the operations on Villeré's canal:‖ in short, the Americans were fully apprized, that their works on both sides of the river would be attacked on the morning of the 8th. "In our camp," says major Latour, "all was composure; the officers were ordered to direct their subalterns to be ready on the first signal. Half the troops passed the

* Latour's War in Louisiana, p. 143.

† Eaton's Life of Jackson, p. 332.

‡ See Plate VII.

§ App. No. 99.

‖ App. No. 102.

night behind the breastwork; relieving each other occasionally. Every one waited for day with anxiety and impatience, but with calm intrepidity; expecting to be vigorously attacked, and knowing that the enemy had then from 12 to 15,000 bayonets to bring into action, besides 2000 sailors, and some marines."* This preliminary puff might pass, but for the statement about the strength of the British forces. We will first point out where the major contradicts himself. His "list of the several corps composing the British army, at the time of its landing on the shores of the Mississippi, with an estimate of their respective force,"—wherein we find the "40th regiment," and a "detachment of the 62d regiment," that did not land till the 11th of January, stated, together, at "1360 men," the "rocket-brigade, artillery, drivers, engineers, sappers and miners," at "1500," and the "royal marines, and sailors taken from the fleet," as high as "3500,"—makes a total of *only* "14450;"† less, by 2000 and upwards, than the amount which he had previously told us was "ready for action." Again; the numbers upon the major's diagram, or plan of the battle of the 8th, run thus: "Main attack of the British, supposed to be between 8 and 9000 strong;"—"Left column of the British,

* Latour's War in Louisiana, p. 154.

† Ibid. his Appendix, No. 44.

supposed 1200 strong." Add to this number the 800 stated as the British force upon the right bank ; and we have, as the total upon both sides of the river, 12500, instead of " from 12 to 15000, besides 2000 sailors, and some marines."

This is the enemy's, now for the British, account of our force. Previously to the attack on the morning of the 8th, we had, including fatigue-parties and piquets, and every description of force on shore, the following rank and file: 14th light dragoons, 295 ; royal artillery, 570 ; sappers and miners, 98 ; staff corps, 57 ; 4th foot, 747 ; 7th, 750 ; 21st, 800 ; 43d, 820 ; 44th, 427 ; 85th, 298 ; 93d, 775 ; 95th, 276 ; and 1st and 5th West India regiments, (blacks,) 1040 ; total, 6953 men ; just 2643 less than major Latour's estimated strength of those 14 corps. By adding 1200, for the seamen and marines from the fleet, we have 8153 for the total amount of the British on shore. Deducting 853 men for the fatigue-parties, piquets, guards at the hospitals, &c. leaves 7300 men for the British force, " ready for action," on both sides of the river, at or before day-light, on the morning of the 8th of January. To this force was added a battery, hastily thrown up, of six 18-pounders ; besides a brigade of 9, 6, and 3-pounders, and one howitzer. With the details of the force at general Jackson's lines, we have nothing to do. The following extract from Mr. O'Connor's book will suffice. "From an official account," says he, "it appeared, that the number of men under command of general Jackson, and actually engaged against the enemy, on the 8th of January, amounted to 4698."* This was on the left bank: on the right bank, we have 400 men, sent across, on the morning of the 8th, under the celebrated French general, Humbert, and 1500,† already on that side, under major-general Morgan and commodore Patterson; making a total force, on both sides of the river, of 6198 men. The American artillery, including the batteries on the opposite bank, and only half the guns of the Louisiana, consisted of upwards of 30 pieces.

For the order of attack, and the disposition of the different corps, we must refer the reader to major-general Lambert's letter.‡ An unavoidable delay had occurred in getting the boats into the Mississippi; where they were required to carry across troops, in order to attack general Morgan's lines: and then a circumstance, which happened at the very onset, gave a fatal turn to the first misfortune. The 44th regiment, owing chiefly to the negligence of its commander, failed to be in readiness with the fascines and ladders. These had been placed in a redoubt, 1200 yards from the enemy's lines; by which

* Hist. of the War, p. 291.

† Eaton's Life of Jackson, p. 336; vide Erratum.

‡ App. No. 96.

redoubt the 44th, in its way from camp to its station, passed, till it arrived at the advanced battery, about 500 yards nearer to the enemy's line. The misunderstanding, for such it was, being now, for the first time, cleared up, the commanding officer of the 44th, lieutenant-colonel Mullins, (only a captain in the regiment,) sent back 300 men, under lieutentant-colonel Debbeig, to bring up the fascines and ladders. Before the 44th returned, the firing had commenced; and many of the men threw down their "heavy" loads, and took to their muskets. *There was not one ladder placed*;* although some were thrown in the ditch. What followed we cannot describe better, than in the sworn depositions of two distinguished officers, examined at colonel Mullins's court-martial. Major sir John Tylden, of the 43d regiment, says:—"On the morning of the 8th of January, I was in the field, as senior officer on the adjutant-general's department. I accompanied sir E. Pakenham, shortly after four o'clock, to the house of major-general Gibbs. Immediately on his arrival, general Gibbs reported to sir E. Pakenham, in my presence, that colonel Mullins had neglected to obey the order given him the evening before, in not having his regiment at the head of the column, with the fascines and ladders, but that he had immediately, on finding it out, sent an officer to the regiment to hurry them on; that the mistake

* Court-martial on lieutenant-colonel Mullins, p. 26.

might be rectified, and that he was in momentary expectation of a report from that regiment. Sir E. Pakenham then ordered me to find out the 44th regiment, and to know if they had got the fascines and ladders, and to ascertain (the probability) of their getting up in their situation in column. I did so, and found the 44th regiment moving off at the redoubt, just before day, in a most irregular and unsoldierlike manner, with the fascines and ladders. I then returned, after some time, to sir E. Pakenham, and reported the circumstance to him; stating that, by the time which had elapsed since I left them, they must have arrived in their situation in column. Shortly after the signal of attack was given, I rode with sir E. Pakenham toward the column. In passing towards the head of the column, we saw several parties of the 44th regiment straggling about the ground with their fascines and ladders; and some of them had, even then, commenced firing. On arriving at the column, a check and confusion had taken place, and the firing was becoming general throughout the whole of the column. General Gibbs came up to sir Edward Pakenham, and said, in my hearing, 'I am sorry to have to report to you, the troops will not obey me; they will not follow me.' At this moment there certainly was great confusion prevailing in the column. Sir E. Pakenham pulled off his hat, and rode to the head of the column, and cheered the men on, and in that act fell. At this time, I had just returned from the other flank of the column, and having been at both flanks, and at the head of the column, I can positively assert, there was not a single man of the 44th regiment in front. I then rode to the rear, to report the death of sir Edward Pakenham. In going to the rear, I saw several parties of the 21st and 44th regiments running to the rear, and firing in all directions, in the most disorderly manner I ever witnessed. I also saw, scattered in several parts of the field, several of the fascines and ladders. I reported the substance of my testimony to major-general sir John Lambert." * — Major M'Dougal, of the 85th regiment, says thus:— "I was aide de camp to major-general Pakenham, and, on the signal of attack being given on the morning of the 8th January, I accompanied him to the front. He expressed himself in the strongest terms, relative to the 44th regiment. The column of attack appeared to be moving in a regular manner; and he expressed his confidence on the event of the attack: however, a firing commenced; and, presently afterwards, I saw many individuals of the 44th regiment, as well as a group of three or four, scattered over the field, some of them running to the rear with the fascines on their shoulders. Sir Edward Pakenham said,—'For shame, recollect you are

* Court-martial on lieutenant-colonel Mullins, p. 10.

British soldiers; this is the road you ought to take;' but with little avail. On getting up to the columns the firing had extended to the rear, and the whole column was a mass of firing and confusion, and the head of the column had checked. Sir Edward Pakenham placed himself in front; and, by his exertions, got the firing very nearly to cease, although not altogether; and the column which he led in person began to move forward. When he had conducted them about 30 or 40 yards, he received a wound, and his horse at the same moment was shot under him; and, almost immediately afterwards, when he had mounted the second horse, he received another shot, which deprived him of life, and, by the fall of their leader, deprived the column of its best chance of recovering success. On his fall, the firing recommenced with all its fury; and, beyond the spot where the general led them, the head of the column did not advance. The ground presented no obstacle to the advance of the column, or any thing that should have occasioned straggling in a corps regularly formed and duly attended to, had the regiment originally been properly formed. At no period in the field did I see any part of the 44th regiment in a body; there were some at the head of the column, many at the flanks and rear of the column: I particularly remarked several of the soldiers of that regiment throwing down the fascines and ladders to commence firing. It is my opinion, that the whole confusion of the column proceeded from the original defective formation of the 44th; the fall of sir Edward Pakenham deprived the column of its best chance of success; and, had the column moved forward according to order, the enemy's lines would have been carried with little loss. When the fire from our column commenced, the fire from the enemy's was but mere spit of fire, nothing to check a moving column."* We may here notice a slight error in major-general Lambert's despatch. It was brigade-major Wilkinson, and not major-general sir Edward Pakenham, who fell on the glacis of the enemy's line. The latter fell near the spot marked on the diagram.†

Had it not been for the misbehaviour of the 44th regiment, sir Edward Pakenham's life might have been spared; and, with such an officer to command in chief, the day must have been ours. The two officers, the best able to succeed him, fell also; one mortally, the other severely wounded. It is idle to accuse the 44th and 21st, (part of which regiment equally misbehaved,) of cowardice. To refute such a charge, it is sufficient to state, that the men of those regiments were chiefly Irishmen. The 21st

* Court-martial on lieutenant-colonel Mullins, p. 8.
† See Plate VII.

and 44th were not, however, as major Latour jeeringly calls them, " Wellington's heroes :" they came from the Mediterranean,—from Tarragona; and were, certainly, the two worst disciplined corps upon the field at New Orleans. The second battalion of the 44th had gained repute under the duke of Wellington, and been always in a high state of discipline: it was at this time in Europe. Where was the proper commanding officer of the first battalion of the 44th? We are sorry to be compelled to say, that colonel Brooke was present, but not at the head of his regiment; owing, it would seem, to some pique or misunderstanding. Comparing his competency with the notorious incompetency of lieutenant-colonel Mullins, colonel Brooke has much to answer for. Major Latour having heard, as he could not fail to do, that the check in the advance of the right British column arose from the want of the fascines and ladders, describes the men as " shouldering their muskets, and all carrying fascines, and some with ladders."* Here he is outdone by Mr. O'Connor; who, in his representation of the action, has actually placed a ladder, and a long one too, directly against the parapet.

Colonel Rennie, of the engineers, at the head of a division of the British left brigade, under major-general Keane, was directed, as we gather

* Latour's War in Louisiana, p. 154.

from the American accounts, (for the British official letter contains no details,) to storm an unfinished redoubt upon the enemy's right. "The detachment ordered against this place," says general Jackson's biographist, "formed the left of general Keane's command. Rennie executed his orders with great bravery; and, urging forward, arrived at the ditch. His advance was greatly annoyed by commodore Patterson's battery on the left bank, and the cannon mounted on the redoubt; but, reaching our works, and passing the ditch, Rennie, sword in hand, leaped on the wall, and, calling to his troops, bade them to follow: he had scarcely spoken, when he fell, by the fatal aim of our riflemen. Pressed by the impetuosity of superior numbers who were mounting the wall, and entering at the embrasures, our troops had retired to the line, in rear of the redoubt. A momentary pause ensued, but only to be interrupted with increased horrors. Captain Beal, with the city riflemen, cool and self possessed, perceiving the enemy in his front, opened upon them, and, at every discharge, brought the object to the ground. To advance, or maintain the point gained, was equally impracticable for the enemy: to retreat or surrender was the only alternative; for they already perceived the division on the right thrown into confusion, and hastily leaving the field."* The situation of these brave fellows, thus abandoned, may be easily conceived: they were, nearly all, killed or taken prisoners. The fire from the musketry ceased at about half-past eight; that from the artillery, not till half-past two in the afternoon. The British loss, on both banks, amounted to 290 killed; 1262 wounded; and 484 missing;† total, not, as the American accounts say, "about 2600," but 2036. As a proof what little opportunity there was, on the part of general Jackson's troops, for displaying any other qualities than skill in the use of the rifle and great guns, the American loss, on the left bank, amounted to no more than seven killed and six wounded; and, on both banks, to only 13 killed, 39 wounded, and 19 missing: total 71.‡

We shall conclude our account of the battle on the left bank of the Mississippi, with the opinions of two American, or rather of one French and one American military officer, upon the quality and behaviour of the British troops; as well as upon the merits of the plan of attack, in which they so unfortunately failed. "It is well known," says major Latour, "that agility is not the distinctive quality of British troops. Their movement is, in general, sluggish and difficult; steady, but too precise; or, at least, more suitable for a pitched battle, or behind intrenchments, than

* Eaton's Life of Jackson, p. 342. † App. No. 100.

‡ App. No. 103.

for an assault. The British soldiers showed, on this occasion, that it is not without reason that they are said to be deficient in agility. The enormous load they had to carry contributed, indeed, not a little to the difficulty of their movement: besides their knapsacks, usually weighing nearly 30 pounds, and their muskets, too heavy by, at least, one-third, almost all of them had to carry a fascine, from nine to 10 inches in diameter, and four feet long, made of sugar-canes, perfectly ripe, and consequently very heavy, or a ladder from 10 to 12 feet long."* "Instead of "almost all," only 300 of the British troops had to carry fascines and ladders; and these were, in truth, so heavy, especially when to be carried, in haste, nearly three quarters of a mile, that most of the men threw down their loads long before they reached the ditch, As there was an abundance of *dry* cane on the spot, it is rather surprising that the ripe or green should have been selected; particularly for the fascines. Owing to the rain that had been falling, as well as to general Jackson's having, by cutting down the levées, flooded the country, the ground over which the troops had to march, was not the best calculated for displaying their "agility." Major Latour proceeds:—"The duty of impartiality, incumbent on him who relates military events, obliges me to observe,

* Latour's War in Louisiana, p. 161.

that the attack made on Jackson's lines, by the British, on the 8th of January, must have been determined on by their generals, without any consideration of the ground, the weather, or the difficulties to be surmounted, before they could storm lines, defended by militia indeed, but by militia whose valor they had already witnessed, with soldiers bending under the weight of their loads; when a man, unincumbered, would, that day, have found it difficult to mount our breast-works, at leizure, and with circumspection, so extremely slippery was the soil. Yet those officers had had time, and abundant opportunity, to observe the ground, on which the troops were to act. Since their arrival on the banks of the Mississippi, they had sufficiently seen the effects of rainy weather, to form a just idea of the difficulty their troops must have experienced, in climbing up our intrenchments, even had the column been allowed to advance, without opposition, as far as the ditch. But they were blinded by their pride."* Major-general Wilkinson, on the same subject, says:—" On this memorable day, sir Edward Pakenham, disdaining to avail himself of local circumstances, or to profit by professional skill, determined to carry New Orleans at the point of the bayonet, in the face of day, exposing himself to showers of canister, and triple ranks of infantry and riflemen. He

* Latour's War in Louisiana, p. 161.

was slaughtered, and repulsed; and, as the whole operations were confined to the perpendicular march of columns against a straight line, defended by stationary batteries and battalions, the subject requires no further elucidation, than that the passive resolution of the American citizen vanquished the active courage of the British veteran."* In justice to sir Edward Pakenham's memory, it is right to state, that the attack was intended to be made before daylight, could the difficult and arduous service of tracking the boats to the Mississippi have been executed in time.†

At last, 50 barges, launches, and pinnaces were launched; and 298 of the 85th regiment, along with about 200 seamen and marines, under the command of colonel Thornton, were crossed over. Three of the boats, armed with carronades, called by that officer "gun-boats"‡ co-operated in the attack. The American force on this side was, as already stated, 1500 men. The progress and successful result of the expedition will be found, fully detailed, in the British and American official accounts.§ By the returns of loss on the 8th, only two of the 85th were killed; 41 wounded; and one missing. The seamen and marines (supposing none to have fallen on the left bank) lost four killed and 35 wounded;

* Wilkinson's Mem. Vol. I. p. 541. † App. No. 96.

‡ App. No. 97. § App. Nos. 97, 98, 101, and 102.

total six killed, 76 wounded, (an unusual proportion,) and one missing; grand total 83. Commodore Patterson's guns, and not the rifles of the flying Kentuckians, "the meritorious conquerors of Tecumseh," occasioned the chief of colonel Thornton's loss. The American loss is not distinctly specified in the returns, but was very trifling. The behaviour of the American troops on the right, shews what we should have had to fear from the "valor" of those on the left bank, had only half of sir Edward's army got behind their works. Colonel Thornton, at the end of his letter, is very positive, that lieutenant-colonel Gubbins, whom, on crossing over to have his wound dressed, he had left, with a force that, including the reinforcement of seamen and marines, did not exceed 700 men, would retain possession of the captured lines. But colonel Dickson, of the artillery, "did not think it could be held with security by a smaller corps than 2000 men."* The consequence of this unfortunate report was, that major-general Lambert, now the commanding officer, ordered the right bank of the river to be instantly evacuated. "I need not tell you," says general Jackson, "with how much eagerness, I immediately regained possession of the position he had thus happily quitted."† Major-general Lambert had previously applied to

* App. No. 96. † App. No. 101.

general Jackson for a suspension of hostilities; in granting which the latter considers, and, apparently, with reason, that he completely outwitted the British general.

Of the six vessels ordered up the Mississippi to bombard Fort-St. Philip, the Herald, two bombs, and Thistle and Pigmy only, could ascend the river. The fort mounted twenty-nine 24-pounders, one 6-pounder, a 13-inch mortar, an 8 and a $5\frac{1}{2}$-inch howitzer; and, in the covert-way, two long 32-pounders, mounted on a level with the water; and was garrisoned by 366 men.* The particulars of the bombardment are given in the American official account: † we have no British account to compare it with, or from which to state our loss on the occasion. It appears that the garrison lost only two men killed, and seven wounded. On the 11th the 40th regiment arrived; but no movement took place in consequence. On the morning of the 15th, a British deserter informed general Jackson that major-general Lambert would retreat in a few days.‡ On the night of the 18th the retreat took place; and the army remained in bivouac, near its first point of disembarkation, unmolested, till the 27th; when the whole re-embarked. Our loss between the 9th and 26th of January, owing to the enemy's cannonade,

* Latour's War in Louis. p. 191. † App. Nos. 107 and 108.

‡ Ibid. p. 179.

amounted to one killed, and five wounded, including lieutenant D'Arcy, of the 43d;* who, according to the American accounts, had both his legs carried off by a shell, at the moment when, after having been on guard for several days in succession, he was taking some repose, stretched on the ground, at the entrance of his bivouac. This makes the loss sustained by the British, from first to last, in this ill-fated expedition, 385 killed; 1516 wounded; and, including the two officers and 37 dragoons taken on the night of the 25th, 591 missing; total, not as general Jackson supposed "4000,"† but 2492: while the American loss, in the same expedition, amounted to 55 killed; 185 wounded; and 93 missing; total 333.‡ Major Latour says:—"The number of *sick* and wounded in the fleet is estimated at 2000."§ Where could he have obtained this fact? Both the army and navy employed on the expedition were, from first to last, healthy beyond example. Supposing all the British wounded to have been disabled, there would still be 5400 troops remaining; enough, surely, if properly employed, to have taken New Orleans: an object of ten-fold more importance now, than when the expedition was first thought of. As at Baltimore, so at New Orleans, the premature fall of a British general saved an American city.

* App. No. 106. † App. No. 104. ‡ App. No. 103.

§ Latour's War in Louisiana, p. 226.

Instead of attributing their good fortune, in this their "Waterloo"* battle, to a succession of blunders and accidents on our part, the Americans boasted, that it was their "superior valor" that had driven away the invaders. If valor did any thing, it was the valor of Frenchmen, Spaniards, natives of New Orleans, "people of colour from St. Domingo," and Irish emigrants, but not,—as the affair on the right bank proved, — of "brave but indiscreet Kentuckians." Among the several names of French generals, we find "Humbert," the "hero of Castlebar," the general "to whom the French government had formerly confided the command of that expedition to Ireland, which will ever be recorded in the glorious pages of history;" † and the same who was authorized by general Jackson, after the battle at New Orleans, to "form a legion, and to enrol in it all the English deserters who were willing to enter the service."‡ The "Mexican field-marshal, Don Juan De Anaya," also fought against us at New Orleans. Generals Coffee and Carroll were both Irishmen, or of Irish extraction. As to general Jackson; he was not quite an Irishman. Both his parents, it appears, emigrated in 1765; and he was born on the 15th of March, 1767, at a place called the Waxsaw settlement, near Camden, in South-Carolina.

* Marengo, Austerlitz, Leipsiz, *New Orleans*, and Waterloo. Wilkinson's Mem. Vol. I. p. 654.

† Latour's War in Louisiana, p. 176. ‡ Ibid. 227.

His mother was "an exemplary woman;" and, says Mr. Eaton, "to the lessons she inculcated on the youthful minds of her sons, was, no doubt, owing, in a great measure, that fixed opposition to British tyranny and oppression, which afterwards so much distinguished them."* We can now account for general Jackson's calling England "the common enemy of mankind, the highway robber of the world."† However, he proved himself at New Orleans, not only an able general, for the description of country in which he had to operate, but, in all his transactions with the British officers, both an honorable, and a courteous enemy. In his official despatches, too, he has left an example of modesty, worthy of imitation by the generality of American commanders, naval as well as military.

Every American history that we have seen, and, probably, every one that has been published since the war, charges the British commander at New Orleans, with having given out, on the morning of the 8th of January, for the parole and countersign, the words—'Booty and Beauty.' The excellent moral character of the late sir Edward Pakenham renders this improbable; and we aver, without fear of contradiction, that, agreeably to the custom of our armies on the peninsula, no parole and countersign was given out at New Orleans. The same sentiment, but expresssed in

* Eaton's Life of Jackson, p. 9. † Ibid. p. 282.

less refined language, may, however, have been uttered by, or in the hearing of, some soldier or sailor, who afterwards deserted to the enemy.

The bad state of the weather delayed the departure of the fleet and troops till the 5th of February; on which day they sailed, and, on the 7th, arrived off Dauphine island. The troops here disembarked, and encamped; except the skeletons of the 4th, 21st, and 44th regiments, which, under the orders of lieutenant-colonel Debbeig, of the 44th, were despatched in boats, to attack Fort-Bowyer. These 600, or, as major Latour will have it, "5000,"* troops landed, early on the morning of the 8th, about three miles in the rear of the fort. The full details of the surrender of Fort-Bowyer, on the "memorable" 12th of February, without a shot having been fired at it, are given in the British and American official accounts.† By the fire opened upon the working parties at the intrenchments, the British lost 13 killed and 18 wounded. Mr. O'Connor cunningly says:—"There were but few lives lost on *either* side."‡ Major Latour has given a plan of the attack; upon which we count 60 ships and other vessels; and between Dauphine island and the Mobile peninsula, no fewer than 8050 British troops.

* Latour's War in Louisiana, p. 209.

† App. Nos. 109. 110. 111. 112. 113. 114. and 115.

‡ History of the War, p. 296.

For the major's puffing remarks we have no room. They will be read with interest by those to whom they are more immediately addressed. But it is doctor Smith, that is entitled to the thanks of his brother-citizens. "The array of 60 sail," says he, "and the parade of 16000 Britons before Fort-Bowyer was a most extraordinary military spectacle."* Extraordinary, indeed! He finds fault with the British, too, for particularizing, among the articles surrendered, "one triangle gin complete," and "500 flints."† How happened doctor Smith not to know, that general Wilkinson, when he obtained possession of this same fort from the Spaniards, inserted in his "inventory of ordnance and munitions of war," —"one wooden spetula," "two tarpaulins," and "one pair of washer-hooks"?‡ Had the American generals that took the forts George and Erie been so precise, particularly as to the "women and children," doctor Smith and his brother historians would have been content with shorter paragraphs in announcing those "brilliant achievements" to the world. About the middle of March, along with major-general Power,§ and one or two reinforcements of troops, arrived the official notification of the treaty of peace; and, agreeably to the first article in it,‖ Fort-Bowyer was restored.

* Hist. of the United States, Vol. III. p. 355.
† App. No. 110. ‡ Wilkinson's Mem. Vol. I. p. 515.
§ See p. 336. ‖ App. No. 116.

Leaving the British troops at Mobile and Cumberland island to find their way home, we shall pass at once to the Canadas. Here additional reinforcements had been arriving, and, along with them, what had been so long vainly hoped for, a competent commander-in-chief. Sir George Murray, however, had scarcely arrived, ere the peace sent him home again. The captured American schooners on Lake Huron had conveyed reinforcements to Michilimacinac; and a British fleet, for the service of that lake, was in rapid progress. A 74 and a new frigate had been launched at Kingston; and two or three frigates and sloops were building for Lake Champlain. The Americans still retained Sackett's Harbor; and we, the forts Niagara and Michilimacinac. The peace deprived us of the two latter; and, considering how the campaign of 1815, as soon as it could be opened, was likely to be conducted on our part, we may say, of the former also.

A full discussion upon the merits of the treaty would, of itself, fill a volume. We cannot, however, read over the ninth article, without pointing to the recent proceedings of the American general Gaines with the Seminole Indians. It is the interest of the United States to destroy, and they will in time destroy, either by the sword or debauchery, every Indian upon the American continent. The United States declared war; invaded Canada; could not take it; and got a peace,—by which they lost their former privileges. How ludicrous now appears the following rhapsody of an American government-editor:—"Canada must be conquered, or we shall stand disgraced in the eyes of the world. It is 'a rod held over our heads;' a fortress which haughtily frowns upon our country, and from which are disseminated throughout the land, the seed of disaffection, sedition, and treason. The national safety and honor and glory are lost, if we do not win this splendid prize." There are some Americans, however, who will find consolation in the concluding words of Mr. Thomson's book. "The operations of the American armies," says he, "were, at the commencement of the war, not quite so successful. Defeat, disgrace, and disaster, in many instances, followed their movements; but the struggle was eventually closed by a succession of achievements, which reflected the highest degree of lustre upon the American name, and ranked the United States among the first and most independent nations of the earth." As the reader has already had detailed to him the "succession of achievements," by which the United States have acquired so high renown, it is unnecessary for us to comment upon this climax of American gasconade.

APPENDIX.

No. 1.

District general order.

District head-quarters,
Kingston, 25th November, 1813.

THE major-general commanding, and president, having received from major-general Vincent a report of the very gallant and patriotic conduct of lieutenant-colonel Bostwick, and an association of 45 officers and men of the militia of the county of Norfolk, in capturing and destroying a band of traitors, who, in violation of their allegiance, and of every principle of honor and honesty, had leagued themselves with the enemies of their country, to plunder and make prisoners the peaceable and well disposed inhabitants of the province, major-general De Rottenburg requests that colonel Bostwick, and every individual of the association, will accept his best thanks for their zeal and loyalty in planning, and gallantry in carrying into execution, this most useful and public spirited enterprise.

The major-general and president hopes, that so striking an instance of the beneficial effects of unanimity and exertion in the cause of their country, will not fail of producing a due effect on the militia of this province. He calls upon them to observe how quickly the energetic conduct of 45 individuals has succeeded in freeing the inhabitants of an extensive district from a numerous and well armed banditti, who would soon have left them neither liberty nor property. He reminds them that, if so much can be effected by so small a number, what may not be expected from the unanimous exertions of the whole population, guided and assisted by a spirit of subordination, and aided by his majesty's troops, against an enemy who comes for no other purpose than to enslave, plunder, and destroy.

By order,
H. N. MOORSOM,
lieutenant A. D. A. G.

No. 2.

From colonel Murray to major-general Vincent.

SIR, Fort-George, Dec. 12, 1813.

Having obtained information that the enemy had determined on driving the country between Fort-George and the advance, and was carrying off the loyal part of the inhabitants, notwithstanding the inclemency of the season, I deemed it my duty to make a rapid and forced march towards him with the light troops under my command, which not only frustrated his designs, but compelled him to evacuate Fort-George, by precipitately crossing the river, and abandoning the whole of the Niagara frontier. On learning our approach, he laid the town of Newark in ashes, passed over his cannon and stores, but failed in an attempt to destroy the fortifications, which are evidently so much strengthened whilst in his possession, as might have enabled general M'Clure (the commanding officer) to have maintained a regular siege; but such was the apparent panic, that he left the whole of his tents standing.

I trust the indefatigable exertions of this handful of men have rendered an essential service to the country, by rescuing from a merciless enemy the inhabitants of an extensive and highly cultivated tract of land, stored with cattle, grain, and provisions, of every description; and it must be an exultation to them to find themselves delivered from the oppression of a lawless banditti, composed of the disaffected of the country, organised under the direct influence of the American government, who carried terror and dismay into every family.

I have the honor to be, &c.

J. MURRAY, colonel.

To major-general Vincent, &c.

No. 3.

From the same to lieutenat-general Drummond.

SIR, Fort-Niagara, Dec. 19, 1813.

In obedience to your honor's commands, directing me to attack Fort-Niagara, with the advance of the army of the right, I resolved upon attempting a surprise. The embarkation commenced on the 18th, at night, and the whole of the troops were landed three miles from the fort early on the following morning, in the following order of attack:—Advanced guard one subaltern and 20 rank and file; grenadiers 100th regiment;

royal artillery, with grenadiers; five companies 100th regiment, under lieutenant-colonel Hamilton, to assault the main gate, and escalade the works adjacent; three companies of the 100th regiment, under captain Martin, to storm the eastern demi-bastion: captain Bailey, with the grenadiers royal Scots, was directed to attack the salient angle of the fortification; and the flank companies of the 41st regiment were ordered to support the principal attack.—Each party was provided with scaling ladders and axes. I have great satisfaction in acquainting your honor, that the fortress was carried by assault in the most resolute and gallant manner, after a short but spirited resistance.

The highly gratifying but difficult duty remains, of endeavouring to do justice to the bravery, intrepidity, and devotion of the 100th regiment to the service of their country, under that gallant officer lieutenant-colonel Hamilton, to whom I feel highly indebted for his cordial assistance. Captain Martin, 100th regiment, who executed the task allotted to him in the most intrepid manner, merits the greatest praise; I have to express my admiration of the valour of the royals, grenadiers, under captain Bailey, whose zeal and gallantry were very conspicuous. The just tribute of my applause is equally due to the flank companies of the 41st regiment, under lieutenant Bullock, who advanced to the attack with great spirit. The royal artillery, under lieutenant Charlton, deserve my particular notice. To captain Elliot, deputy-assistant-quarter-master-general, who conducted one of the columns of attack, and superintended the embarkation, I feel highly obliged. I cannot pass over the brilliant services of lieutenant Dawson and captain Fawcett, 100th, in command of the advance and grenadiers, who gallantly executed the orders entrusted to them, by entirely cutting off two of the enemy's piquets, and surprising the sentries on the glacis and at the gate, by which means the watch-word was obtained, and the entrance into the fort greatly facilitated, to which may be attributed in a great degree our trifling loss. I beg leave to recommend these meritorious officers to your honor's protection. The scientific knowledge of lieutenant Gengruben, royal engineers, in suggesting arrangements previous to the attack, and for securing the fort afterwards, I cannot too highly appreciate. The unwearied exertions of acting quarter-master Pilkington, 100th regiment, in bringing forward the materials requisite for the attack, demand my acknowledgements. Captain Kirby, lieutenants Ball, Scroos, and Hamilton, of the different provincial corps, deserve my thanks. My staff-adjutant, Mr. Brampton, will have the honor of presenting this despatch, and the standard of the American garrison; to his intelligence, valor, and friendly assistance, not only on this trying occasion, but on many former, I feel most grateful. Our force consisted of about 500 rank and file. Annexed is a return of our casualties, and the enemy's loss in killed, wounded, and prisoners. The ordnance and commissariat stores are so immense, that it is totally out of my power to forward to you a correct statement for some days, but 27 pieces of cannon, of different calibres, are on the works, and upwards of 3000 stand of arms and many rifles in the arsenal. The store-houses are full of cloathing and camp equipage of every description.

J. MURRAY, colonel.

His honor lieutenant-gen. Drummond, &c. &c. &c.

Return of killed and wounded in an assault of Fort-Niagara, at day-break, on the morning of the 19th of December, 1813.

General staff;—1 officer, wounded.
Royal artillery;—1 staff, wounded.
41*st foot*;—1 rank and file, wounded.
100*th foot*;—1 lieutenant, 5 rank and file, killed; 2 rank and file, wounded.

Names of officers killed and wounded.

Killed—100*th foot*;—Lieutenant Nowlan.
Wounded;—Col. Murray, commanding, severely (not dangerously).
Royal artillery;—Assistant-surgeon Ogilvie, slightly.

J. HARVEY,
lieut.-col., and deputy-assistant-gen.

Return of the enemy's loss in killed, wounded, and prisoners, who fell into our hands, in an assault on Fort-Niagara, on the morning of the 19th of December, 1813.

Killed;—65.
Wounded;—1 lieutenant, 1 assistant-surgeon, 12 rank and file.
Prisoners;—1 captain, 9 lieutenants, 2 ensigns, 1 surgeon, 1 commissary, 12 serjeants, 318 rank and file.

J. HARVEY, lieut.-col., and dep.-adjt.-gen.
E. BARNES, adj.-gen. North America.

No. 4.

From brigadier-general M'Clure to the American secretary at war.

Head-quarters, Buffaloe,
Dec. 22, 1813.

Sir,

I regret to be under the necessity of announcing to you the mortifying intelligence of the loss of Fort-Niagara. On the morning of the 19th instant, about four o'clock, the enemy crossed the river at the Five mile Meadows in great force, consisting of regulars and Indians, who made their way undiscovered to the garrison, which, from the most correct information I can collect, was completely surprised. Our men were nearly all asleep in their tents; the enemy rushed in, and commenced a most horrid slaughter. Such as escaped the fury of the first contest, retired to the old mess-house, where they kept up a destructive fire on the enemy until a want of ammunition compelled them to surrender. Although our force was very inferior, and comparatively small indeed, I am induced to think that the disaster is not attributable to any want of troops, but to gross neglect in the commanding officer of the fort, captain Leonard, in not preparing, being ready, and looking out for, the expected attack.

I have not been able to ascertain correctly the number of killed and wounded. About 20 regulars have escaped out of the fort, some badly wounded. Lieutenant Beck, 24th regiment, is killed, and it is said three others.

You will perceive, Sir, by the enclosed general orders, that I apprehended an attack, and made the necessary arrangement to meet it; but have reason to believe, from information received by those who have made their escape, that the commandant did not in any respect comply with those orders.

On the same morning a detachment of militia, under major Bennett, stationed at Lewistown Heights, was attacked by a party of savages; but the major and his little corps, by making a desperate charge, effected their retreat, after being surrounded by several hundreds, with the loss of six or eight, who doubtless were killed; among whom were two sons of captain Jones, Indian interpreter. The villages of Youngstown, Lewistown, Manchester, and the Indian Tuscarora village, were reduced to ashes, and the inoffensive inhabitants who could not escape, were, without regard to age or sex, inhumanly butchered, by savages headed by British officers painted. A British officer, who is taken prisoner, avows that many small children were murdered by their Indians.

Major Mallory, who was stationed at Schlosser, with about 40 Canadian volunteers, advanced to Lewistown Heights, and compelled the advanced guard of the enemy to fall back to the foot of the mountain. The major is a meritorious officer; he fought the enemy two days, and contested every inch of ground to the Tantawanty Creek. In these actions lieutenant Lowe, 23d regiment of the United States army, and eight of the Canadian volunteers, were killed. I had myself, three days previous to the attack on the Niagara, left it with a view of providing for the defence of this place, Black Rock, and the other villages on this frontier.

I came here with the troops, and have called out the militia of Gennessee, Niagara, and Chatauqua counties, *en masse.*

This place was then thought to be in imminent danger, as well as the shipping, but I have no doubt is now perfectly secure. Volunteers are coming in great numbers; they are, however, a species of troops that cannot be expected to continue in the service for a long time. In a few days 1000 detached militia, lately drafted, will be on.

I have the honor to be, &c.

G. M'CLURE, brig.-gen. com.

Hon. J. Armstrong, secretary at war.

No. 5.

First American general order.

Head-quarters, Fort-Niagara, December 12, 1813.

Captain Leonard will, as soon as possible, have a proportion of hand-grenades in the different block-houses, and give directions to the officers of the infantry where they should be posted with their men, in case of an attack; and should they not be able to maintain the out-works, to repair to the block and mess-houses, and have every thing arranged in such a manner as though he expected an immediate attack.

Much is expected from captain Leonard, from his long experience and knowledge of duty; and the general feels confident he will be well supported by captain Lomas, of the artillery, as well as the officers of the infantry.

By order of brig.-gen. M'Clure,

DONALD FRASER,

lieutenant 15 U. S. inf., and vol. aid de camp.

No. 6.

From major-general Riall to lieutenant-general Drummond.

Niagara frontier, near Fort-Erie,

Sir, Jan. 1, 1814.

I have the honor to report to you, that, agreeably to the instructions contained in your letter of the 29th ult., and your general order of that day, to pass the river Niagara, for the purpose of attacking the enemy's force, collected at Black Rock and Buffalo; and carring into execution the other objects therein mentioned, I crossed the river in the following night, with four companies of the king's regiment, and the light company of the 89th, under lieutenant-colonel Ogilvie; 250 men of the 41st regiment, and the grenadiers of the 100th, under major Friend; together with about 50 militia volunteers and a body of Indian warriors. The troops completed their landing about 12 o'clock, nearly two miles below Black Rock; the light infantry of the 89th being in advance, surprised and captured the greater part of a piquet of the enemy, and secured the bridge over the Conguichity Creek, the boards of which had been loosened, and were ready to be carried off had there been time given for it. I immediately established the 41st and 100th grenadiers in position beyond the bridge, for the purpose of perfectly securing its passage: the enemy made some attempts during the night upon this advanced position, but were repulsed with loss.

At day-break I moved forward, the king's regiment and light company of the 89th leading, the 41st and grenadiers of the 100th being in reserve. The enemy had by this time opened a very heavy fire of cannon and musketry on the Royal Scots, under lieutenant-colonel Gordon, who were destined to land above Black Rock, for the purpose of turning his position, while he should be attacked in front by the troops who landed below; several of the boats having grounded, I am sorry to say this regiment suffered some loss, and was not able to effect its landing in sufficient time to fully accomplish the object intended, though covered by the whole of our field-guns, under captain Bridge, which were placed on the opposite bank of the river.

The king's and 89th, having in the meantime gained the town, commenced a very spirited attack upon the enemy, who were in great force, and very strongly posted. The reserve being arrived on the ground, the whole were shortly engaged. The enemy maintained his position with very considerable obstinacy for some time; but such was the spirited and determined advance of our troops, that he was at length compelled to give way, was driven through his batteries, in which were a 24-pounder, three 12-pounders, and one 9-pounder, and pursued to the town of Buffalo, about two miles distant; he here shewed a large body of infantry and cavalry, and attempted to oppose our advance by the fire of a field piece, posted on the height, which commanded the road; but finding this ineffectual, he fled in all directions, and betaking himself to the woods, further pursuit was useless. He left behind him one 6-pounder brass field-piece, and one iron 18 and one iron 6-pounder, which fell into our hands. I then proceeded to execute the ulterior object of the expedition, and detached captain Robinson, of the king's, with two companies, to destroy the two schooners and sloop, (part of the enemy's late squadron,) that were on shore a little below the town, with the stores they had on board, which he effectually completed. The town itself, (the inhabitants having previously left it,) and the whole of the public stores, containing considerable quantities of cloathing, spirits, and flour, which I had not the means of conveying away, were then set on fire, and totally consumed; as was also the village of Black Rock, on the evening it was evacuated. In obedience to your further instructions, I have directed lieutenant-colonel Gordon to move down the river to Fort-Niagara, with a party of the 19th light dragoons, under major Lisle, a detachment of the royal Scots, and the 89th light company, and destroy the remaining cover of the enemy upon his frontier, which he has reported to have been effectually done. From every account I have been able to collect, the enemy's force opposed to us was not less than from 2000 to 2500 men; their loss in killed and wounded, I should imagine from 3 to 400; but from the nature of the country, being mostly covered with wood, it is difficult to ascertain it precisely; the same reason will account for our not having been able to make a greater number of prisoners than 130.

I have great satisfaction in stating to you the good conduct of the whole of the regular troops and volunteer militia; but I must particularly mention the steadiness and bravery of the king's regiment, and 89th light infantry. They were most gallantly led to the attack by lieutenant-colonel Ogilvie, of the king's, who, I am sorry to say, received a severe wound, which will for a time deprive the service of a very brave and intelligent officer. After lieutenant-colonel Ogilvie was wounded, the command of the regiment devolved on captain Robinson, who, by a very judicious movement to his right, with the three battalion companies, made a considerable impression on the left of the enemy's position. I have every reason to be satisfied with lieutenant-colonel Gordon, in the command of the royal Scots, and have much to regret, that the accidental grounding of his boats deprived me of the full benefit of his services; and I have also to mention my approbation of the conduct of major Frend, commanding the 41st, as well as that of captain Fawcett, of the 100th grenadiers, who was unfortunately wounded. Captain Barden, of the 89th, and captain Brunter, of the king's light infantry companies, conducted themselves in the most exemplary manner. Lieutenant-colonel Elliott, in this, as well as on other occasions, is entitled to my highest commendations, for his zeal and activity as superintendant of the Indian department; and I am happy to add, that, through his exertions, and that of his officers, no act of cruelty, as far as I could learn, was committed by the Indians towards any of their prisoners.

I cannot close this report without mentioning, in terms of the warmest praise, the good conduct of my aide-de-camp, captain Holland, from whom I received the most able assistance throughout the whole of these operations. Nor can I omit mentioning my obligations to you for acceding to the request of your aide-de-camp, captain Jervoise, to accompany me. He was extremely active and zealous, and rendered me very essential service. I enclose a return of the killed, wounded, and missing, and of the ordnance captured at Black Rock and Buffalo.

P. RIALL, major-general.

Lieutenant-general Drummond, commanding
the forces, Upper Canada.

Return of the killed, wounded, and missing, of the troops of the right division, under the command of major-general Rial, in the attack on Black Rock and Buffalo, on the 30th of December, 1813.

Killed—royal Scots;—13 rank and file.
King's regiment;—7 rank and file.
41st foot;—2 rank and file.
89th light infantry;—3 rank and file.
Volunteer militia;—3 rank and file.
Indian warriors;—3 rank and file.

Wounded—royal Scots;—3 serjeants, 29 rank and file.
King's regiment;—2 officers, 14 rank and file.
41st foot;—5 rank and file.
89th foot; (*light infantry*;)—5 rank and file.
100th foot; (*grenadiers*;)—1 officer, 4 rank and file.
Volunteer militia;—1 officer, 5 rank and file.
Indian warriors;—3 rank and file.

Missing—royal Scots;—6 rank and file.
41st foot;—3 rank and file.

Names of officers wounded.

King's regiment;—Lieutenent-colonel Ogilvie, severely; (not dangerously;) lieutenant Young, slightly.
100th foot; (*grenadiers*;)—Capt. Fawcett, severely; not dangerously.
Volunteer militia;—Captain Scroos, slightly.

J. HARVEY,
Lieut.-colonel, and deputy-adjutant-general.

Return of ordnance captured at Black Rock and Buffalo, on the 30th of December, 1813.

One brass 6-pounder field-piece, with carriage, complete; one iron 24-pounder, one iron 18-pounder, one iron 12-pounder, one 9-pounder, one iron 6-pounder.

C. BRIDGE, captain, R. A.

No. 7.

Extract of a letter from major-general Hall to governor Tompkins; dated head-quarters, Niagara frontier, Dec. 30th, 1812, *7 o'clock, P.M.*

I have only time to acknowledge the receipt of your letter of the 25th inst., and to add, that this frontier is wholly desolate. The British crossed over, supported by a strong party of Indians, a little before day this morning, near Black Rock; they were met by the militia under my command with spirit; but, overpowered by the numbers and discipline of the enemy, the militia gave way, and fled on every side; every attempt to rally them was ineffectual.

The enemy's purpose was obtained, and the flourishing village of Buffalo is laid in ruins. The Niagara frontier now lies open and naked to our enemies. Your judgment will direct you what is most proper in this emergency. I am exhausted with fatigue, and must defer particulars till to-morrow. Many valuable lives are lost.

No. 8.

From rear-admiral Cockburn to admiral Warren.

His majesty's sloop Fantome, in the Elk River,
Sir, 20th April, 1813.

I have the honor to acquaint you, that, having yesterday gained information of the depôt of flour (alluded to in your note to me of the 23d inst.) being, with some military and other stores, situated at a place called French-Town, a considerable distance up the river Elk, I caused his majesty's brigs, Fantome, and Mohawk, and the Dolphin, Racer, and Highflyer tenders, to be moored, yesterday evening, as far within the entrance of this river as could be prudently effected after dark; and at 11 o'clock last night, the detachment of marines now in the advanced squadron, consisting of about 150 men, under captains Wybourn and Carter, of that corps, with five artillery-men, under first-lieutenant Robertson of the artillery, (who eagerly volunteered his valuable assistance on this occasion,) proceeded in the boats of the squadron, the whole being under the immediate direction of lieutenant G. A. Westphall, first of the Marlborough, to take and destroy the aforesaid stores: the Highflyer tender, under the command of lieutenant T. Lewis, being directed to follow, for the support and protection of the boats, as far and as closely as he might find it practicable.

Being ignorant of the way, the boats were unfortunately led up the Bohemia River, instead of keeping in the Elk; and, it being daylight before this error was rectified, they did not reach the destined place till between 8 and 9 o'clock this morning, which occasioned the enemy to have full warning of their approach, and gave him time to collect his force, and make his arrangements for the defence of his stores and town; for the security of which, a 6-gun battery had lately been erected, and from whence a heavy fire was opened upon our boats the moment they approached within its reach; but the launches, with their carronades, under the orders of lieute. Nicholas Alexander, first of the Dragon, pulling resolutely up to the work, keeping up at the same time a constant and well-directed fire on it; and the marines being in the act of disembarking on the right, the Americans judged it prudent to quit their battery, and to retreat precipitately into the country, abandoning to their fate French-Town and its depôts of stores; the whole of the latter, therefore, consisting of much flour, a large quantity of army-cloathing, of saddles, bridles, and other equipments for cavalry, &c. &c., together with various articles of merchandize, were immediately set fire to, and entirely consumed, as were five vessels lying near the place; and the guns of the battery being too heavy to bring away, were disabled as effectually as possible by lieutenant Robertson and his artillery-men; after which, my orders being completely fulfilled, the boats returned down the river without molestation; and I am happy to add, that one seamen, of the Maidstone, wounded in the arm by a grape-shot, is the only casualty we have sustained.

To lieutenant G. A. Westphall, who has so gallantly conducted, and so ably executed, this service, my highest encomiums and best acknowledgements are due; and I trust, sir, you will deem him to have also thereby merited your favorable consideration and notice. It is likewise my pleasing duty to acquaint you, that he speaks in the highest terms of the zeal and good conduct of every officer and man employed with him on this occasion; but particularly of the very great assistance he derived from lieutenant Robertson, of the artillery; lieutenant Alexander, of the Dragon; lieutenant Lewis, of the Highflyer; and captains Wybourn and Carter of the royal marines.

I have now anchored the above-mentioned brigs and tenders near a farm, on the right bank of this river, where there appears to be a considerable quantity of cattle, which I intend embarking for the use of the fleet under your command; and if I meet with no resistance or impediment in so doing, I shall give the owner bills on the victualling-office for the fair value of whatsoever is so taken; but should resistance be made, I shall consider them as prize of war, which I trust will meet your approbation; and I purpose taking on board a further supply for the fleet to-morrow, on similar terms, from Specucie Island, which lies a little below Havre-de-Grace, and which I have been informed is also well stocked.

I have the honor to be, &c.

G. COCKBURN, rear-admiral.

To the right hon. admiral Sir J. B. Warren, bart. K. B. &c.

No. 9.

From same to same.

His majesty's ship Maidstone,
Tuesday-night, 3d of May, 1813, at anchor off
Turkey Point.

Sir,

I have the honor to inform you, that, whilst anchoring the brigs and tenders off Specucie Island, agreeably to my intentions notified to you in my official report of the 29th ultimo, No. 10, I observed guns fired, and American colours hoisted, at a battery lately erected at Havre-de-grace, at the entrance of Susquehanna River. This, of course, immediately gave to the place an importance which I had not before attached to it, and I therefore determined on attacking it after the completion of our operations at the island; consequently, having sounded in the direction towards it, and found that the shallowness of the water would only admit of its being approached by boats, I directed their assembling under lieutenant Westphall, (first of the Marlborough,) last night at 12 o'clock, alongside the Fantome: when our detachments of marines, consisting of about 150 men, (as before,) under captains Wybourn and Carter, with a small party of artillerymen, under lieutenant Robinson, of the artillery, embarked in them; and the whole being under the immediate direction of captain Lawrence, of the Fantome, (who, with much zeal and readiness, took upon himself, at my request, the conducting of this service,) proceeded toward Havre-de-Grace, to take up, under cover of the night, the necessary position for commencing the attack at the dawn of day. The Dolphin and Highflyer tenders, commanded by lieutenants Hutchinson and Lewis, followed for the support of the boats, but the shoalness of the water prevented their getting within six miles of the place. Captain Lawrence, however, having got up with the boats, and having very ably and judiciously placed them during the dark, a warm fire was opened on the place at day-light from our launches and rocket-boats, which was smartly returned from the battery for a short time; but the launches constantly closing with it, and their fire rather increasing than decreasing, that from the battery soon began to slacken; and captain Lawrence observing this, very judiciously directed the landing of the marines on the left; which movement, added to the hot fire they were under, induced the Americans to commence withdrawing from the battery, to take shelter in the town.

Lieutenant G. A. Westphall, who had taken his station in the rocket-boat close to the battery, therefore now judging the moment to be favourable, pulled directly up under the work, and landing with his boat's crew, got immediate possession of it, turned their own guns on them, and thereby soon obliged them to retreat, with their whole force, to the farthest extremity of the town, whither, (the marines having by this time landed,) they were pursued closely; and no longer feeling themselves equal to an open and manly resistance, they commenced a teazing and irritating fire from behind the houses, walls, trees, &c.: from which, I am sorry to say, my gallant first-lieutenant received a shot through his hand whilst leading the pursuing party; he, however, continued to head the advance, with which he soon succeeded in dislodging the whole of the enemy from their lurking-places, and driving them for shelter to the neighbouring woods; and whilst performing which service, he had the satisfaction to overtake, and with his remaining hand to make prisoner and bring in a captain of their militia. We also took an ensign and some armed individuals; but the rest of the force, which had been opposed to us, having penetrated into the woods, I did not judge it prudent to allow of their being further followed with our small numbers; therefore, after setting fire to some of the houses, to cause the proprietors, (who had deserted them, and formed part of the militia who had fled to the woods,) to understand, and feel, what they were liable to bring upon themselves, by building batteries, and acting towards us with so much useless rancour, I embarked in the boats the guns from the battery, and having also taken and destroyed about 130 stand of small arms, I detached a small division of boats up the Susquehanna, to take and destroy whatever they might meet with in it, and proceeded myself with the remaining boats under captain Lawrence, in search of a cannon foundry, which I had gained intelligence of, whilst on shore at Havre-de-Grace, as being situated about three or four miles to the northward, where we found it accordingly; and getting possession of it without difficulty, commenced instantly its destruction, and that of the guns and other materials we found there, to complete which, occupied us during the remainder of the day, as there were several buildings, and much complicated heavy machinery, attached to it; it was known by the name of Cecil, or Principio foundry, and was one of the most valuable works of the kind in America; the destruction of it, therefore, at this moment, will, I trust, prove of much national importance.

In the margin* I have stated the ordnance taken and disabled by our small division this day, during the whole of which we have been on shore in the centre of the enemy's country, and on his high road between Baltimore and Philadelphia. The boats which I sent up the Susquehanna, returned after destroying five vessels on it, and a large store of flour; when every thing being completed to my utmost wishes, the whole division re-embarked and returned to the ships, where we arrived at 10 o'clock, after having been 22 hours in constant exertion, without nourishment of any kind; and, I have much pleasure in being able to add, that, excepting lieutenant Westphall's wound, we have not suffered any casualty whatever.

The judicious dispositions made by captain Lawrence, of the Fantome, during the preceding night, and the able manner in which he conducted the attack of Havre in the morning, added to the gallantry, zeal, and attention, shewn by him during this whole day, most justly entitle him to my highest encomiums and acknowledgements, and will, I trust, ensure to him your approbation; and I have the pleasure to add, that he speaks in the most favorable manner of the good conduct of all the officers and men employed in the boats under his immediate orders, particularly of lieutenants Alexander and Reed, of the Dragon and Fantome, who each commanded a division; of lieutenant G. A. Westphall, whose exemplary and gallant conduct it has been necessary for me already to notice in detailing to you the operations of the day. I shall only now add that, from a thorough knowledge of his merits, (he having served many years with me as first lieutenant,) I always, on similar occasions, expected much from him, but this day he even outstripped those expectations; and though in considerable pain from his wound, he insisted on continuing to assist me to the last moment with his able exertions. I therefore, sir, cannot but entertain a confident hope that his services of to-day, and the wound he has received, added to what he so successfully executed at Frenchtown, (as detailed in my letter to you of the 29th ultimo,) will obtain for him your favorable consideration

* Taken from the battery at Havre-de-Grace—6 guns, 12 and 6-pounders.

Disabled, in battery for protection of foundry—5 guns, 24-pounders.

Disabled, ready for sending away from foundry—28 guns, 32-pounders.

Disabled, in boring-house and foundry—8 guns and 4 carronades of different calibres.

Total—51 guns, and 130 stand of small arms.

and notice, and that of my lords commissioners of the admiralty. I should be wanting in justice did I not also mention to you, particularly, the able assistance again afforded me by lieutenant Robertson, of the artillery, who is ever a volunteer where service is to be performed, and always foremost in performing such service, being equally conspicuous for his gallantry and ability; and he also obliged me by superintending the destruction of the ordnance taken at the foundry. To captains Wyborn and Carter, who commanded the marines, and shewed much skill in the management of them, every praise is likewise due, as are my acknowledgments to lieutenant Lewis, of the Highflyer, who, not being able to bring his vessel near enough to render assistance, came himself with his usual active zeal to offer his personal services. And it is my pleasing duty to have to report to you, in addition, that all the other officers and men seemed to vie with each other in the cheerful and zealous discharge of their duty, and I have, therefore, the satisfaction of recommending their general good conduct, on this occasion, to your notice accordingly. I have the honor to be, &c.

G. COCKBURN, rear-adm.

To the right hon. admiral sir J. B. Warren, bart. and K.B. &c.

No. 10.

From same to same.

H.M.S. Maidstone, off the Sassafras river, May 6th, 1813.

SIR,

I have the honor to acquaint you, that understanding Georgetown and Frederickstown, situated up the Sassafras river, were places of some trade and importance, and the Sassafras being the only river or place of shelter for vessels at this upper extremity of the Chesapeake, which I had not examined and cleared, I directed, last night, the assembling of the boats alongside the Mohawk, from whence with the marines, as before, under captains Wybourn and Carter, with my friend lieutenant Robertson, of the artillery, and his small party, they proceeded up this river, being placed by me for this operation, under the immediate directions of captain Byng of the Mohawk.

I intended that they should arrive before the above-mentioned towns by dawn of day, but in this I was frustrated by the intricacy of the river, our total want of local knowledge in it, the darkness of the night, and the great distance the towns lay up it; it, therefore, unavoidably became late in the morning before we approached them, when, having intercepted a small boat with two of the inhabitants, I directed captain Byng to halt our boats about two miles below the town, and I sent forward the two Americans in their boat to warn their countrymen against acting in the same rash manner the people of Havre-de-Grace had done; assuring them, if they did, that their towns would enevitably meet with a similar fate; but, on the contrary, if they did not attempt resistance, no injury should be done to them or their towns; that vessels and public property only would be seized; that the strictest discipline would be maintained; and that, whatever provisions or other property of individuals I might require for the use of the squadron, should be instantly paid for in its fullest value. After having allowed sufficient time for this message to be digested, and their resolution taken thereon, I directed the boats to advance, and I am sorry to say, I soon found the more unwise alternative was adopted; for on our reaching within about a mile of the town, between two projecting elevated points of the river, a most heavy fire of musketry was opened on us from about 400 men, divided and entrenched on the two opposite banks, aided by one long gun. The launches and rocket-boats smartly returned this fire with good effect, and with the other boats and the marines I pushed a-shore immediately above the enemy's position, thereby ensuring the capture of the towns or the bringing him to a decided action. He determined, however, not to risk the latter; for the moment he discerned we had gained the shore, and that the marines had fixed their bayonets, he fled with his whole force to the woods, and was neither seen nor heard of afterwards, though several parties were sent out to ascertain whether he had taken up any new position, or what had become of him. I gave him, however, the mortification of seeing, from whereever he had hid himself, that I was keeping my word with respect to the towns, which (excepting the houses of those who had continued peaceably in them, and had taken no part in the attack made on us) were forthwith destroyed, as were four vessels laying in the river, and some stores of sugar, of lumber, of leather, and of other merchandize. I then directed the re-embarkation of our small force, and we proceeded down the river again, to a town I had observed, situated in a branch of it, about half way up, and here I had the satisfaction to find, that what had passed at Havre, Georgetown, and Fredericks-town, had its effect, and led these people to understand, that they had more to hope for from our generosity, than from erecting batteries, and opposing us by means within their power; the inhabitants of this place having met me at landing, to say that they had not permitted either guns or militia to be stationed there, and that whilst there I should not meet with any opposition whatever. I therefore landed with the officers and a small guard only, and having ascertained that there was no public property of any kind, or warlike stores, and having allowed of such articles as we stood in need of being embarked in the boats on payment to the owner of their full value, I again re-embarked, leaving the people of this place well pleased with the wisdom of their determination on their mode of receiving us. I also had a deputation from Charlestown, in the north-east river, to assure me that that place is considered by them at your mercy, and that neither guns nor militia-men shall be suffered there; and as I am assured that all the places in the upper part of the Chesapeake have adopted similar resolutions, and that there is now neither public property, vessels, nor warlike stores remaining in this neighbourhood, I propose returning to you with the light squadron to-morrow morning.

I am sorry to say the hot fire we were under this morning cost us five men wounded, one only, however, severely; and I have much satisfaction in being able to bear testimony to you of the zeal, gallantry, and good conduct of the different officers and men serving in this division. To captain Byng, of the Mohawk, who conducted the various arrangements, on this occasion, with equal skill and bravery, every possible praise is most justly due, as well as to captains Wybourn and Carter, lieutenant Robertson, of the artillery, and lieutenant Lewis, of the Highflyer; lieutenant Alexander, of the Dragon, the senior officer under captain Byng, in command of the boats, deserves also that I should particularly notice him to you for his steadiness, correctness, and the great ability with which he always executes whatever service is entrusted to him; and I must beg permission of seizing this opportunity of stating to you how much I have been indebted, since on this service, to captain Burdett, of this ship, who was good enough to receive me on board the Maidstone when I found it impracticable to advance higher in the Marlborough, and has invariably accompanied me on every occasion whilst directing these various operations, and rendered me always the most able, prompt, and efficacious assistance.

I have the honor to be, &c.

G. COCKBURN, rear-adm.

To the right hon. admiral sir J. B. Warren, Bart. K.B. &c.

No. 11.

From lieutenant Crerie to captain Travis.

SIR, His majesty's ship Narcissus, June 13, 1813.

Your gallant and desperate attempt to defend your vessel against more than double your number, on the night of the

12th instant, excited such admiration on the part of your opponents, as I have seldom witnessed, and induced me to return you the sword you had so nobly used, in testimony of mine. Our poor fellows have severely suffered, occasioned chiefly, if not solely, by the precaution you had taken to prevent surprise; in short, I am at a loss which to admire most, the previous engagement on board the Surveyor, or the determined manner by which her deck was disputed, inch by inch.

I am, sir, with much respect, &c.

JOHN CRERIE.

Capt. S. Travis, U. S. cutter, Surveyor.

No. 12.

From commodore Cassin to the American secretary of the navy.

(LETTER I.)

SIR, Navy yard, Gosport, June 21, 1813.

On Saturday, at 11 P. M. captain Tarbell moved with the flotilla under his command, consisting of 15 gun-boats, in two divisions, lieutenant John M. Gardner 1st division, and lieutenant Robert Henley the 2d, manned from the frigate, and 50 musketeers, ordered from Craney island by general Taylor, and proceeded down the river; but adverse winds and squalls prevented his approaching the enemy until Sunday morning at four, when the flotilla commenced a heavy galling fire on a frigate, at about three quarters of a mile distance, lying well up the roads, two other frigates lying in sight. At half past four, a breeze sprung up from E.N.E. which enabled the two frigates to get under way—one a razee or very heavy ship, and the other a frigate—and to come nearer into action. The boats, in consequence of their approach, hauled off, though keeping up a well directed fire on the razee and the other ship, which gave us several broadsides. The frigate first engaged, supposed to be the Junon, was certainly severely handled—had the calm continued one half hour, that frigate must have fallen into our hands, or been destroyed. She must have slipped her mooring so as to drop nearer the razee, who had all sail set, coming up to her with the other frigate. The action continued one hour and a half with three ships. Shortly after the action, the razee got alongside of the ship, and had her upon a deep careen in a little time, with a number of boats and stages round her. I am satisfied considerable damage was done to her, for she was silenced some time, until the razee opened her fire, when she commenced again. Our loss is very trifling. Mr. Allison, master's mate, on board 139, was killed early in the action, by an 18-pound ball, which passed through him and lodged in the mast. No. 154 had a shot between wind and water. No. 67 had her franklin shot away, and several of them had some of their sweeps and their stancheons shot away—but two men slightly injured from the sweeps. On the flood tide several ships of the line and frigates came into the roads, and we did expect an attack last night. There are now in the roads 13 ships of the line and frigates, one brig and several tenders.

I cannot say too much for the officers and crews on this occasion; for every man appeared to go into action with so much cheerfulness, apparently to do their duty, resolved to conquer. I had a better opportunity of discovering their actions than any one else, being in my boat the whole of the action.

I have the honor to be, &c.

Hon. W. Jones, &c. JOHN CASSIN.

(Letter II.)

Sir, Navy yard, Gosport, June 23, 1813.

I have the honor to inform you, that on the 20th the enemy got under way, in all 13 sail, and dropped up to the mouth of James' river, one ship bearing a flag at the mizen. At 5 P.M. they were discovered making great preparation with troops for landing, having a number of boats for the purpose. Finding Craney island rather weakly manned, captain Tarbell directed lieutenants Neal, Shubrick, and Sanders, with 100 seamen, on shore, at 11 P.M. to a small battery on the N.W. side of the island.

Tuesday 22d, at dawn, the enemy were discovered landing round the point of Nansemond river; at 8 A.M. the barges attempted to land in front of the island, out of reach of the shot from the gun-boats, when lieutenants Neal, Shubrick, and Sanders with the sailors, and lieutenant Breckenbridge with the marines of the Constellation, 150 in number, opened the fire, which was so well directed, that the enemy were glad to get off, after sinking three of their largest boats. One of them, called the Centepede, admiral Warren's boat, 50 feet in length, carried 75 men, the greater part of whom were lost by her sinking. Twenty soldiers and sailors were saved, and the boat hauled up.

The officers of the Constellation fired their 18-pounder more like riflemen than artillerists. I never saw such shooting, and seriously believe they saved the island.

I have the honor to be, &c.

Hon. W. Jones, &c. JOHN CASSIN.

The number of the enemy engaged in the attack was nearly 3000.

No. 13.

From admiral Warren to Mr. Croker.

San Domingo, Hampton-roads,
Sir, Chesapeake, June 24, 1813.

I request you will inform their lordships, that, from the information received of the enemy's fortifying Craney Island, and it being necessary to obtain possession of that place, to enable the light ships and vessels to proceed up the narrow channel towards Norfolk, to transport the troops over on that side for them to attack the new fort and lines, in the rear of which the Constellation frigate was anchored, I directed the troops under sir Sydney Beckwith to be landed upon the continent within the nearest point to that place, and a reinforcement of seamen and marines from the ships; but upon approaching the island, from the extreme shoalness of the water on the sea side, and the difficulty of getting across from the land, as well as the island itself being fortified with a number of guns and men from the frigate and militia, and flanked by 15 gun-boats, I considered, in consequence of the representation of the officer commanding the troops, of the difficulty of their passing over from the land, that the persevering in the attempt would cost more men than the number with us would permit, as the other forts must have been stormed before the frigate and dock-yard could have been destroyed; I therefore ordered the troops to be re-embarked.

I am happy to say, the loss in the above affair (returns of which are enclosed) has not been considerable, and only two boats sunk.

I have to regret, that captain Hanshett, of his majesty's ship Diadem, who volunteered his services, and led the division of boats with great gallantry, was severely wounded by a ball in the thigh.

The officers and men behaved with much bravery, and if it had been possible to have got at the enemy, I am persuaded would have soon gained the place.

I have the honor to be, &c.

J. W. Croker, esq. J. B. WARREN.

A return of officers, seamen, and marines, belonging to his majesty's ships, killed, wounded, and missing, in the attack on Craney island, June 22d.

Killed;—None.
Wounded;—1 officer and 7 seamen.
Missing;—10 seamen.

Name of the officer wounded.

Captain Hanchett, of his majesty's ship Diadem, severely, but not dangerously.

J. B. WARREN.

A return of the killed, wounded, and missing, of the officers, non-commissioned officers, drummers, and rank and file, in the affair with the enemy near Craney island, June 22d.

1st battalion royal marines and rocket artillery;—1 rank and file wounded.

2d battalion royal marines;—2 rank and file, killed; 1 captain, 4 rank file, wounded; 7 rank and file, missing.

102d regiment;—1 serjeant, killed; 1 serjeant, wounded.

1st and 2d company Canadian chasseurs;—1 lieutenant, wounded; 2 serjeants, 2 drummers, 41 rank and file, missing.

Total—3 killed; 8 wounded; 52 missing.

SYDNEY BECKWITH, quarter-master-gen.

No. 14.

From same to same.

San Domingo, Hampton-roads, Chesapeake,
June 27th, 1813.

SIR,

I request you will inform their lordships, that the enemy having a post at Hampton, defended by a considerable corps, commanding the communication between the upper part of the country and Norfolk; I considered it advisable, and with a view to cut off their resources, to direct it to be attacked by the troops composing the flying corps attached to this squadron; and having instructed rear-admiral Cockburn to conduct the naval part of the expedition, and placed captain Pechell with the Mohawk sloop and launches, as a covering force, under his orders, the troops were disembarked with the greatest zeal and alacrity.

Sir Sydney Beckwith commanding the troops, having most ably attacked and defeated the enemy's force, and took their guns, colours, and camp, I refer their lordships to the quarter-master-general's report, (which is enclosed,) and that will explain the gallantry and behavior of the several officers and men employed upon this occasion, and I trust will entitle them to the favor of his royal highness the prince regent, and the lord's commissioners of the Admiralty.

Sir Sydney Beckwith, having reported to me that the defences of the town were entirely destroyed, and the enemy completely dispersed in the neighbourhood, I ordered the troops to be re-embarked, which was performed with the utmost good order by the several officers of the squadron under the orders of rear-admiral Cockburn. I have the honor to be,

JOHN BORLASE WARREN.

John Wilson Croker, esq.

No. 15.

From quarter-master-general sir Sydney Beckwith to admiral Warren.

His majesty's ship San Domingo, Hampton-roads,
SIR, June 28, 1813.

I have the honor to report to you, that in compliance with your orders to attack the enemy in town and camp at Hampton, the troops under my command were put into light sailing vessels and boats, during the night of the 25th instant, and by the excellent arrangements of rear-admiral Cockburn, who was pleased in person to superintend the advance under lieutenant-colonel Napier, consisting of the 102d regiment, two companies of Canadian Chasseurs, three companies of marines from the squadron, with two 6-pounders from the marine artillery, were landed half an hour before day-light the next morning, about two miles to the westward of the town, and the royal marine battalions, under lieutenant-colonel Williams, were brought on shore so expeditiously that the column was speedily enabled to move forward.

With a view to turn the enemy's position, our march was directed towards the great road, leading from the country into the rear of the town. Whilst the troops moved off in this direction, rear-admiral Cockburn, to engage the enemy's attention, ordered the armed launches and rocket-boats to commence a fire upon their batteries; this succeeded so completely, that the head of our advanced guard had cleared a wood, and were already on the enemy's flank before our approach was perceived. They then moved from their camp to their position in rear of the town, and here they were vigorously attacked by lieutenant-colonel Napier, and the advance; unable to stand which, they continued their march to the rear of the town, when a detachment, under lieutenant-colonel Williams, conducted by captain Powell, assistant-quarter-master-general, pushed through the town, and forced their way across a bridge of planks into the enemy's encampment, of which, and the batteries, immediate possession was gained. In the mean time some artillerymen stormed and took the enemy's remaining field-pieces.

Enclosed I have the honor to transmit a return of ordnance taken. Lieutenant-colonel Williams will have the honor of delivering to you a stand of colours of the 68th regiment, James city light infantry, and one of the 1st battalion 85th regiment. The exact numbers of the enemy it is difficult to ascertain.

From the woody country, and the strength of their positions, our troops have sustained some loss; that of the enemy was very considerable. Every exertion was made to collect the wounded Americans, who were attended by a surgeon of their own, and by the British surgeons, who performed amputations on such as required it, and afforded every assistance in their power. The dead bodies of such as could be collected were also carefully buried.

I beg leave on this occasion to express the obligations I owe to lieutenant-colonel Napier, and lieutenant-colonel Williams, for their kind and able assistance; to major Malcolm and captain Smith, and all the officers and men, whose zeal and spirited conduct entitle them to my best acknowledgements.

I have the honor to be, &c.

SYDNEY BECKWITH, Q.M.G.

Return of ordnance stores taken in Hampton, on the 25th of June, 1813.

Four 12-pounder guns on travelling carriages, three 6-pounder guns on travelling carriages, with timbers and a proportion of ammunition, for each of the above calibres.

Three covered waggons and their horses.

T. A. PARKE, captain,
and senior officer R. M. artillery.

A return of the killed, wounded, and missing, at Hampton, the 26th of June, 1813.

Royal marine artillery;—1 rank and file, killed; 4 rank and file, wounded.

Ships' 3 companies of royal marines;—1 rank and file, wounded; 1 rank and file, missing.

1st and 2d Canadian chasseurs;—3 rank and file, killed; 13 rank and file, wounded; 6 rank and file, missing.

1st battalion royal marines;—1 rank and file, killed; 1 lieutenant, 1 rank and file, wounded.

2d battalion royal marines;—1 lieutenant, 1 serjeant, 6 rank and file, wounded; 3 rank and file, missing.

Total—5 killed; 33 wounded; 10 missing.

SYDNEY BECKWITH, Q. M. G.

Admiral Sir J. B. Warren,
&c. &c. &c.

No. 16.

From colonel Butler to general Harrison.

Dear sir,

By lieutenant Shannon, of the 27th regiment United States' infantry, I have the honor of informing you, that a detachment of the troops under my command, led by captain Holmes, of the 24th United States' infantry, have obtained a signal victory over the enemy.

The affair took place on the 4th instant, about 100 miles from this place, on the river de French. Our force consisted of no more than 160 rangers and mounted infantry. The enemy, from their own acknowledgement, had about 240. The fine light company of the royal Scots is totally destroyed; they led the attack most gallantly, and their commander fell within ten paces of our front line. The light company of the 89th has also suffered severely; one officer of that company fell, one is a prisoner, and another is said to be badly wounded.

In killed, wounded, and prisoners, the enemy lost about 80, whilst on our part there were but four killed, and four wounded. This great disparity in the loss on each side, is to be attributed to the very judicious position occupied by captain Holmes, who compelled the enemy to attack him at great disadvantage. This even more gallantly merits the laurel.

Captain Holmes has just returned, and will furnish a detailed account of the expedition, which shall immediately be transmitted to you. Very respectfully,

your most obedient servant,

H. BUTLER,

Major-general Harrison. lieut.-col. commandant Detroit.

Enemy's forces, as stated by the prisoners.

Royal Scots,	101
89th regiment,	45
Militia,	50
Indians,	40 to 60
	236

No. 17.

Minutes of a council of war held at Champlain the 29th of March, 1814.

Present—Brigadier-general Macomb, brigadier-general Bissell, brigadier-general Smith, colonel Atkinson, colonel Miller, colonel Cummings, major Pitts, major Totten.

Major-general Wilkinson states to the council, that, from the best information he can collect, the enemy has assembled at the Isle aux Noix and La Colle Mill 2500 men, composed of about 2000 regular troops and 500 militia, of whom, after leaving a garrison of 200 men at Isle aux Noix, 1800 regulars and 500 militia may be brought into action. The corps of the United States, now at this place, consists of 3999 combatants, including 100 cavalry, and 304 artillerists, with 11 pieces of artillery. The objects of the enemy are unknown, and the two corps are separated nine miles. Under these circumstances the major-general submits the following questions for the consideration and opinion of the council.

First—Shall we attack the enemy? and in such case do the council approve the order of march and battle hereunto annexed, with the general order of the day?

Second—When and by what route shall the attack be made, on the plan of the intermediate country hereunto annexed?

Third—Shall a single attack be made with our force combined; or shall two attacks be made; or shall we feint on the right by the shore of the Sorel, or to the left by Odell's mill, to favor the main attack?

The general will be happy to adopt any advantageous change which may be proposed by the council, or be governed by their opinions.

The council is of opinion, that the light troops should cover a reconnoissance towards La Colle Mill; and, if it is found practicable, the position should be attacked, and the enemy's works destroyed; that the whole army move to support the light troops; that the order of battle is approved, and the manner and mode of attack must be left entirely with the commanding general.

ALEX. MACOMB,
TH. A. SMITH,
D. BISSELL,
R. PURDY,
JAMES MILLER,
T. H. PITTS,
H. ATKINSON,
JOSEPH G. TOTTEN.

Under existing circumstances my opinion is, that we go as far as La Colle Mill, designated in the map, to meet the enemy there, and destroy their block-house and the mill in which they are quartered.

M. SMITH, col. 29th inf.

No. 18.

American general order of the 29th of March.

Head-quarters, Champlain, 29th March, 1814.

The army will enter Canada to-morrow to meet the enemy, who has approached in force to the vicinity of the national line of demarkation; the arms and ammunition are therefore to be critically examined, and the men completed to 60 rounds. The commanding officers of corps and companies will be held responsible for the exact fulfilment of this essential order. The troops to be completed to four days' cooked provisions, exclusive of the present; and it is recommended to the gentlemen in commission to make same provision. No baggage will be taken forward, excepting the bedding of the officers. Let every officer, and every man, take the resolution to return victorious, or not at all: for, with double the force of the enemy, this army must not give ground.

Brigadier-general Macomb having joined with his command, the formation of the troops must necessarily be modified. They are therefore to be formed into three brigades; the first, under general Macomb, consisting of his present command, with the addition of colonel M. Smith's consolidated regiment; second and third, under the command of brigadier-general Smith and Bissell, consisting of the troops already consigned to them. The order of march and battle will be furnished the brigadier-generals, and commanding officers of regiments, by the adjutant-general.

The transport permit will be immediately returned for, and distributed by, regiments.

On the march, when approaching the enemy, or during an action, the men are to be profoundly silent, and will resolutely execute the commands they may receive from the officers. In every movement which may be made, the ranks are to be unbroken, and there must be no running forward or shouting. An officer will be posted on the right of each platoon, and a tried serjeant will form a supernumerary rank, and will instantly put to death any man who goes back. This formation is to take place by regiments and brigades, in the course of the day, when the officers are to be posted.

Let every one perfectly understand his place; and let all bear in mind what they owe to their own honor and to a beloved country, contending for its rights, and its very independence as a nation.

The officers must be careful that the men do not throw away their ammunition: one deliberate shot being worth half a dozen hurried ones; and they are to give to the troops the example of courage in every exigency which may happen.

In battle, there must be no contest for rank or station, but every corps must march promptly and directly to the spot, which it may be directed to occupy. The troops will be under arms at reveillée to-morrow morning, and will be ready to march at a moment's warning. All orders from the adjutant and inspector-general's department; from captain Rees, assistant-deputy-quarter-master-general; and major Lush and captain Nourse, extra aides de camp to general Wilkinson, will be respected as coming from the commanding general himself.

Signed, by order, W. CUMMINGS, adjutant-gen.

No. 19.

From lieutenant-colonel Williams to sir G. Prevost.

SIR, La Cole, March 13, 1814.

I beg leave to acquaint you, that I have just received from major Handcock, of the 13th regiment, commanding at the block-house on La Colle river, a report, stating that the out-posts on the roads from Burtonville and La Colle mill, leading from Odell-town, were attacked at an early hour yesterday morning by the enemy in great force, collected from Plattsburg and Burlington, under the command of major-general Wilkinson. The attack on the Burtonville road was soon over, when the enemy shewed themselves on the road from the mill that leads direct to Odell-town, where they drove in a piquet stationed in advance of La Colle, about a mile and a half distant; and soon after the enemy established a battery of three guns (12 pounders) in the wood. With this artillery they began to fire on the mill, when major Handcock, hearing of the arrival of the flank companies of the 13th regiment at the block-house, ordered an attack on the guns; which, however, was not successful, from the wood being so thick and so filled with men. Soon after, another opportunity presented itself, when the Canadian grenadier company, and a company of the voltigeurs, attempted the guns; but the very great superiority of the enemy's numbers, hid in the woods, prevented their taking them.

I have to regret the loss of many brave and good soldiers in these two attacks, and am particularly sorry to lose the service, for a short time, of captain Ellard, of the 13th regiment, from being wounded, while gallantly leading his company. The enemy withdrew their artillery towards night-fall, and retired, towards morning, from the mill, taking the road to Odell-town.

Major Handcock speaks in high terms of obligation to captain Ritter, of the frontier light infantry, who, from his knowledge of the country, was of great benefit. The marine detachment, under lieutenants Caldwell and Barton, the Canadian grenadier company, and the company of voltigeurs, as well as all the troops employed: the major expresses himself in high terms of praise for their conduct, so honorable to the service.

Major Handcock feels exceedingly indebted to captain Pring, R. N. for his ready and prompt assistance, in mooring up the sloop and gun-boats from Isle au Noix, to the entrance of the La Colle river, the fire from which was so destructive.

Lieutenants Caswick and Hicks, of the royal navy, were most actively zealous in forwarding two guns from the boats, and getting them up to the mill.

To major Handcock the greatest praise is due, for his most gallant defence of the mill against such superior numbers; and I earnestly trust it will meet the approbation of his excellency the commander in chief of the forces. I have the honor to transmit a list of the killed and wounded of the British: that of the enemy, from all accounts I can collect from the inhabitants, must have been far greater.

I have the honor to be, &c.

WILLIAM WILLIAMS,
lieut.-col. 13th regiment,
commanding at St. John's.

List of killed, wounded, and missing, in action at La Colle mill, on the 30th of March, 1814.

13th grenadiers;—8 rank and file, killed; 1 captain, 1 subaltern, 1 serjeant, 31 rank and file, wounded; 1 rank and file, missing.

13th light infantry;—1 rank and file, killed; 1 serjeant, 8 rank and file, wounded; 1 rank and file, missing.

13th, *captain Blake's company*;—1 rank and file, killed.

Canadian grenadiers;—1 rank and file, killed; 3 rank and file, wounded; 2 rank and file, missing.

Canadian voltigeurs;—1 rank and file, wounded.

Total—11 rank and file, killed; 1 captain, 1 subaltern, 1 serjeant, 43 rank and file, wounded; 4 rank and file, missing.

Officers wounded.

13th regiment;—Captain Ellard; ensign Whitford, slightly.

Note—1 Indian warrior killed, 1 wounded.

R. B. HANDCOCK, major.

No. 20.

From lieutenant-general Drummond to Sir George Prevost.

H. M. S. Prince Regent, Lake Ontario,
off Oswego, May 7, 1814.

Sir,

I am happy to have to announce to your excellency the complete success of the expedition against Oswego. The troops mentioned in my despatch of the 3d instant; viz. six companies of De Watteville's regiment, under lieutenant-colonel Fischer, the light company of the Glengarry light infantry, under captain M'Millan, and the whole of the second battalion royal marines, under lieutenant-colonel Malcolm, having been embarked with a detachment of the royal artillery, under captain Cruttenden, with two field-pieces, a detachment of the rocket company under lieutenant Stevens, and a detachment of sappers and miners under lieutenant Gosset, of the royal engineers, on the evening of the 3d instant, I proceeded on board the Prince Regent at day-light on the 4th, and the squadron immediately sailed; the wind being variable, we did not arrive off Oswego until noon the following day. The ships lay-to within long gun-shot of the battery, and the gun-boats under captain Collier were sent close in, for the purpose of inducing the enemy to shew his fire, and particularly the number and position of his guns. This service was performed in the most gallant manner, the boats taking a position within point-blank shot of the fort, which returned the fire from four guns, one of them heavy. The enemy did not appear to have any guns mounted on the town-side of the river.

Having sufficiently reconnoitred the place, arrangements were made for its attack, which it was designed should take place at eight o'clock that evening; but at sun-set a very heavy squall blowing directly on the shore, obliged the squadron to get under weigh, and prevented our return until next morning; when the following disposition was made of the troops and squadron by commodore sir J. Yeo and myself. The Princess Charlotte, Wolfe,* and Royal George,† to engage the batteries, as close as the depth of water would admit of their approaching the shore; the Sir Sidney Smith‡ schooner, to scour the town, and keep in check a large body of militia, who might attempt to pass over into the fort; the Moira§ and Melville¶ brigs, to tow the boats with the troops, and then cover their landing, by scouring the woods on the low point towards the foot of the hill, by which it was intended to advance to the assault of the fort.

Captain O'Connor had the direction of the boats and gun-boats destined to land the troops, which consisted of the flank companies of De Watteville's regiment, the company of the Glengarry light infantry, and the second battalion of the royal marines, being all that could be landed at one embarkation. The four battalion companies of the regiment of De Watteville, and the detachment of artillery remaining in reserve on board the Princess Charlotte and Sir Sidney Smith schooner.

As soon as every thing was ready, the ships opened their fire, and the boats pushed for the point of disembarkation, in the most regular order. The landing was effected under a heavy fire from the fort, as well as from a considerable body of the enemy, drawn up on the brow of the hill and in the woods. The immediate command of the troops was entrusted to lieute-

* Montreal. † Niagara. ‡ Magnet. § Charwell. ¶ Star.

nant-colonel Fischer, of the regiment of De Watteville, of whose gallant, cool, and judicious conduct, as well as of the distinguished bravery, steadiness, and discipline of every officer and soldier composing this small force, I was a witness, having, with commodore sir James Yeo, the deputy-adjutant-general, and the officers of my staff, landed with the troops.

I refer your excellency to lieutenant-colonel Fischer's letter enclosed, for an account of the operations. The place was gained in ten minutes from the moment the troops advanced. The fort being every where almost open, the whole of the garrison, consisting of the third battalion of artillery, about 400 strong, and some hundred militia, effected their escape, with the exception of about 60 men, half of them severely wounded.

I enclose a return of our loss, amongst which I have to regret that of captain Haltaway, of the royal marines. Your excellency will lament to observe in the list the name of that gallant, judicious, and excellent officer, captain Mulcaster, of the royal navy, who landed at the head of 200 volunteer seamen from the fleet, and received a severe and dangerous wound, when within a few yards of the guns, which he was advancing to storm, which I fear will deprive the squadron of his valuable assistance for some time at least.

In noticing the co-operation of the naval branch of the service, I have the highest satisfaction in assuring your excellency, that I have throughout this, as well as on every other occasion, experienced the most zealous, cordial, and able support from sir James Yeo. It will be for him to do justice to the merits of those under his command; but I may nevertheless be permitted to observe, that nothing could exceed the coolness and gallantry in action, or the unwearied exertions on shore, of the captains, officers, and crews of the whole squadron.

I enclose a memorandum of the captured articles that have been brought away, in which your excellency will perceive with satisfaction seven heavy guns, that were intended for the enemy's new ship. Three 32-pounders were sunk by the enemy in the river, as well as a large quantity of cordage, and other naval stores. The loss to them, therefore, has been very great; and I am sanguine in believing that by this blow, they have been deprived of the means of completing the armament, and particularly the equipment, of the large man of war, an object of the greatest importance.

Every object of the expedition having been effected, and the captured stores embarked, the troops returned in the most perfect order on board their respective ships, at four o'clock this morning, when the squadron immediately sailed, the barracks in the town, as well as those in the fort, having been previously burnt, together with the platforms, bridge, &c.

and the works in every other respect dismantled and destroyed, as far as was practicable.

I cannot close this despatch without offering to your excellency's notice the admirable and judicious manner in which lieutenant-colonel Fischer formed the troops, and led them to the attack; the cool and gallant conduct of lieutenant-colonel Malcolm, at the head of the second battalion royal marines; the intrepidity of captain De Bersey, of the regiment De Watteville, who commanded the advance; the zeal and energy of lieutenant-colonel Pearson, inspecting field-officer, who, with major Smelt, of the 103d regiment, had obtained a passage on board the squadron to Niagara, and volunteered their services on the occasion; the gallantry of captain M'Millan, of the Glengarry light infantry, who covered the left flank of the troops in the advance; and the activity and judgment of captain Cruttenden, royal artillery; brevet-major De Courten, of the regiment De Watteville; lieutenant Stevens, of the rocket company; lieutenant Gosset, royal engineers; each in their respective situations.

Lieutenant-colonel Malcolm has reported in high terms the conduct of lieutenant Lawrie, of the royal marines, who was at the head of the first men who entered the fort; and I had an opportunity of witnessing the bravery of lieutenant Hewett, of that corps, who climbed the flag-staff, and pulled down the American ensign which was nailed to it. To lieutenant-colonel Harvey, deputy-adjutant-general, my warmest approbation is most justly due, for his unremitting zeal and useful assistance. The services of this intelligent and experienced officer have been so frequently brought under your excellency's observation before, that it would be superfluous my making any comment on the high estimation in which I hold his valuable exertions.

Captain Jervois, my aide de camp, and lieutenant-colonel Hagermane, my provincial aide de camp, the only officers of my personal staff who accompanied me, rendered me every assistance.

Captain Jervois, who will deliver to your excellency, with this despatch, the American flag taken at Oswego, is fully able to afford every further information you may require; and I avail myself of the present opportunity strongly to recommend this officer to the favorable consideration of his royal highness the commander in chief.

I have the honor to be, &c.

GORDON DRUMMOND.

No. 21.

From lieutenant-colonel Fischer to lieutenant-colonel Harvey.

H. M. S. Prince Regent, off Oswego,
Sir, Lake Ontario, May 7.

It is with heartfelt satifaction that I have the honor to report to you, for the information of lieutenant-general Drummond, commanding, that the troops placed under my orders for the purpose of storming the fort at Oswego, have completely succeeded in this service.

It will be superfluous for me to enter into any details of the operations, as the lieutenant-general has personally witnessed the conduct of the whole party; and the grateful task only remains to point out for his approbation, the distinguished bravery and discipline of the troops.

The second battalion of royal marines formed their column in the most regular manner, and, by their steady and rapid advance, carried the fort in a very short time. In fact, nothing could surpass the gallantry of that battalion, commanded by lieutenant-colonel Malcolm; to whose cool and deliberate conduct our success is greatly to be attributed.

The lieutenant-colonel reported to me, in high terms, the conduct of lieutenant James Laurie, who was at the head of the first men who entered the fort. The two flank companies of De Watteville's, under captain De Bersey, behaved with spirit, though labouring with more difficulties during their formation, on account of the badness of the landing place, and the more direct opposition of the enemy. The company of Glengarry light infantry, under captain M'Millan, behaved in an equally distinquished manner, by clearing the wood, and driving the enemy into the fort. I beg leave to make my personal acknowledgements to staff-adjutant Greig, and lieutenant and adjutant Mermet, of De Watteville's, for their zeal and attention to me during the day's service. Nor can I forbear to mention the regular behavior of the whole of the troops during their stay on shore, and the most perfect order in which the re-embarkation of the troops has been executed, and every service performed.

I enclose herewith the return of killed and wounded, as sent to me by the different corps.

I have the honor to be, &c.

V. FISCHER,
lieut.-col. De Watteville's regiment.

Lieut.-col. Harvey,
deputy-adjuant-general,

Return of killed and wounded of the troops in action with the enemy at Oswego, on the 6th of May, 1814.

2d batt. royal marines;—1 captain, 2 serjeants, 4 rank and file, killed.

De Watteville's regiment;—1 drummer, 7 rank and file, killed.

2d battalion royal marines;—1 serjeant, 32 rank and file, wounded.

De Watteville's regiment;—1 captain, 1 subaltern, 1 serjeant, 17 rank and file, wounded.

Glengarry fencibles;—9 rank and file, wounded.

Total—1 captain, 2 serjeants, 1 drummer, 15 rank and file, killed; 1 captain, 1 subaltern, 2 serjeants, 58 rank and file, wounded.

Officers killed.

2d battalion royal marines:—Captain William Holtaway.

Officers wounded.

De Watteville's regiment;—Captain Lendergrew, severely; lieutenant Victor May, dangerously (since dead).

J. HARVEY,
lieut.-col. dep.-adj.-gen.

Return of the killed and wounded of the royal navy at Oswego, May 6.

3 seamen, killed; 2 captains, 1 lieutenant, 1 master, 7 seamen, wounded.

Total—3 killed; 11 wounded.

Officers wounded.

Captain Mulcaster, dangerously; captain Popham, lieutenant Griffin, severely; Mr. Richardson, master, arm amputated.

J. LAWRIE, sec.

No. 22.

His majesty's brig Magnet, (late Sir Sidney Smith,)
Off Oswego, U. S. May 7.

Return of ordnance and ordnance-stores, taken and destroyed at Oswego, Lake-Ontario, the 6th May, 1814, by his majesty's troops under the command of lieut.-gen. Drummond.

Taken;—3 32-pounder iron guns, 4 24-pounder iron guns, 1 12-pounder iron gun, 1 6-pounder iron gun.—Total 9.

Destroyed;—1 heavy 12-pounder, 1 heavy 6-pounder.—Total 2.

Shot;—81 42-pounder, round; 32 32-pounder, round; 36 42-pounder, canister; 42 32-pounder, canister; 30 24-pounder, canister; 12 42-pounder, grape; 48 32-pounder, grape; 18 24-pounder, grape.

Eight barrels of gunpowder, and all the shot of small caliber in the fort, and stores, thrown into the river.

EDWARD CRUTTENDEN, captain,
commanding royal artillery.

E. BAYNES, adjutant-general.

Memorandum of provisions stores, &c. captured.

One thousand and forty-five barrels of flour, pork, potatoes, salt, tallow, &c. &c. 70 coils of rope and cordage; tar, blocks, (large and small,) 2 small schooners, with several boats, and other smaller craft.

NOAH FREER, mil. Sec.

No. 23.

From sir James L. Yeo to Mr. Croker.

SIR,

My letter of the 15th April last will have informed their lordships, that his majesty's ships, Prince Regent and Princess Charlotte, were launched on the preceding day. I now have the satisfaction to acquaint you, for their lordships' information, that the squadron, by the unremitting exertions of the officers and men under my command, were ready on the 3d instant, when it was determined by lieutenant-general Drummond and myself, that an immediate attack should be made on the forts and town of Oswego: which, in point of position, is the most formidable I have seen in Upper Canada; and where the enemy had, by river navigation, collected from the interior several heavy guns, and naval stores for the ships, and large depôts of provisions for their army.

At noon, on the 5th, we got off the port, and were on the point of landing, when a heavy gale from the N. W. obliged me to gain an offing. On the morning of the 6th, every thing being ready, 140 troops, 200 seamen, armed with pikes, under captain Mulcaster, and 400 marines, were put into the boats. The Montreal and Niagara took their stations a-breast, and within a quarter of a mile of the fort; the Magnet, opposite the town; and the Star and Charwell, to cover the landing, which was effected under a most heavy fire of round, grape, and musketry, kept up with great spirit. Our men having to ascend a very steep and long hill, were consequently exposed to a destructive fire. Their gallantry overcoming every difficulty, they soon gained the summit of the hill; and, throwing themselves into the fossé, mounted the ramparts on all sides, vying with each other who should be foremost. Lieutenant Laurie, my secretary, was the first who gained the ramparts; and lieutenant Hewitt climbed the flag-staff under a heavy fire, and in the most gallant style struck the American colours, which had been nailed to the mast. My gallant and much-esteemed friend, captain Mulcaster, led the seamen to the assault with his accustomed bravery; but, I lament to say, he received a dangerous wound in the act of entering the fort, which I apprehend will, for a considerable time, deprive me of his valuable services. Mr. Scott, my first-lieutenant, who was next in command, nobly led them on, and soon gained the ramparts. Captain O'Connor, of the Prince Regent, to whom I entrusted the landing of the troops, displayed great ability and cool judgment: the boats being under a heavy fire from all points.

Captain Popham, of the Montreal, anchored his ship in a most gallant style, sustaining the whole fire until we gained the shore. She was set on fire three times by red hot shot, and much cut up in her hull, masts, and rigging; captain Popham received a severe wound in his right hand, and speaks in high terms of Mr. Richardson, the master, who, from a severe wound in the left arm, was obliged to undergo amputation at the shoulder-joint.

Captain Spilsbury, of the Niagara; captain Dobbs, of the Charwell; captain Anthony, of the Star; and captain Collier, in the Magnet, behaved much to my satisfaction. The second battalion of royal marines excited the admiration of all; they were led by the gallant colonel Malcolm, and suffered severely. Captain Hollaway, doing duty in the Princess Charlotte, gallantly fell at the head of his company. Having landed with the seamen and marines, I had great pleasure in witnessing, not only the zeal and prompt attention of the officers to my orders, but also the intrepid bravery of the men, whose good and temperate conduct under circumstances of great temptation, (being a whole night in the town, employed loading the captured vessels, with ordnance, naval stores, and provisions,) most justly claim my high approbation and acknowledgment. And I here beg leave to recommend to their lordships' notice the service of all; of my first-lieutenant, Mr. Scott; and of my aide de camp, acting lieutenant Yeo, to whom I beg leave to refer their lordships for information; nor should the meritorions exertions of acting lieutenant Griffin, severely wounded in the arm, or Mr. Brown, both of whom were attached to the storming party, be omitted. It is a great source of satisfaction to me to acquaint their lordships, that I have on this, and in all other occasions, received from lieutenant Drummond that support and attention, which never fail in securing perfect cordiality between the two services.

I herewith transmit a list of the killed and wounded, and of the ordnance, naval stores, and provisions, captured and destroyed, by the combined attack on the 6th instant.

I have the honor to be, &c.

JAMES LUCAS YEO,

Commodore and commander ia chief.

J. W. Croker, esq. &c.

A list of officers and seamen, of his majesty's fleet on Lake-Ontario, killed and wounded at Oswego on the 6th May, 1814.

Three seamen, killed; 2 captains, 1 lieutenant, 1 master, 7 seamen, wounded.

Total—3 killed, 11 wounded.

A statement of ordnance, and naval stores and provisions, brought off and destroyed, in a combined attack of the sea and land forces on the town and fort of Oswego, on the 6th may, 1814.

Ordnance stores brought off;—Three long 32-pounder guns; four long 24-pounders.

A quantity of various kinds of Ordnance stores.

Naval stores and provisions; 3 schooners; 800 barrels of flour, 500 barrels of pork, 600 barrels of salt, 500 barrels of bread.

A quantity of large rope.

Destroyed;—Three long 24-pounder guns, one long 12-pounder gun, two long 6-pounder guns.

One schooner, and all barracks and other public buildings.

J. L. YEO,
Commodore and commander in chief.

No. 24.

American general order.

Head quarters, Sackett's Harbor,
May 12, 1814.

Major-general Brown has the satisfaction to announce to the forces under his command, that the detachments stationed at Oswego, under the immediate orders of lieutenant-colonel Mitchell, of the third artillery, by their gallant and highly military conduct, in sustaining the fire of the whole British fleet of this lake for nearly two days, and contending with the vastly superior numbers of the enemy on the land, as long as the interest of the country, or the honor of their profession, required; and then, effecting their retreat in good order, in the face of this superior force of the enterprising and accomplished foe, to the depôt of naval stores, which it became their duty to defend, have established for themselves a name in arms, worthy of the gallant nation in whose cause they fight, and highly honorable to the army. Lieutenant-colonel Mitchell had, in all, less than 300 men; and the force of the enemy, by land and water, exceeded 3000. R. JONES, assist.-adjt.-gen.

No. 25.

American general order.

Adjutant-general's office, left division,
July 2, 1814.

Major-general Brown has the satisfaction to announce to the troops of his division on this frontier, that he is authorized by the orders of his government to put them in motion against the enemy. The first and second brigades, with the corps of artillery, will cross the strait before them this night, or as early to-morrow as possible. The necessary instructions have been given to the brigadiers, and by them to the commanding officers of regiments and corps.

Upon entering Canada, the laws of war will govern; men found in arms, or otherwise engaged in the service of the enemy, will be treated as enemies; those behaving peaceably, and following their private occupations, will be treated as friends. Private property, in all cases, will be held sacred; public property, whenever found, will be seized and disposed of by the commanding general. Our utmost protection will be given to all who actually join, or who evince a desire, to join us.

Plundering is prohibited. The major-general does not apprehend any difficulty on this account, with the regular army and volunteers, who press to the standard of their country to avenge her wrongs, and to gain a name in arms. Profligate men, who follow the army for plunder, must not expect that they will escape the vengeance of the gallant spirits who are struggling to exalt the national character. Any plunderer shall be punished with death who may be found violating this order.

By order of the major-general.

C. K. GARDNER, adjt.-gen.

No. 26.

From major-general Riall to lieutenant-gen. sir G. Drummond.

SIR, Chippeway, July 6.

I have the honor to inform you, that the enemy effected a landing on the morning of the 3d instant at the ferry, opposite Black Rock, having driven in the piquet of the garrison of Fort-Erie. I was made acquainted with the circumstance about eight in the morning, and gave orders for the immediate advance to Chippeway of five companies of the royal Scots, under lieutenant-colonel Gordon, to reinforce the garrison of that place. Lieutenant-colonel Pearson had moved forward from thence with the light companies of the 100th, some militia, and a few Indians, to reconnoitre their position and numbers; he found them posted on the ridge parallel with the river, near the ferry, and in strong force. I received instructions from major Buck, that they had also landed a considerable force above Fort-Erie. In consequence of the king's regiment, which I had every reason to expect the day before from York, not having arrived, I was prevented from making an attack that night.

The following morning, the 4th, a body of their troops were reported to be advancing by the river; I moved to reconnoitre, and found them to be in considerable force, with cavalry and artillery, and a large body of riflemen. Lietenant-colonel Pearson was in advance during this reconnoisance with the light company of the royal Scots, and the flank company of the 100th, and a few of the 19th light dragoons, four of whom, and eight horses, were wounded in a skirmish with the enemy's riflemen.

Having been joined by the king's regiment on the morning of the 5th, I made my dispositions for attack at four oclock in the afternoon. The light companies of the royal Scots, and 100th regiment, with the second Lincoln militia, formed the advance under lieutenant-colonel Pearson. The Indian warriors were, throughout, on our right flank in the woods. The troops moved in three columns, the third (the king's regiment) being in advance. The enemy had taken up a position with his right resting on some buildings and orchards, close on the river Niagara, and strongly supported by artillery; his left towards the wood, having a considerable body of riflemen and Indians in front of it.

Our Indians and militia were shortly engaged with the enemy's riflemen and Indians, who at first checked their advance; but the light troops being brought to their support, they succeeded, after a sharp contest, in dislodging them, in a very handsome style. I placed two light 24-pounders, and $5\frac{1}{2}$-inch howitzer, against the right of the enemy's position, and formed the royal Scots and 100th regiment, with the intention of making a movement upon his left, which deployed with the greatest regularity, and opened a very heavy fire. I immediately moved up the king's regiment to the right, while the royal Scots and 100th regiment were directed to charge the enemy in front, for which they advanced with the greatest gallantry, under a most destructive fire. I am sorry to say, however, in this attempt they suffered so severely, that I was obliged to withdraw them, finding their further efforts against the superior numbers of the enemy would be unavailing.—Lieutenant-colonel Gordon, and lieutenant-colonel the marquis of Tweedale, commanding these regiments, being wounded, as were most of the officers belonging to each. I directed a retreat to be made upon Cippeway, which was conducted with good order and regularity, covered by the king's regiment, under major Evans, and the light troops under lieutenant-colonel Pearson; and I have pleasure in saying, that not a single prisoner fell into the enemy's hands, except those who were disabled from wounds. From the report of some prisoners, we have made the enemy's force to amount to about 6000 men, with a very numerous train of artillery, having been augmented by a very large body of troops, which moved down from Fort-Erie immediately before the commencement of the action. Our own force, in regular troops, amounted to about 1500,* exclusive of the militia and Indians, of which last description there was not above 300. Fort-Erie, I understand, surrendered upon capitulation on the 3d instant. Although this affair was not attended with the success which I had hoped for, it will be highly gratifying to you to learn, that the officers and men behaved with the greatest gallantry. I am particularly indebted to lieutenant-colonel Pearson for the very great assistance I have received from him, and for the manner in which he led his light troops into the action. Lieutenant-colonel Gordon, and lieutenant-colonel the marquis of Tweedale, and major Evans, commanding the king's regiment, merit my warmest praise for the good example they shewed at the head of their respective regiments.

The artillery, under the command of captain Mackonochie, was ably served, and directed with good effect; and I am particularly obliged to major Lisle, of the 19th light dragoons, for the manner in which he covered and protected one of the 24-pounders which had been disabled. I have reason to be highly satisfied with the zeal, activity, and intelligence, of captain Holland, my aide de camp, captain Eliot, deputy-assistant-quarter-master-general; staff-adjutant Greig, and lieutenant Fox, of the royal Scots, who acted as major of brigade during the absence of major Glegg, at Fort-George. The conduct of lieutenant-colonel Dixon, of the 2d Lincoln militia, has been most exemplary; and I am very much indebted to him for it on this, as well as on other occasions, in which he has evinced the greatest zeal for his majesty's service. The conduct of the officers and men of this regiment has also been highly praiseworthy. Lieutenant colonel Pearson has reported to me, in the most favourable terms, the excellent manner in which lieutenant Horton, with a part of the 19th light dragoons, observed the motions of the enemy, while he occupied the position he took on his first-landing, and during his advance to this place.

I have, &c.
P. RIALL, major-gen.

* 1st royal Scots, 500; 1st batt. King's, 480; 100th regiment, 450; with one troop of the 19th light dragoons, and a proportion of royal artillery.

No. 27.

Return of the killed, wounded, and missing, of the right division, in action with the enemy, in advance of Chippeway, July 5, 1814.

Killed.—Royal artillery ;—1 rank and file.
1st, or royal Scots;—1 captain, 4 serjeants, 58 rank and file.
8th, or king's regiment ;—3 rank and file.
100th regiment ;—3 subalterns, 3 serjeants, 64 rank and file.
Militia ;—2 captains, 1 subaltern, 9 rank and file.
Total killed—3 captains, 3 subalterns, 7 serjeants, 135 rank and file.

Wounded—General staff ;—1 captain.
Royal artillery ;—4 rank and file.
Royal artillery drivers ;—1 subaltern.
19th light dragoons ;—1 serjeant, 5 rank and file.
1st, or royal Scots ;—1 field-officer, 2 captains, 7 subalterns, 4 serjeants, 121 rank and file.
8th, or king's regiment;—1 subaltern, 1 serjeant, 22 rank and file.
100th regiment;—1 field-officer, 2 captains, 6 subalterns, 11 serjeants, 114 rank and file.
Militia ;—1 field-officer, 3 subalterns, 1 serjeant, 11 rank and file.
Total wounded—3 field-officers, 5 captains, 18 subalterns, 18 serjeants, 277 rank and file.

Missing—1st, or royal Scots;—30 rank and file.
100th regiment ;—1 subaltern.
Militia ;—1 serjeant, 14 rank and file.
Total missing—1 subaltern, 1 serjeant, 44 rank and file.
Horses—2 killed, 1 missing.—Total, 3.

N. B. The men returned missing, are supposed to be killed or wounded.
One 24-pounder limber blown up ; 2 tumbrils damaged.

EDWARD BAYNES.
Adjutant-general North America.

Names of officers killed and wounded.

Killed—1st battalion, royal Scots ;—Captain Bailey.
100th regiment ;—Lieutenant Gibbon, ensign Rea.
Militia;—Captains Rowe and Tomey, lieutenant M'Donnel.

Wounded—General staff;—Captain Holland, aide de camp to major-general Riall, severely (not dangerously).
Royal artillery drivers ;—Lieutenant Jack, slightly.
1st battalion, royal Scots;—Lieutenant-colonel Gordon, slightly ; captains Bird and Wilson, severely, and prisoners ; lieutenant W. Campbell, severely ; lieutenants Fox, Jackson, and Hendrick, severely ; (not dangerously;) Lieutenant M'Donald, slightly ; lieutenant A. Campbell, severely ; lieutenant Connel, severely.
8th regiment ;—Lieutenant Boyd.
100th regiment;—Lieutenant-colonel the marquis of Tweedale, severely ; (not dangerously ;) captain Sherrard, severely ; (not dangerously;) captain Sleigh, severely ; lieutenants Williams, Lyon, and Valentine ; lieutenant Fortune, wounded and missing, supposed prisoner ; ensigns Clarke and Johnson ; adjutant Kingston.

No. 28.

From Major-general Brown to the American secretary at war.

SIR, Chippeway Plains, July 6, 1814.

Excuse my silence; I have been much engaged: Fort-Erie did not, as I assured you it should not, detain me a single day. At 11 o'clock on the night of the 4th, I arrived at this place with the reserve, general Scott having taken the position about noon with the van. My arrangements for turning and taking in the rear the enemy's position east of Chippeway was made; when major-jeneral Riall, suspecting our intention, and adhering to the rule, that it is better to give than to receive an attack, came from behind his works about 5 o'clock in the afternoon of the 5th in order of battle. We did not baulk him. Before 6 o'clock his line was broken and his forces defeated, leaving on the field 400 killed and wounded. He was closely pressed, and would have been utterly ruined, but for the proximity of his works, whither he fled for shelter.

The wounded of the enemy, and those of our own army, must be attended to. They will be removed to Buffaloe. This, with my limited means of transportation, will take a day or two, after which I shall advance, not doubting but that the gallant and accomplished troops I lead, will break down all opposition between me and Lake Ontario, when, if met by the fleet, all is well—if not, under the favour of heaven, we shall behave in a way to avoid disgrace. My detailed report shall be made in a day or two. I am, with the highest respect, &c.

Hon. secretary of War. JACOB BROWN.

No. 29.

American return of killed, wounded, and missing, in the affair of Chippeway, July 5th, 1815

Artillery;—4 rank and file, killed; 8 ditto, wounded; and 8 rank and file, missing.

9th regiment;—13 rank and file, killed; 1 captain, 2 subalterns, 2 serjeants, 39 rank and file, wounded.

11th ditto;—1 serjeant, 14 rank and file, killed; 1 colonel, 1 subaltern, 6 serjeants, 52 rank and file, wounded.

19th ditto;—3 rank and file, killed; 2 ditto, wounded.

22d ditto;—8 rank and file, killed; 1 captain, 2 subalterns, 2 serjeants, 41 rank and file, wounded.

25th ditto;—1 serjeant, 4 rank and file, killed; 1 captain, 2 subalterns, 4 serjeants, 62 rank and file, wounded.

Militia;—3 rank and file, killed; 2 ditto, wounded; 1 lieutenant-colonel, 1 major, 1 captain, 2 serjeants, 2 rank and file, missing.

Indians;—9 rank and file, killed; 4 ditto, wounded; 10 ditto, missing.

Total;—2 serjeants, 58 rank and file, killed; 1 colonel, 3 captains, 7 subalterns, 14 serjeants, 210 rank and file, wounded; 1 lieutenant-colonel, 1 major, 1 captain, 2 serjeants, 14 rank and file, missing.

No. 30.

From lieutenant-general Drummond to sir G. Prevost.

Head-quarters, near Niagara Falls,
July 27, 1814.

SIR,

I embarked on board his majesty's schooner Netley, at York, on Sunday evening, the 24th intant, and reached Niagara at day-break the following morning. Finding, from lieutenant-colonel Tucker, that major-general Riall was understood to be moving towards the Falls of Niagara, to support the advance of his division, which he had pushed on to that place on the preceding evening, I ordered lieutenant-colonel Morrison, with the 89th regiment and a detachment of the royals and king's, drawn from Fort George and Mississaga, to proceed to the same point in order that, with the united force, I might act against the enemy (posted at Street's Creek, with his advance at Chippeway) on my arrival, if it should be found expedient. I ordered lieutenant-colonel Tucker, at the same time, to proceed up the right bank of the river, with 300 of the 41st, about 200 of the royal Scots, and a body of Indian warriors, supported (on the river) by a party of armed seamen, under captain Dobbs, royal navy. The object of this movement was to disperse, or capture, a body of the enemy, encamped at Lewistown. Some unavoidable delay having occurred in the march of the troops up the right bank, the enemy had moved off previous to lieutenant-colonel Tucker's arrival. I have to express myself satisfied with the exertions of that officer.

Having refreshed the troops at Queenstown, and having brought across the 41st, royals, and Indians, I sent back the 41st and 100th regiments, to form the garrisons of forts George, Mississaga, and Niagara, under lieutenant-colonel Tucker, and moved with the 89th, and detachments of the royals and king's, and light company of the 41st, in all about 800 men, to join major-general Riall's division at the Falls.

When arrived within a few miles of that position, I met a report from major-general Riall, that the enemy was advancing in great force. I immediately pushed on, and joined the head of lieutenant-colonel Morrison's columns just as it reached the road leading to the Beaver Dam, over the summit of the hill at Lundy's Lane. Instead of the whole of major-general Riall's division, which I expected to have found occupying this position, I found it almost in the occupation of the enemy, whose columns were within 600 yards of the top of the hill, and the surrounding woods filled with his light troops. The advance of major-general Riall's division, consisting of the Glengarry light infantry and incorporated militia, having commenced a retreat upon Fort George, I countermanded these corps, and formed the 89th regiment, the royal Scots detachment, and the 41st light company, in the rear of the hill, their left resting on the great road; my two 24-pounder brass field guns a little advanced, in front of the centre, on the summit of the hill; the Glengarry light infantry on the right; the battalion of incorporated militia, and the detachment of the king's regiment on the left of the great road; the squadron of the 19th light dragoons in the rear of the left, on the road. I had scarcely completed this formation when the whole front was warmly and closely engaged. The enemy's principal efforts were directed against our left and centre. After repeated attacks, the troops on the left were partially forced back, and the enemy gained a momentary possession of the road. This gave him, however, no material advantage, as the troops which had been forced back formed in the rear of the 89th regiment, fronting the road, and securing the flank. It was during this short interval that major-general Riall, having received a severe wound, was intercepted as he was passing to the rear, by a party of the enemy's cavalry, and taken prisoner. In the centre, the repeated and determined attacks of the enemy were met by the 89th regiment, the detachments of the royals and king's, and the light company of the 41st regiment, with the most perfect steadiness and intrepid gallantry, and the enemy was constantly repulsed with very heavy loss. In so determined a manner were their attacks directed against our guns, that our artillerymen were bayonetted by the enemy while in the act of loading, and the muzzles of the enemy's guns were advanced within a few yards of our's. The darkness of the night, during this extraordinary conflict, occasioned several uncommon incidents: our troops having for a moment been pushed back, some of our guns remained for a few minutes in the enemy's hands; they, however, were not only quickly recovered, but the two pieces (a 6-pounder and a 5½ inch howitzer) which the enemy had brought up, were captured by us, together with several tumbrils, and in limbering up our guns at one period, one of the enemy's 6-pounders was put by mistake on a limber of ours, and one of our 6-pounders limbered on one of his: by which means the pieces were exchanged; and thus, though we captured two of his guns, yet, as he obtained one of ours, we have gained only one gun.

About 9 o'clock, (the action having commenced at 6,) there was a short intermission of firing, during which it appears the enemy was employed in bringing up the whole of his remaining force; and he shortly afterwards renewed his attack with fresh troops, but was every where repulsed with equal gallantry and success. About this period the remainder of major-general Riall's division, which had been ordered to retire on the advance of the enemy, consisting of the 103d regiment, under colonel Scott; the head-quarter division of the royal Scots; the head-quarter division of the 8th, or king's; flank companies of the 104th; and some detachments of militia, under lieutenant-colonel Hamilton, inspecting field officer, joined the troops engaged; and I placed them in a second line, with the exception of the royal Scots and flank companies of the 104th, with which I prolonged my line in front to the right, where I was apprehensive of the enemy outflanking me.

The enemy's efforts to carry the hill were continued till about midnight, when he had suffered so severely from the superior steadiness and discipline of his majesty's troops, that he gave up the contest, and retreated with great precipitation to his camp beyond the Chippeway. On the following day he abandoned his camp, threw the greater part of his baggage, camp equipage, and provisions, into the Rapids, and having set fire to Street's mills, and destroyed the bridge at Chippeway, continued his retreat in great disorder towards Fort-Erie. My light troops, cavalry, and Indians, are detached in pursuit, and to harass his retreat, which I doubt not he will continue until he reaches his own shore.

The loss sustained by the enemy in this severe action cannot be estimated at less than 1500 men, including several hundred of prisoners left in our hands; his two commanding generals, Brown and Scott, are said to be wounded, his whole force, which has never been rated at less than 5000, having been engaged.

Enclosed I have the honor to transmit a return of our loss, which has been very considerable. The number of troops under my command did not, for the first three hours, exceed 1600 men; and the addition of the troops under colonel Scott, did not encrease it to more than 2800 of every description.

A very difficult, but at the same time a most gratifying duty remains, that of endeavouring to do justice to the merits of the officers and soldiers by whose valor and discipline this important success has been obtained. I was, very early in the action, deprived of the service of major-general Riall, who, I regret to learn, has suffered the amputation of his arm* in the enemy's possession: his bravery, zeal, and activity, have always been conspicuous.

To lieutenant-colonel Harvey, deputy-adjutant-general, I am so deeply indebted for his valuable assistance previous to, as well as his able and energetic exertions during, this severe contest, that I feel myself called upon to point your excellency's attention to the distinguished merits of this highly deserving officer, whose services have been particularly conspicuous in every affair that has taken place since his arrival in this province. The zeal and intelligence displayed by major Glegg, assistant-adjutant-general, deserve my warmest approbation. I much regret the loss of a very intelligent and promising young officer, lieutenant Moorsom, 104th regiment, deputy-assistant-adjutant-general, who was killed towards the close of the action. The active exertions of captain Eliot, deputy-assistant-quarter-master-general, of whose gallantry and conduct I had occasion on two former instances to remark, were conspicuous. Major Maule and lieutenant Le Breton, of the quarter-master-general's department, were extremely useful to me; the latter was severely wounded.

Amongst the officers from whose active exertions I derived the greatest assistance, I cannot omit to mention my aides de camp, captains Jervoise and Loring, and captain Holland, aide de camp to major-general Riall. Captain Loring was unfortunately taken prisoner by some of the enemy's dragoons, whilst in the execution of an order.

In reviewing the action from its commencement, the first object which presents itself, as deserving of notice, is the steadiness and good countenance of the squadron of the 19th light dragoons, under major Lisle, and the very creditable and excellent defence made by the incorporated militia-battalion, under lieutenant-colonel Robinson, who was dangerously wounded, and a detachment of the 8th (king's) regiment, under colonel Campbell. Major Kirby succeeded lieutenant-colonel Robinson in the command of the incorporated militia-battalion, and continued very gallantly to direct its efforts. This battalion has only been organized a few months, and, much to the credit of captain Robinson, of the king's regiment, (provincial lieutenant-colonel,) has attained a highly respectable degree of discipline.

In the reiterated and determined attacks which the enemy made on our centre, for the purpose of gaining, at once, the

* It was afterwards ascertained, that major-general Riall, though severely wounded, did not lose his arm.

crest of the position, and our guns, the steadiness and intrepidity displayed by the troops allotted for the defence of that post, were never surpassed; they consisted of the 2d battalion of the 89th regiment, commanded by lieutenant-colonel Morrison, and after the lieutenant-colonel had been obliged to retire from the field by a severe wound, by major Clifford; a detachment of the royal Scotts, under lieutenant Hemphill, and after he was killed, lieutenant Fraser; a detachment of the 8th, (or King's,) under captain Campbell; light company 41st regiment, under captain Glew; with some detachments of militia under lieutenant-colonel Parry, 103d regiment. These troops repeatedly, when hard pressed, formed round the colours of the 89th regiment, and invariably repulsed the desperate efforts made against them. On the right, the steadiness and good countenance of the 1st battalion royal Scots, under lieutenant Gordon, on some very trying occasions, excited my admiration. The king's regiment, 1st battalion, under major Evans, behaved with equal gallantry and firmness, as did the light company of the royals, detached under captain Stewart; the grenadiers of the 103d, detached under captain Browne; and the flank companies of the 104th, under captain Leonard; the Glengarry light infantry, under lieutenant-colonel Battersby, displayed most valuable qualities as light troops; colonel Scott, major Smelt, and the officers of the 103d, deserve credit for their exertions in rallying that regiment, after it had been thrown into momentary disorder.

Lieutenant-colonel Pearson, inspecting field-officer, directed the advance with great intelligence; and lieutenant-colonel Drummond, of the 104th, heving gone forward with my permission, early in the day, made himself actively useful in different parts of the field, under my direction. These officers are entitled to my best thanks, as is lieutenant-colonel Hamilton, inspecting field-officer, for his exertions after his arrival with the troops under colonel Scott. The field-artillery, so long as there was light, was well served.

The credit of its efficient state is due to captain Mackonachie, who has had charge of it since his arrival with this division. Captain M'Lauchlan, who has charge of the batteries at Fort-Mississaga, volunteered his services in the field on this occasion. He was severely wounded. Lieutenant Tomkins deserves much credit for the way in which the two brass 24-pounders, of which he had charge, were served; as does serjeant Austin, of the rocket company, who directed the Congreve rockets, which did much execution. The zeal, loyalty, and bravery with which the militia of this part of the province had come forward to co-operate with his majesty's troops in the expulsion of the enemy, and their conspicuous gallantry in this, and in the action of the 5th instant, claim my warmest thanks.

I cannot conclude this despatch without recommending, in the strongest terms, the following officers, whose conduct during the late operations has called for marked approbation; and I am induced to hope that your excellency will be pleased to submit their names for promotion to the most favorable consideration of his royal highness the prince regent; viz. captain Jervoise, my aide de camp; captain Robinson, 8th (king's) regiment, (provincial lieutenant-colonel,) commanding the incorporated militia; captain Eliot, deputy assistant-quarter-master-general; captain Holland, aide-de-camp to major-general Riall; and captain Glew, 41st regiment.

This despatch will be delivered to you by captain Jervoise, my aide de camp, who is fully competent to give your excellency every further information you may require.

I have the honor to be, &c.

GORDON DRUMMOND,
lieutenant-general.

His excellency sir G. Prevost,
&c. &c. &c.

No. 31.

Return of the killed, wounded, missing, and taken prisoners, of the right division of the army in Upper Canada, under the command of lieuteuant-general Drummond, in action with the enemy near the Falls of Niagara, 25th of July, 1814.

General Staff;—1 deputy assistant-adjutant-general, killed; 1 lieutenant-general, 1 major-general, 1 inspecting field-officer, 1 deputy assistant quarter-master-general, wounded; 1 aide de camp, prisoner.

19th light dragoons;—3 horses killed; 2 rank and file, 10 horses, wounded; 1 rank and file, 1 horse, missing.

Provincial light dragoons;—2 rank and file, 3 horses, missing; 1 captain, prisoner.

Royal engineers;—1 subaltern, missing.

Royal artillery;—1 captain, 12 rank and file, wounded; 7 rank and file, missing.

Royal marine-artillery;—1 serjeant, 1 rank and file, prisoners.

Royal artillery drivers;—11 horses killed; 3 rank and file, 4 horses wounded; 1 rank and file, 8 horses, missing.

N.B.—Two privates, 41st regiment, and 2 privates of the 89th regiment, attached to royal artillery drivers, missing, not included.

1st, or royal Scots;—1 subaltern, 15 rank and file, killed; 1 captain, 2 subalterns; 6 serjeants, 1 drummer, 106 rank and file, wounded; 2 subalterns, 3 serjeants, 1 drummer, 35 rank and file, missing.

8th (or king's) regiment;—12 rank and file, killed; 3 subalterns, 3 serjeants, 54 rank and file, wounded; 1 quarter-master, 12 rank and file, missing.

41st regiment;—3 rank and file, killed; 2 serjeants, 1 drummer, 31 rank and file, wounded.

89th regiment;—1 captain, 1 subaltern, 1 serjeant, 26 rank and file, killed; 1 lieutenant-colonel, 10 subalterns, 9 serjeants, 2 drummers, 166 rank and file, wounded; 3 serjeants, 4 drummers, 2 rank and file, missing; 1 captain, prisoner.

103d regiment;—6 rank and file, killed; 1 subaltern, 3 serjeants, 1 drummer, 42 rank and file, wounded; 1 rank and file, missing; 1 captain, 2 subalterns, 1 serjeant, 2 rank and file, prisoners.

104th regiment;—1 rank and file, killed; 5 rank and file, wounded.

Glengarry light infantry;—1 serjeant, 3 rank and file, killed; 1 subaltern, 3 serjeants, 27 rank and file, wounded; 2 serjeants, 6 rank and file, missing; 1 subaltern, 2 serjeants, 11 rank and file, prisoners.

Incorporated militia;—1 subaltern, 2 serjeants, 4 rank and file, killed; 1 lieutenant-colonel, 3 captains, 4 subalterns, 3 serjeants, 32 rank and file, wounded; 3 serjeants, 72 rank and file, missing; 1 captain, 1 subaltern, 1 quarter-master, 14 rank and file, prisoners.

1st Lincoln militia;—1 rank and file, killed.

2d Lincoln militia;—1 subaltern, wounded.

4th Lincoln militia;—1 captain, 1 subaltern, 2 serjeants, 1 rank and file, wounded; 1 captain, 1 quarter-master, missing.

5th Lincoln militia;—1 major, 1 serjeant, 2 rank and file, wounded.

2d York militia;—1 major, 2 captains, 2 subalterns, 4 rank and file, wounded.

General total—1 captain, 3 subalterns, 1 deputy assistant-adjutant-general, 4 serjeants, 75 rank and file, killed; 1 lieutenant-general, 1 major-general, 1 inspecting field-officer, 1 deputy assistant-quarter-master-general, 2 lieutenant-colonels, 8 captains, 25 subalterns, 31 serjeants, 5 drummers, 482 rank and file, wounded; 1 captain, 3 subalterns, 2 quarter-masters, 11 serjeants, 5 drummers, 171 rank and file, missing; 1 aide de camp, 4 captains, 4 subalterns, 1 quarter-master, 4 serjeants, 28 rank and file, prisoners; 14 horses, killed; 14 horses, wounded; 12 horses, missing.

Total killed,	84
Total wounded,	559
Total missing,	193
Total prisoners,	42
Total,	——878

Names of officers killed, wounded, and prisoners.

Officers killed—General Staff;—Lieutenant Moorsom, deputy assistant-adjutant-general.

Royal Scots;—Lieutenant Hemphill.

89th regiment;—Captain Spunner, lieutenant Latham.

Incorporated militia;—Ensign Campbell.

Officers wounded—General staff;—Lieutenant-general Drummond, severely; (not dangerously;) major-general Riall, severely, and prisoner; lieutenant-colonel Pearson, slightly; lieutenant Le Breton, severely.

Royal artillery;—Captain Maclachlan, dangerously.

Royal Scots;—Captain Brereton, slightly; lieutenant Haswell, severely; (not dangerously;) lieutenant Fraser, severely, (not dangerously,) and missing.

8th (or king's) regiment;—Lieutenant Noell, ensign Swayne, slightly; ensign M'Donald, severely.

89th regiment;—Lieutenant-colonel Morrison, lieutenants Sanderson, Steele, Pearce, Taylor, Lloyd, and Miles, severely; (not dangerously;) lieutenant Redmond, adjutant Hopper, slightly; lieutenant Grey, ensign Saunders, dangerously.

103d regiment;—Litutenant Langhorn, slightly.

Glengarry light infantry;—Lieutenant R. Kerr, slightly.

Incorporated militia;—Lieutenant-colonel Robinson, dangerously; captain Fraser, severely; captain Washburn, slightly; captain M'Donald, severely; (left arm amputated;) lieutenant M'Dougall, mortally; lieutenant Ratan, severely; lieutenant Hamilton, slightly; ensign M'Donald, severely.

2d Lincoln militia;—Adjutant, Thompson, slightly.

4th Lincoln militia;—Captain W. Nellis, ensign Kennedy, slightly.

5th Lincoln militia;—Major Hath, severely.

2d York militia;—Major Simons, severely; captain Mackay, slightly; captain Rockman, severely.

Officers missing - Royal engineers;—Lieutenant Yall.

Royal Scots;—Lieutenant Clyne; lieutenant Lamont, supposed to be prisoner.

8th (or King's) regiment;—Quarter-master G. Kirnan.

4th Lincoln militia;—Captain H. Nellis, quarter-master Bell.

Officers prisoners—General staff;—Captain Loring, aide de camp to lieutenant-general Drummond.

103d regiment;—Captain Brown; lieutenant Montgomery, and wounded; ensign Lyon.

Glengarry light infantry;—Ensign Robins.

Incorporated militia;—Captain M'Lean, ensign Whort; and quarter-master Thompson.

Provincial light dragoons;—Capt. Merritt.

89th regiment;—Captain Gore.

EDWARD BAYNES, adj.-gen.
J. HARVEY, lieut.-col.
dep.-adj. gen.

No. 32.

From major.gen. Brown to the American secretary at war.

SIR, (No date.)

Confined as I was, and have been, since the last engagement with the enemy, I fear that the account I am about to give may be less full and satisfactory than under other circumstances it might have been made. I particularly fear that the conduct of the gallant men it was my good fortune to lead will not be noticed in a way due to their fame, and the honor of our country.

You are already apprised, that the army had, on the 25th

ult. taken a position at Chippeway. About noon of that day, colonel Swift, who was posted at Lewistown, advised me, by express, that the enemy appeared in considerable force in Queenstown, and on its heights; that four of the enemy's fleet had arrived on the preceding night, and were then lying near Fort Niagara; and that a number of boats were in view, moving up the streight. Within a few minutes after this intelligence had been received, I was further informed by captain Denmon, of the quarter-master's department. that the enemy were landing at Lewistown, and that our baggage and stores at Schlosser, and on their way thither, were in danger of immediate capture.

It is proper here to mention, that having received advices as late as the 20th, from general Gaines, that our fleet was then in port, and the commodore sick, we ceased to look for co-operation from that quarter, and determined to disencumber ourselves of baggage, and march directly to Burlington Heights. To mask this intention, and to draw from Schlosser a small supply of provisions, I fell back upon Chippeway. As this arrangement, under the encreased force of the enemy, left much at hazard on our side of the Niagara, and as it appeared by the before stated information, that the enemy was about to avail himself of it, I conceived that the most effectual method of recalling him from this object was to put myself in motion towards Queenstown. General Scott, with the 1st brigade, Towson's artillery, and all the dragoons and mounted men, were accordingly put in march on the road leading thither, with orders to report if the enemy appeared, and to call for assistance, if that was necessary.

On the general's arrival at the falls, he learned that the enemy was in force directly in his front, a narrow piece of wood alone intercepting his view of them. Waiting only to give this information, he advanced upon them. By the time assistant-adjutant-general Jones had delivered this message, the action began, and before the remaining part of the division had crossed the Chippeway, it had become close and general between the advanced corps. Though general Ripley with the 2d brigade, major Hindman with the corps of artillery, and general Porter, at the head of his command, had respectively pressed forward with ardor, it was not less than an hour before they were brought to sustain general Scott, during which time his command most skilfully and gallantly maintained the conflict. Upon my arrival I found that the general had passed the wood, and engaged the enemy on the Queenstown road, and on the ground to the left of it, with the 9th, 11th, and 22d regiments, and Towson's artillery.

The 25th had been thrown to the right, to be governed by circumstances. Apprehending that these corps were much exhausted, and knowing that they had suffered severely, I determined to interpose a new line with the advancing troops, and thus disengage general Scott, and hold his brigade in reserve. Orders were accordingly given to general Ripley. The enemy's artillery at this moment occupied a hill which gave him great advantages, and was the key of the whole position. It was supported by a line of infantry. To secure the victory, it was necessary to carry this artillery, and seize the height. This duty was assigned to colonel Miller, while, to favor its execution, the 1st regiment, under the command of colonel Nicholas, was directed to menace and amuse the infantry. To my great mortification, this regiment, after a discharge or two, gave way, and retreated some distance before it could be rallied, though it is believed the officers of the regiment exerted themselves to shorten the distance.

In the mean time, colonel Miller, without regard to this occurrence, advanced steadily and gallantly to his object, and carried the height and the cannon. General Ripley brought up the 23d (which had also faultered) to his support, and the enemy disappeared from before them. The 1st regiment was now brought into a line on the left of the 21st, and the detachments of the 17th and 19th, general Porter occupying, with his command, the extreme left. About this time colonel Miller carried the enemy's cannon.

The 25th regiment, under major Jessup, was engaged in a most obstinate conflict with all that remained to dispute with us the field of battle. The major, as has been already stated, had been ordered by general Scott, at the commencement of the action, to take ground to his right. He had succeeded in turning the enemy's left flank,—had captured (by a detachment under captain Ketchum) general Riall, and sundry other officers, and shewed himsalf again to his own army, in a blaze of fire, which defeated or destroyed a very superior force of the enemy. He was ordered to form on the right of the 2d regiment. The enemy rallying his forces, and, as is believed, having received reinforcements, now attempted to drive us from our position, and regain his artillery. Our line was unshaken, and the enemy repulsed. Two other attempts, having the same object, had the same issue. General Scott was again engaged in repelling the former of these; and the last I saw of him on the field of battle, he was near the head of his column, and giving to its march a direction that would have placed him on the enemy's right. It was with great pleasure I saw the good order and intrepidity of general Porter's volunteers from the moment of their arrival, but during the last charge of the enemy those qualities were conspicuous.

Stimulated by the examples set them by their gallant leader, by major Wood, of the Pennsylvania corps, by colonel Dobbin, of New York, and by their officers generally, they precipitated themselves upon the enemy's line, and made all the prisoners which were taken at this point of the action.

Having been for some time wounded, and being a good deal exhausted by loss of blood, it became my wish to devolve the command on general Scott, and retire from the field; but on inquiry I had the misfortune to learn, that he was disabled by wounds; I therefore kept my post, and had the satisfaction to see the enemy's last effort repulsed. I now consigned the command to general Ripley.

While retiring from the field, I saw and felt that the victory was complete on our part, if proper measures were promptly adopted to secure it. The exhaustion of the men was, however, such as made some refreshment necessary. They particularly required water. I was myself extremely sensible of the want of this necessary article. I therefore believed it proper that general Ripley and the troops should return to camp, after bringing off the dead, the wounded, and the artillery; and in this I saw no difficulty, as the enemy had entirely ceased to act. Within an hour after my arrival in camp, I was informed that general Ripley had returned without annoyance, and in good order. I now sent for him, and, after giving him my reasons for the measure I was about to adopt, ordered him to put the troops into the best possible condition; to give them the necessary refreshment; to take with him the piquets and camp guards, and every other description of force, to put himself on the field of battle as the day dawned, and there to meet and beat the enemy if he again appeared. To this order he made no objection, and I relied upon its execution.. It was not executed. I feel most sensibly how inadequate are my powers in speaking of the troops, to do justice either to their merits or to my own sense of them. Under abler direction, they might have done more and better.

From the preceding detail, you have now evidence of the distinguished gallantry of generals Scott and Porter, of colonel Miller and major Jessop.

Of the 1st brigade, the chief, with his aide de camp, Worth, his major of brigade, Smith, and every commander of battalion were wounded.

The 2d brigade suffered less; but, as a brigade, their conduct entitled them to the applause of their country. After the enemy's strong position had been carried by the 21st and the detachments of the 17th and 19th, the 1st and 23d assumed a new character. They could not again be shaken or dismayed.

Major M'Farland, of the latter, fell nobly at the head of his battalion.

Under the command of general Porter, the militia volunteers of Pennsylvania and New York stood undismayed amidst the hottest fire, and repulsed the veterans opposed to them. The Canadian volunteers, commanded by colonel Wilcox, are reported by general Porter as having merited and received his approbation.

The corps of artillery, commanded by major Hindman, behaved with its usual gallantry. Captain Towson's company, attached to the 1st brigade, was the first and last engaged, and during the whole conflict maintained that high character which they had previously won by their skill and valor. Captains Biddle and Ritchie were both wounded early in the action, but refused to quit the field. The latter declared that he never would leave his piece; and, true to his engagement, fell by its side, covered with wounds.

The staff of the army had its peculiar merit and distinction; colonel Gardner, adjutant-general, though ill, was on horseback, and did all in his power; his assistant, major Jones, was very active and useful. My gallant aides de camp, Austin and Spencer, had many and critical duties to perform, in the discharge of which the latter fell. I shall ever think of this young man with pride and regret; regret that his career has been so short,—pride that it has been so noble and distinguished.

The engineers, majors Macrae and Wood, were greatly distinguished on this day, and their high military talents exerted with great effect; they were much under my eye, and near my person, and to their assistance a great deal is fairly to be ascribed; I must earnestly recommend them, as worthy of the highest trust and confidence. The staff of generals Ripley and Porter discovered great zeal and attention to duty. Lieutenant E. B. Randolph, of the 20th regiment, is entitled to notice; his courage was conspicuous.

I enclose a return of our loss; those noted as missing may generally be numbered with the dead. The enemy had but little opportunity of making prisoners.

I have the honor to be, sir, &c.

JACOB BROWN.

Hon. John Armstrong, secretary at war.

No. 33.

Return of the killed, wounded, and missing, of the division of the army under the command of major-general Brown, at the battle of Bridgewater, July 25th, 1814.

General staff;—1 major-general, 1 brigadier-general, 2 aides de camp, 1 brigade-major, wounded; 1 brigade-major, missing.

Light dragoons;—1 rank and file, killed; 2 rank and file, wounded.

Artillery;—1 captain, 9 rank and file, killed; 1 captain, 2 subalterns, 1 serjeant, 1 musician, 30 rank and file, wounded; 1 rank and file, missing.

1st regiment infantry;—11 rank and file, killed; 2 subalterns, 18 rank and file, wounded; and 2 rank and file, missing.

9th ditto;—1 captain, 2 subalterns, 1 serjeant, 12 rank and file, killed; 1 major, 1 captain, 1 paymaster, 1 quarter-master, 5 subalterns, 7 serjeants, 74 rank and file, wounded; one subaltern, 3 serjeants, 11 rank and file, missing.

11th regiment;—1 captain, 2 serjeants, 25 rank and file, killed; 1 major, 1 captain, 5 subalterns, 9 serjeants, 1 musician, 85 rank and file, wounded; 1 subaltern, 2 rank and file, missing.

21st regiment;—1 subaltern, 2 serjeants, 12 rank and file, killed; 1 captain, 5 subalterns, 1 serjeant, 63 rank and file, wounded; 19 rank and file, missing.

22d regiment;—2 serjeants, 34 rank and file, killed; 1 colonel, 2 captains, 4 subalterns, 9 serjeants, 1 musician, 73 rank and file, wounded; 3 subalterns, 2 serjeants, 12 rank and file, missing.

23d regiment;—1 major, 2 serjeants, 7 rank and file, killed; 1 captain, 6 subalterns, 1 serjeant, 44 rank and file, wounded; 3 serjeants, 24 rank and file, missing.

25th regiment;—1 captain, 1 subaltern, 26 rank and file, killed; 1 major, 1 adjutant, 1 quarter-master, 1 subaltern, 6 serjeants, 56 rank and file, wounded; 1 serjeant, 14 rank and file, missing.

Canadian volunteers;—1 rank and file, killed; 2 rank and file, wounded; 8 rank and file, missing.

Pennsylvania regiment;—1 adjutant, 1 serjeant, 9 rank and file, killed; 1 major, 1 quarter-master, 1 subaltern, 21 rank and file, wounded; 1 captain, missing.

New York militia;—1 captain, 3 rank and file, killed; 1 lieutenant-colonel, 1 subaltern, 2 serjeants, 10 rank and file, wounded; 1 subaltern, missing.

Total—Killed, 1 major, 5 captains, 1 adjutant, 4 subalterns, 10 serjeants, 150 rank and file. Wounded, 1 major-general, 1 brigadier-general, 2 aides de camp, 1 brigade-major, 1 colonel, 1 lieutenant-colonel, 4 majors, 7 captains, 1 adjutant, 1 paymaster, 3 quarter-masters, 32 subalterns, 36 serjeants, 3 musicians, 478 rank and file. Missing, 1 brigade-major, 1 captain, 6 subalterns, 9 serjeants, 93 rank and file.

No. 34.

From lieutenant Conkling to captain Kennedy.

Fort-George, Upper Canada,
Sir, Aug. 16, 1814.

With extreme regret I have to make known to you the circumstances attending the capture of the Ohio and Somers. On the night of the 12th, between the hours of 11 and 12, the boats were seen a short distance a-head of the Somers, and were hailed from that vessel: they answered "provision-boats," which deceived the officer of the deck, as our army-boats had been in the habit of passing and repassing throughout the night, and enabled them to drift athwart his hawse, and cut his cables; at the same time pouring in a heavy fire, before he discovered who they were. Instantaneously they were along-side of me, and notwithstanding my exertions, aided by Mr. M'Cally, acting sailing-master, (who was soon disabled,) I was unable to repulse them, but for a moment. I maintained the quarter-deck until my sword fell, in consequence of a shot in the shoulder, and nearly all on deck either wounded or surrounded with bayonets. As their force was an overwhelming one, I thought farther resistance vain, and gave up the vessel, with the satisfaction of having performed my duty, and defended my vessel to the last.

List of killed and wounded.

Ohio;---Killed, 1; wounded, 6.
Somers;---Wounded, 2.

The enemy's loss in killed and wounded is much more considerable; among the killed is the commanding officer of the Netley, (lying here,) captain Ratcliffe; he fell in attempting to come over my quarter. Notwithstanding the number of muskets and pistols which were fired, and the bustle inseparable from enterprises of the kind, neither the fort nor the Porcupine attempted to fire, as we drifted past them; nor did we receive a shot until past Black Rock, though they might have destroyed us with ease. Respectfully, your obedient servant,

A. M. CONKLING.

We expect to be sent to Montreal, and perhaps to Quebec directly.

Edward P. Kennedy, esq. commanding the
United States naval force on Lake Erie.

No. 35.

From lieutenant general Drummond to sir George Prevost.

SIR, Camp before Fort-Erie, August 15, 1814.

Having reason to believe that a sufficient impression had been produced on the works of the enemy's fort, by the fire of the battery which I had opened on it on the morning of the 13th, and by which the stone building was much injured, and the general outline of the parapet and embrazures very much altered, I was determined on assaulting the place; and accordingly made the necessary arrangements for attacking it, by a heavy column directed to the entrenchments on the side of Snak-hill, and by two columns to advance from the battery, and assault the fort and entrenchments on this side.

The troops destined to attack by Snake-hill, (which consisted of the king's regiment and that of De Watteville's, with the flank companies of the 89th and 100th regiments, under lieutenant-colonel Fischer, of the regiment of De Watteville,) marched at four o'clock yesterday afternoon, in order to gain the vicinity of the point of attack in sufficient time.

It is with the deepest regret I have to report the failure of both attacks, which were made two hours before day-light this morning. A copy of lieutenant-colonel Fischer's report, herewith enclosed, will enable your excellency to form a tolerable correct judgment of the cause of the failure of that attack; had the head of the column, which had entered the place without difficulty or opposition, been supported, the enemy must have fled from his works, (which were all taken, as was contemplated in the instructions, in reverse,) or have surrendered.

The attack on the fort and entrenchments leading from it to the lake, was made at the same moment by two columns, one under lieutenant-colonel Drummond, 104th regiment, consisting of the flank companies 41st and 104th regiments, and a body of seamen and marines, under captain Dobbs, of the royal navy, on the fort; the other under colonel Scott, 103d, consisting of the 103d regiment, supported by two companies of the royals, was destined to attack the entrenchments. These columns advanced to the attack as soon as the firing upon colonel Fischer's column was heard, and succeeded after a desperate resistance, in making a lodgement in the fort through the embrazures of the demi-bastion, the guns of which they had actually turned against the enemy, who still maintained the stone building, when, most unfortunately, some ammunition, which had been placed under the platform, caught fire from the firing of the guns in the rear, and a most tremendous explosion followed, by which almost all the troops which had entered the place were dreadfully mangled. Panic was instantly communicated to the troops, who could not be persuaded that the explosion was accidental, and the enemy, at the same time, pressing forward, and commencing a heavy fire of musketry, the fort was abandoned, and our troops retreated towards the battery. I immediately pushed out the 1st battalion royals, to support and cover the retreat, a service which that valuable corps executed with great steadiness.

Our loss has been severe in killed and wounded: and I am sorry to add that almost all those returned "missing," may be considered as wounded or killed by the explosion, and left in the hands of the enemy.

The failure of these most important attacks has been occasioned by circumstances which may be considered as almost justifying the momentary panic which they produced, and which introduced a degree of confusion into the columns which, in the darkness of the night, the utmost exertions of the officers were ineffectual in removing.

The officers appear invariably to have behaved with the most perfect coolness and bravery; nor could any thing exceed the steadiness and order with which the advance of lieutenant-colonel Fischer's brigade was made, until emerging from a thick wood, it found itself suddenly stopped by an abattis, and within a heavy fire of musketry and guns from behind a formidable entrenchment. With regard to the centre and left columns, under colonel Scott and lieutenant-colonel Drummond, the persevering gallantry of both officers and men, until the unfortunate explosion, could not be surpassed. Colonel Scott, 103d, and lieutenant-colonel Drummond, 104th regiments, who commanded the centre and left attacks, were unfortunately killed, and your excellency will perceive that almost every officer of those columns was either killed or wounded by the enemy's fire, or by the explosion.

My thanks are due to the under mentioned officers; viz. to lieutenant-colonel Fischer, who commanded the right attack; to major Coore, aide de camp to your excellency, who accompanied that column; major Evans, of the king's, commanding the advance; major Villatte, De Watteville's; captain Basden, light company 89th; lieutenant Murray, light company 100th; I also beg to add the name of captain Powell, of the Glengarry light infantry, employed on the staff as deputy-assistant in the quarter-master-general's department, who conducted lieutenant-colonel Fischer's column, and first entered the enemy's entrenchments, and by his coolness and gallantry particularly distinguished himself; major Villatte, of De Watteville's regiment, who led the column of attack and entered the entrenchments; as did lieutenant Young of the king's regiment, with about 50 men of the light companies of the king's and De Watteville's regiments: captain Powell reports that serjeant Powell, of the 19th dragoons, who was perfectly acquainted with the ground, volunteered to act as a guide, and preceeded the leading sub-division in the most intrepid style. In the centre and left columns, the exertions of major Smelt, 103d regiment, who succeeded to the command of the left column, on the death of colonel Scott; captains Leonard and Shore, of the 104th flank companies; captains Glew, Bullock, and O'Keefe, 41st flank companies; captain Dobbs, royal navy, commanding a party of volunteer seamen and marines, are entitled to my acknowledgments (they are all wounded). Nor can I omit mentioning, in the strongest terms of approbation, the active, zealous, and useful exertions of captain Eliot, of the 103d regiment, deputy assistant-quarter-master-general, who was unfortunately wounded and taken prisoner; and captain Barney, of the 89th regiment, who had volunteered his services as a temporary assistant in the engineer department, and conducted the centre column to the attack, in which he received two dangerous wounds.

To major Phillot, commanding the royal artillery, and captain Sabine, who commanded the battery as well as the field-guns, and to the officers and men of that valuable branch of the service, serving under them, I have to express my entire approbation of their skill and exertions. Lieutenant Charlton, royal artillery, entered the fort with the centre column, fired several rounds upon the enemy from his own guns, and was wounded by the explosion. The ability and exertions of lieutenant Philpot, royal engineers, and the officers and men of that department, claim my best acknowledgments.

To lieutenant-colonel Tucker, who commanded the reserve, and to lieutenant-colonel Pearson, inspecting field-officer, and lieutenant-colonel Battersby, Glengarry light infantry, and captain Walker, incorporated militia, I am greatly indebted for their active and unremitted attention to the security of the out-posts.

To the deputy adjutant-general, and deputy quarter-master-general, lieutenant-colonel Harvey, and lieutenant-colonel Myers, and to the officers of their departments, respectively, as well as to captain Foster, my military secretary, and the officers of my personal staff, I am under the greatest obligations for the assistance they have afforded me. My acknowledgments are due to captain D'Alson, of the 90th regiment, brigade-major to the right division, and to lieutenant-colonel Nichol, quarter-master-general of militia, the exertions of deputy commissioner-general Turquand, and the officers of that department, for the supply of the troops; and the care and attention of staff-surgeon O'Maly, and the medical officers of the division, to the sick and wounded, also claim my thanks.

I have the honor to be, &c.

GORDON DRUMMOND,

lieutenant-general.

His excellency sir George Prevost, bart. &c.

No. 36.

From lieutenant-Colonel Fischer to lieutenant-general sir Gordon Drummond.

SIR, Camp, August 15, 1814.

I have the honour to report to you, for the information of lieutenant-general Drummond, that, in compliance with the instructions I received, the brigade under my command, consisting of the 8th and De Watteville's regiment, the light companies of the 89th and 100th, with a detachment of artillery, attacked this morning, at 2 o'clock, the position of the enemy on Snake-hill, and, to my great concern, failed in its attempt.

The flank companies of the brigade, who were formed under the orders of major Evans, of the king's regiment, for the purpose of turning the position between Snake-hill and the lake, met with a check at the abattis, which was found impenetrable, and was prevented by it to support major De Villatte, of De Watteville's, and captain Powell of the quarter-master-general's department, who, actually with a few men, had turned the enemy's battery.

The column of support, consisting of the remainder of De Watteville's and the king's regiment, forming the reserve, in marching too near the lake, found themselves entangled between the rocks and the water, and, by the retreat of the flank companies, were thrown into such confusion, as to render it impossible to give them any kind of formation during the darkness of the night, at which time they were exposed to a most galling fire of the enemy's battery, and the numerous parties in the abattis; and I am perfectly convinced that the great number of missing, are men killed or severely wounded, at that time, when it was impossible to give them any assistance.

After day-break the troops formed, and retired to the camp. I enclose a return of casualties.

J. FISCHER,

Lieutenant-colonel De Watteville's regt.

No. 37.

Return of killed, wounded, and missing, of the right division, in the assault of Fort-Erie, the 15th of August, 1814.

Killed—Royal artillery;—1 rank and file.
Royal marine artillery;—1 rank and file.
1st, or royal Scots; 1 captain.
8th, or king's own;—1 lieutenant, 1 serjeant, 15 rank and file.
89th light company;—1 rank and file.
103d regiment;—1 lieutenant-colonel.
104th regiment;—1 lieutenant-colonel.
Watteville's regiment;—1 drummer, 33 rank and file.

Wounded—General staff;—1 deputy-assistant-quarter-master-general.
Royal artillery;—1 rank and file.
Royal navy;—1 captain, 1 lieutenant, 1 master, 12 seamen.
Royal marines;—10 rank and file.
1st, or royal Scots;—1 captain, 1 lieutenant, 2 serjeants, 16 rank and file.
8th, or king's own;—1 lieutenant, 14 rank and file.
41st flank companies;—2 captains, 1 lieutenant, 1 ensign, 2 serjeants, 33 rank and file.
89th light company;—1 captain, 1 rank and file.
100th light company;—2 rank and file.
103d regiment;—1 major, 2 captains, 6 lieutenants, 1 ensign, 10 serjeants, 1 drummer, 120 rank and file.
104th regiment;—1 captain, 1 lieutenant, 2 serjeants, 2 drummers, 23 rank and file.
Watteville's regiment;—1 serjeant, 26 rank and file.
Glengarry light infantry;—1 rank and file.

Missing—General staff;—1 deputy-assistant-quarter-master-general.
Royal artillery;—2 rank and file.
Royal navy;—1 midshipman, 7 seamen.
Royal marines;—3 serjeants, 17 rank and file.
1st, or royal Scots;—49 rank and file.
8th, or king's own;—1 serjeant, 15 rank and file.
41st flank companies;—1 lieutenant, 1 ensign, 3 serjeants, 37 rank and file.
89th light company;—3 rank and file.
100th light company.—1 lieutenant, 2 serjeants, 5 rank and file.
103d regiment; 1 captain, 1 lieutenant, 1 ensign, 1 adjutant, 30 serjeants, 3 drummers, 246 rank and file.

The number returned missing, the greater part supposed killed by the explosion of a magazine.

104th regiment; 1 serjeant, 23 rank and file.
Watteville's regiment;—1 serjeant, 82 rank and file.
Incorporated militia;—1 rank and file.

Total—Killed;—2 lieutenant-colonels, 1 captain, 1 lieutenant, 1 serjeant, 1 Drummer, 51 rank and file.

Wounded;—1 deputy-assistant-quarter-master-general, 1 major, 8 captains, 11 lieutenants, 2 ensigns, 1 master, 12 seamen, 20 serjeants, 3 drummers, 250 rank and file.

Missing;—1 deputy-assistant-quarter-master-general, 1 captain, 8 lieutenants, 2 ensigns, 1 midshipman, 1 adjutant, 7 seamen, 41 serjeants, 3 drummers, 479 rank and file.

Names of officers, killed, wounded, and missing.

Killed—1st, or royal Scots;—Captain Torrens.

8th regiment;—Lieutenant Noel.

103d regiment;—Colonel Scott.

104th regiment;—Lieutenant-colonel Drummond.

Wounded—General staff;—Captain Powell, deputy-assistant-quarter-master-general, slight contusion.

Royal navy;—Captain Dobbs, lieutenant Stevenson, slightly; Mr. Harris, master, severely.

1st, or royal Scots;—Captain Rowan severely; lieutenant Vaughan, slightly.

8th regiment;—Lieutenant Young, slightly.

41st flank companies;—Captains Glew and Bullock, severely; lieutenant Hailes, slightly; ensign Townshend, severely.

89th regiment;—Captain Barney, severely.

100th regiment;—Volunteer Fraser, severely.

103d regiment;—Major Smolt, severely; captain Gardiner, severely; captain Coleclough, severely, and prisoner; lieutenant Fallon, severely; lieutenant Charlton, severely, and prisoner; lieutenant Coppage, jun. dangerously; lieutenant Meagher, slightly; lieutenants Burrows and Hazin, severely; ensign Nash, severely.

104th flank companies;—Captain Leonard, lieutenant M'Laughlan, severely.

Missing—General staff;—Captain Elliot, deputy-assistant-quarter-master-general.

Royal Navy;—Mr. Hyde, midshipman.

41st flank companies;—Lieutenant Garner, ensign Hall.

100th light company;—Lieutenant Murray, wounded and prisoner.

103d regiment;—Captain Irwin, lieutenant Kaye, ensign Huey, lieutenant and adjutant Pettit.

J. HARVEY, lieut-col.
Deputy-adjutant-general.

No. 38.

From brigadier-general Gaines to the American secretary at war.

DEAR SIR,

My heart is gladdened with gratitude to heaven and joy to my country, to have it in my power to inform you, that the gallant army, under my command, has this morning beaten the enemy, commanded by lieutenant-general Drummond, after a severe conflict of near three hours, commencing at 2 o'clock, A.M. They attacked us on each flank, got possession of the salient bastion of Old Fort Erie, which was regained at the point of the bayonet with a dreadful slaughter. The enemy's loss, in killed and prisoners, is about 600—near 300 killed. Our loss is considerable, but I think not one-tenth part as great as that of the enemy. I will not detain the express to give you the particulars. I am preparing my force to follow up the blow. With great respect and esteem,

Your obedient servant,

EDMUND P. GAINES,

Brigadier-general, commanding.

Hon. J. Armstrong,
Secretary at war.

No. 39.

From lieutenant-colonel M'Kay to lieutenant-colonel M'Douall.

Prairie du Chien, Fort M'Kay,
July 27, 1814.

SIR,

I have the honor to communicate to you, that I arrived here on the 17th instant at 12 o'clock; my force amounting to 650 men: of which, 150 were Michigan fencibles, Canadian volunteers, and officers of the Indian department, the remainder Indians.

I found that the enemy had a small fort, situated on a height immediately behind the village, with two blockhouses, perfectly safe from Indians, and that they had six pieces of cannon, and 60 or 70 effective men, officers included. That, lying at anchor in the middle of the Mississippi, directly in front of the fort, there was a very large gun-boat, called governor Clark, gun-boat No. 1, mounting 14 pieces of cannon, some 6 and 3 pounders, and a number of cohorns, manned with 70 or 80 men with muskets, and measuring 70 feet keel. This floating blockhouse is so constructed, that she can be rowed in any direction, the men on board being perfectly safe from small arms, while they can use their own to the greatest advantage.

At half-past 12 o'clock, I sent captain Anderson with a flag of truce, to invite them to surrender, which they refused. My intention was not to have made an attack till next morning at day-light; but, it being impossible to controul the Indians, I ordered our gun to play upon the gun-boat, which she did with a surprizing good effect; for, in the course of three hours the time the action lasted, she fired 86 rounds, two-thirds of which went into the governor Clark. They kept up a constant fire upon us, both from the boat and fort. We were an hour between two fires, having run our gun up within musket-shot of the fort, from whence we beat the boat out of her station. She cut her cable and ran down the current, and was sheltered under the island. We were obliged to desist, it being impossible, with our little barges, to attempt to board her, and our only gun in pursuit of her would have exposed our whole camp to the enemy; she therefore made her escape.

On the 19th, finding there were only six rounds of round shot remaining, including three of the enemy's we had picked up, the day was employed in making lead bullets for the gun, and throwing up two breast-works: one within 700 yards, and the other within 450 yards of the fort. At six in the evening, every thing being prepared, I marched to the first breastwork, from whence I intended to throw in the remaining six rounds. At the moment, the first ball was about being put into the cannon, a white flag was put out at the fort, and immediately an officer came down with a note and surrendered. It being too late, I deferred making them deliver up their arms in form till morning, but immediately placed a strong guard in the fort, and took possession of the artillery. From the time of our landing till they surrendered, the Indians kept up a constant, but perfectly useless fire, upon the fort; the distance from whence they fired was too great to do execution, even had the enemy been exposed to view.

I am happy to inform you, that every man in the Michigan fencibles, Canadian volunteers, and officers in the Indian department, behaved as well as I could possibly wish; and, though in the midst of a hot fire, not a man was even wounded, except three Indians; that is, one Puant, one Fallsovine, and one Scoux, all severely, but not dangerously.

One lieutenant, 24th U. S. regiment; one militia captain, one militia lieutenant, three serjeants, three corporals, two musicians, 53 privates, one commissary, and one interpreter, have been made prisoners. One iron 6-pounder, mounted on a garrison carriage; one iron 3-pounder, on a field-carriage; three swivels, 61 stand of arms, four swords, one field-carriage for 6-pounder, and a good deal of ammunition; 28 barrels of pork, and 46 barrels of flour: these are the principal articles found in the fort when surrendered.

I will now take the liberty to request your particular attention to captains Rollette and Anderson; the former for his activity in many instances, but particulatly during the action. The action having commenced unexpectedly, he ran down from the upper end of the village, with his company, through the heat of the fire, to receive orders; and before and since, in being instrumental in preserving the citizens from being quite ruined by pillaging Indians; and the latter, for his unwearied attention in keeping every thing in order during the route, and his activity in following up the cannon during the action, and asssisting in transporting the ammunition. Lieutenant Portier, of captain Anderson's company; lieutenants Graham and Brisbois, of the Indian department; captain Dean, of the Prairie du Chien militia; and lieutenant Powell, of the Green Bay, all acted with courage and activity, so becoming Canadian militia or volunteers. The interpreters also behaved well, but particularly M. St. Germain, from the Saulte St. Marie, and M. Rouville, Scoux interpeter: they absolutely prevented their Indians committing any outrage in the plundering way. Commissary Honoré, who acted as lietenant in captain Rollette's company, whose singular activity in saving and keeping an exact account of provisions, surprised me, and without which we must unavoidably have lost much of that essential article. The Michigan fencibles, who manned the gun, behaved with great courage, coolness, and regularity. As to the serjeant of artillery, too much cannot be said of him; for the fate of the day, and our success, were to be attributed, in a great measure, to his courage, and well-managed firing.

Since writing the foregoing, a few Sanks have arrived from the rapids, at the Rock river, with two Canadians, and bring the following information: On the 21st instant, six American barges, three of which were armed, were coming up and encamped in the rapids; that, in the course of the night, the party of Indians having the four bags of gunpowder I sent from this on the 17th, reached them. The barges being encamped at short distances from each other, they, on the 22d, early in the morning, attacked the lowest, and killed about 100 persons, took five pieces of cannon, and burnt the barge: the other barges seeing this disaster, and knowing there were British troops here, ran off. This is, perhaps, one of the most brilliant actions, fought by Indians only, since the commencement of the war. I have, &c.

W. M'KAY, lieutenant-colonel.

Lieut.-col. M'Douall, commanding at Michilimacinac.

No. 40.

From lieutenant-colonel M'Douall to sir George Prevost.

Sir, Michilimacinac, August 14, 1814.

I have reported to lieutenant-general Drummond the particulars of the attack made by the enemy on this post on the 4th instant. My situation was embarrassing. I knew that they could land upwards of 1000 men; and, after manning the guns at the fort, I had only a disposable force of 140 to meet them, which I determined to do, in order as much as possible to encourage the Indians, and having the fullest confidence in the little detachment of the Newfoundland regiment. The position I took up was excellent, but at an unavoidable and too great a distance from the forts, in each of which I was only able to leave 25 militiamen. There were likewise roads upon my flanks, every inch of which was known to the enemy, by means of the people formerly residents of this island, which were with them. I could not afford to detach a man to guard them.

My position was rather too extensive for such a handful of men. The ground was commanding, and, in front, clear as I could wish it. On both our flanks and rear, a thick wood. My utmost wish was, that the Indians would only prevent the enemy from gaining the woods upon our flanks, which would have forced them upon the open ground in our front. A natural breastwork protected my men from every shot; and I had told them that, on a close approach of the enemy, they were to pour in a volley, and immediately charge; numerous as they were, all were fully confident of the result.

On the advance of the enemy, my 6-pounder and 3-pounder opened a heavy fire upon them, but not with the effect they should have had: being not well manned, and for want of an artillery-officer, which would have been invaluable to us. They moved slowly and cautiously, declining to meet me in the open ground, but gradually gaining my left flank; which the Indians permitted, even in the woods, without firing a shot. I was even obliged to weaken my small front, by detaching the Michigan fencibles to oppose a party of the enemy, which were advancing to the woods on my right. I now received accounts from major Crawford, of the militia, that the enemy's two large ships had anchored in the rear of my left, and that troops were moving by a road in that direction towards the forts. I, therefore, immediately moved, to place myself between them and the enemy, and took up a position effectually covering them; from whence, collecting the greater part of the Indians who had retired, and taking with me major Crawford and about 50 militia, I again advanced to support a party of the Fallsovine Indians; who, with their gallant chief, Thomas, had commenced a spirited attack upon the enemy; who, in a short time, lost their second in command and several other officers; seventeen of which we counted dead upon the field, besides what they carried off, and a considerable number wounded. The enemy retired in the utmost haste and confusion, followed by the troops, till they found shelter under the very powerful broadside of their ships, anchored within a few yards of the shore. They re-embarked that evening, and the vessels immediately hauled off.

I have the honour, &c.

R. M'DOUALL, lieutenant colonel.

His excellency sir George Prevost, &c.

No. 41.

From lieutenant Bulger to lieutenant-colonel M'Douall.

SIR, Michilimacinac, September 7, 1814.

I have the honor to report to you the particulars of the capture of the United States' schooners, Scorpion and Tigress, by a detachment from this garrison, under the command of lieutenant Worsley, of the royal navy, and myself.

In obedience to your orders, we left Michilimacinac on the evening of the 1st instant, in four boats, one of which was manned by seamen under lieutenant Worsley, the others by a detachment of the royal Newfoundland regiment, under myself, lieutenants Armstrong, and Radenherst. We arrived near the Détour about sun-set on the following day; but nothing was attempted that night, as the enemy's position had not been correctly ascertained. The troops remained the whole of the 3d instant concealed amongst the roads, and about 6 o'clock that evening began to move towards the enemy. We had to row about six miles, during which the most perfect order and silence reigned. The Indians which accompanied us from Machinac, were left about three miles in the rear. About 9 o'clock at night we discerned the enemy, and had approached to within 100 yards of them before they hailed us. On receiving no answer, they opened a smart fire upon us, both of musketry and of the 24-pounder. All opposition, however, was in vain; and in the course of five minutes, the enemy's vessel was boarded and carried, by lieutenant Worsley and lieutenant Armstrong on the starboard-side, and my boat and lieutenant Radenhurst's on the larboard. She proved to be the Tigress, commanded by sailing-master Champlin, mounting one long 24-pounder, and with a complement of 30 men. The defence of this vessel did credit to her officers, who were all severely wounded. She had three men wounded and three missing, supposed to have been killed and thrown immediately overboard. Our loss is two seamen killed, and several soldiers and seamen slightly wounded.

On the morning of the 4th instant the prisoners were sent in a boat to Machinac, under a guard, and we prepared to attack the other schooner, which we understood was anchored 15 miles further down. The position of the Tigress was not altered; and, the better to carry on the deception, the American pendant was kept flying. On the 5th instant, we discerned the enemy's schooner beating up to us; the soldiers I directed to keep below, or to lie down on the deck, to avoid being seen. Every thing succeeded to our wish; the enemy came to anchor about two miles from us in the night; and, as day dawned on the 6th instant, we slipt our cable, and ran down under our jib and foresail. Every thing was so well managed by lieutenant Worsley, that we were within ten yards of the enemy before they discovered us. It was then too late; for, in the course of five minutes, her deck was covered with our men, and the British flag hoisted over the American. She proved to be the Scorpion, commanded by lieutenant Turner, of the United States' navy; carrying one long 24-pounder in her hold, with a complement of 32 men. She had two men killed, and two wounded. I enclose a return of our killed and wounded, and am happy to say that the latter are but slight.

To the admirable good conduct and management of lieutenant Worsley, of the royal navy, the success is to be in a great measure attributed; but I must assure you, that every officer and man did his duty.

I have the honor to be, &c.

A. H. BULGER,

lieutenant royal Newfoundland regiment.

To lieutenant-colonel M'Douall, &c. &c.

Return of killed and wounded of the troops, employed in the capture of the United States' schooners, Scorpion and Tigress, on the 3d and 6th of September, 1814.

Royal artillery;—1 rank and file, wounded.
Royal Newfoundland regiment;—1 lieutenant, 6 rank and file, wounded.

Officer wounded.

Lieutenant Bulger, slightly.
N. B. Three seamen killed.

No. 42.

From Sir George Prevost to Earl Bathurst.

Head-quarters, Plattsburg, State of New York,
MY LORD, Sept. 11, 1814.

Upon the arrival of the reinforcements from the Garonne, I lost no time in assembling three brigades on the frontier of

Lower Canada, extending from the river Richelieu to the St. Lawrence, and in forming them into a division under the command of major-general De Rottenburg, for the purpose of carrying into effect his royal highness the prince regent's commands, which had been conveyed to me by your lordship in your despatch of the 3d of June last.

As the troops concentrated and approached the line of separation between this province and the United States, the American army abandoned its entrenched camp on the river Chazy, at Champlain; a position I immediately seized, and occupied in force on the 3d instant. The following day, the whole of the left division advanced to the village of Chazy, without meeting the least opposition from the enemy.

On the 5th, it halted within eight miles of this place, having surmounted the difficulties created by the obstructions in the road from the felling of trees and the removal of bridges. The next day the division moved upon Plattsburg, in two columns, on parallel roads; the right column led by major-general Power's brigade, supported by four companies of light infantry and a demi-brigade, under major-general Robinson; the left by major-general Brisbane's brigade.

The enemy's militia, supported by his regulars, attempted to impede the advance of the right column, but they were driven before it from all their positions, and the column entered Plattsburg. This rapid movement having reversed the strong position taken up by the enemy at Dead creek, it was precipitately abandoned by him, and his gun-boats alone left to defend the ford, and to prevent our restoring the bridges, which had been imperfectly destroyed—an inconvenience soon surmounted.

Here I found the enemy in the occupation of an elevated ridge of land on the south branch (bank) of the Saranac, crowned with three strong redoubts and other field works, and block-houses armed with heavy ordnance, with their flotilla* at anchor out of gun-shot from the shore, consisting of a ship, a brig, a schooner, a sloop, and ten gun-boats.

I immediately communicated this circumstance to captain Downie, who had been recently appointed to command the vessels † on Lake Champlain, consisting of a ship, a brig, two sloops, and 12 gun-boats, and requested his co-operation, and in the mean time batteries were constructed for the guns brought from the rear.

On the morning of the 11th, our flotilla was seen over the isthmus which joins Cumberland-head with the main-land,

* The Saratoga, 26 guns; Surprise, 20 guns; Thunderer, 16 guns; Preble, 7 guns: 10 gun boats, 14 guns.

† The Confiance, 36 guns: Linnet, 18 guns; Broke, 10 guns; Shannon, 10 guns; 12 gun-boats, 16 guns.

steering for Plattsburg Bay. I immediately ordered that part of the brigade under major-general Robinson, which had been brought forward, consisting of our light infantry companies, third battalion 27th and 76th regiments, and major-general Power's brigade, consisting of the third, fifth, and the first battalion of the 27th and 58th regiments, to force the fords of the Saranac, and advance, provided with scaling-ladders, to escalade the enemy's works upon the heights; this force was placed under the command of major-general Robinson. The batteries opened their fire the instant the ships engaged.

It is now with deep concern I inform your lordship, that notwithstanding the intrepid valor with which captain Downie led his flotilla into action, my most sanguinary hopes of complete success were, not long afterwards, blasted, by a combination, as appeared to us, of unfortunate events, to which naval warfare is peculiarly exposed Scarcely had his majesty's troops forced a passage across the Saranac, and ascended the height on which stand the enemy's works, when I had the extreme mortification to hear the shout of victory from the enemy's works, in consequence of the British flag being lowered on board the Confiance and Linnet, and to see our gun-boats seeking their safety in flight. This unlooked-for event deprived me of the co-operation of the fleet, without which the further prosecution of the service was become impracticable, I did not hesitate to arrest the course of the troops advancing to the attack, because the most complete success would have been unavailing, and the possession of the enemy's works offered no advantage to compensate for the loss we must have sustained in acquiring possession of them.

I have ordered the batteries to be dismantled, the guns withdrawn, and the baggage, with the wounded men who can be removed, to be sent to the rear, in order that the troops may return to Chazy to-morrow, and on the following day to Champlain, where I propose to halt until I have ascertained the use the enemy propose making of the naval ascendancy they have acquired on Lake Champlain.

I have the honor to transmit herewith returns of the loss sustained by the left division of this army in its advance to Plattsburg, and in forcing a passage across the river Saranac.

I have the the honor, &c.

GEORGE PREVOST.

Earl Bathurst, &c.

No. 43.

Return of killed, wounded, and missing, of the left division, under the command of major-general De Rottenburg, in action with the enemy from the 6th to the 14th of September, inclusive.

General staff;—1 general staff, wounded.

19th light dragoons; 1 rank and file, 2 horses, wounded; 5 rank and file, 6 horses, missing.

Royal artillery; 1 serjeant, 1 rank and file, 1 horse, killed; 3 rank and file, wounded.

3d foot;—1 captain, 1 ensign, killed; 4 lieutenants, 1 serjeant, 34 rank and file, wounded; 2 rank and file missing.

5th foot;—1 rank and file, killed; 1 rank and file, wounded.

8th foot, 2d battalion;—1 rank and file, wounded.

13th foot;—2 rank and file, wounded.

27th foot, 1st battalion;—3 rank and file, killed; 1 serjeant, 13 rank and file, wounded; 1 rank and file, missing.

27th foot, 3d battalion;—1 serjeant, 2 rank and file, killed; 3 serjeants, 11 rank and file, wounded; 4 rank and file, missing.

49th foot;—3 rank and file, wounded.

58th foot; 4 rank and file, killed; 1 captain, 2 lieutenants, 1 serjeant, 29 rank and file, wounded.

76th foot;—1 captain, 1 serjeant, 10 rank and file, killed: 3 rank and file, wounded; 3 lieutenants, 2 serjeants, 1 drummer, 20 rank and file, missing.

88th foot;—9 rank and file, wounded.

De Meuron's regiment;—1 serjeant, 5 rank and file, killed; 1 serjeant, 14 rank and file, wounded; 9 rank and file, missing.

Canadian chasseurs;—4 rank and file, killed; 10 rank and file, wounded; 1 lieutenant, 7 rank and file, missing.

39th foot;—1 rank and file, wounded.

Total;—2 captains, 1 ensign, 4 serjeants, 30 rank and file, 1 horse, killed; 1 general staff, 1 captain, 6 lieutenants, 7 serjeants, 135 rank and file, 2 horses, wounded; 4 lieutenants, 2 serjeants, 1 drummer, 48 rank and file, 6 horses, missing.

Names of officers, killed, wounded, and missing.

Killed—3d foot;—Captain (brevet lieutenant-colonel) I. Willington, ensign J. Chapman.

76th foot;—Captain J. Purchase.

Wounded—General staff;—Captain T. Crosse, aide de camp to major-general De Rottenburg, slightly.

3d foot;—Lieutenant R. Kingsbury, severely; (since dead;) lieutenant J. West, severely; lieutenants G. Benson, and J. Horne, slightly.

58th foot;—Captain L. Westropp, severely; lieutenant C. Brokier, slightly; lieutenant and adjutant —— Lewis, slightly.

Missing—76th foot;—Lieutenants G. Hutch, G. Ogilvie, and E. Marchington.

Canadian chasseurs;—Lieutenant E. Vigneau.

EDWARD BAYNES,
Adjutant-general North America.

No. 44.

From sir James Lucas Yeo to Mr. Croker,

H. M. S. St. Lawrence, Kingston,
SIR, September 24, 1814.

I have the honor to transmit, for the information of the lords commissioners of the admiralty, a copy of a letter from captain Pring, late commander of his majesty's brig Linnet.

It appears to me, and I have good reason to believe, that captain Downie was urged, and his ship hurried into action, before she was in a fit state to meet the enemy.

I am also of opinion, that there was not the least necessity for our squadron giving the enemy such decided advantages, by going into their bay to engage them. Even had they been successful, it would not in the least have assisted the troops in storming the batteries; whereas, had our troops taken their batteries first, it would have obliged the enemy's squadron to quit the bay, and give ours a fair chance.

I have the honor, to be, &c.
JAMES LUCAS YEO,
Commmodore and commander in chief.

J. W. Croker, esq. &c. &c. &c.

No. 45.

From major-general Macombe to the American secretary at war.

SIR, Plattsburg, Sept. 15, 1814.

The governor-general of the Canadas, sir George Prevost, having collected all the disposable force in Lower Canada, with a view of conquering the country as far as Crown Point, and Ticonderago, entered the territories of the United States on the 1st of the month, and occupied the village of Champlain: there he avowed his intentions, and issued orders and proclamations, tending to dissuade the people from their allegiance, and inviting them to furnish his army with provisions. He immediately began to impress the waggons and teams in the vicinity, and loaded them with his heavy baggage and stores. From this I was persuaded he intended to attack this place. I had but just returned from the lines, where I had commanded a fine brigade, which was broken up to form the division under major-general Izard, and ordered to the westward. Being senior officer, he left me in command; and, except the four companies of the 6th regiment, I had not an organized battalion among those remaining. The garrison was composed of convalescents and recruits of the new regiments, all in the greatest confusion, as well as the ordnance and stores, and the works in no state of defence. To create an emulation and zeal among the officers and men in completing the works, I divided them into detachments, and placed them near the several forts; declaring in orders, that each detachment was the garrison of its own work, and bound to defend it to the last extremity. The enemy advanced cautiously and by short marches, and our soldiers worked day and night, so that by the time he made his appearance before the place we were prepared to receive him. General Izard named the principal work Fort-Moreau; and, to remind the troops of the actions of their brave countrymen, I called the redoubt on the right Fort-Brown, and that on the left Fort-Scott. Besides these three works, we had two block-houses strongly fortified. Finding, on examining the returns of the garrison, that our force did not exceed 1500 effective men for duty, and well informed that the enemy had as many thousands, I called on general Mooers, of the New York militia, and arranged with him plans for bringing forth the militia *en masse*. The inhabitants of the village fled with their families and effects, except a few worthy citizens and some boys, who formed themselves into a party, received rifles, and were exceedingly useful. By the 4th of the month, general Mooers collected about 700 militia, and advanced seven miles on the Beckman-town road, to watch the motions of the enemy, and to skirmish with him as he advanced; also to obstruct the roads with fallen trees, and to break up the bridges. On the lake-road, at Dead creek bridge, I posted 200 men, under captain Sproul, of the 13th regiment, with orders to abattis the woods, to place obstructions in the road, and to fortify himself: to this party I added two field-pieces. In advance of that position was lieutenant-colonel Appling, with 110 riflemen, watching the movements of the enemy, and procuring intelligence. It was ascertained, that before day-light on the 6th, the enemy would advance in two columns, on the two roads before mentioned, dividing at Sampson's a little below Chazy village. The column on the Beckman-town road proceeded most rapidly; the militia skirmished with his advanced parties, and except a few brave men, fell back most precipitately in the greatest disorder, notwithstanding the British troops did not deign to fire on them, except by their flankers and advanced patroles. The night previous, I ordered major Wool to advance with a detachment of 250 men to support the militia, and set them an example of firmness; also captain Leonard, of the light-artillery, was directed to proceed with two pieces to be on the ground before day; yet he did not make his appearance until eight o'clock, when the enemy had approached within two miles of the village. With his conduct, therefore, I am not well pleased. Major Wool, with his party, disputed the road with great obstinacy, but the militia could not be prevailed on to stand, notwithstanding the exertions of their general and staff-officers; although the fields were divided by strong stone walls, and they were told that the enemy could not possibly cut them off. The state dragoons of New York wear red coats; and they being on the heights to watch the enemy, gave constant alarm to the militia, who mistook them for the enemy, and feared his getting in their rear

Finding the enemy's columns had penetrated within a mile of Plattsburg, I despatched my aide de camp, lieutenant Root, to bring off the detachment at Dead creek, and to inform lieutenant-colonel Appling that I wished him to fall on the enemy's right flank. The colonel fortunately arrived just in time to save his retreat, and to fall in with the head of a column debouching from the woods. Here he poured in a destructive fire from his riflemen at rest, and continued to annoy the enemy until he formed a junction with major Wool. The field-pieces did considerable execution among the enemy's columns. So undaunted, however, was the enemy, that he never deployed in his whole march, always pressing on in column. Finding that every road was full of troops, crowding on us on all sides, I ordered the field-pieces to retire across the bridge, and form a battery for its protection, and to cover the retreat of the infantry, which was accordingly done, and the parties of Appling and Wool, as well as that of Sproul, retired, alternately keeping up a brisk fire until they got under cover of the works. The enemy's light troops occupied the houses near the bridge, and kept up a constant firing from the windows and balconies, and annoyed us much. I ordered them to be driven out with hot shot, which soon put the houses in flames, and obliged those sharp-shooters to retire. The whole day, until it was too late to see, the enemy's light troops endeavoured to drive our guards from the bridge, but they suffered dearly for their perseverance. An attempt was also made to cross the upper bridge, where the militia handsomely drove them back. The column which marched by the lake-road was much impeded by the obstructions, and the removal of the bridge at Dead creek; and, as it passed the creek and beach, the gallies kept up a lively and galling fire. Our troops being now all on the south side of the Saranac, I directed the planks to be taken off the bridges and piled up in the form of breast-works, to cover our parties intended for disputing the passage, which afterwards enabled us to hold the bridges against very superior numbers. From the 7th to the 14th, the enemy was employed in getting on his battering-train, and erecting his batteries and approaches, and constantly skirmishing at the bridges and fords. By this time the militia of New York and the volunteers of Vermont were pouring in from all quarters. I advised general Mooers to keep his force along the Saranac to prevent the enemy's crossing the river, and to send a strong body in his rear to harass him day and night, and keep him in continual alarm. The militia behaved with great spirit after the first day, and the volunteers of Vermont were exceedingly serviceable. Our regular troops, notwithstanding the constant skirmishing, and repeated endeavours of the enemy to cross the river, kept at their work day and night, strengthening the defences, and evinced a determination to hold out to the last extremity. It was reported that the enemy only waited the arrival of his flotilla to make a general attack. About eight in the morning of the 11th, as was expected, the flotilla appeared in sight round Cumberland Head, and at nine bore down and engaged at anchor in the bay off the town. At the same instant the batteries were opened on us, and continued throwing bomb-shells, shrapnells, balls, and Congreve rockets, until sun-set, when the bombardment ceased, every battery of the enemy being silenced by the superiority of our fire. The naval engagement lasted but two hours, in full view of both armies. Three efforts were made by the enemy to pass the river at the commencement of the cannonade and bombardment, with a view of assaulting the works, and they had prepared for that purpose an immense number of scaling-ladders. One attempt to cross was made at the village bridge, another at the upper bridge, and a third at a ford about three miles from the works. At the two first he was repulsed by the regulars—at the ford by the brave volunteers and militia, where he suffered severely in killed, wounded, and prisoners: a considerable body crossed the stream, but were either killed, taken, or driven back. The woods at this place were very favorable to the operations of the militia. A whole company of the 76th regiment was here destroyed, the three lieutenants and 27 men prisoners, the captain and the rest killed. I cannot forego the pleasure of here stating the gallant conduct of captain M'Glassin, of the 15th regiment, who was ordered to ford the river, and attack a party constructing a battery on the right of the enemy's line, within 500 yards of Fort-Brown, which he handsomely executed at midnight, with 50 men; drove off the working party, consisting of 150, and defeated a covering party of the same number, killing one officer and six men in the charge, and wounding many. At dusk the enemy withdrew his artillery from the batteries, and raised the siege; and at nine, under cover of the night, sent off, in a great hurry, all the baggage he could find transport for, and also his artillery. At two the next morning the whole army precipitately retreated, leaving the sick and wounded to our generosity; and the governor left a note with a surgeon, requesting the humane attention of the commanding-general.

Vast quantities of provision were left behind and destroyed; also an immense quantity of bomb-shells, cannon-balls, grape-shot, ammunition, flints, &c. entrenching tools of all sorts, also tents and marquees. A great deal has been found concealed in ponds and creeks, and buried in the ground, and a vast quantity carried off by the inhabitants. Such was the precipitance of his retreat, that he arrived at Chazy, a distance of eight miles, before we discovered he had gone. The light troops, volunteers, and militia, pursued immediately on learning of his flight, and some of the mounted men made prisoners five dragoons of the 19th regiment, and several others of the rear-guard. A continual fall of rain and a violent storm prevented further pursuit. Upwards of 300 deserters have come in, and many are hourly arriving. We have buried the British officers of the army and navy with the honors of war, and shewn every attention and kindness to those who have fallen into our hands. The conduct of the officers, non-commissioned officers, and soldiers of my command, during the trying occasion, cannot be represented in too high terms.

ALEX. MACOMB.

The loss of the enemy in killed, wounded, prisoners, and deserters, since his first appearance, cannot fall short of 2500.

Hon. I. Armstrong.

No. 46.

From major-general De Watteville, to lieutenant-general Drummond.

Camp before Fort-Erie,
Sept. 19, 1814.

Sir,

I have the honor to report to you, that the enemy attacked, on the 17th in the afternoon at three o'clock, our position before Fort-Erie, the 2d brigade, under colonel Fischer, composed of the 8th and de Watteville's regiments, being on duty.

Under cover of a heavy fire of his artillery from Fort-Erie, and much favored by the nature of the ground, and also by the state of the weather, the rain falling in torrents at the moment of his approach, the enemy succeeded in turning the right of our line of piquets, without being perceived, and with a very considerable force, attacked both the piquets and support, in their flank and rear: at the same time, another of the enemy's columns attacked, in front, the piquets between No. 2 and No. 3 batteries, and, having succeeded in penetrating by No. 4 piquet, part of his force turned to his left, and thereby surrounded our right, and got almost immediate possession of No. 3 battery. The enemy then directed his attacks, with a very superior force, towards No. 2 battery; but the obstinate resistance made by the piquets, under every possible disadvantage, delayed considerably his getting possession of No. 2 battery; in which, however, he at last succeeded.

As soon as the alarm was given, the 1st brigade, being next for support, composed of the royal Scots, the 82d and 89th regiments, under lieutenant-colonel Gordon, received orders to march forward; and also the light demi-brigade under lieutenant-colonel Pearson: the 6th regiment remaining in reserve, under lieutenant-colonel Campbell. From the Concession-road, the royal Scots, with the 89th as support, moved by the new road, and met the enemy near the block-house, on the right of No. 3 battery; whom they engaged, and, by their steady and intrepid conduct, checked his further progress. The 82d regiment, and three companies of the 6th regiment, were detached to the left, in order to support Nos. 1 and 2 batteries. The enemy having, at that time, possession of No. 2 battery, and still pushing forward, seven companies of the 82d, under major Proctor, and the three companies of the 6th, under major Taylor, received directions to oppose the enemy's forces, and immediatrly charged them with the most intredid bravery, driving them back across our entrenchments; and also from No. 2 battery, thereby preventing their destroying it, or damaging its guns in a considerable degree. Lieutenant-colonel Pearson, with the Glengarry light infantry, under lieutenant-colonel Battersby, pushed forward by the centre-road, and attacked, and carried, with great gallantry, the new entrenchment, then in full possession of the enemy.

The enemy, being thus repulsed at every point, was forced to retire with precipitation to their works, leaving several prisoners, and a number of their wounded in our hands. By five o'clock the entrenchments were again occupied, and the line of piquets established, as it had been previous to the enemy's attack.

I have the honor to enclose a return of casualties, and the report of the officer commanding the royal artillery, respecting the damage done to the ordnance and the batteries, during the time they were in the enemy's possession.

I have the honor to be, &c.

L. DE WATTEVILLE, major-gen.

Lieut.-general Drummond, &c.

No. 47.

Return of casualties of the right division of the army, in action with the enemy; camp before Fort-Erie, Sept. 17, 1814.

Royal artillery;—9 rank and file, missing.

Additional gunners, De Watteville's regiment;—1 rank and file, wounded; 10 rank and file, missing.

1st, or royal Scots;—8 rank and file, killed; 1 lieutenant-colonel, 1 lieutenant, 1 serjeant, 30 rank and file, wounded; 2 serjeants, 15 rank and file, missing.

6th foot;—1 captain, 1 serjeant, 13 rank and file, killed; 1 lieutenant, 1 serjeant, 25 rank and file, wounded; 1 serjeant, 10 rank and file, missing.

8th foot;—1 lieutenant, 1 serjeant, 12 rank and file, killed; 1 lieutenant, 12 rank and file, wounded; 1 captain, 1 lieutenant, 1 ensign, 8 serjeants, 63 rank and file, missing.

82d foot;—2 serjeants, 10 rank and file, killed; 5 captains, 4 lieutenants, 1 ensign, 5 serjeants, 33 rank and file, wounded; 8 rank and file, missing.

89th foot;—1 rank and file, killed; 1 serjeant, 2 rank and file, wounded; 1 serjeant, 19 rank and file, missing.

De Watteville's regiment;—1 lieutenant, 3 serjeants, 58 rank and file, killed; 1 lieutenant-colonel, 1 captain, 3 lieutenants, 4 serjeants, 1 drummer, 26 rank and file, wounded; 2 majors, 3 captains, 2 lieutenants, 1 adjutant, 1 assistant-surgeon, 9 serjeants, 2 drummers, 146 rank and file, missing.

Glengarry light infantry;—3 rank and file, killed; 1 serjeant, 18 rank and file, wounded.

Grand total—1 captain, 2 lieutenants, 7 serjeants, 105 rank and file, killed; 3 lieutenant-colonels, 3 captains, 10 lieutenants, 1 ensign, 13 serjeants, 1 drummer, 147 rank and file, wounded; 2 majors, 4 captains, 3 lieutenants, 2 ensigns, 1 adjutant, 1 assistant-surgeon, 21 serjeants, 2 drummers, 280 rank and file, missing.

Names of officers.

Killed.

6th foot;—Captain R. D. Patterson.

8th foot;—Lieutenant Barston.

De Watteville's regiment;—Lieutenant Pelliehody.

Wounded.

Royal Scots;—Lieutenant-colonel J. Gordon, severely; lieutenant G. Ratledge, since dead.

6th foot;—Lieutenant Andrews, severely.

8th foot;—Lieutenant Lowry, severely.

82d foot;—Captain I. M. Wright, since dead; captain E. Marshall, slightly; lieutenant H. Pigott, W. Mason, and Robert Latham, severely; lieutenant G. Harman, slightly; ensign C. Langford, since dead.

De Watteville's regiment;—Lieutenant-colonel Fischer, severely;

captain Mittelholzer, severely; lieutenant Gingins, severely; lieutenant Steiger, slightly; lieutenant La Pierre, severely.

Staff;—Lieutenant-colonel Thomas Pearson, inspecting field-officer, severely.

Missing—8th foot;—Captain Bradbridge, lieutenant M'Nair, ensign Matthewson.

De Watteville's regiment;---Major De Villatte, major Winter, wounded; captain Zehender, Hecken, and Steiger; lieutenant De Berry, lieutenant Hecken, wounded; adjutant Thermet; assistant-surgeon Gorbea.

No. 48.

From lieutenant-colonel Pilkington to lieutenant-general sir John C. Sherbrooke.

Moose Island, Passamaquaddy Bay,
July 12, 1814.

SIR,

Having sailed from Halifax on the 5th instant, accompanied by lieutenant-colonel Nicolls, of the royal engineers, and a detachment of the royal artillery, under the command of captain Dunn, I have the honour to acquaint your excellency, that we arrived at Shelburne, the place of rendezvous, on the evening of the 7th instant, where I found captain sir Thomas Hardy, in his majesty's ship Ramillies, with two transports, having on board the 102d regiment, under the command of lieutenant-colonel Herries, which had arrived the day before. I did not fail to lay before Sir Thomas Hardy my instructions, and to consult with him the best means of carrying them into execution.

As we concurred in opinion that the success of the enterprise, with which we were entrusted, would very materially depend upon our reaching the point of attack previous to the enemy being apprised of our intentions, that officer, with his accustomed alacrity and decision, directed the ships of war and transports to get under weigh early on the following morning; and we yesterday, about 3 o'clock P.M., anchored near to the town of Eastport.

On our approach to this island, lieutenant Oats (your excellency's aide de camp, whom you had permitted to accompany me on this service) was detached in a boat, bearing a flag of truce, with a summons, (copy of which is transmitted,) addressed to the officer commanding, requiring that Moose Island should be surrendered to his Britannic majesty. This proposal was not accepted; in consequence of which, the troops, which were already in the boats, pulled off under the superintendance of captain Senhouse, of the royal navy, whose arrangements were so judicious, as to insure a successful issue. But, previous to reaching the shore, the colours of the enemy on Fort-Sullivan were hauled down: and on our landing, the capitulation was agreed to, of which the copy is inclosed.

We found in the fort a detachment of the 40th regiment of American infantry, consisting of six officers and about 80 men, under the command of major Putman, who surrendered themselves prisoners of war.

This fort is situated on an eminence commanding the entrance to the anchorage, and within it is a block-house, and also four long 18-pounders, one 18-pound carronade, and four field-pieces. The extent of the island is about four miles in length and two in breadth, and in a great state of cultivation. The militia amount to about 250, and the population is calculated at 1500.

We have also occupied Allen's and Frederick Island, so that the whole of the islands in this bay are now subject to the British flag.

It is very satisfactory to me to add, that this service has been effected, without any loss or casualty among the troops employed in it.

To captain sir Thomas Hardy, I consider myself under the greatest obligations; having experienced every possible co-operation, with an offer to disembark, from his squadrom, any proportion of seamen or marines which I considered necessary.

I beg to acknowledge my thanks to you in allowing your aide de camp, lieutenant Oats, to accompany me upon this service. He has been a great assistant to me, and will have the honor of delivering this despatch. He has also in his possession the colours and standard found in Fort-Sullivan.

I have the honor to be, &c.

A. PILKINGTON, lieut.-col.
deputy-adjutant-general.

Lieut.-general
Sir J. C. Sherbrook, K. B.

No. 49.

From captain Hardy, R. N., and lieutenant-colonel Pilkington, to the American commander at Moose Island.

On board of his majesty's ship Ramillies, off Moose Island, July 11, 1814.

Sir,

As we are perfectly apprised of the weakness of the fort and garrison under your command, and your inability to defend Moose Island against the ships and troops of his Britannic majesty placed under our directions, we are induced, from the humane consideration of avoiding the effusion of blood, and from a regard to you and the inhabitants of the island, to prevent, if in our power, the distresses and calamities which will befall them in case of resistance. We, therefore, allow you five minutes, from the time this summons is delivered, to decide upon an answer.

In the event of your not agreeing to capitulate on liberal terms, we shall deeply lament being compelled to resort to those coercive measures, which may cause destruction to the town of Eastport, but which will ultimately assure us possession of the island.

T. M. HARDY, captain of H.M.S Ramillies.
A. PILKINGTON, lieut.-col. commanding.

To the officers commanding the United States' troops
on Moose Island.

No. 50.

From major Putman to captain Hardy, and lieutenant-colonel Pilkington.

GENTLEMEN, Fort Sullivan, July 11, 1814.

Conformably to your demand, I have surrendered Fort-Sullivan with all the public property.

This I have done to stop the effusion of blood and in consideration of your superior forces. I am, gentlemen, &c.

P. PUTMAN, major, commanding.

P. S. I hope, gentlemen, every respect will be paid to the defenceless inhabitants of this island, and the private property of the officers. P. P.

No. 51.

Articles of capitulation.

Article I. The officers and troops of the United States, at present on Moose island, are to surrender themselves prisoners of war, and are to deliver up the forts, buildings, arms, ammunition, stores, and effects, with exact inventories thereof, belonging to the American government; and they are thereby transferred to his Britannic majesty, in the same manner and possession, as has been held heretofore by the American government.

Art. II. The garrison of the island shall be prisoners of war, until regularly exchanged; they will march out of the fort with the honors of war, and pile their arms at such place as will be appointed for that purpose; the officers will be permitted to proceed to the United States on their parole.

No. 52.

Return of ordnance and stores found in Fort-Sullivan, surrendered to his majesty's forces under the command of lieutenant-colonel Pilkington.

Iron guns;—four 18-pounders, with standing carriages, side arms; two unserviceable 9-pounders, two 12-pounder carronades without carriages.

Brass guns;—two serviceable and two unserviceable light 6-pounders, with travelling carriages, side arms, &c.

Forty-two paper cartridges, filled with six pounds of powder, 5 flannel ditto, ditto; 3176 unserviceable musket-ball cartridges.

Four hundred and fifty-two loose round 18-pounder shot; fifty-five 18-pounder grape shot, three hundred and eighty-nine loose round 6-pounder, ninety-five 6-pounder case shot.

Six barrels of horned powder, containing one hundred pounds each; 100 muskets, with bayonets, belts, slings, and complete swords, with belts, scabbards, &c.

Seventy-two incomplete tents, one United States' ensign.

W. DUNN, capt. royal artillery company.

No. 53.

From lieutenant-general sir I. C. Sherbrooke to earl Bathurst.

Castine at the entrance of the Penobscot,
Sept. 18, 1814.

MY LORD,

I have now the honor to inform your lordship, that after closing my despatch of the 25th ult. in which I mentioned my intention of proceeding to the Penobscot, rear-admiral Griffiths and myself lost no time in sailing from Halifax, with such a naval force as he deemed necessary, and the troops as per margin, (viz. 1st company of royal artillery, two rifle companies of the 7th battalion 60th regiment, 29th, 62d, and 98th regiments,) to accompany the object we had in view.

Very early in the morning of the 30th we fell in with the Rifleman sloop of war, when captain Pearse informed us, that the United States' frigate, the Adams, had got into the Penobscot, but from the apprehension of being attacked by our cruizers, if she remained at the entrance of the river, she had run up as high as Hampden, where she had landed her guns, and mounted them on shore for her protection.

On leaving Halifax it was my original intention to have taken possession of Machias, on our way hither, but on receiving this intelligence, the admiral and myself were of opinion that no time should be lost in proceeding to our destination, and we arrived here very early on the morning of the 1st instant.

The fort of Castine, which is situated upon a peninsula of the eastern side of the Penobscot, near the entrance of that river, was summoned a little after sun-rise, but the American officer refused to surrender it, and immediately opened a fire from four 24-pounders upon a small schooner that had been sent with lieutenant-colonel Nichols (commanding royal engineers) to reconnoitre the work.

Arrangements were immediately made for disembarking the troops, but before a landing could be effected, the enemy blew up the magazine, and escaped up the Majetaquadous river, carrying off in the boats with them two field-pieces.

As we had no means of ascertaining what force the Americans had on this peninsula, I landed a detachment of the royal artillery, with two rifle-companies of the 60th and 98th regiments, under colonel Douglas, in the rear of it, with orders to secure the isthmus, and to take possession of the heights which command the town; but I soon learned there were no regulars at Castine, except the party which had blown up the magazine and escaped, and that the militia, which were assembled there, had dispersed immediately upon our landing.

Rear-admiral Griffith and myself next turned our attention to obtaining possession of the Adams, or if that could not be done, destroying her. The arrangement for this service having been made, the rear-admiral entrusted the execution of it to captain Barrie, royal navy, and as the co-operation of a land force was necessary, I directed lieutenant-colonel John, with a detachment of artillery, the flank companies of the 29th, 62d, and 98th regiments, and one rifle company of the 60th, to accompany and co-operate with captain Barrie on this occasion; but as Hampden is 27 miles above Castine, it appeared to me a necessary measure of precaution first to occupy a post on the western bank, which might afford support, if necessary, to the force going up the river, and at the same time prevent the armed population, which is very numerous to the southward and to the westward, from annoying the British in their operations against the Adams.

Upon inquiry, I found that Belfast, which is upon the high road leading from Hampden to Boston, and which perfectly commands the bridge, was likely to answer both these purposes, and I consequently directed major-general Gosselin to occupy that place with the 29th regiment, and maintain it till further orders.

As soon as this was accomplished, and the tide served, rear-admiral Griffith directed captain Barrie to proceed to his destination, and the remainder of the troops were landed that evening at Castine.

Understanding that a strong party of militia from the neighbouring township had assembled at about four miles from Castine, on the road leading to Blue-hill, I sent out a strong patrole on the morning of the 2d, before day-break; on arriving at the place, I was informed that the militia of the county was assembled there on the alarm guns being fired at the fort at Castine, upon our first appearance; but that the main body had since dispersed, and went to their respective homes. Some stragglers were however left, who fired upon our advanced guard, and then took to the woods; a few of them were made prisoners. No intelligence having reached us from captain Barrie, on Saturday night, I marched with about 700 men and two light field-pieces, upon Buckstown, at three o'clock, on Sunday morning the 4th instant, for the purpose of learning what progress he had made, and of affording him assistance if required. This place is about 18 miles higher up the Ponobscot than Castine, and on the eastern bank of the river. Rear-admiral Griffith accompanied me on this occasion, and we had reason to believe that the light guns which had been taken from Castine were secreted in the neighbourhood of Buckstown. We threatened to destroy the town unless they were given up, and the two brass 3-pounders on travelling-carriages were in consequence brought to us in the course of the day, and are now in our possession.

At Buckstown, we received very satisfactory accounts of the success which had attended the force employed up the river. We learned that captain Barrie had proceeded from Hampton up to Bangor; and the admiral sent an officer in a boat from Buckstown to communicate with him: when, finding there was no necessity for the troops remaining longer at Buckstown, they marched back to Castine the next day.

Having ascertained that the object of the expedition up the Penobseot had been obtained, it was no longer necessary for me to occupy Belfast. I, therefore, on the evening of the 6th, directed major-general Gosselin to embark the troops, and to join me here.

Machias being the only place now remaining where the enemy had a post between the Penobscot and Passamaquaddy bay, I ordered lieutenant-colonel Pilkington to proceed with a detachment of royal artillery and the 29th regiment to occupy it; and as naval assistance was required, rear-admiral Griffith directed captain Parker, of the Tenedos, to co-operate with lieutenant-colonel Pilkington upon this occasion.

On the morning of the 9th, captain Barrie, with lieutenant-colonel John, and the troops which had been employed with him up the Penobscot, returned to Castine. It seems, the enemy blew up the Adams, on his strong position at Hampden being attacked; but all his artillery, two stands of colours, and a standard, with several merchant vessels, fell into our hands. This, I am happy to say, was accomplished with very little loss on our part; and your lordship will perceive, by the return sent herewith, that the only officer wounded in this affair, is captain Gall, of the 29th grenadiers.

Herewith I have the honor to transmit a copy of the report, made to me by lieutenant-colonel John on this occasion, in which your lordship will be pleased to observe, that the lieutenant-colonel speaks very highly of the gallantry and good conduct displayed by the troops upon this expedition, under very trying circumstances. And I beg to call your lordship's attention to the names of those officers upon whom lieutenant-colonel John particularly bestows praise. The enterprise and intrepidity manifested by lieutenant-colonel John, and the discipline and gallantry displayed by the troops under him, reflect great honor upon them, and demand my warmest acknowledgments; and I have to request your lordship will take a favourable opportunity of bringing the meritorious and successful services, performed by the troops employed on this occasion, under the view of his royal highness the prince regent.

As rear-admiral Griffith will, no doubt, make a detailed report of the naval operations on this occasion, I forbear touching upon this subject, further than to solicit your lordship's attention to that part of colonel John's report, in which he "attributes the success of this enterprise to the masterly arrangements of captain Barrie, royal navy, who conducted it."

I have much pleasure in reporting to your lordship, that the most perfect unanimity and good understanding has prevailed between the naval and military branches of the service, during the whole progress of this expedition.

I feel it my duty to express, in the strongest terms, the great obligations I am under to rear-admiral Griffith, for his judicious advice, and ready co-operation, on every occasion. And my thanks are likewise due to all the captains of the ships employed, for the assistance they have so willingly afforded the troops, and from which the happiest results have been experienced.

I have reason to be well satisfied with the gallantry and good conduct of the troops, and have to offer my thanks to major-general Gosselin, colonel Douglas, and the commanding officers of corps, for the alacrity shown by them, and strict discipline which has been maintained.

To the heads of departments, and to the officers of the general and of my personal staff, I am much indebted for the zealous manner in which they have discharged their respective duties.

Major Addison, my military secretary, will have the honor of delivering this despatch. He has been with me during the whole of these operations, and is well enabled to afford your lordship any information you may require.

I have entrusted the colours and standard taken from the enemy to major Addison, who will receive your lordship's commands respecting the further disposal of them ; and I take the liberty of recommending him as a deserving officer to your lordship's protection. I have, &c.

J. C. SHERBROOKE.

N. B. The returns of killed, wounded, and missing, and of artillery, and of ordnance stores taken, are inclosed.

No. 54.

From lieutenant-colonel John to lieutenant-general sir J. C. Sherbrooke.

Bangor, on the Penobscot river,
Sept. 3, 1814.

Sir,

In compliance with your excellency's orders of the 1st instant, I sailed from Castine with the detachment of royal artillery, the flank companies of the 29th, 62d, and 98th regiments, and one rifle company of the 7th battalion 60th regiment, which composed the force your excellency did me the honor to place under my command, for the purpose of co-operating with captain Barrie, of the royal navy, in an expedition up this river.

On the morning of the 2d, having proceeded above the town of Frankfort, we discovered some of the enemy on their march towards Hamden, by the eastern shore, which induced me to order brevet-major Crosdaile, with a detachment of the 98th, and some riflemen of the 60th regiment, under lieutenant Wallace, to land and intercept them, which was accomplished ; and that detachment of the enemy (as I have since learned) were prevented from joining the main body assembled at Hamden. On this occasion the enemy had one man killed, and some wounded. Major Crosdaile re-embarked without any loss. We arrived off Bald Head cove, three miles distant from Hamden, about five o'clock that evening, when captain Barrie agreed with me in determining to land the troops immediately. Having discovered that the enemy's piquets were advantageously posted on the north side of the cove, I directed brevet-major Riddle, with the grenadiers of the 62d, and captain Ward, with the rifle company of the 60th, to dislodge them, and take up that ground, which duty was performed under major Riddle's directions, in a most complete and satisfactory manner, by about seven o'clock; and before ten at night, the whole of the troops, including 80 marines under captain Carter, (whom captain Barrie had done me the honor to attach to my command,) were landed and bivouacked for the night, during which it rained incessantly. We got under arms at five o'clock this morning, the rifle-company forming the advance under captain Ward; brevet-major Keith, with the light company of the 62d, bringing up the rear, and the detachment of marines, under captain Carter, moving upon my flanks, while captain Barrie, with the ships and gun-boats under his command, advanced at the same time up the river, on my right, towards Hamden. In addition to the detachment of royal artillery under lieutenant Garston, captain Barrie had landed one 6-pounder, a 5½-inch-howitzer, and a rocket apparatus, with a detachment of sailors under lieutenants Symonds, Botely, and Slade, and Mr. Sparling, master of his majesty's ship Bulwark.

The fog was so thick, it was impossible to form a correct idea of the features of the country, or to reconnoitre the enemy, whose number were reported to be 1400, under the command of brigadier-general Blake. Between seven and eight o'clock, our skirmishers in advance were so sharply engaged with the enemy, as to induce me to send forward one-half of the light company of the 29th regiment, under captain Coaker, to their support. The column had not advanced much further, before I discovered the enemy drawn out in line, occupying a very strong and advantageous position in front of the town of Hamden, his left flanked by a high hill commanding the road and river, on which were mounted several heavy pieces of cannon; his right extending considerably beyond our left, resting upon a strong point *d'appui*, with an 18-pounder and some light field-pieces in advance of his centre, so pointed as completely to rake the road, and a narrow bridge at the foot of a hill, by which we were obliged to advance upon his position. As soon as he perceived our column approaching, he opened a very heavy and continued fire of grape and musquetry upon us; we however soon crossed the bridge, deployed, and charged up the hill to get possession of his guns, one of which we found had already fallen into the hands of captain Ward's riflemen in advance.

The enemy's fire now began to slacken, and we pushed on rapidly, and succeeded in driving him at all points from his position; while captain Coaker, with the light company of the 29th, had gained possession of the hill on the left, from whence it was discovered that the Adams frigate was on fire, and that the enemy had deserted the battery which defended her.

We were now in complete possession of the enemy's position above, and captain Barrie with the gun-boats had secured that below the hill. Upon this occasion 20 pieces of cannon fell into our hands, of the naval and military force, the return of which I enclose; after which captain Barrie and myself determined on pursuing the enemy towards Bangor, which place we reached without opposition; and here two brass 3-pounders, and three stands of colours fell into our possession. Brigadier-general Blake, also in this town, surrendered himself prisoner; and, with other prisoners to the amount of 121, were admitted to their paroles. Eighty prisoners taken at Hamden are in our custody. The loss sustained by the enemy I have not had it in my power correctly to ascertain; report states it to be from 30 to 40 in killed, wounded, and missing.

Our own loss, I am happy to add, is but small; viz. 1 rank and file, killed; 1 captain, 7 rank and file, wounded; 1 rank and file, missing. Captain Gell, of the 29th, was wounded when leading the column, which deprived me of his active and useful assistance; but, I am happy to add, he is recovering.

I cannot close this despatch without mentioning, in the highest terms, all the troops placed under my command. They have merited my highest praise for their zeal and gallantry, which were conspicuous in the extreme. I feel most particularly indebted to brevet-major Riddall, of the 62d regiment, second in command; to brevet-major Keith, of the same regiment; brevet-major Croasdaile and captain M'Pherson, of the 98th; captains Gell and Coaker, of the 29th; and captain Ward, of the 7th battalion 60th regiment. The royal artillery was directed in the most judicious manner by lieutenant Garston, from whom I derived the ablest support. I cannot speak too highly of captain Carter and the officers and marines under his directions. He moved them in the ablest manner to the annoyance of the enemy, and so as to meet my fullest approval.

Nothing could exceed the zeal and perseverance of lieutenants Symonds, Botely, and Slade, and Mr. Sparling, of the royal navy, with the detachment of seamen under their command.

From captain Barrie I have received the ablest assistance and support; and it is to his masterly arrangement of the plan that I feel indebted for its success. Nothing could be more cordial than the co-operation of the naval and military forces on this service in every instance.

Captain Carnagie, of the royal navy, who most handsomely volunteered his services with this expedition, was in action with the troops at Hamden; and I feel most particularly indebted to him for his exertions and the assistance he afforded me on this occasion. I am also greatly indebted to lieutenant Du Chatelet, of the 7th battalion, 60th regiment, who acted as major of brigade to the troops, in which capacity he rendered me very essential service. I have the honor, &c.

HENRY JOHN, lieut.-col.

No. 55.

Return of ordnance and stores taken.

Castine, Sept. 10, 1814.

Guns;—4 iron 24-pounders, 27 iron (ship) 18-pounders, 4 12-pounders, 4 brass 3-pounders.

Carriages;—4 traversing 24-pounders, 8 standing 18-pounders, 2 travelling 12-pounders with limbers, 4 travelling 3-pounders with limbers.

Sponges;—8 24-pounders, 20 18-pounders, 2 12-pounders, 4 3-pounders.

Ladles;—2 24-pounders, 3 12-pounders, 1 3-pounder.

Wadhooks:—2 24-pounders, 3 12-pounders, 1 8-pounder.

Shot;—236 round 24-pounders, 500 round 18-pounders. 1 ammunition-waggon, 1 ammunition-cart. 12 common handspikes. 40 barrels of powder.

Wads;—20 24-pounders, 70 18-pounders.

N. B.—The magazine in fort Castine was blown up by the enemy.

The vessel on board of which the powder was, ran on shore, and the whole destroyed.

Eleven of the 18-pounders were destroyed by order of lieutenant-colonel John, not having time to bring them off.

GEORGE CRAWFORD, major,
commanding royal artil.

Lieut.-gen. Sir J. C. Sherbrooke.

No. 56.

Return of the killed, wounded, and missing, in the affair at Hamden, on the 3d of September, 1814, with the force under the command of lieutenant-colonel John, 60th regiment.

Killed.—29th regiment;—1 rank and file.

Wounded—29th regiment;—1 captain, 2 rank and file.

62d regiment;—1 rank and file.

98th regiment;—4 rank and file.

Missing—62d regiment;—1 rank and file.

Name of officer wounded—29th regiment;—Captain Gell, severely (not dangerously).

A. PILKINGTON, Dep.-adj.-gen.

No. 57.

From lieutenant-colonel Pilkington to lieutenant-general sir J.´C. Sherbrooke.

SIR, Machias, Sept. 14, 1814.

I have the honor to acquaint your excellency, that I sailed from Penobscot bay, with the brigade you was pleased to place under my command, consisting of a detachment of royal artillery, with a howitzer, the battalion companies of the 29th regiment, and a party of the 7th battalion of the 60th foot, on the morning of the 9th instant; and arrived at Buck's harbor, about 10 miles from this place, on the following evening.

As the enemy fired several alarm guns on our approaching the shore, it was evident he was apprehensive of an attack: I therefore deemed it expedient to disembark the troops with as little delay as possible; and captain Hyde Parker, commanding the naval force, appointed captain Stanfell to superintend this duty, and it was executed by that officer with the utmost promptitude and decision.

Upon reaching the shore, I ascertained that there was only a pathway through the woods by which we could advance and take Fort O'Brien and the battery in reverse; and as the guns of these works commanded the passage of the river, upon which the town is situated, I decided upon possessing ourselves of them, if practicable, during the night.

We moved forward at ten o'clock P. M. and, after a most tedious and harassing march, only arrived near to the fort at break of day, although the distance does not exceed five miles.

The advanced guard, which consisted of two companies of the 29th regiment, and a detachment of riflemen of the 60th regiment, under major Tod, of the former corps, immediately drove in the enemy's piquets, and upon pursuing him closely, found the fort had been evacuated, leaving their colours, about five minutes before we entered it. Within it, and the battery, there are two 24-pounders, three 18-pounders, several dismounted guns, and a block-house. The party which escaped amounted to about 70 men of the 40th regiment of American infantry, and 30 of the embodied militia; the retreat was so rapid that I was not enabled to take any prisoners. I undestand there were a few wounded, but they secreted themselves in the wood.

Having secured the fort, we lost no time in advancing upon Machias, which was taken without any resistance; and also two field-pieces.

The boats of the squadron, under the command of lieutenant Bouchier, of the royal navy, and the royal marines, under lieutenant Welchman, were detached to the eastern side of the river, and were of essential service in taking two field-pieces in that quarter.

Notwithstanding that the militia were not assembled to any extent in the vicinity of the town, I was making the necessary arrangements to advance into the interior of the country, when I received a letter from brigadier-general Brewer, commanding the district, wherein he engages that the militia forces within the county of Washington shall not bear arms, or in any way serve against his Britannic majesty during the present war. A similar offer having been made by the civil officers and principal citizens of the county, a cessation of arms was agreed upon, and the county of Washington has passed under the dominion of his Britannic majesty.

I beg leave to congratulate you upon the importance of this accession of territory which has been wrested from the enemy; it embraces about 100 miles of sea-coast, and includes that intermediate tract of country which separates the province of New Brunswick from Lower Canada.

We have taken 26 pieces of ordnance, (serviceable and unserviceable,) with a proportion of arms and ammunition, returns of which are enclosed; and I have the pleasing satisfaction to add, that this service has been effected without the loss of a man on our part.

I cannot refrain from expressing, in the strongest manner, the admirable steadiness and good conduct of the 29th regiment, under major Hodge. The advance, under major Tod, are also entitled to my warmest thanks.

A detachment of 30 seamen from his majesty's ship Bacchante, under Mr. Bruce, master's mate, were attached to the royal artillery, under the command of lieutenant Daniel, of that corps, for the purpose of dragging the howitzer, as no other means could be procured to bring it forward; and to their unwearied exertions, and the judicious arrangement of lieutenant Daniel, I am indebted for having a 5½ inch howitzer conveyed through a country the most difficult of access I ever witnessed.

To captain Parker, of his majesty's ship Tenedos, who commanded the squadron, I feel every obligation; and I can assure you the most cordial understanding has subsisted between the two branches of the service.

I have the honor to be, &c.

A. PILKINGTON,

lieut.-col. dep. adj.-gen.

To lieut.-gen. Sir J. C. Sherbrooke, K. B. &c.

Return of ordnance, arms, ammunition, &c. taken at Machias by the troops under the command of lieutenant-colonel Pilkington, 11th September, 1814.

Ordnance—Fort O'Brien;—2 18-pounders, mounted on garrison carriages, complete; 1 18-pounder carronade, mounted on garrison carriage, complete; 1 serviceable dismounted 24-pounder; 1 dismounted serviceable 18-pounder carronade.

Point Battery;—2 24-pounders, mounted on garrison carriages, complete.

East Machias;—2 brass 4-pounders, mounted, and harness, complete.

Machias;—2 iron 4-pounders, on travelling carriages, complete; 5 24-pounders, 10 18-pounders, rendered partly unserviceable by the enemy, and completely destroyed by us.

Total—26.

Arms;—164 muskets, 99 bayonets, 100 pouches, 41 belt, 2 drums.

Ammunition;—20 barrels of serviceable gunpowder.

75 paper cartridges filled for 18 and 24-pounders,

2938 musket-ball cartridges.

3 barrels of grape and case-shot.

553 round shot for 18 and 24-pounders.

6 kegs of gunpowder, 25lbs each.

28 paper cartridges filled for 4-pounders.

J. DANIEL, lieut. royal artil.

No. 58.

From rear-admiral Griffith to vice-admiral Cochrane.

H.M.S. Endymion, off Castine, entrance of the Penobscot river, September 9, 1814.

Sir,

My letter of the 23d of August from Halifax, by the Rover, will have made you acquainted with my intention of accompanying the expedition, then about to proceed under the command of his excellency sir John Coape Sherbrooke, K.B. for this place.

I have now the honor to inform you, that I put to sea on the 26th ultimo, with the ships and sloop named in the margin,* and ten sail of transports, having the troops on board, and arrived off the Metinicus Islands on the morning of the 31st, where I was joined by the Bulwark, Tenedos, Rifleman, Peruvian, and Pictou. From captain Pearce, of the Rifleman, I learned that the United States' frigate Adams had, a few days before, got into Penobscot; but not considering herself in safety there, had gone on to Hamden, a place 27 miles higher up the river, where her guns had been landed, and the position was fortifying for her protection.

Towards evening, the wind being fair and the weather

* Dragon, Endymion, Bacchante, and Sylph.

favorable, the fleet made sail up the Penobscot Bay, captain Parker in the Tenedos leading. We passed between the Metinicus and Green islands about midnight; and steering through the channel formed by the Fox's islands and Owl's head, ran up to the eastward of Long island, and found ourselves at daylight in the morning in sight of the fort and town of Castine. As we approached, some shew of resistance was made, and a few shots were fired; but the fort was soon after abandoned and blown up. At about 8 A.M. the men of war and transports were anchored a little to the northward of the peninsula of Castine, and the smaller vessels taking a station nearer in for covering the landing, the troops were put on shore, and took possession of the town and works without opposition.

The general wishing to occupy a post at Belfast, on the western side of the bay, (through which the high road from Boston runs,) for the purpose of cutting off all communication with that side of the country, the Bacchante and Rifleman were detached with the troops destined for this service, and quiet possession was taken, and held, of that town, as long as was thought necessary.

Arrangements were immediately made for attacking the frigate at Hamden, and the general having proffered every military assistance, 600 picked men, under the command of lieutenant-colonel John, of the 60th regiment, were embarked the same afternoon, on board his majesty's sloops Peruvian and Sylph, and a small transport. To this force were added the marines of the Dragon, and as many armed boats from the squadron as was thought necessary for disembarking the troops and covering their landing, and the whole placed under the command of captain Barrie, of the Dragon; and the lieutenant-colonel made sail up the river at 6 o'clock that evening.

I have the honour to enclose captain Barrie's account of his proceedings; and, taking into consideration the enemy's force, and the formidable strength of his position, too much praise cannot be given him, and the officers and men under his command, for the judgment, decision, and gallantry, with which this little enterprise has been achieved.

So soon as accounts were received from captain Barrie, that the Adams was destroyed, and the force assembled for her protection dispersed, the troops stationed at Belfast were embarked, and arrangements made for sending them to take possession of Machias, the only place occupied by the enemy's troops, between this and Passamaquaddy bay. I directed captain Parker, of H.M.S. Tenedos, to receive on board lieutenant-colonel Pilkington, deputy-adjutant-general, who is appointed to command, and a small detachment of artillery and riflemen, and to take under his command the Bacchante, Rifleman, and Pictou schooner, and proceed to the attack of that place. He sailed on the 6th instant, and most likely, by this time, the troops are in possession of it. After destroying the defences, they are directed to return here.

The inhabitants of several townships east of this, have sent deputations here to tender their submission to the British authority: and such of them as could give reasonable security, that their arms would be used only for the protection of their persons and property, have been allowed to retain them. This indulgence was absolutely necessary, in order to secure the quiet and unoffending against violence and outrage from their less peaceable neighbours, and for the maintenance of the peace and tranquillity of the country. All property on shore, *bonâ fide* belonging to the inhabitants of the country in our possession, has been respected. All public property, and all property a-float, have been confiscated.

Sir John Sherbrooke, conceiving it to be of importance that the government should be informed, without delay, of our successes here, has requested that a vessel of war may take his despatches to England.

I have in compliance with his wishes, appropriated the Martin for that service, and captain Senhouse will take a copy of this letter to the secretary of the admiralty.

I have honor to be, &c.
EDWARD GRIFFITH.

To vice-admiral the hon.
sir Alexander Cochrane, K.B., &c.

No. 59.

From captain Barrie to rear-admiral Griffith.

H.M. sloop Sylph, off Bangor, in the Penobscot,
September 3, 1814.

SIR,

Having received on board the ships named, in the margin,* a detachment of 20 men of the royal artillery, with one $5\frac{1}{2}$-inch howitzer, commanded by lieutenant Garsten; a party of 80 marines commanded by captain Carter, of the dragon; the flank companies of the 29th, 62d, and 98th regiments, under the command of captains Gell and Caker; majors Riddall, Keith, and Croasdaile, and captain Macpherson; also, a rifle company of the 7th battalion of the 60th regiment, commanded by captain Ward; and the whole under the orders of lieutenant-

* H.M.S. Peruvian and Sylph, Dragon tender, and the Harmony transport.

colonel John, of the 60th regiment; I proceeded, agreeably to your order, with the utmost despath, up the Penobscot. Light variable winds, a most intricate channel, of which we were perfectly ignorant, and thick foggy weather, prevented my arriving off Frankfort before 2 P.M. of the 2d instant. Here colonel John and myself thought it advisable to send a message to the inhabitants; and, having received their answer, we pushed on towards Hamden, where we received intelligence that the enemy had strongly fortified himself. On our way up, several troops were observed on the east side of the river, making for Brewer: these were driven into the woods, without any loss on our side, by a party under the orders of major Croasdaile, and the guns from the boats. The enemy had one killed, and several wounded.

At 5 P.M. of the 2d instant, we arrived off Ball's-head cove, distant three miles from Hamden. Colonel John and myself landed on the south side of the cove to reconnoitre the ground, and obtain intelligence. Having gained the hills, we discovered the enemy's piquets advantageously posted near the highway leading to Hamden, on the north side of the cove.

We immediately determined to land 150 men, under major Riddall, to drive in the piquets, and take up their ground. This object was obtained by 7 o'clock; and, notwithstanding every difficulty, the whole of the troops were landed on the north side of the cove by 10 o'clock; but it was found impossible to land the artillery at the same place. The troops bivouacked on the ground taken possession of by major Riddall. It rained incessantly during the night. At day-break this morning, the fog cleared away for about a quarter of an hour, which enabled me to reconnoitre the enemy by water; and I found a landing-place for the artillery about two-thirds of a mile from Ball's-head. Off this place the troops halted, till the artillery were mounted; and, by 6, the whole advanced towards Hamden.

The boats under the immediate command of lieutenant Pedler, the first of the Dragon, agreeably to a previous arrangement with colonel John, advanced in line with the right flank of the army. The Peruvian, Sylph, Dragon's tender, and Harmony transport, were kept a little in the rear in reserve.

Our information stated the enemy's force at 1400 men, and he had chosen a most excellent position on a high hill. About a quarter of a mile to the southward of the Adams' frigate, he had mounted eight 18-pounders. This fort was calculated to command both the highway, by which our troops had to advance, and the river. On a wharf close to the Adams, he had mounted fifteen 18-pounders, which completely commanded the river, which, at this place, is not above three cables' lengths wide, and the land on each side is high and well wooded.

A rocket-boat, under my immediate direction, but manœuvred by Mr. Ginton, gunner, and Mr. Small, midshipman, of the Dragon, was advanced about a quarter of a mile a-head of the line of boats.

So soon as the boats got within gun-shot, the enemy opened his fire upon them from the hill and wharf, which was warmly returned. Our rockets were generally well-directed, and evidently threw the enemy into confusion. Meantime, our troops stormed the hill with the utmost gallantry. Before the boats got within good grape-shot distance of the wharf-battery, the enemy set fire to the Adams, and he run from his guns the moment our troops carried the hill.

I joined the army about ten minutes after this event. Colonel John and myself immediately determined to leave a sufficient force in possession of the hill, and to pursue the enemy, who was then in sight on the Bangor road, flying at full speed. The boats and ships pushed up the river, preserving their original position with the army. The enemy was too nimble for us, and most of them escaped into the woods on our left.

On approaching Bangor, the inhabitants, who had opposed us at Hamden, threw off their military character; and, as magistrates, select men, &c. made an unconditional surrender of the town. Here, the pursuit stopped. About two hours afterwards, brigadier-general Blake came into the town to deliver himself as a prisoner; the general, and other prisoners, amounting to 191, were admitted to their parole.

Enclosed, I have the honor to forward you lists of the vessels we have captured or destroyed, and other necessary reports. I am happy to inform you, our loss consists only of one seaman, belonging to the Dragon, killed; captain Gell, of the 29th, and seven privates, wounded; one rank and file, missing.

I cannot close my report, without expressing my highest admiration of the very gallant conduct of colonel John, and the officers and soldiers under his command; for, exclusive of the battery before-mentioned, they had difficulties to contend with on their left, which did not fall under my observation, as the enemy's field-pieces in that direction were masked. The utmost cordiality existed between the two services; and I shall ever feel obliged to colonel John for his ready co-operation in every thing that was proposed. The officer and men bore the privations, inseperable from our confined means of accommodation, with a cheerfulness that entitles them to my warmest thanks.

Though the enemy abandoned his batteries before the ships be brought to act against them, yet I am not less obliged to captains Kippen and Dickens, of the Peruvian and Sylph; acting-lieutenant Pearson, who commanded the Dragon's tender; lieutenant Woodin, of the Dragon; and Mr. Barnett, master of the Harmony; their zeal and indefatigable exertions in bringing up their vessels, through the most intricate navigation, were eminently conspicuous. Colonel John speaks highly in praise of captain Carter, and the detachment of royal marines under his orders; and also of the seamen attached to the artillery, under the command of lieutenants Simmonds, Motley, L. State, and Mr. Spurling, master of the Bulwark.

I have, on other occasions of service, found it a pleasing part of my duty to commend the services of lieutenant Pedler, first of the Dragon; in this instance, he commanded the boat-part of the expedition most fully to my satisfaction; he was ably seconded by lieutenants Perceval, of the Tenedos, and Ormond, of the Endymion; and Mr. Ansel, master's mate of the Dragon; this last gentleman has passed his examination nearly five years, and is an active officer, well worthy of your patronage; but, in particularising him, I do not mean to detract from the other petty-officers and seaman employed in the boats; for they all most zealously performed their duty, and are equally entitled to my warmest acknowledgments. I am also most particularly indebted to the active and zealous exertion of lieutenant Carnegie, who was a volunteer on this occasion.

I can form no estimate of the enemy's absolute loss. From different stragglers I learn, that, exclusive of killed and missing, upwards of 30 lay wounded in the woods.

I have the honor to be, &c.

ROBERT BARRIE, capt of H.M.S. Dragon.

No. 60.

CAPITULATION.

To captain Hyde Parker, commanding the naval force, and lieutenant-colonel Andrew Pilkington, commanding the land force of his Britannic majesty, now at Machias.

GENTLEMEN,

The forces under your command having captured the forts in the neighbourhood of Machias, and taken possession of the territory adjacent within the county of Washington, and the situation of the county being such between the Penobscot river and the Passamaquaddy bay, as to preclude the hope that an adequate force can be furnished by the United States for its protection, we propose a capitulation, and offer for ourselves, and in behalf of the officers and soldiers of the brigade within the county of Washington, to give our parole of honor, that we will not, directly, or indirectly, bear arms, or in any way serve, against his Britannic majesty, king George the Third, king of the united kingdom of Great Britain and Ireland, his sussessors and allies, during the present war between Great Britain and the United States, upon condition we have your assurance, that, while we remain in this situation, and consider ourselves under the British government until further orders, we shall have the safe and full enjoyment of our private property, and be protected in the exercise of our usual occupations.

JOHN BREWER, brigadier-general 2d brigade, 10th division, for the officers and soldiers of the 3d regiment in the said brigade.

JAMES CAMPBELL, lieutenant-colonel, commanding 1st regiment, 2d brigade, 10th division, for himself, officers, and soldiers, in the said regiment.

These terms have been granted and approved of by us,

HYDE PARKER, capt. H.M.S. Tenedos.
A. PILKINGTON, lieutenant.-colonel, commanding.

Machias, Sept. 13, 1814.

No. 61.

List of vessels captured and destroyed in the Penobscot, and of those left on the stocks, as near as I am able to ascertain.

Captured and brought away;—2 ships, 1 brig, 6 schooners, 3 sloops.

Destroyed at Hamden;—The Adams frigate, of 26 guns, 18-pounders, and two ships, one of them armed; burnt by the enemy.

Destroyed at Bangor;—1 ship, 1 brig, 3 schooners, and 1 sloop; burnt by us.

Lost since in our possession;—A copper-bottomed brig, pierced for 18 guns, and the Decatur privateer, pierced for 16 guns.

Note.—The powder and wine captured at Hamden were put on board those vessels.

Left on the stocks at Bangor;—2 ships, 2 brigs, and 2 schooners.

At Brewer;—1 ship, 1 brig, and 1 schooner.

At Arrinuton;—1 ship, one schooner, on the stocks.

Left at Hamden;—1 ship, 1 Hermaphrodite brig, and 2 schooners; also, 1 brig and 1 schooner on the stocks.

Left at Fremford on the stocks;—1 schooner and some small craft.

To rear-admiral Griffith. R. BARRIE.

Return of ordnance taken from the enemy on the 3d of Sept. 1814

Taken at Hamden;—23 iron 18-pounders, 2 iron 12-pounders; 41 18-pounders destroyed, 14 brought away.

Taken at Bangor, and brought away;—2 3-pounder brass guns, 1 iron 3-pounder.

Total brought away—17.

Embarked;—1 ammunition cart, 500 18-pound shot, about 40 barrels of powder, and a quantity of wads, &c. &c.

ROBERT GASTEN, lieut. royal artillery.

Robert Barrie.

Return of small arms not collected, supposed about 100.

EDWARD GRIFFITH.

No. 62.

From rear-admiral Cockburn to vice-admiral Cochrane.

H. M. sloop Manly, off Nottingham,
Patuxent, Aug. 27, 1814.

SIR,

I have the honor to inform you, that, agreeably to the intentions I notified to you in my letter of the 22d instant,* I proceeded by land, on the morning of the 23d, to Upper Marlborough, to meet and confer with major-general Ross, as to our further operations against the enemy; and as we were not long in agreeing on the propriety of making an immediate attempt on the city of Washington.

In conformity, therefore, with the wishes of the general, I instantly sent orders for our marine and naval forces, at Pig-point, to be forthwith moved over to Mount Calvert, and for the marine-artillery, and a proportion of the seamen, to be there landed, and with the utmost possible expedition to join the army, which I also most readily agreed to accompany.

The major-general then made his dispositions, and arranged that captain Robyns, with the marines of the ships, should retain possession of Upper Marlborough, and that the marine-artillery and seamen should follow the army to the ground it was to occupy for the night. The army then moved on, and bivouacked before dark about five miles nearer Washington.

In the night, captain Palmer of the Hebrus, and captain Money of the Traave, joined us with the seamen and with the marine-artillery, under Captain Harrison. Captain Wainwright of the Tonnant, had accompanied me the day before, as had also lieutenant James Scott, acting first lieutenant of the Albion.

* James's Nav. Occurr. App. No. 81.

At day-light, on the morning of the 24th, the major-general again put the army in motion, directing his march upon Bladensburg; on reaching which place, with the advanced brigade, the enemy was observed drawn up in force on a rising ground beyond the town; and by the fire he soon opened on us as we entered the place, gave us to understand he was well protected by artillery. General Ross, however, did not hesitate in immediately advancing to attack him; although our troops were almost exhausted with the fatigue of the march they had just made, and but a small proportion of our little army had yet got up. This dashing measure was, however, I am happy to add, crowned with the success it merited; for, in spite of the galling fire of the enemy, our troops advanced steadily on both his flanks, and in his front; and, as soon as they arrived on even ground with him, he fled in every direction, leaving behind him 10 pieces of cannon, and a considerable number of killed and wounded; amongst the latter commodore Barney, and several other officers. Some other prisoners were also taken, though not many, owing to the swiftness with which the enemy went off, and the fatigue our army had previously undergone.

It would, sir, be deemed presumption in me to attempt to give you particular details respecting the nature of this battle; I shall, therefore, only remark generally, that the enemy, 8000 strong, on ground he had chosen as best adapted for him to defend, where he had time to erect his batteries, and concert all his measures, was dislodged, as soon as reached, and a victory gained over him, by a division of the British army, not amounting to more than 1500 men, headed by our gallant general, whose brilliant achievements of this day it is beyond my power to do justice to, and indeed no possible comment could enhance.

The seamen, with the guns, were, to their great mortification, with the rear-division, during this short, but decisive action. Those, however, attached to the rocket-brigade, were in the battle; and I remarked, with much pleasure, the precision with which the rockets were thrown by them, under the direction of first-lieutenant Lawrence, of the marine-artillery. Mr. Jeremiah M'Daniel, master's mate of the Tonnant, a very fine young man, who was attached to this party, being severely wounded, I beg permission to recommend him to your favorable consideration. The company of marines I have on so many occasions had cause to mention to you, commanded by first-lieutenant Stephens, was also in the action, as were the colonial marines, under the temporary command of captain Reed, of the 6th West India regiment, (these companes being attached to the light brigade,) and they respectively behaved with their accustomed zeal and bravery. None other of the naval department were fortunate enough to arrive up in time to take their share in this battle, excepting captain Palmer, of the Hebrus, with his aide de camp, Mr. Arthur Wakefield, midshipman of that ship, and lieutenant James Scott, first of the Albion, who acted as my aide de camp, and remained with me during the whole time.

The contest being completely ended, and the enemy having retired from the field, the general gave the army about two hours rest, when he again moved forward on Washington. It was, however, dark before we reached that city; and, on the general, myself, and some officers advancing a short way past the first houses of the town, without being accompanied by the troops, the enemy opened upon us a heavy fire of musketry, from the capitol and two other houses; these were therefore almost immediately stormed by our people, taken possession of, and set on fire; after which the town submitted without further resistance.

The enemy himself, on our entering the town, set fire to the navy-yard, (filled with naval stores,) a frigate of the largest class almost ready for launching, and a sloop of war lying off it; as he did also the fort which protected the sea-approach to Washington.

On taking possession of the city, we also set fire to the president's palace, the treasury, and the war-office; and, in the morning, captain Wainwright went with a party to see that the destruction in the navy-yard was complete; when he destroyed whatever stores and buildings had escaped the flames of the preceding night. A large quantity of ammunition and ordnance stores were likewise destroyed by us in the arsenal; as were about 200 pieces of artillery of different calibres, as well as a vast quantity of small-arms. Two rope-walks of a very extensive nature, full of tar-rope, &c. situated at a considerable distance from the yard, were likewise set fire to and consumed. In short, sir, I do not believe a vestige of public property, or a store of any kind, which could be converted to the use of the government, escaped destruction: the bridges across the Eastern Branch and the Potomac were likewise destroyed.

This general devastation being completed during the day of the 25th, we marched again, at nine that night, on our return, by Bladensburg, to Upper Marlborough.

We arrived yesterday evening at the latter, without molestation of any sort, indeed without a single musket having been fired; and this morning we moved on to this place, where I have found his majesty's sloop Manly, the tenders, and the boats, and I have hoisted my flag, *pro tempore*, in the former.

The troops will probably march to-morrow, or the next day at farthest, to Benedict for re-embarkation, and this flotilla will of course join you at the same time.

In closing, sir, my statement to you, of the arduous and highly important operations of this last week, I have a most pleasing duty to perform, in assuring you of the good conduct of the officers and men who have been serving under me. I have been particularly indebted, whilst on this service, to captain Wainwright of the Tonnant, for the assistance he has invariably afforded me; and to captains Palmer and Money, for their exertions during the march to and from Washington. To captain Nourse, who has commanded the flotilla during my absence, my acknowledgments are also most justly due, as well as to captains Sullivan, Badcock, Somerville, Ramsay, and Bruce, who have acted in it under him.

Lieutenant James Scott, now first of the Albion, has, on this occasion, rendered me essential services; and as I have had reason so often of late to mention to you the gallant and meritorious conduct of this officer, I trust you will permit me to seize this opportunity of recommending him particularly to your favorable notice and consideration.

Captain Robins, (the senior officer of marines with the fleet,) who has had, during these operations, the marines of the ships united under his orders, has executed ably and zealously the several services with which he has been entrusted, and is entitled to my best acknowledgments accordingly; as is also captain Harrison of the marine-artillery, who, with the officers and men attached to him, accompanied the army to and from Washington.

Mr. Dobie, surgeon of the Melpomene, volunteered his professional services on this occasion, and rendered much assistance to the wounded on the field of battle, as well as to many of the men taken ill on the line of march.

One colonial marine killed, 1 master's mate, 2 serjeants, and 3 colonial marines wounded, are the casualties sustained by the naval department; a general list of the killed and wounded of the whole army will, of course, accompany the report of the major-general. I have the honor to be, &c.

G. COCKBURN, rear-admiral.

Vice-admiral the hon.
Sir A Cochrane, K. B. &c.

P.S. Two long 6-pounder guns, intended for a battery at Nottingham, were taken off, and put on board the Brune, and one taken at Upper Marlborough was destroyed.

No. 63

From major-general Ross to earl Bathurst.

Tonnant, in the Patuxent,
My Lord, Aug. 30, 1814.

I have the honor to communicate to your lordship, that on the 24th instant, after defeating the army of the United States on that day, the troops under my command entered and took possession of the city of Washington.

It was determined between sir Alexander Cochrane and myself, to disembark the army at the village of Benedict, on the right bank of the Patuxent, with the intention of co-operating with rear-admiral Cockburn, in an attack upon a flotilla of the enemy's gun-boats, under the command of commodore Barney. On the 20th instant, the army commenced its march, having landed the previous day without opposition: on the 21st it reached Nottingham, and on the 22d moved on to Upper Marlborough, a few miles distant from Pig point, on the Patuxent, where admiral Cockburn fell in with, and defeated the flotilla, taking and destroying the whole. Having advanced within 16 miles of Washington, and ascertained the force of the enemy to be such as might authorize an attempt at carrying his capital, I determined to make it, and accordingly put the troops in movement on the evening of the 23d. A corps of about 1200 men appeared to oppose us, but retired after firing a few shots. On the 24th, the troops resumed their march, and reached Bladensburg, a village situate on the left bank of the eastern branch of the Potomac, about five miles from Washington.

On the opposite side of that river, the enemy was discovered strongly posted on very commanding heights, formed in two lines, his advance occupying a fortified house, which, with artillery, covered the bridge over the eastern branch, which the British had to pass. A broad and straight road leading from the bridge to Washington, ran through the enemy's position, which was carefully defended by artillery and riflemen.

The disposition for the attack being made, it was commenced with so much impetuosity by the light brigade, consisting of the 85th light infantry, and the light infantry companies of the army under the command of colonel Thornton, that the fortified house was shortly carried, the enemy retiring to the higher grounds.

In support of the light brigade, I ordered up a brigade under the command of colonel Brooke, who, with the 44th regiment, attacked the enemy's left, the 4th regiment pressing his right with such effect, as to cause him to abandon his guns. His first line giving way, was driven on the second, which, yielding to the irresistible attack of the bayonet, and the well-directed discharge of rockets, got into confusion and fled, leaving the British masters of the field. The rapid flight of the enemy, and his knowledge of the country, precluded the possibility of many prisoners being taken, more particularly as the troops had, during the day, undergone considerable fatigue.

The enemy's army, amounting to 8 or 9000 men, with 3 or 400 cavalry, was under the command of general Winder, being formed of troops drawn from Baltimore and Pennsylvania. His artillery, 10 pieces of which fell into our hands, was commanded by commodore Barney, who was wounded and taken prisoner. The artillery I directed to be destroyed.

Having halted the army for a short time, I determined to march upon Washington, and reached that city at eight o'clock that night. Judging it of consequence to complete the destruction of the public buildings with the least possible delay, so that the army might retire without loss of time, the following buildings were set fire to and consumed,—the capitol, including the Senate-house and House of Representation, the Arsenal, the Dock-yard, Treasury, War-office, President's Palace, Rope-walk, and the great bridge across the Potomac: in the dock-yard a frigate nearly ready to be launched, and a sloop of war, were consumed. The two bridges leading to Washington over the eastern branch had been destroyed by the enemy, who apprehended an attack from that quarter. The object of the expedition being accomplished, I determined, before any greater force of the enemy could be assembled, to withdraw the troops, and accordingly commenced retiring on the night of the 25th. On the evening of the 29th we reached Benedict, and re-embarked the following day. In the performance of the operation I have detailed, it is with the utmost satisfaction I observe to your lordship, that cheerfulness in undergoing fatigue, and anxiety for the accomplishment of the object, were conspicuous in all ranks.

To sir A. Cochrane my thanks are due, for his ready compliance with every wish connected with the welfare of the troops and the success of the expedition. To rear-admiral Cockburn, who suggested the attack upon Washington, and who accompanied the army, I confess the greatest obligation for his cordial co-operation and advice.

Colonel Thornton, who led the attack, is entitled to every praise for the noble example he set, which was so well followed by lieutenant-colonel Wood and the 85th light infantry, and by major Jones, of the 4th foot, with the light companies attached to the light brigade. I have to express my approbation of the spirited conduct of colonel Brooke, and of his brigade: the

44th regiment, which he led, distinguished itself under the command of lieutenant-colonel Mullens; the gallantry of the 4th foot, under the command of major Faunce, being equally conspicuous.

The exertions of captain Mitchell, of the royal artillery, in bringing the guns into action, were unremitting; to him, and to the detachment under his command, including captain Deacon's rocket brigade, and the marine rocket corps, I feel every obligation. Captain Lempriere, of the royal artillery, mounted a small detachment of the artillery drivers, which proved of great utility. The assistance afforded by captain Blanchard, of the royal engineers, in the duties of his department, was of great advantage. To the zealous exertions of captains Wainwright, Palmer, and Money, of the royal navy, and to those of the officers and seamen who landed with them, the service is highly indebted: the latter, captain Money, had charge of the seamen attached to the marine artillery. To captain M'Dougall, of the 85th foot, who acted as my aide de camp, in consequence of the indisposition of my aide de camp captain Falls, and to the officers of my staff, I feel much indebted.

I must beg leave to call your lordship's attention to the zeal and indefatigable exertions of lieutenant Evans, acting deputy quarter-master-general. The intelligence displayed by that officer, in circumstances of considerable difficulty, induces me to hope he will meet with some distinguished mark of approbation. I have reason to be satisfied with the arrangements of assistant-commissary-general Lawrence.

An attack upon an enemy so strongly posted, could not be effected without loss. I have to lament that the wounds received by colonel Thornton, and the other officers and soldiers left at Bladensburg, were such as prevented their removal. As many of the wounded as could be brought off were removed, the others being left with medical care and attendants. The arrangements made by staff surgeon Baxter for their accommodation, have been as satisfactory as circumstances would admit of. The agent for British prisoners of war very fortunately residing at Bladensburg, I have recommended the wounded officers and men to his particular attention, and trust to his being able to effect their exchange when sufficiently recovered.

Captain Smith, assistant adjutant-general to the troops, who will have the honor to deliver this despatch, I beg leave to recommend to your lordship's protection, as an officer of much merit and great promise, and capable of affording any further information that may be requisite. Sanguine in hoping for the approbation of his royal highness the prince regent, and of his majesty's government, as to the conduct of the troops under my command, I have, &c. R. ROSS, maj.-gen.

I beg leave to enclose herewith a return of the killed, wounded, and missing in the action of the 24th instant, together with a statement of the ordnance, ammunition, and ordnance stores taken from the enemy between the 19th and 25th of August, and likewise sketches of the scene of action and of the line of march.

No. 64.

Return of killed, wounded, and missing, of the troops under the command of major-general Ross, in action with the enemy on the 24th Aug. 1814, on the heights above Bladensburg.

Washington, Aug. 25, 1814.

General staff;—4 horses, killed.

Royal artillery;—4 horses, killed; 6 rank and file, 8 horses, wounded.

Royal marines artillery;—1 rank and file, killed; 1 serjeant, wounded.

Royal sappers and miners;—1 serjeant, 1 rank and file, killed.

4th regiment;—1 lieutenant, 2 serjeants, 21 rank and file, 1 horse, killed; 5 lieutenants, 2 ensigns, 6 serjeants, 50 rank and file, wounded.

21st regiment;—2 rank and file, killed; 1 captain, 1 lieutenant, 11 rank and file, wounded.

44th regiment;—1 serjeant, 13 rank and file, killed; 35 rank and file, wounded.

2d battalion royal marines;—5 rank and file, killed.

85th light infantry;—1 captain, 1 lieutenant, 1 serjeant, 12 rank and file, 1 horse, killed; 2 lieutenant-colonels, 1 major, 8 lieutenants, 2 serjeants, 51 rank and file, wounded.

Colonial company;—1 rank and file, killed; 2 rank and file, wounded.

6th West India regiment;—1 serjeant, wounded.

Total—1 captain, 2 lieutenants, 5 serjeants, 56 rank and file, 10 horses, killed; 2 lieutenant-colonels, 1 major, 1 captain, 14 lieutenants, 2 ensigns, 10 serjeants, 155 rank and file, 8 horses, wounded.

Names of officers killed and wounded.

Killed—85th light infantry;—Captain D. S. Hamilton, lieutenant G. P. R. Codd.

4th, or king's own;—Lieutenant Thomas Woodward.

Wounded—85th light infantry;—Colonel William Thornton, severely; left at Bladensburg;) lieutenant-colonel William Thornton, severely; (left at Bladensburg;) lieutenant-colonel William Wood, severely; (left at Bladensburg;) major George Brown, severely (left at Bladensburg).

21st fusileers;—Captain R. Rennie, severely, not dangerously.

4th regiment;—Lieutenant E. P. Hopkins, severely; lieutenant I. K. Mackenzie, slightly; lieutenant John Stavely, severely; (left at Bladensburg;) lieutenant Peter Boulby, lieutenant Frederick Field, slightly.

21st fusileers;—Lieutenant James Grace, slightly.

85th regiment;—Lieutenant William Villiers, lieutenant John Burrell, severely; lieutenant F. Mansell, slightly; lieutenant G. F. S. O'Connor, lieutenant Frederick Gascoyne, severely; lieutenant William Hickson, lieutenant G. R. Gleig, slightly; lieutenant Croveby, severely.

4th regiment;—Ensign James Buchannan, severely; (left at Bladensburg;) Ensign William Reddock, severely.

H. G. SMITH, D. A. A. G.

No. 65.

Return of ordnance, ammunition, and ordnance-stores, taken from the enemy by the army under the command of major-general Robert Ross, between the 19th and 25th of August, 1814.

August 19.—1 24-pound carronade.

August 22.—1 6-pound field-gun, with carriage complete; 156 stand of arms, with cartouches, &c. &c.

August 24, *at Bladensburg.*—2 18-pounders, 5 12-pounders, 3 6-pounders, with field-carriages; a quantity of ammunition for the above; 220 stand of arms.

August 25, *at Washington.*—Brass: 6 18-pounders, mounted on traversing platforms; 5 12-pounders, 4 4-pounders, 1 5½ inch howitzer, 1 5½ inch mortar. Iron: 26 32-pounders, 36 24-pounders, 34 18-pounders, 27 12-pounders, 2 18-pounders, mounted on traversing platforms; 19 12-pounders, on ship-carriages; 3 13-inch mortars, 2 8-inch howitzers, 1 42-pound gun, 5 32-pound carronades, 5 18-pound carronades, 13 12-pound guns, 2 9-pound guns, 2 6-pound guns.

Total amount of cannon taken—206; 500 barrels of powder; 100000 rounds of musket-ball cartridges; 40 barrels of fine-grained powder; a large quantity of ammunition of different natures made up.

The navy-yard and arsenal having been set on fire by the enemy before they retired, an immense quantity of stores of every description was destroyed; of which no account could be taken. Seven or eight very heavy explosions during the night denoted that there had been large magazines of powder.

F. G. J. WILLIAMS,
lieutenant royal artillery, A. Q. M.
J. MICHELL,
captain commanding artillery.

N. B. The remains of near 2000 stand of arms were discovered, which had been destroyed by the enemy.

No. 66.

From brigadier-general Winder to the secretary at war.

SIR, Baltimore, Aug. 27, 1814.

When the enemy arrived at the mouth of the Potomac, of all the militia which I had been authorized to assemble, there were but about 1700 in the field, from 13 to 1400 under general Stransbury near this place, and 250 at Bladensburg, under lieutenant-colonel Kramer; the slow progress of draft, and the imperfect organization, with the ineffectiveness of the laws to compel them to turn out, rendered it impossible to have procured more.

The militia of this state and of the contiguous parts of Virginia and Pennsylvania were called on *en masse*, but the former militia law of Pennsylvania had expired the 1st of June, or July, and the one adopted in its place is not to take effect in organizing the militia before October. No aid, therefore, has been received from that state.

After all the force that could be put at my disposal in that short time, and making such dispositions as I deemed best calculated to present the most respectable force at whatever point the enemy might strike, I was enabled (by the most active and harassing movements of the troops) to interpose before the enemy at Bladensburg, about 5000 men, including 350 regulars and commodore Barney's command. Much the largest portion of this force arrived on the ground when the enemy were in sight, and were disposed of to support, in the best manner, the position which general Sansbury had taken. They had barely reached the ground before the action commenced, which was about one o'clock P. M. of the 24th instant, and continued about an hour. The contest was not as obstinately maintained as could have been desired, but was, by parts of the troops, sustained with great spirit and with prodigious effect; and had the whole of our force been equally firm, I am induced to believe that the enemy would have been repulsed, notwithstanding all the disadvantages under which we fought. The artillery from Baltimore, supported by major Pinkney's rifle battalion, and a part of captain Doughty's from the navy-yard, were in advance to command the pass of the bridge at Bladensburg, and played upon the enemy, as I have since learned, with very destructive effect. But the rifle troops were obliged, after some time, to retire, and of course the artillery. Superior numbers, however, rushed upon them, and made their retreat necessary, not, however, without great loss on the part of the enemy. Major Pinkney received a severe wound in his right arm after he had retired to the left flank of Stansbury's brigade. The right and centre of Stansbury's brigade, consisting of lieutenant-colonel Ragan's and Shuler's regiments, generally gave way very soon afterwards, with the exception of about 40 rallied by colonel Ragan, after having lost his horse, and the whole or a part of captain Shower's company, both of whom general Stansbury represents to have made, even thus deserted, a gallant stand. The fall which lieutenant-colonel Ragan received from his horse, together with his great efforts to maintain his position, rendered him unable to follow the retreat; we have therefore to lament that this gallant and excellent officer has been taken prisoner; he has, however, been paroled, and I met him here, recovering from the bruises occasioned by his fall. The loss of his services at this moment is serious.

The 5th Baltimore regiment, under lieutenant-colonel Stenet, being the left of brigadier-general Stansbury's brigade, still, however, stood their ground, and except for a moment, when part of them recoiled a few steps, remained firm, and stood until ordered to retreat, with a view to prevent their being outflanked.

The reserve, under brigadier-general Smith, of the district of Columbia, with the militia of the city and George town, with the regulars and some detachments of Maryland militia, flanked on their right by commodore Barney and his brave fellows, and lieutenant-colonel Beal, still were to the right on the hill, and maintained the contest for some time with great effect.

It is not with me to report the conduct of commodore Barney and his command, nor can I speak from observation, being too remote; but the concurrent testimony of all who did observe them, does them the highest justice for their brave resistance, and the destructive effect they produced on the enemy. Commodore Barney, after having lost his horse, took post near one of his guns, and there unfortunately received a severe wound in the thigh, and he also fell into the hands of the enemy. Captain Miller, of the marines, was wounded in the arm fighting bravely. From the best intelligence, there remains but little doubt that the enemy lost at least 400 killed and wounded, and of these a very unusual portion killed.

Our loss cannot, I think, be estimated at more than from 30 to 40 killed, and 50 to 60 wounded. They took altogether about 120 prisoners.

You will readily understand that it is impossible for me to speak minutely of the merit or demerit of particular troops so little known to me from their recent and hasty assemblage. My subsequent movements for the purposes of preserving as much of my force as possible, gaining reinforcements, and protecting this place, you already know.

I am, with very great respect, sir, your obedient servant,

W. H. WINDER,

Hon. J. Armstrong, sec. of war. brig.-gen. 10th mil. dist.

N. B. We have to lament that captain Sterett, of the 5th Baltimore regiment, has also been wounded, but is doing well. Other officers, no doubt, deserve notice, but I am as yet unable to particularize.

No. 67.

American estimate of public property destroyed at Washington.

The committee appointed by the American congress to inquire into the circumstances attending the capture of Washington, and the destruction consequent on that event, after giving a statement of the operations in the navy-yard, report the following estimate of the public property destroyed:—

	Dollars.
The capitol, including all costs,	787163
President's house,	234334
Public offices,	93613
	1115110

But the committee remark, as the walls of the capitol and president's house are good, they suppose that the sum of 460000 dollars will be sufficient to place the buildings in the situation they were in previous to their destruction.

The losses sustained in the navy-yard are thus estimated:—

	Dollars.
In moveable property,	417745
In buildings and fixtures	91425
	509170

The committee then proceed to the recapitulation of the losses in the navy-yard, with an estimate of the real losses. After deducting the value recovered from the original value of the articles, the total amount is 417745 dollars, 51 cents.

The original value of the articles destroyed was 678219 dollars, 71 cents, of which 260465 dollars and 20 cents value were recovered, in anchors, musket-barrels, locks, copper, timber, &c.

No. 68.

From vice-admiral Cochrane to Mr. Monroe.

His majesty's ship the Tonnant, in the
Patuxent river, Aug. 18, 1814.

SIR,

Having been called on by the governor-general of the Canadas to aid him in carrying into effect measures of retaliation against the inhabitants of the United States, for the wanton destruction committed by their army in Upper Canada, it has become imperiously my duty, conformably with the nature of the governor-general's application, to issue to the naval force under my command, an order to destroy and lay waste such towns and districts upon the coast as may be found assailable.

I had hoped that this contest would have terminated, without my being obliged to resort to severities which are contrary to the usages of civilized warfare; and as it has been with extreme reluctance and concern that I have found myself compelled to adopt this system of devastation, I shall be equally gratified if the conduct of the executive of the United States will authorize my staying such proceedings, by making reparation to the suffering inhabitants of Upper Canada; thereby manifesting that if the destructive measures pursued by their army were ever sanctioned, they will no longer be permitted by the government.

I have the honor to be, sir, with much consideration, your most obedient humble servant,

ALEXANDER COCHRANE,
vice-admiral and commander in chief of his Britannic majesty's ships and vessels upon the North American station.

The hon James Monroe, secretary of state, &c. Washington.

No. 69.

From Mr. Monroe to sir Alexander Cochrane.

SIR, Department of state, Sept. 6, 1814.

I have had the honor to receive your letter of the 18th of August, stating that having been called on by the governor-general of the Canadas, to aid him in carrying into effect measures of retaliation against the inhabitants of the United States, for the wanton desolation committed by their army in Upper Canada, it has become your duty, conformably with the nature of the governor-general's application, to issue to the naval force under your command, an order to destroy and lay waste such towns and districts upon the coast as may be found assailable.

It is seen with the greatest surprise, that this system of devastation which has been practised by the British forces, so manifestly contrary to the usage of civilized warfare, is placed by you on the ground of retaliation. No sooner were the United States compelled to resort to war against Great Britain, than they resolved to wage it in a manner most consonant to the principles of humanity, and to those friendly relations which it was desirable to preserve between the two nations, after the restoration of peace. They perceived, however, with the deepest regret, that a spirit alike just and humane was neither cherished nor acted on by your government. Such an assertion would not be hazarded, if it were not supported by facts, the proof of which has perhaps already carried the same conviction to other nations that it has to the people of these states.

Without dwelling on the deplorable cruelties committed by the savages in the British ranks, and in British pay, on American prisoners, at the river Raisin, which to this day have never been disavowed, or atoned, I refer, as more immediately connected with the subject of your letter, to the wanton desolation that was committed at Havre-de-Grace, and at George town, early in the spring of 1813. These villeges were burnt and ravaged by the naval forces of Great Britain, to the ruin of their unarmed inhabitants, who saw with astonishment they derived no protection to their property from the laws of war. During the same season, scenes of invasion and pillage, carried on under the same authority, were witnessed all along the waters of the Chesapeake, to an extent inflicting the most serious private distress, and under circumstances that justified the suspicion, that revenge and cupidity, rather than the manly motives that should dictate the hostility of a high-minded foe, led to their perpetration. The late destruction of the houses of government in this city, is another act which comes necessarily into view. In the wars of modern Europe, no examples of the kind, even among nations the most hostile to each other, can be traced. In the course of 10 years past, the capitals of the principal powers of the Continent of Europe have been conquered, and occupied alternately by the victorious armies of each other, and no instance of such wanton and unjustifiable destruction has been seen. We must go back to distant and barbarous ages to find a parallel for the acts of which I complain. Although these acts of desolation invited, if they did not impose on, the government the necessity of retaliation, yet in no instance has it been authorized. The burning of the village of Newark, in Upper Canada, posterior to the early outrages above enumerated, was not executed on that principle. The village of Newark adjoined Fort-George, and its destruction was justified by the officer who ordered it, on the ground that it became necessary in the military operations there. The act, however, was disavowed by the government. The burning which took place at Long-point was unauthorized by the government, and the conduct of the officer subjected to the investigation of a military tribunal. For the burning of St. David's, committed by stragglers, the officer who commanded in that quarter was dismissed without a trial, for not preventing it.

I am commanded by the president distinctly to state, that it as little comports with any orders issued to the military and naval commanders of the United States, as it does with the established and known humanity of the American nation, to pursue a system which it appears you have adopted. The government owes to itself, and to the principles which it has ever held sacred, to disavow, as justly chargeable to it, any such wanton, cruel, and unjustifiable warfare.

Whatever unauthorized irregularity may have been committed by any of its troops, it would have been ready, acting on these principles of sacred and eternal obligation, to disavow, and as far as might be practicable, to repair. But in the plan of desolating warfare which your letter so explicitly makes known, and which is attempted to be excused on a plea so utterly groundless, the president perceives a spirit of deep-rooted hostility, which, without the evidence of such facts, he could not have believed existed, or would have been carried to such an extremity.

For the reparation of injuries, of whatever nature they may be, not sanctioned by the law of nations, which the naval or military forces of either power may have committed against the other, this government will always be ready to enter into reciprocal arrangements. It is presumed that your government will neither expect or propose any which are not reciprocal.

Should your government adhere to a system of desolation so contrary to the views and practice of the United States, so revolting to humanity, and repugnant to the sentiments and usages of the civilized world, whilst it will be seen with the deepest regret, it must and will be met with a determination and constancy becoming a free people, contending in a just cause for their essential rights, and their dearest interests.

I have the honor to be, with great consideration, sir, your most obedient humble servant,

JAMES MONROE.

Vice-admiral sir Alexander Cochrane, commander in chief of his Britannic majesty's ships and vessels.

No. 70.

Mr. Madison's Proclamation.

Whereas, the enemy, by sudden incursion, have succeeded in invading the capital of the nation, defended at the moment by troops less numerous than their own, and almost entirely of the militia; during their possession of which, though for a single day only, they wantonly destroyed the public edifices, having no relation in their structure to operations of war, nor used at the time for military annoyance; some of these edifices being also costly monuments of state, and of arts; and the others, depositories of the public archives, not only precious to the nation, as the memorials of its origin and its early transactions, but interesting to all nations, as contributions to the general stock of historical instruction and political science.

And, whereas, advantage has been taken of the loss of a fort, more immediately guarding the neighbouring town of Alexandria, to place the town within a range of a naval force, too long and too much in the habit of abusing its superiority, wherever it can be applied, to require, as the alternative of a general conflagration, an undisturbed plunder of private property, which has been executed in a manner peculiarly distressing to the inhabitants, who had inconsiderately cast themselves on the justice and generosity of the victor.

And, whereas, it now appears, by a direct communication from the British naval commander on the American station, to be his avowed purpose to employ the force under his direction, in destroying and laying waste such towns and districts upon the coast as may be found assailable; adding, to this declaration, the insulting pretext, that it is in retaliation for a wanton destruction committed by the army of the United States in Upper Canada; when it is notorious, that no destruction has been committed, which, notwithstanding the multiplied outrages previously committed by the enemy, was not unauthorized, and promptly shewn to be so, and that the United States have been as constant in their endeavours to reclaim the enemy from such outrages, by the contrast of their own example, as they have been ready to terminate, on reasonable conditions, the war itself.

And, whereas, these proceedings and declared purposes, which exhibit a deliberate disregard of the principles of humanity, and the rules of civilized warfare, and which must give to the existing war a character of extended devastation and barbarism, at the very moment of negociation for peace, invited by the enemy himself, leave no prospect of safety to any thing within the reach of his predatory and incendiary operations, but in a manly and universal determination to chastise and expel the invader.

Now, therefore, I, James Madison, president of the United States, do issue this my proclamation, exhorting all the good people, therefore, to unite their hearts and hands in giving effect to the ample means possessed for that purpose. I enjoin it on all officers, civil and military, to exert themselves in executing the duties with which they are respectively charged. And, more especially, I require the officers, commanding the respective military districts, to be vigilant and alert in providing for the defence thereof; for the more effectual accomplishment of which, they are authorized to call to the defence of exposed and threatened places, proportions of the militia, most convenient thereto, whether they be, or be not, parts of the quotas detached for the service of the United States, under requisitions of the general government.

On an occasion which appeals so forcibly to the proud feelings and patriotic devotion of the American people, none will forget what they owe to themselves; what they owe to their country; and the high destinies which await it; what to the glory acquired now, and to be maintained by their sons, with the augmented strength and resources with which time and Heaven have blessed them. In testimony whereof, I have hereunto set my hand, and caused the seal of the United States to be affixed to these presents. Done at Washington, Sept. 1, 1814.

By the president, JAMES MADISON.

JAMES MUNROE, secretary of state.

No. 71.

From colonel Brooke to earl Bathurst.

On board H.M.S. Tonnant, Chesapeake,
MY LORD, September 17, 1814.

I have the honor to inform your lordship, that the division of troops under the command of major-general Ross effected a disembarkation on the morning of the 12th of September, near North Point, on the left point of the Patapsco river, distant from Baltimore about 13 miles, with the view of pushing a reconnoissance, in co-operation with the naval forces, to that town, and acting thereon as the enemy's strength and positions might be found to dictate.

The approach on this side to Baltimore, lays through a small peninsula, formed by the Patapsco and Black river, and generally from two to three miles broad, while it narrows in some places to less than half a mile.

Three miles from North point, the enemy had entrenched himself quite across this neck of land, towards which (the disembarkation having been completed at an early hour) the troops advanced.

The enemy was actively employed in the completion of this work,—deepening the ditch, and strengthening its front by a low abattis; both which, however, he precipitately abandoned on the approach of our skirmishers, leaving in our hands some few dragoons, being part of his rear-guard.

About two miles beyond this point our advance became engaged; the country was here closely wooded, and the enemy's riflemen were enabled to conceal themselves. At this moment, the gallant general Ross received a wound in his breast, which proved mortal. He only survived to recommend a young and unprovided family to the protection of his king and country.

Thus fell, at an early age, one of the brightest ornaments of his profession; one who, whether at the head of a rigiment, a brigade, or corps, had alike displayed the talents of command; who was not less beloved in his private than enthusiastically admired in his public character; and whose only fault, if it may be deemed so, was an excess of gallantry, enterprise, and devotion to the service.

If ever it were permitted to a soldier, to lament those who fall in battle, we may indeed, in this instance, claim that melancholy privilege.

Thus it is, that the honor of addressing your lordship, and the command of this army, have devolved upon me; duties which, under any other circumstances, might have been embraced as the most enviable gifts of fortune; and here I venture to solicit, through your lordship, his royal highness the prince regent's consideration to the circumstances of my succeeding, during operations of so much moment, to an officer of such high and established merit.

Our advance continuing to press forward, the enemy's light troops were pushed to within five miles of Baltimore, where a corps of about 6000 men, six pieces of artillery, and some hundred cavalry, were discovered posted under cover of a wood, drawn up in a very dense order, and lining a strong paling, which crossed the main road nearly at right angles. The creeks and inlets of the Patapsco and Black rivers, which approach each other at this point, will in some measure account for the contracted nature of the enemy's position.

I immediately ordered the necessary dispositions for a general attack. The light brigade, under the command of major Jones, of the 4th, consisting of the 85th light infantry, under major Gubbins, and the light companies of the army, under major Pringle, of the 21st, covered the whole of the front, driving the enemy's skirmishers with great loss on his main body. The 4th regiment, under major Faunce, by a detour through some hollow ways, gained, unperceived, a lodgement close upon the enemy's left. The remainder of the right brigade, under the command of the honorable lieutenant-colonel Mullins, consisting of the 44th regiment, under major Johnson, the marines of the fleet under captain Robbins, and a detachment of seamen under captain Money, of the Trave, formed a line along the enemy's front; while the left brigade, under colonel Paterson, consisting of the 21st regiment, commanded by major Whitaker, the 2d battalion of marines by lieutenant-colonel Malcolm, and a detachment of marines by major Lewis, remained in columns on the road, with orders to deploy to his left, and press the enemy's right, the moment the ground became sufficiently open to admit of that movement.

In this order, the signal being given, the whole of the troops advanced rapidly to the charge. In less than 15 minutes, the enemy's force being utterly broken and dispersed, fled in every direction over the country, leaving on the field two pieces of cannon, with a considerable number of killed, wounded, and prisoners.

The enemy lost, in this short but brilliant affair, from 500 to 600 in killed and wounded; while, at the most moderate compuation he is at least 1000 *hors de combat*. The 5th regiment of militia, in particular, has been represented as nearly annihilated.

The day being now far advanced, and the troops (as is always the case on the first march after disembarkation) much fatigued, we halted for the night on the ground of which the enemy had been dispossessed. Here, I received a communication from vice-admiral the honorable sir A. Cochrane, informing me that the frigates, bomb-ships, and flotilla of the fleet, would, on the ensuing morning, take their stations as previously proposed.

At day-break, on the 13th, the army again advanced, and at 10 o'clock I occupied a favorable position eastward of Baltimore, distant about a mile and a half, and from whence I could reconnoitre, at my leisure, the defences of that town.

Baltimore is completely surrounded by strong but detached hills, on which the enemy had constructed a chain of pallisaded redoubts, connected by a small breast-work; I have, however, reason to think, that the defence to the northward and westward of the place, were in a very unfinished state. Chinkapin hill, which lay in front of our position, completely commands the town; this was the strongest part of the line, and here the enemy seemed most apprehensive of an attack. These works were defended, according to the best information which we could obtain, by about 15000 men, with a large train of artillery.

Judging it perfectly feasible, with the description of forces under my command, I made arrangements for a night-attack, during which the superiority of the enemy's artillery would not have been so much felt; and captain M'Dougall, the bearer of these despatches, will have the honor to point out to your lordship those particular points of the line which I had proposed to act on. During the evening, however, I received a communication from the commander in chief of the naval forces, by which I was informed, that, in consequence of the entrance to the harbor being closed up by vessels sunk for that purpose by the enemy, a naval co-operation against the town and camp was found impracticable.

Under these circumstances, and keeping in view your lordships instructions, it was agreed, between the vice-admiral and myself, that the capture of the town would not have been a sufficient equivalent to the loss which might probably be sustained in storming the heights.

Having formed this resolution; after compelling the enemy to sink upwards of 20 vessels in different parts of the harbor; causing the citizens to remove almost the whole of their property to places of more security inland; obliging the government to concentrate all the military force of the surrounding states; harassing the militia, and forcing them to collect from any remote districts; causing the enemy to burn a valuable rope-walk, with other public buildings, in order to clear the glacis in front of their redoubts, besides having beaten and routed them in a general action, I retired on the 14th, three miles from the position which I had occupied, where I halted during some hours.

This tardy movement was partly caused by an expectation that the enemy might possibly be induced to move out of the entrenchments and follow us; but he profited by the lesson which he had received on the 12th; and towards the evening I retired the troops about three miles and a half further, where I took up my ground for the night.

Having ascertained, at a late hour on the morning of the 15th, that the enemy had no disposition to quit his entrenchments, I moved down and re-embarked the army at North Point, not leaving a man behind, and carrying with me about 200 prisoners, being persons of the best families in the city, and which number might have been very considerably increased, was not the fatigue of the troops an object principally to be avoided.

I have now to remark to your lordship, that nothing could surpass the zeal, unanimity, and ardour, displayed by every description of force, whether naval, military, or marine, during the whole of these operations.

I am highly indebted to vice-admiral sir A. Cochrane, commander in chief of the naval forces, for the active assistance and zealons co-operation which he was ready, upon every occasion, to afford me; a disposition conspicuous in every branch of the naval service, and which cannot fail to ensure success to every combined operation of this armament.

Captain Edward Crofton, commanding the brigade of seamen appointed to the small arms, for the animated and enthusiastic example which he held forth to his men, deserves my approbation; as do also captains Nourse, Money, Sullivan, and Ramsay, R.N., for the steadiness and good order which they maintained in their several directions.

I feel every obligation to rear-admiral Cockburn, for the counsel and assistance which he afforded me, and from which I derived the most signal benefit.

To colonel Paterson, for the steady manner in which he brought his column into action, I give my best thanks.

The honorable lieutenant-colonel Mullins deserved every approbation for the excellent order in which he led that part of the right brigade under his command, while charging the enemy in line.

Major Jones, commanding the light brigade, merits my best acknowledgments, for the active and skilful dispositions by which he covered all the movements of the army.

The distinguished gallantry of captain De Bathe, of the 95th light infantry, has been particularly reported to me, and I beg to record my own knowledge of similar conduct on former occasions.

To major Faunce, of the 4th regiment, for the manner in which he gained and turned the enemy's left, as well as for the excellent discipline maintained in that regiment, every particular praise is due.

The exertions of major Gubbins, commanding the 85th light infantry; and of major Kenny, commanding the light companies, were highly commendable.

Captain Mitchell, commanding the royal artillery; captain Carmichael, a meritorious officer of that corps; and lieutenant Lawrence, of the marine artillery, are entitled to my best thanks; as is captain Blanchard, commanding royal engineers, for the abilities he displayed in his particular branch of the service.

To lieutenant Evans, of the 3d dragoons, acting deputy-quarter-master-general to this army, for the unremitting zeal, activity, and perfect intelligence, which he evinced in the discharge of the various and difficult duties of his department, I feel warmly indebted; and I beg to solicit, through your lordship, a promotion suitable to the high professional merits of this officer.

Captain M'Dougall, aide de camp to the late general Ross, (and who has acted as assistant-adjutant-general in the absence of major Debbeig through indisposition,) is the bearer of these despatches; and having been in the confidence of general Ross, as well as in mine, will be found perfectly capable of giving your lordship any further information relative to the operations of this army which you may require: he is an officer of great merit and promise, and I beg to recommend him to your lordship's protection. I have the honor to be, &c.

ARTHUR BROOKE, colonel commanding.

No. 72.

Return of the killed and wounded, in action with the enemy, near Baltimore, on the 12th of September, 1814.

General staff;—1 major-general, 2 horses, killed; 1 horse, wounded.

Royal artillery;—6 rank and file, wounded.

Royal marine-artillery;—1 rank and file, killed; 3 rank and file, wounded.

4th regiment, 1st batt;—1 serjeant, 1 rank and file, killed; 3 serjeants, 10 rank and file, wounded.

21st regiment, 1st batt.;—1 subaltern, 1 serjeant, 9 rank and file, killed; 1 captain, 1 subaltern, 2 serjeants, 77 rank and file, wounded.

44th regiment, 1st batt.;—11 rank and file, killed; 3 captains, 2 subalterns, 5 serjeants, 78 rank rand file, wounded.

85th light infantry;—3 rank and file, killed; 2 captains, 1 subaltern, 26 rank and file, wounded.

Royal marines, 2d batt.;—4 rank and file, killed; 10 rank and file, wounded.

Royal marines, 3d batt.;—2 rank and file, killed; 1 serjeant, 9 rank and file, wounded.

Detachments of royal marines, from the ships, attached to the 2d battalion;—2 rank and file, killed; 1 rank and file, wounded.

Detachments of royal marines, under the command of captain Robyns;—2 rank and file, killed; 1 captain, 9 rank and file, wounded.

Total;—1 general staff, 1 subaltern, 2 serjeants, 35 rank and file, killed; 7 captains, 4 subalterns, 11 serjeants, and 229 rank and file, wounded.

Names of officers killed and wounded.

Killed;—General Staff;—Major-general Robert Ross.

21st fusileers;—Lieutenant Gracie.

Wounded;—*21st fusileers*;—Brigade-major Renny, slightly; lieutenant Leavoeq, severely.

44th regiment;—Brigade-major Cruice, slightly; captain Hamilton Greenshields, dangerously (since dead); captain George Hill, lieutenant Richard Cruice, ensign J. White, severely.

85th light infantry;—Captains W. P. De Bathe and J. D. Hicks, lieutenant G. Wellings, slightly.

Royal marines;—Captain John Robyns, severely.

HENRY DEBBEIG, major, A.D.A gen.

No. 73.

From sir Alexander Cochrane to Mr. Croker.

SIR, H.M.S. Tonnant, Chesapeake, Sept. 17. 1814.

I request that you will be pleased to inform my lords commissioners of the admiralty, that the approaching equinoctial new moon rendering it unsafe to proceed immediately out of the Chesapeake with the combined expedition, to act upon the plans which had been concerted previous to the departure of the Iphigenia; major-general Ross and myself resolved to occupy the intermediate time to advantage, by making a demonstration upon the city of Baltimore which might be converted into a real attack, should circumstances appear to justify it; and, as our arrangements were soon made, I proceeded up this river, and anchored off the mouth of the Patapsco, on the 11th instant, where the frigates and smaller vessels entered at a convenient distance for landing the troops.

At an early hour the next morning, the disembarkation of the army was effected without opposition, having attached to it a brigade of 600 seamen, under captain E. Crofton, (late of the Leopard,) the second battalion of marines, the marines of the squadron, and the colonial black marines. Rear-admiral Cockburn accompanied the general, to advise and arrange as might be deemed necessary for our combined efforts.

So soon as the army moved forward, I hoisted my flag in the Surprise, and with the remainder of the frigates, bombs, sloops, and the rocket-ship, passed further up the river, to render what co-operation could be found practicable.

While the bomb-vessels were working up, in order that we might open our fire upon the enemy's fort at day-break next morning, an account was brought to me, that major-general Ross, when reconnoitring the enemy, had received a mortal wound by a musket-ball, which closed his glorious career before he could be brought off to the ship.

It is a tribute due to the memory of this gallant and respected officer, to pause in my relation, while I lament the loss that his majesty's service and the army, of which he was one of the brightest ornaments, have sustained by his death. The unanimity and the zeal, which he manifested on every occasion, while I had the honor of serving with him, gave life and ease to the most arduous undertakings. Too heedless of his personal security when in the field, his devotion to the care and honor of his army has caused the termination of his valuable life. The major-general has left a wife and family, for whom I am confident his grateful country will provide.

The skirmishes which had deprived the army of its brave

general, was a prelude to a most decisive victory over the flower of the enemy's troops. Colonel Brooke, on whom the command devolved, having pushed forward our force to within five miles of Baltimore, where the enemy, about 6000 or 7000, had taken up an advanced position, strengthened by field-pieces, and where he had disposed himself, apparently with the intention of making a determined resistance, fell upon the enemy with such impetuosity, that he was obliged soon to give way, and fly in every direction, leaving on the field of battle a considerable number of killed and wounded, and two pieces of cannon.

For the particulars of this brilliant affair, I beg leave to refer their lordships to rear-admiral Cockburn's despatch, transmitted herewith.

At day-break the next morning, the bombs having taken their stations within shell-range, supported by the Surprise, with the other frigates and sloops, opened their fire upon the fort that protected the entrance of the harbor, and I had now an opportunity of observing the strength and preparations of the enemy.

The approach to the town on the land-side was defended by commanding heights, upon which was constructed a chain of redoubts, connected by a breast-work, with a ditch in front, an extensive train of artillery, and a shew of force that was reported to be from 15 to 20,000 men.

The entrance by sea, within which the town is retired nearly three miles, was entirely obstructed by a barrier of vessels sunk at the mouth of the harbor, defended inside by gun-boats, flanked on the right by a strong and regular fortification, and on the left by a battery of several heavy guns.

These preparations rendering it impracticable to afford any essential co-operation by sea, I considered that an attack on the enemy's strong position by the army only, with such disparity of force, though confident of success, might risk a greater loss than the possession of the town would compensate for, while holding in view the ulterior operations of this force in the contemplation of his majesty's government; and therefore, as the primary object of our movement had been already fully accomplished, I communicated my observations to colonel Brooke, who, coinciding with me in opinion, it was mutually agreed that we should withdraw.

The following morning, the army began leisurely to retire; and so salutary was the effect produced on the enemy by the defeat he had experienced, that, notwithstanding every opportunity was offered for his repeating the conflict, with an infinite superiority, our troops re-embarked without molestation. The ships of war dropped down as the army retired.

The result of this demonstration has been the defeat of the

army of the enemy, the destruction, by themselves, of a quantity of shipping, the burning of an extensive rope-walk, and other public erections; the causing of them to remove their property from the city, and, above all, the collecting and harassing of the armed inhabitants from the surrounding country; producing a total stagnation of their commerce, and heaping upon them considerable expenses, at the same time effectually drawing off their attention and support from other important quarters.

It has been a source of the greatest gratification to me, the continuance of that unanimity existing between the two services, which I have before noticed to their lordships; and I have reason to assure them, that the command of the army has fallen upon a most zealous and able officer in colonel Brooke, who has followed up the system of cordiality that had been so beneficially adopted by his much-lamented chief.

Rear-admiral Cockburn, to whom I had confided that part of the naval service which was connected with the army, evinced his usual zeal and ability, and executed his important trust to my entire satisfaction.

Rear-admiral Malcolm, who regulated the collection, debarkation, and re-embarkation of the troops, and the supplies they required, has merited my best thanks for his indefatigable exertions; and I have to express my acknowledgments for the counsel and assistance which, in all our operations, I have received from rear-admiral Codrington, the captain of the fleet.

The captains of the squadron, who were employed on the various duties a-float, were all emulous to promote the service in which they were engaged, and, with the officers acting under them, are entitled to my fullest approbation.

I beg leave to call the attention of their lordships to the report rear-admiral Cockburn has made, of the meritorious and gallant conduct of the naval brigade; as well as to the accompanying letter from colonel Brooke, expressing his obligation to captain Edward Crofton, who commanded, and captains T. B. Sullivan, Rowland, Money, and Robert Ramsay, who had charge of divisions; and I have to recommend these officers, together with those who are particularly noticed by the rear-admiral, to their lordship's favorable consideration.

Captain Robyns, of the royal marines, who commanded the marines of the squadron on this occasion, and in the operations against Washington, being severely wounded, I beg leave to bring him to their lordship's recollection, as having been frequently noticed for his gallant conduct during the services in the Chesapeake, and to recommend him, with lieutenant Sampson Marshall, of the Diadem, who is dangerously wounded, to their lordships' favor and protection.

First-lieutenant John Lawrence, of the royal marine artillery, who commanded the rocket-brigade, has again rendered essential service, and is highly spoken of by colonel Brooke.

Captain Edward Crofton, who will have the honor of delivering this despatch, is competent to explain any further particulars; and I beg leave to recommend him to their lordships' protection, as a most zealous and intelligent officer.

I have the honor to be, &c.

ALEXANDER COCHRANE,

Vice-admiral, and commander in chief.

To John Wilson Croker, Esq. &c.

No. 74.

From rear-admiral Cockburn to sir Alexander Cochrane.

H. M. S. Severn, in the Patapsco,

Sir, 15th Sept. 1814.

In furtherance of the instructions I had the honor to receive from you on the 11th instant, I landed at day-light on the 12th with major-general Ross, and the force under his command, at a place the general and myself had previously fixed upon, near to North-point, at the entrance of the Patapsco; and, in conformity with his wishes, I determined on remaining on shore, and accompanying the army, to render him every assistance within my power during the contemplated movements and operations; therefore, so soon as our landing was completed, I directed captain Nourse, of this ship, to advance up the Patapsco with the frigate, sloops, and bomb-ships, to bombard the fort, and threaten the water-approach to Baltimore, and I moved on with the army and seamen (under captain Edward Crofton) attached to it, on the direct road leading to the above-mentioned town.

We had advanced about five miles, (without any other occurrence than taking prisoners a few light-horsemen,) when the general and myself, being with the advanced guard, observed a division of the enemy posted at a turning of the road, extending into a wood on our left; a sharp fire was almost immediately opened upon it, and as quickly returned with considerable effect by our advanced guard, which pressing steadily forward, soon obliged the enemy to run off with the utmost precipitation, leaving behind him several men killed and wounded; but it is with the most heartfelt sorrow I have to add, that in this short and desultory skirmish, my gallant and highly valued friend, the major-general, received a musket-ball through his arm into his breast, which proved fatal to him on his way to the water-side for re-embarkation.

Our country, sir, has lost in him one of its best and bravest soldiers; and those who knew him, as I did, a friend most honored and beloved; and I trust, sir, I may be forgiven for considering it a sacred duty I owe to him to mention here, that whilst his wounds were binding up, and we were placing him on the bearer which was to carry him off the field, he assured me that the wonnds he had received in the performance of his duty to his country, caused him not a pang; but he felt alone anxiety for a wife and family, dearer to him than his life; whom, in the event of the fatal termination he foresaw, he recommended to the protection and notice of his majesty's government, and the country.

Colonel Brooke, on whom the command of the army now devolved, having come up, and the body of our troops having closed with the advance, the whole proceeded forward about two miles further, where we observed the enemy in force drawn up before us; (apparently about 6000 or 7000 strong;) on perceiving our army, he filed off into a large and extensive wood on his right, from which he commenced a cannonade on us from his field-pieces, and drew up his men behind a thick paling, where he appeared determined to make his stand. Our field guns answered his with an evident advantage; and so soon as colonel Brooke had made the necessary dispositions, the attack was ordered, and executed in the highest style possible. The enemy opened his musketry on us from his whole line, immediately we approached within reach of it, and kept up his fire till we reached and entered the wood, when he gave way in every direction, and was chased by us a considerable distance with great slaughter, abandoning his post of the Meeting-house, situated in this wood, and leaving all his wounded, and two of his field-guns, in our possession.

An advance of this description, against superior numbers of an enemy so posted, could not be effected without loss. I have the honor to enclose a return of what has been suffered by those of the naval department, acting with the army on this occasion; and it is, sir, with the greatest pride and pleasure I report to you, that the brigade of seamen with small arms, commanded by captain E. Crofton, assisted by captains Sullivan, Money, and Ramsay, (the three senior commanders with the fleet), who commanded divisions under him, behaved with a gallantry and steadiness which would have done honor to the oldest troops, and which attracted the admiration of the army. The seamen under Mr. Jackson, master's mate of the Tonnant, attached to the rocket brigade, commanded by the first-lieutenant Lawrence, of the marines, behaved also with equal skill and bravery. The marines, landed from the ships under the command of captain Robyns, the senior officer of that corps, belonging to the fleet, behaved with their usual gallantry.

Although, sir, in making to you my report of this action, I

know it is right I should confine myself to mentioning only the conduct of those belonging to the naval department, yet I may be excused for venturing further to state to you, generally, the high admiration with which I viewed the conduct of the whole army, and the ability and gallantry with which it was managed, and headed, by its brave colonel, which insured to it the success it met with.

The night being fast approaching, and the troops much fatigued, colonel Brooke determined on remaining for the night on the field of battle; and, on the morning of the 13th, leaving a small guard at the Meeting-house to collect and protect the wounded, we again moved forwards towards Baltimore; on approaching which, it was found to be defended by extremely strong works on every side, and immediately in front of us by an extensive hill, on which was an entrenched camp, and great quanties of artillery; and the information we collected, added to what we observed, gave us to believe there were at least, within their works, from 15 to 20,000 men. Colonel Brooke lost no time in reconnoitring these defences; after which, he made his arrangement for storming, during the ensuing night, with his gallant little army, the entrenched camp in our front, notwithstanding all the difficulties which it presented. The subsequent communications which we opened with you, however, induced him to relinquish again the idea, and therefore yesterday morning the army retired leisurely to the Meeting-house, where it halted for some hours to make the necessary arrangements respecting the wounded and the prisoners taken on the 12th, which being completed, it made a further short movement in the evening towards the place where it had dis-embarked, and where it arrived this morning for re-embarkation, without suffering the slightest molestation from the enemy; who, in spite of his superiority of number, did not even venture to look at us during the slow and deliberate retreat.

As you, sir, were in person with the advanced frigates, sloops, and bomb-vessels, and as, from the road the army took, I did not see them after quitting the beach, it would be superfluous for me to make any report to you respecting them I have now, therefore, only to assure you of my entire satisfaction and approbation of the conduct of every officer and man employed under me, during the operations above detailed, and to express to you how particularly I consider myself indebted to captain Edward Crofton, (acting captain of the Royal Oak,) for the gallantry, ability, and zeal, with which he led on the brigade of seamen in the action of the 12th, and executed all the other services with which he has been entrusted since our landing; to captain White, (acting captain of the Albion,) who attended me as my aide de camp the whole time, and rendered me every possible assistance; to captains Sullivan, Money, and Ramsay, who commanded divisions of the brigade of seamen; to lieutenant James Scott, of the Albion, whom I have had much frequent cause to mention to you on former occasions, and who in the battle of the 12th commanded a division of seamen, and behaved most gallantly, occasionally also acting as an extra aide de camp to myself. Captain Robyns, who commanded the marines of the fleet, and who was severely wounded during the engagement, I also beg to recommend to your favourable notice and consideration, as well as lieutenant George C. Urmston, of the Albion, whom I placed in command of the smaller boats, to endeavour to keep up a communication between the army and navy, which he effected by great perseverance, and thereby rendered us most essential service. In short, sir, every individual seemed animated with equal anxiety to distinguish himself by good conduct on this occasion, and I trust, therefore, the whole will be deemed worthy of your approbation.

Captain Nourse, of the Severn, was good enough to receive my flag for this service; he rendered me great assistance in getting the ships to the different stations within the river, and when the storming of the fortified hill was contemplated, he hastened to my assistance with a reinforcement of seamen and marines; and I should consider myself wanting in candour and justice did I not particularly point out, sir, to you, the high opinion I entertain of the enterprise and ability of this valuable officer, not only for his conduct on this occasion, but on the very many others on which I have employed him since with me in the Chesapeake. I have the honour to be, &c.

GEORGE COCKBURN, rear-admiral.

Vice-admiral the hon. sir A. Cochrane, K.B.
Commander in chief.

No. 75.

Colonel Brooke to the same.

On board his majesty's ship Tonnant,
September 15, 1814

Dear sir,

I beg leave to be allowed to state to you, how much I feel indebted to captain Crofton, commanding the brigade of sailors from his majesty's ships under your command; as also to captains Sullivan, Money, and Ramsay, for their very great exertions in performing every formation made by his majesty's troops, having seen myself those officers expose themselves to the hottest of the enemy's fire, to keep their men in the line of march, with the disciplined troops. The obedient and steady conduct of the sailors, believe me, sir, excited the admiration of every individual of the army, as well as my greatest gratitude.

Believe me to be, dear sir,

ARTHUR BROOKE, col.-com.

Vice-admiral the hon. sir A. Cochrane, K.B. commander-in-chief.

No. 76.

A return of killed and wounded belonging to the navy, disembarked with the army under major-general Ross, September, 12, 1814.

Tonnant;—1 petty officer, 5 seaman, 3 marines, wounded.

Albion;—3 seamen killed; 1 petty officer, 8 seamen, 6 marines, wounded.

Ramillies;—2 marines killed; 4 petty officers, 6 seamen, 4 marines, wounded.

Diadem;—1 officer, 2 seamen, wounded.

Melpomene;—1 petty officer killed.

Trave;—1 seaman wounded.

Madagascar;—1 marine killed; 1 marine wounded.

Royal Oak;—1 marine wounded.

Total killed—1 petty officer, 3 seamen, 3 marines.

Total wounded—1 officer, 6 petty officers, 22 seamen, 15 marines.

Names of officers killed and wounded.

Killed—Melpomene;—Mr. William, (or Arthur) Edmonson, clerk.

Wounded—Tonnant;—captain Robyns, royal marines, severely; Mr. Charles Ogle, midshipman, severely.

Diadem;—lieutenant S. Marshall, severely.

Albion;—John Billett, quarter-master, severely.

Ramillies;—Robert Wafton (or Watton) boatswain's-mate, severely; Henry Bakewell yeoman of the powder-room, badly; John Prickett, ship's corporal, slightly.

G. COCKBURN, rear-admiral.

No. 77.

From major-general Smith, to the American secretary at war. *(Extract.)*

About the time general Stricker had taken the ground just mentioned, he was joined by brigadier-general Winder, who had been stationed on the west side of the city, but was now ordered to march with general Douglas's brigade of Virginia militia, and the United States' dragoons, under captain Bird, and take post on the left of general Stricker. During these movements, the brigades of generals Stansbury and Foreman, the seamen and marines under commodore Rodgers, the Pennsylvania volunteers under colonels Cobean and Findley, the Baltimore artillery under colonel Harris, and the marine artillery under captain Stiles, manned the trenches and the batteries—all prepared to receive the enemy. We remained in this situation during the night.

On Tuesday, the enemy appeared in front of my entrenchments, at the distance of two miles, on the Philadelphia road, from whence he had a full view of our position. He manœuvred during the morning towards our left, as if with the intention of making a circuitous march, and coming down on the Harford or York roads. Generals Winder and Stricker were ordered to adapt their movement to those of the enemy, so as to baffle this supposed intention. They executed this order with great skill and judgment, by taking an advantageous position, stretching from my left across the country, when the enemy was likely to approach the quarter he seemed to threaten. This movement induced the enemy to concentrate his forces (between one and two o'clock), in my front, pushing his advance to within a mile of us, driving in our videttes, and showing an intention of attacking us that evening. I immediately drew generals Winder and Striker nearer to the left of my entrenchments, and to the right of the enemy, with the intention of their falling on his right or rear, should he attack me; or, if he declined it, of attacking him in the morning. To this movement, and to the strength of my defence, which the enemy had the fairest opportunity of observing, I am induced to attribute his retreat, which was commenced at half-past one o'clock on Wednesday morning. In this he was so favored by the extreme darkness, and a continued rain, that we did not discover it until day-light.

I have now the pleasure of calling your attention to the brave commander of Fort M'Henry, major Armistead, and to the operations confined to that quarter. The enemy made his approach by water at the same time that his army was advancing on the land, and commenced a discharge of bombs and rockets at the fort, as soon as he got within range of it. The situation of major Armistead was peculiarly trying—the enemy having taken his position such a distance, as to render offensive operations on the part of the fort entirely fruitless, whilst their bombs and rockets were every moment falling in and about it —the officers and men, at the same time, entirely exposed. The vessels, however, had the temerity to approach somewhat nearer—they were as soon compelled to withdraw. During the night, whilst the enemy on land was retreating, and whilst the bombardment was most severe, two or three rocket vessels and barges succeeded in getting up the Ferry Branch, but they were soon compelled to retire, by the forts in that quarter, commanded by lieutenant Newcomb, of the navy, and lieutenant Webster, of the flotilla. These forts also destroyed one of the barges, with all on board. The barges and battery at the Lazaretto, under the command of lieutenant Rutter, of the flotilla, kept up a brisk, and it is believed, a successful fire, during the hottest period of the bombardment.

No. 78.

From Captain Lockyer to vice-admiral Cochrane.

His Majesty's sloop Sophie, Cat island Roads, Dec. 18, 1814.

SIR,

I beg leave to inform you, that in pursuance of your orders, the boats of the squadron which you did me the honour to place under my command, were formed into three divisions, (the first headed by myself, the second by captain Montressor of the Manly, and the third by captain Roberts of the Meteor,) and proceeded on the night of the 12th instant from the frigate's anchorage, in quest of the enemy's flotilla.

After a very tedious row of thirty-six hours, during which the enemy attempted to escape from us, the wind fortunately obliged him to anchor off St. Joseph's island, and nearing him on the morning of the 14th, I discovered his force to consist of five gun-vessels of the largest dimensions, which were moored in a line a-breast, with springs on their cables, and boarding nettings triced up, evidently prepared for our reception.

Observing, also, as we approached the flotilla, an armed sloop endeavouring to join them, captain Roberts, who volunteered to take her with part of his division, succeeded in cutting her off and capturing her without much opposition.

About 10 o'clock, having closed to within long gun-shot, I directed the boats to come to a grapnel, and the people to get their breakfasts; and, as soon as they had finished, we again took to our oars, and pulling up to the enemy against a strong current, running at the rate of nearly three miles an hour exposed to a heavy and destructive fire of round and grape, about noon I had the satisfaction of closing with the commodore in the Seahorse's barge.

After several minutes' obstinate resistance, in which the greater part of the officers and crew of this boat were either killed or wounded, myself amongst the latter, severely, we succeeded in boarding, and being seconded by the Seahorse's first barge, commanded by Mr. White, midshipman, and aided by the boats of the Tonnant, commanded by lieutenant Tatnell, we soon carried her, and turned her guns with good effect upon the remaining four.

During this time captain Montresor's division was making every possible exertion to close with the enemy, and with the assistance of the other boats, then joined by captain Roberts, in about five minutes we had possossion of the whole of the flotilla.

I have to lament the loss of many of my brave and gallant companions, who gloriously fell in this attack; but, considering the great strength of the enemy's vessels (whose force is underneath described) and their state of preparation, we have by no means suffered so severely as might have been expected.

I am under the greatest obligations to the officers, seamen, and marines, I had the honor to command on this occasion, to whose gallantry and exertions the service is indebted for the capture of these vessels; any comments of mine would fall short of the praise due to them: I am especially indebted to captains Montresor and Roberts for their advice and assistance: they are entitled to more than I can say of them, and have my best thanks for the admirable style in which they pushed on with their divisions to the capture of the remainder of the enemy's flotilla.

In an expedition of this kind, where so many were concerned, and so much personal exertion and bravery was displayed, I find it impossible to particularize every individual who distinguished himself, and deserves to be well spoken of, but I feel it my duty to mention those whose behaviour fell immediately under my own eye.

Lieutenant George Pratt, second of the Seahorse, who commanded that ship's boats, and was in the same boat with me, conducted himself to that admiration which I cannot sufficiently express; in his attempt to board the enemy, he was several times severely wounded, and at last so dangerously, that I fear the service will be deprived of this gallant and promising young officer.

I cannot omit to mention, also, the conduct of lieutenants Tatnell and Roberts, of the Tonnant, particularly the former, who, after having his boat sunk alongside, got into another, and gallantly pushed on to the attack of the remainder of the flotilla. Lieutenant Roberts was wounded in closing with the enemy. I have the honor to be, &c.

NICH. LOCKYER, captain.

Vice-admiral the Hon. Sir Alexander Cochrane,
commander-in-chief, &c. &c. &c.

No. 1.—Gun-vessel, 1 long 24-pounder, 4 12-pounder carronades, and 4 swivels, with a complement of 45 men; captain Jones, commodore.

No. 2.—Gun-vessel, 1 long 32-pounder, 6 long 6-pounders, 2 5-inch howitzers, and four swivels, with a complement of 45 men; lieutenant M'Ives.

No. 3.—Gun-vessel, 1 long 24-pounder, 4 long 6-pounders, and 4 swivels, with a complement of 45 men.

No. 4.—Gun-vessel, 1 long 24-pounder, 4 12-pounder carronades, with a complement of 45 men.

No. 5.—Gun-vessel, 1 long 24-pounder, 4 12-pounder carronades, with a complement of 45 men.

No. 6.—Armed sloop, 1 long 6-pounder, 2 12-pounder carronades, with a complement of 20 men.

NICHOLAS LOCKYER, captain.

No. 79.

A list of the killed and wounded in the boats of his majesty's ships at the capture of the American gun-vessels near New Orleans.

Tonnant;—1 able seaman, 2 ordinary seamen, killed; 1 lieutenant, 4 midshipmen, 4 able seamen, 4 ordinary, 2 landmen, 3 private marines, wounded.

Norge;—1 quarter-master killed: 1 master's-mate, 4 able seamen, 3 ordinary seamen, 1 private marine, wounded.

Bedford;—1 seaman killed; 2 lieutenants, 1 master's-mate, 2 seamen, wounded.

Royal Oak;—1 seaman wounded.

Ramillies; —4 seamen killed; 9 seamen wounded.

Armide;—1 seaman killed.

Cydnus;—1 midshipman, 1 seaman, 2 private marines, wounded.

Seahorse;—1 midshipman, 1 volunteer of the 1st class, 1 able seaman, 1 ordinary seaman, 1 private marine, killed; 1 lieutenant, 2 midshipmen, 1 lieutenant of marines, 7 able seamen, 7 ordinary seamen, 1 landman, 4 private marines, wounded.

Trave;—1 volunteer of the 1st class, 1 captain of the foretop, killed; 1 private marine wounded.

Sophie;—1 captain wounded.

Meteor;—3 seamen wounded.

Belle Poule;—2 seamen wounded.

Gorgon—1 master's-mate wounded.

Total—3 midshipmen, 13 seamen, 1 private marine, killed; 1 captain, 4 lieutenants, 1 lieutenant of marines, 3 master's-mates, 7 midshipmen, 50 seamen, 11 marines, wounded.

Grand Total—17 killed; 77 wounded.

No. 80.

From lieutenant Jones to commodore Patterson.

SIR, New Orleans, 12th March, 1815.

Having sufficiently recovered my strength, I do myself the honor of reporting to you the particulars of the capture of the division of United States' gun boats late under my command.

On the 12th December, 1814, the enemy's fleet off Ship island increased to such a force as to render it no longer safe or prudent for me to continue on that part of the lakes with the small force which I commanded. I therefore determined to gain a station near the Malheureux islands as soon as possible, which situation would better enable me to oppose a further penetration of the enemy up the lakes, and at the same time afford me an opportunity of retreating to the Petite Coquilles if necessary.

At 10, A.M. on the 13th I discovered a large flotilla of barges had left the fleet, (shaping their course towards the Pass Christian,) which I supposed to be a disembarkation of troops intended to land at that place. About 2, P.M. the enemy's flotilla having gained the Pass Christian, and continuing their course to the westward, convinced me that an attack on the gun-boats was designed. At this time the water in the lakes was uncommonly low, owing to the westerly wind which had prevailed for a number of days previous, and which still continued from the same quarter. Nos. 150, 162 and 163, although in the best channel, were in 12 or 18 inches less water than their draught. Every effort was made to get them a-float by throwing overboard all articles of weight that could be dispensed with. At 3 30, the flood-tide had commenced; got under weigh, making the best of my way towards the Petite Coquilles. At 3 45, the enemy despatched three boats to cut out the schooner Seahorse, which had been sent into the bay St. Louis that morning to assist in the removal of the public stores, which I had previously ordered. There finding a removal impracticable, I ordered preparations to be made for their destruction, least they should fall into the enemy's hands. A few discharges of grape-shot from the Seahorse compelled the three boats, which had attacked her, to retire out of reach of her guns, until they were joined by four others, when the attack was recommenced by the seven boats. Mr. Johnson having chosen an advantageous position near the two 6-pounders mounted on the bank, maintained a sharp action for near 30 minutes, when the enemy hauled off, having one boat apparently much injured, and with the loss of several men killed and wounded. At 7 30, an explosion at the bay, and soon after a large fire, induced me to believe the Seahorse was blown up and the public store-house set on fire, which has proved to be the fact.

About 1 A.M. on the 14th, the wind having entirely died away, and our vessels become unmanageable, came to anchor in the west-end of Malheureux island's passage. At daylight next morning, still a perfect calm, the enemy's flotilla was about nine miles from us at anchor, but soon got in motion and rapidly advanced on us. The want of wind, and the strong ebb-tide which was setting through the pass, left me but one alternative, which was, to put myself in the most advantageous position, to give the enemy as warm a reception as possible. The commanders were all called on board and made acquainted with my intentions, and the position which each vessel was to take, the whole to form a close line a-breast across the channel, anchored by the stern with springs on the cable, &c. &c. Thus we remained anxiously awaiting an attack from the advancing foe, whose force I now clearly distinguished to be composed of 42 heavy launches and gun-barges, with three light gigs, manned with upwards of 1000 men and officers. About 9 30, the Alligator (tender) which was to the southward and eastward, and endeavouring to join the division, was captured by several of the enemy's barges, when the whole flotilla came-to, with their grapnels a little out of reach of our shot, apparently making arrangements for the attack. At 10 30, the enemy weighed, forming a line a-breast in open order, and steering direct for our line, which was unfortunately in some degree broken by the force of the current, driving Nos. 156 and 163 about 100 yards in advance. As soon as the enemy came within reach of our shot, a deliberate fire from our long guns was opened upon him, but without much effect, the objects being of so small a size. At 10 minutes before 11, the enemy opened a fire from the whole of his line, when the action became general and destructive on both sides. About 11 49, the advance boats of the enemy, three in number, attempted to board No. 156, but were repulsed with the loss of nearly every officer killed or wounded, and two boats sunk. A second attempt to board was then made by four other boats, which shared almost a similar fate. At this moment I received a severe wound in my left shoulder, which compelled me to quit the deck, leaving it in charge of Mr. George Parker, master's-mate, who gallantly defended the vessel until he was severely wounded, when the enemy, by his superior number, succeeded in gaining possession of the deck about 10 minutes past 12 o'clock. The enemy immediately turned the guns of his prize on the other gun-boats, and fired several shot previous to striking the American colours. The action continued with unabating severity until 40 minutes past 12 o'clock, when it terminated with the surrender of No. 23, all the other vessels having previously fallen into the hands of the enemy.

In this unequal contest our loss in killed and wounded has been trifling, compared to that of the enemy.

Enclosed you will receive a list of the killed and wounded, and a correct statement of the force which I had the honor to command at the commencement of the action, together with an estimate of the force I had to contend against, as acknowledged by the enemy, which will enable you to decide how far the honor of our country's flag has been supported in this conflict.

I have the honor to be, &c.

THOMAS AP CATESBY JONES.

No. 81.

Statement of the effective forces of a division of the United States' gun-boats under the command of lieutenant-commanding Thomas Ap Catesby Jones, at the commencement of the action, with a flotilla of English gun-boats, on the 14th December 1814.

Gun-boat No. 5, 5 guns, 36 men, sailing-master John D. Ferris: gun-boat 23, 5 guns, 39 men, lieutenant Isaac M'Keeve; gun-boat No. 156, 5 guns, 41 men, lieutenant-commandant Thomas A. C. Jones; gun-boat 162, 5 guns, 35 men, lieutenant Robert Spedden; gun-boat 163, 3 guns, 31 men, sailing-master George Ulrick.

Total—23 guns, 182 men.

N.B The schooner Seahorse, had one 6-pounder, and 14 men, sailing-master William Johnson, commander; none killed or wounded.

The sloop Alligator (tender) had one 4-pounder and eight men, sailing-master Richard S Shepperd, commander.

THOMAS AP CATESBY JONES.

No. 82.

Statement of the British forces which were engaged in the capture of the late United States' gun boats, Nos. 23, 156, 5, 162, *and* 163, *near the Malheureux islands, lake Borgne,* 14*th December*, 1814.

Forty launches and barges, mounting one carronade, each of 12, 18, and 24 caliber.

One launch, mounting one long brass 12-pounder.

One launch, mounting one long brass 9-pounder.

Three gigs, with small-arms only.

Total number of boats—45.

Total number of cannon—43.

The above flotilla was manned with 1200 men and officers, commanded by captain Lockyer, who received three severe wounds in the action. The enemy, as usual, will not acknowledge his loss on this occasion in boats or men; but from the nature of the action, and the observations made by our officers, while prisoners in their fleet, his loss in killed and wounded may be justly estimated to exceed 300, among whom are an unusual proportion of officers.

No. 83.

From major-general Keane to major-general the honorable sir Edward Pakenham.

Camp on the left bank of the Mississippi, nine miles from New Orleans, December 26, 1814.

SIR,

I have the honor to inform you, that between the 17th and 22d instant, the troops destined for the attack of New Orleans, were collected at Isle aux Poix, which is the entrance of the Pearl river.

Having learnt that it was possible to effect a landing at the head of the bayou Catalan, which runs into lake Borgne, I directed major Forrest, assistant-quarter-master-general, to have it reconnoitred. Lieutenant Peddie, of that department, accompanied by the honorable captain Spencer of the navy, ascertained on the night of 18th, that boats could reach the head of the bayou, from which a communication might be made to the high road, on the left bank of the Mississippi, leading to New Orleans.

On the morning of the 22d, every arrangement being made by vice-admiral the honorable sir Alexander Cochrane, I determined to attempt it. The light brigade, composed of the 85th and 95th regiments, captain Lane's rocketeers, 100 sappers and miners, and the 4th regiment as a support, the whole under the command of colonel Thornton, were placed in the boats, and the 21st, 44th, and 93d regiments, under colonel Brooke, and a large proportion of artillery under major Munro, were embarked in small vessels.

At 10 A.M. on the 22d, we sailed from Pearl River and reached the head of the bayou at day-light next morning. A landing was immediately effected without any other opposition than the country presented; captain Blanchard of the royal engineers, in the course of two hours, opened a communication through several fields of reeds, intersected by deep muddy ditches, bordered by a low swampy wood; colonel Thornton then advanced and gained the high road, taking up a position with the right resting on the road, and the left on the Mississippi. In this situation I intended to remain untill the boats returned for the rest of the troops to the vessels, some of which grounded at a great distance.

At about eight o'clock in the evening when the men, much fatigued by the length of time they had been in the boats, were asleep in their bivouac, a heavy flanking fire of round and grape-shot was opened upon them, by a large schooner and two gun-vessels, which had dropped down the river from the town and anchored a-breast of our fires; immediate steps were necessary to cover the men, and colonel Thornton, in the most prompt and judicious manner, placed his brigade under the inward slope of the bank of the river, as did also lieutenant-colonel Brooke, of the 4th regiment, behind some buildings which were near that corps. This movemont was so rapid that the troops suffered no more than a single casualty.

The 3-pounders being the only guns up, the success of a few 12-pound rockets, directed by captain Lane, was tried against these vessels; but the ground on which it was necessary to lay them not being even, they were found not to answer, and their firing was ceased.

A most vigorous attack was then made on the advanced front and right flank piquets, the former of the 95th, under captain Hallan, the latter the 85th, under captain Schaw; these officers, and their respective piquets, conducted themselve with firmness, and checked the enemy for a considerable time, but renewing their attack with a large force, and pressing at these points, colonel Thornton judged it necessary to move up the remainder of both corps. The 85th regiment was commanded by brevet-major Gubbins, whose conduct cannot be too much commended. On the approach of his regiment to the point of attack, the enemy, favored by the darkness of the night, concealed themselves under a high fence which separated the fields, and calling to the men as friends, under pretence of being part of our own force, offered to assist them in getting over, which was no sooner accomplished than the 85th found itself in the midst of very superior numbers, who, discovering themselves, called on the regiment immediately to surrender—the answer was an instantaneous attack; a more extraordinary conflict has perhaps never occurred, absolutely hand to hand both officers and men. It terminated in the repulse of the enemy with the capture of 30 prisoners. A similar finesse was attempted with the 95th regiment, which met the same treatment.

The enemy finding his reiterated attacks were repulsed by colonel Thornton, at half-past 10 o'clock advanced a large column against our centre; perceiving his intention, I directed colonel Stovin to order lieutenant-colonel Dale, with 130 men of the 93d regiment, who had just reached the camp, to move forward and use the bayonet, holding the 4th regiment in hand, formed in line, as my last reserve. Colonel Dale endeavoured to execute his orders, but the crafty enemy would not meet him, seeing the steadiness of his small body, gave it a heavy fire, and quickly retired. Colonel Brooke, with four companies of the 21st regiment, fortunately appeared at that moment on our right flank, and sufficiently secured it from further attack.

The enemy now determined on making a last effort, and, collecting the whole of his force, formed an extensive line, and moved directly against the light brigade. At first this line drove in all the advanced posts, but colonel Thornton, whose noble exertions had guaranteed all former success, was at hand; he rallied his brave comrades round him, and moving forward with a firm determination of charging, appalled the enemy, who, from the lesson he had received on the same ground in the early part of the evening, thought it prudent to retire, and did not again dare to advance.

It was now 12 o'clock, and the firing ceased on both sides. From the best information I can obtain, the enemy's force amounted to 5000 men, and was commanded by major-general Jackson: judging from the number left on the field, his loss must have been severe. I now beg leave to inclose a list of our casualties on that night, and have only to hope it will appear to you, that every officer and soldier on shore did his duty.

To sir Alexander Cochrane I feel particularly obliged for his very friendly counsels and ready compliance with every wish I expressed respecting the service or welfare of the troops.

To rear-admiral Malcolm, and the several captains employed in the landing, &c. I confess the greatest obligation. I must leave it to the vice-admiral to do them the justice they so much deserve, for I cannot find words to express the exertions made by every branch of the navy, since the period of our arrival on this coast.

In the attack made on the centre, lieutenant-colonel Stovin, assistant-adjutant-general, received a severe wound, which deprived me of his able services; to him and major Forrest, assistant-quarter-master-general, I feel greatly indebted; they are both officers of great merit. Colonel Brooke is entitled to every praise for securing our right flank.

To colonel Thornton I feel particularly grateful; his conduct on the night of the 23d I shall ever admire and honor. He headed his brigade in the most spirited manner, and afforded it a brilliant example of active courage and cool determination.

I have every reason to be satisfied with lieutenant-colonel Brooke, commanding the 4th regiment; as also with major

Mitchell, of the 95th, who was unfortunately taken prisoner at the close of the affair.

The exertions of major Munroe, of the royal artillery, were unremitting; to him, and the officers under his command, I feel every obligation. The assistance given by captain Blanchard, and the officers of the royal engineers, was most conspicuous, and entitle them to my best thanks.

Brevet-major Hooper, acting deputy assistant-adjutant-general, was attached to the light brigade. Colonel Thornton states, that he derived the greatest benefit from his activity, zeal, and judgment. I regret to have to add that he was very severely wounded, and had his leg amputated in the course of the night.

The indefatigable zeal and intelligence displayed by lieutenants Peddie and Evans, of the quarter-master-general's department, entitle them to the most favorable consideration.

Assistant-commissary-general Wemyss's arrangements were satisfactory, and deputy-inspector Thompson claims my best acknowledgements, for the care and attention shewn to the wounded, the whole of whom were collected, dressed, and comfortably lodged, before two in the morning.

Major Mills, of the 14th light dragoons, accompanied me on shore; from him, captain Persse, my aide de camp; and the honorable lieutenant Curzon, naval aide de camp, I received every assistance.

Trusting that the steps I pursued while in command will meet your approbation,

I have the honor to be, &c.

JOHN KEANE, maj.-gen.

No. 84.

Return of casualties in action with the enemy near New Orleans, on the 23d and 24th December, 1814.

General staff;—1 lieutenant-colonel, 1 major, 1 lieutenant, wounded.

Royal artillery; 2 rank and file, killed; 1 lieutenant, 7 rank and file, wounded.

Royal engineers, sappers and miners; 1 rank and file missing.

4th foot;—1 captain, 1 lieutenant, 1 serjeant, 1 drummer, 1 rank and file, killed; 1 lieutenant, 14 rank and file, wounded.

21st foot;—1 captain, 2 rank and file, killed: 1 serjeant, 2 drummers, 8 rank and file, wounded; 2 rank and file, missing.

85th foot; 2 captains, 11 rank and file, killed; 1 captain, 3 lieutenants, 4 serjeants, 2 drummers, 57 rank and file, wounded; 1 lieutenants, 1 ensign, 1 serjeant, 16 rank and file, missing.

93d foot;—1 rank and file, wounded.

95th foot;—6 serjeants, 17 rank and file, killed; 1 captain, 2 lieutenants, 5 serjeants, 54 rank and file, wounded; 1 major, 2 serjeants, 39 rank and file, missing.

Total;—4 captains, 1 lieutenant, 7 serjeants, 1 drummer, 33 rank and file, killed; 1 lieutenant-colonel, 1 major, 2 captains, 8 lieutenants, 10 serjeants, 4 drummers, 141 rank and file, wounded; 1 major, 1 lieutenant, 1 ensign, 3 serjeants, 58 rank and file, missing.

Names of the officers killed, wounded, and missing.

Killed—4th foot;—Captain Francis Johnstone, lieutenant John Sutherland.

21st foot;—Captain William Conran.

85th foot;—Captains Charles Grey and Charles Harris

Wounded—general staff;—Lieutenant-colonel Stovin, 28th foot, assistant-adjutant-general, severely, but not dangerously; major Hooper, 87th foot, deputy assistant-adjutant general, severely; (leg amputated;) lieutenant Delacy Evans, 3d dragoons, deputy assistant-quarter-master-general, severely.

Royal Artillery;—Lieutenant James Christie, severely.

4th foot;—Lieutenant Thomas Moody, severely.

85th foot;—Captain James Knox, lieutenants George Willings, Frederick Maunsell, and William Hickson, severely.

95th foot;—Captain William Hallen, lieutenant Daniel Forbes, severely; lieutenant W. J. G. Farmer, slightly.

Missing—85th foot;—Lieutenant William Walker, ensign George Ashton.

95th foot—Major Samuel Mitchell.

FRED. STOVIN, lieut.-col. dep. adj.-gen.

No. 85.

From major-general Jackson to the American secretary at war.

Head-quarters, 7th military district, camp below New Orleans, 27th Dec. A.M.

SIR,

The loss of our gun-boats near the pass of the Rigolets, having given the enemy command of lake Borgne, he was enabled to choose his point of attack. It became therefore an object of importance to obstruct the numerous bayous and canals leading from that lake to the highlands on the Mississippi. This important service was committed, in the first instance, to a detachment from the 7th regiment, afterwards to colonel Delaronde of the Louisiana militia, and lastly, to make all sure, to major-general Villeré, commanding the district between the river and the lakes, and who, being a native of the country, was presumed to be best acquainted with all those passes. Unfortunately, however, a piquet which the general had established at the mouth of the bayou Bienvenu, and which, notwithstanding my orders, had been left unobstructed, was completely surprised, and the enemy penetrated through a canal leading to his farm, about two leagues below the city, and succeeded in cutting off a company of militia stationed there. The intelligence was communicated to me about two o'clock on the 23d. My force, at this time, consisted of parts of the 7th and 44th regiments, not exceeding 600 together, the city militia, a part of general Coffee's brigade of mounted gun-men, and the detached militia from the western division of Tennessee, under the command of major.general Carroll—these two last corps were stationed four miles above the city. Apprehending a double attack by the way of Chef-Menteur, I left general Carroll's force, and the militia of the city, posted on the Gentilly road; and at 5 o'clock P. M. marched to meet the enemy, whom I was resolved to attack in his first position, with major Hind's dragoons, general Coffee's brigade, parts of the 7th and 44th regiments, the uniform companies of militia under the command of major Plauche, 200 men of colour (chiefly from St. Domingo) raised by colonel Savary, and acting under the command of major Daquin, and a detachment of artillery under the direction of colonel M'Rea, with two 6-pounders, under the command of lieutenant Spots—not exceeding in all 1500. I arrived near the enemy's encampment about seven, and immediately made my dispositions for the attack. His forces amounting at that time on land to about 3000, extended half a mile on the river, and in the rear nearly to the wood. General Coffee was ordered to turn their right, while, with the residue of the force, I attacked his strongest position on the left, near the river. Commodore Patterson having dropped down the river in the schooner Carolina, was directed to open a fire upon their camp, which he executed at about half after seven. This being the signal of attack, general Coffee's men, with their usual impetuosity, rushed on the enemy's right, and entered their camp, while our right advanced with equal ardor. There can be but little doubt that we should have succeeded on that occasion, with our inferior force, in destroying or capturing the enemy, had not a thick fog, which arose about eight o'clock, occasioned some confusion among the different corps. Fearing the consequences, under this circumstance, of the further prosecution of a night attack with troops then acting tagether for the first time, I contented myself with lying on the field that night; and at four in the morning assumed a stronger position about two miles nearer to the city. At this position I remain encamped, waiting the arrival of the Kentucky militia, and other reinforcements. As the safety of the city will depend on the fate of this army, it must not be incautiously exposed.

In this affair, the whole corps under my command deserve the greatest credit. The best compliment I can pay to general

Coffee and his brigade, is to say they behaved as they have always done while under my command. The 7th, led by major Peire, and the 44th, commanded by colonel Ross, distinguished themselves. The battalion of city militia, commanded by major Plauche, realized my anticipations, and behaved like veterans. Savary's volunteers manifested great bravery; and the company of city riflemen, having penetrated into the midst of the enemy's camp, were surrounded, and fought their way out with the greatest heroism, bringing with them a number of prisoners. The two field-pieces were well served by the officer commanding them.

All my officers in the line did their duty, and I have every reason to be satisfied with the whole of my field and staff. Colonels Butler and Piatt, and major Chotard, by their intrepidity, saved the artillery. Colonel Haynes was every where that duty or danger called. I was deprived of the services of one of my aides, captain Butler, whom I was obliged to station, to his great regret, in town. Captain Reid, my other aide, and Messrs. Livingston, Duplessis and Davezac, who had volunteered their services, faced danger wherever it was to be met, and carried my orders with the utmost promptitude.

We made one major, two subalterns, and 63 privates prisoners; and the enemy's loss in killed and wounded must have been at least ——. My own loss I have not as yet been able to ascertain with exactness, but suppose it to amount to 100 in killed, wounded, and missing. Among the former I have to lament the loss of colonel Lauderdale, of general Coffee's brigade, who fell while bravely fighting. Colonels Dyer and Gibson, of the same corps, were wounded; and major Kavenaugh taken prisoner.

Colonel Delaronde, major Villeré of the Louisiana militia, major Latour of engineers, having no command, volunteered their services, as did Drs. Kerr and Flood, and were of great assistance to me.

I have the honor to be, &c.

ANDREW JACKSON.

No. 86.

Report of the killed, wounded, and missing, of the army under the command of major-general Andrew Jackson, in the action of the 23d of December, 1814, with the enemy.

Killed;—artillerymen, 1; 7th United States' infantry, 1 lieutenant, 1 serjeant, 1 corporal, 4 privates; 44th ditto, 7 privates; general

Coffee's brigade volunteer mounted gun-men, 1 lieutenant-colonel, 1 captain, 1 lieutenant, 2 serjeants, 4 privates.—Total, 24.

Wounded;—general staff, 1 colonel; 7th United States' infantry, 1 captain, 1 ensign, 1 serjeant, 2 corporals, 23 privates; 44th ditto, 2 lieutenants, 3 serjeants, 2 corporals, 19 privates; general Coffee's brigade, 1 colonel, 2 lieutenant-colonels, 1 captain, 2 lieutenants, 1 quarter-master-serjeant, 3 serjeants, 2 corporals, 1 musician, 30 privates; New Orleans volunteer corps, 1 captain, 2 serjeants, 7 privates; volunteers of colour, 1 adjutant and 6 privates.—Total, wounded, 115.

Missing;—general Coffee's brigade, 1 major, 2 captains, 3 lieutenants, 1 quarter-master, 3 ensigns or cornets, 4 serjeants, 1 corporal, 2 musicians, 57 privates.—Total, missing, 74.

No. 87.

From commodore Patterson to the American secretary of the navy.

SIR, U. S. ship Louisiana, Dec. 28, 1814.

I have the honor to inform you, that on the 23d instant, while at the bayou St. John, examining the batteries erecting there by the navy, under the superintendance of captain Henley, of the Carolina, I learnt that information had been received by general Jackson, that the enemy had penetrated through bayou Bienvenu with a large force, and effected a landing at general Villeré's plantation on the banks of the Mississippi, which upon application to the general proved to be true. The alarm was immediately given in town, and the troops put in motion; I repaired on board the United States' schooner Carolina, with captain Henley, and after ordering the Louisiana, commanded by lieutenant-commandant C. B. Thompson, to follow me, at 4 P. M. weighed, and it being calm, dropped down with the current; at about half past six I received a request from general Jackson, through Mr. Edward Livingston, his aide de camp, to anchor a-breast of the enemy's camp, which he pointed out, and opened a fire upon them. It continuing calm, got out sweeps, and a few minutes after, having been frequently hailed by the enemy's sentinels, anchored, veered out a long scope of cable, sheered close in shore a-breast of their camp, and commenced a heavy (and as I have since learned most destructive) fire from our starboard battery and small arms, which was returned most spiritedly by the enemy with Congreve rockets and musketry from their whole force, when after about 40 minutes of most incessant fire, the enemy was silenced; the fire from our battery was continued till nine o'clock upon the enemy's flank while engaged in the field with our army, at which hour ceased firing, supposing, from the distance of the enemy's fire, (for it was too dark to see any thing on shore,) that they had retreated beyond the range of our guns—weighed and swept across the river, in hopes of a breeze the next morning, to enable me to renew the attack upon the enemy, should they be returned to their encampment; but was disappointed on the 24th, by a light air from north-north-west, which, towards the evening, hauled toward north-west, and blew a heavy gale, compelling me to remain during the 24th, 25th, and 26th, at anchor in a position a-breast of the enemy, although every possible exertion was made by captain Henley to warp the schooner up, without success, from the extreme rapidity of the current occasioned by the very uncommon rise of the river. On the afternoon of the 26th, at the request of general Jackson, I visited him at his head-quarters, and went from thence to town, to equip and arm with two 32-pounders, such merchant vessels in port, as I might find capable of supporting them. During the 24th, 25th, and 26th, fired at the enemy whenever they could be seen. Owing to the calmness of the night of the 23d, the Louisiana could not join me till the morning of the 24th, when she fortunately anchored about one mile above the Carolina. By the fire from the enemy on the night of the 23d, one man only was wounded, and very little injury done to the hull, sails, and rigging; in her bulwarks were a great number of musket-balls, several in her masts and top-masts, and through her main-sail. Nothing could exceed the incessant fire from the Carolina, which alone can be attributed to the high state of discipline to which captain Henley has brought her crew. Of him, lieutenants Norris and Crawley, and sailing-master Haller, I cannot speak in too high terms; the petty officers and crew behaved with that cool determined courage and zeal which has so strongly characterized the American tars in the present war. I have the honor to be, &c.

D. T. PATTERSON.

No. 88.

From captain Henley to commodore Patterson.

Sir, New Orleans, Dec. 28, 1814.

I have the honor to inform you, that after you left here on the 26th instant, in pursuance to your order, every possible exertion was made to move the schooner Carolina higher up the river, and near general Jackson's camp, without success; the wind being at N.N.W. and blowing fresh, and too scant to get under weigh, and the current too rapid to move her by warping, which I had endeavoured to do with my crew.

At day-light on the morning of the 27th the enemy opened upon the Carolina a battery of five guns, from which they threw shells and hot shot; returned their fire with the long 12-pounder, the only gun on board which could reach across the river, the remainder of her battery being light 12-pound carronades.

The air being light and at north, rendered it impossible to get under way; the second shot fired by the enemy lodged in the schooner's main-hold under her cables, and in such a situation as not to be come at, and fired her, which rapidly progressed. Finding that hot shot were passing through her cabin and filling room, which contained a considerable quantity of powder; her bulwarks all knocked down by the enemy's shot, the vessel in a sinking situation, and the fire increasing, and expecting every moment that she would blow up, at a little after sun-rise I reluctantly gave orders for the crew to abandon her, which was effected, with the loss of one killed and six wounded. A short time after I had succeeded in getting the crew on shore, I had the extreme mortification of seeing her blow up.

It affords me great pleasure to acknowledge the able assistance I received from lieutenants Norris and Crawley, and sailing-master Haller, and to say that my officers and crew behaved on this occasion, as well as on the 23d, when under your own eye, in a most gallant manner.

Almost every article of clothing belonging to the officers and crew, from the rapid progress of the fire, was involved in the destruction of the vessel. I have the honor to be, &c.

JOHN D. HENLEY.

P. S. I have not made out a detailed account of the action on the night of the 23d, as you were on board during the whole action.

No. 89.

From major-general Jackson to the American secretary at war.

Head-quarters, seventh military district,
Sir, Camp below New Orleans, Dec. 29, 1814.

The enemy succeeded on the 27th in blowing up the Carolina (she being becalmed) by means of hot shot from a land battery which he had erected in the night. Emboldened by this event, he marched his whole force the next day up the levee, in the hope of driving us from our position, and with this view, opened upon us, at the distance of about half a mile, his bombs and rockets. He was repulsed, however, with considerable loss; not less, it is believed, than 120 in killed. Our's was inconsiderable; not exceeding half a dozen killed, and a dozen wounded.

Since then he has not ventured to repeat his attempt, though lying close together. There has been frequent skirmishing between our piquets.

I lament that I have not the means of carrying on more offensive operations. The Kentucky troops have not arrived, and my effective force at this point does not exceed 3000. Their's must be at least double; 60 prisoners and deserters agreeing in the statement that 7000 landed from their boats.

ANDREW JACKSON.

No. 90.

From commodore Patterson to the American secretary of the navy.

U. S. ship Louisiana, four miles below New Orleans,
SIR, 29th December, 1814.

I have the honor to inform you, that on the morning of the 28th instant, at about half past seven, perceived our advanced guard retreating towards our lines—the enemy pursuing; fired shot, shells, and rockets, from field artillery, with which they advanced on the road behind the levee; sprung the ship to bring the starboard guns to bear upon the enemy; at 25 minutes past eight A. M. the enemy opened their fire upon the ship with shells, hot shot, and rockets, which was instantly returned with great spirit, and much apparent effect, and continued without intermission until one P. M. when the enemy slackened their fire, and retreated with a part of their artillery from each of their batteries, evidently with great loss. Two attempts were made to screen one heavy piece of ordnance mounted behind the levee, with which they threw hot shot at the ship, and which had been a long time abandoned before they succeeded in recovering it, and then it must have been with very great loss, as I distinctly saw, with the aid of my glass, several shot strike in the midst of the men (seamen) who were employed dragging it away. At three P. M. the enemy were silenced; at four P. M. ceased firing from the ship, the enemy having retired beyond the range of her guns. Many of their shot passed over the ship, and their shells burst over her decks, which were strewed with their fragments; yet, after an incessant cannonading of upwards of seven hours, during which time 800 shot were fired from the ship, one man only was wounded slightly, by a piece of a shell, and one shot passed between the bowsprit and heel of the jib-boom.

The enemy drew up his whole force, evidently with an intention of assaulting general Jackson's lines, under cover of his heavy cannon; but his cannonading being so warmly returned from the lines and ship Louisiana, caused him, I presume, to abandon his project, as he retired without making the attempt. You will have learned by my former letters, that the crew of the Louisiana is composed of men of all nations, (English excepted,) taken from the streets of New Orleans not a fortnight before the battle; yet I never knew guns better served, or a more animated fire, than was supported from her.

Lieutenant C. C. B. Thompson deserves great credit for the discipline to which in so short a time he had brought such men, two-thirds of whom do not understand English.

General Jackson having applied for officers and seamen to work the heavy cannon on his lines furnished by me, lieutenants Norris and Crawley, of the late schooner Carolina, instantly volunteered, and with the greater part of her crew were sent to those cannon, which they served during the action herein detailed. The enemy must have suffered a great loss in that day's action, by the heavy fire from this ship and general Jackson's lines, where the cannon was of heavy calibre, and served with great spirit.

I have the honor to be, with great consideration and respect, your obedient servant,

DANIEL T. PATTERSON.

No. 91.

Report of the killed, wounded, and missing, of the army under the command of major-general Andrew Jackson, in the action of the 28th of December, 1814.

Killed—General Coffee's brigade, 1 private; New Orleans volunteer company, 1 private; general Carroll's division of Tennesse militia, 1 colonel, 1 serjeant, 5 privates

Total—9.

Wounded;—Marines, 1 major; New Orleans volunteer company, 3 privates; general Carroll's division, 1 lieutenant, 3 privates.

Total wounded—8.

Total killed, wounded, and missing, on this day—17.

No. 92.

From commodore Patterson to the American secretary of the navy.

Marine batteries, five miles below New Orleans,
SIR, January 2, 1815.

Finding the advantageous effect which resulted from the flanking fire of the enemy from the Louisiana, as detailed in my letter of the 29th ultimo, I that night had brought down from the navy yard, and mounted in silence, a 24-pounder on shore, in a position where it could most annoy the enemy when throwing up works on the levee or in the field. On the 30th opened upon the enemy with the 24-pounder, which drove them from their works, the ship firing at the same time upon their advance, which retired from the levee, and sheltered itself behind houses, &c. The great effect produced by the gun on shore, induced me on the 31st to land from the Louisiana two 12-pounders, which I mounted behind the levee in the most advantageous position, to harass the flank of the enemy in his approaches to our lines, and to aid our right. At four A. M. the enemy opened a fire upon the left of our line with artillery and musketry, which was returned most spiritedly with artillery and musketry. At two P. M. the enemy having retired, the firing ceased.

On the first instant, at 10 A. M. after a very thick fog, the enemy commenced a heavy cannonading upon general Jackson's lines and my battery, from batteries they had thrown up during the preceding night on the levee; which was returned from our lines and my battery, and terminated, after a most incessant fire from both parties of nearly five hours, in the enemy being silenced and driven from their works; many of their shells went immediately over my battery, and their shot passed through my breast-work and embrazures, without injuring a man. On this, as on the 28th, I am happy to say, that my officers and men behaved to my entire satisfaction; but I beg leave particularly to name acting lieutenant Campbell, acting sailing-master John Gates, acting midshipman Philip Philibert, of the Louisiana, and sailing-master Haller, of the late schooner Carolina. I did not drop the Louisiana down within the range of their shot, having learnt from deserters that a furnace of shot was kept in constant readiness at each of their batteries, to burn her; and the guns being of much greater effect on shore, her men were drawn to man them, and I was particularly desirous to preserve her from the hot shot, as I deemed her of incalculable service to cover the army in the event of general Jackson retiring from his present line to those which he had thrown up in his rear. I have the honor to be, &c.

DANIEL T. PATTERSON.

No. 93.

Return of the killed, wounded, and missing, of the army under the command of major-general Andrew Jackson, in the action of the 1st of January, 1814.

Killed;—Artillery, navy, and volunteers, at batteries, 8 privates; 44th ditto, 1 private; general Coffee's brigade, 1 serjeant; general Carroll's division, 1 private.

Total—11.

Wounded;—Artillery, navy, and volunteers at batteries, 8; 7th United States' infantry, 1 private; 44th ditto, 3; general Coffee's brigade, 2; New Orleans' volunteers, 3 privates; general Carroll's division, 1 sergeant, 2 privates; volunteers of colour, 1 lieutenant, 1 serjeant, 1 private.

Total—23.

Total of killed, wounded, and missing this day—34.

No. 94.

Return of casualties between the 25th and 31st Dec. 1814.

Royal artillery;—4 rank and file, killed; 1 lieutenant, 5 rank and file, wounded.

Royal engineers, sappers and miners;—1 rank and file, wounded.

4th foot ;—4 rank and file, wounded.

21st foot ;—1 rank and file, killed; 1 rank and file, wounded.

44th foot ;—2 rank and file, wounded; 1 rank and file, missing.

85th foot ;—1 drummer, 3 rank and file, killed; 2 ensigns, 11 rank and file, wounded.

93d foot ;—2 rank and file, killed; 5 rank and file, wounded.

95th foot;—3 rank and file, killed; 1 serjeant, 3 rank and file, wounded; 1 rank and file, missing.

1st West India regiment ;— 1 captain, killed.

5th ditto;—1 rank and file, killed; 2 rank and file, wounded.

Total—1 captain, 1 drummer, 14 rank and file, killed; 1 lieutenant, 2 ensigns, 1 serjeant, 34 rank and file, wounded; 2 rank and file, missing.

Names of officers killed and wounded.

Killed.

1st West India regiment ;—Captain Francis Collings.

Wounded.

Royal artillery;—Lieutenant B. L. Poynter, slightly.

85th foot ;—Ensign sir Frederick Eden, bart. severely; (since dead;) ensign Thomas Ormsby, slightly.

FRED STOVIN, lieut.-col.
dep. adj.-gen.

No. 95.

Return of casualties between the 1st and 5th January, 1815.

Royal artillery;—1 lieutenant, 1 serjeant, 9 rank and file, killed; 12 rank and file, wounded.

Royal engineers, sappers, and miners;—1 lieutenant, killed.

21st foot;—1 rank and file, killed; 1 lieutenant, 4 rank and file, wounded.

44th foot;—1 lieutenant, 1 rank and file, killed; 3 rank and file, wounded.

85th foot;—2 rank and file, killed; 2 lieutenants, 4 rank and file, wounded.

93d foot;—1 serjeant, 8 rank and file, killed; 1 lieutenant, 10 rank and file, wounded.

95th foot;—1 rank and file, killed; 2 rank and file, missing.

5th West India regiment;—4 rank and file, killed; 2 rank and file, wounded.

Total—3 lieutenants, 2 serjeants, 27 rank and file, killed; 4 lieutenants, 40 rank and file, wounded; 2 rank and file, missing.

Names of officers killed and wounded.

Killed.

Royal artillery;—Lieutenant Alexander Ramsay.

Royal engineers;—Lieutenant Peter Wright.

44th foot;—Lieutenant John Blakeney.

Wounded.

21st foot;—Lieutenant John Leavock, slightly.

85th foot;—Lieutenant Robert Charlton, severely; lieutenant J. W. Boys, slightly.

93d foot;—Lieutenant Andrew Phaup, severely (since dead).

FRED. STOVIN, lieut.-col.
dep.-adj.-gen.

No. 96.

From major-general Lambert to earl Bathurst.

Camp, in front of the enemy's lines, below New Orleans, Jan. 10, 1815.

My lord,

It becomes my duty to lay before your lordship, the proceedings of the force lately employed on the coast of Louisiana, under the command of major-general the honourable Sir E. M. Pakenham, K.B. and acting in concert with vice-admiral the honorable sir A. Cochrane, K.B.

The report which I enclose from major-general Keane, will put your lordship in possession of the occurrences which took place until the arrival of major-general the honorable sir

E. Parkenham to assume the command; from that period I send an extract of the journal of major Forrest, assistant-quarter-master-general, up to the time of the joining of the troops, (which sailed on the 26th of October last under my command,) and which was on the 6th January; and from that period, I shall detail, as well as I am able, the subsequent events.

I found the army in position, in a flat country, with the Mississippi on its left, and a thick extensive wood on its right, and open to its front, from which the enemy's line was quite distinguishable.

It seems sir E. Pakenham had waited for the arrival of the fusiliers and 43d regiment, in order to make a general attack upon the enemy's line; and on the 8th, the army was formed for that object.

In order to give your lordship as clear a view as I can, I shall state the position of the enemy. On the left bank of the river it was simply a straight line of about a front of 1000 yards with a parapet, the right resting on the river, and the left on a wood which had been made impracticable for any body of troops to pass. This line was strengthened by flank works, and had a canal of about four feet deep generally, but not altogether of an equal width; it was supposed to narrow towards their left: about eight heavy guns were in position on this line. The Mississippi is here about 800 yards across; and they had on the right bank a heavy battery of 12 guns, which enfiladed the whole front of the position on the left bank.

Preparations were made on our side, by very considerable labor, to clear out and widen a canal that communicated with a stream by which the boats had passed up to the place of dis-embarkation, to open it into the Mississippi, by which means troops could be got over to the right bank, and the co-operation of armed boats could be secured.

The disposition for the attack was as follows:—a corps, consisting of the 85th light infantry, 200 seamen, and 400 marines, the 5th West India regiment, and four pieces of artillery, under the command of colonel Thornton, of the 85th, was to pass over during the night, and move along the right bank towards New Orleans, clearing its front until it reached the flanking battery of the enemy on that side, which it had orders to carry.

The assailing of the enemy's line in front of us, was to be made by the brigade composed of the 4th, 21st, and 44th regiments, with three companies of the 95th under major-general Gibbs, and by the 3d brigade, consisting of the 93d, two companies of the 95th, and two companies of the fusileers, and 43d, under major-general Keane; some black troops were destined to skirmish in the wood on the right; the principal attack was to be made by major-general Gibbs; the 1st brigade, consisting of the fusileers and 43d, formed the reserve; the attacking columns were to be provided with fascines, scaling-ladders, and rafts; the whole to be at their stations before daylight. An advanced battery in our front, of six 18-pounders, was thrown up during the night, about 800 yards from the enemy's line. The attack was to be made at the earliest hour. Unlooked-for difficulties, increased by the falling of the river, occasioned considerable delay in the entrance of the armed boats, and those destined to land colonel Thornton's corps, by which four or five hours were lost, and it was not until past five in the morning, that the 1st division, consisting of 500 men, were over. The *ensemble* of the general movement was lost, and in a point which was of the last importance to the attack on the left bank of the river, although colonel Thornton, as your lordship will see in his report, which I enclose, ably executed in every particular his instructions, and fully justified the confidence the commander of the forces placed in his abilities. The delay attending that corps occasioned some on the left bank, and the attack did not take place until the columns were discernible from the enemy's lines at more than 200 yards distance; as they advanced, a continued and most galling fire was opened from every part of their line, and from the battery on the right bank.

The brave commander of the forces, who never in his life could refrain from being at the post of honor, and sharing the dangers to which the troops were exposed, as soon as from his station he had made the signal for the troops to advance, galloped on to the front to animate them by his presence, and he was seen, with his hat off, encouraging them on the crest of the glacis; it was there (almost at the same time) he received two wounds, one in his knee, and another, which was almost instantly fatal, in his body; he fell in the arms of major M'Dougall, his aide de camp. The effect of this in the sight of the troops, together with major-general Gibbs and major-general Keane being both borne off wounded at the same time, with many other commanding officers, and further, the preparations to aid in crossing the ditch not being so forward as they ought to have been, from, perhaps, the men being wounded who were carrying them, caused a wavering in the column, which in such a situation became irreparable; and as I advanced with the reserve, at about 250 yards from the line, I had the mortification to observe the whole falling back upon me in the greatest confusion.

In this situation, finding that no impression had been made, that though many men had reached the ditch, and were either drowned or obliged to surrender, and that it was impossible to restore order in the regiments where they were, I placed the reserve in position, until I could obtain such information as to determine me how to act to the best of my judgment, and whether or not I should resume the attack, and if so, I felt it could be done only by the reserve. The confidence I have in the corps composing it would have encouraged me greatly, though not without loss, which might have made the attempt of serious consequence, as I know it was the opinion of the late distinguished commander of the forces, that the carrying of the first line would not be the least arduous service. After making the best reflections I was capable of, I kept the ground the troops then held, and went to meet vice-admiral sir Alexander Cochrane, and to tell him, that under all the circumstances I did not think it prudent to renew the attack that day. At about 10 o'clock, I learnt of the success of colonel Thornton's corps on the right bank. I sent the commanding officer of the artillery, colonel Dickson, to examine the situation of the battery, and to report if it was tenable; but informing me that he did not think it could be held with security by a smaller corps than 2000 men, I consequently ordered lieutenant-colonel Gubbins, on whom the command had devolved, (colonel Thornton being wounded,) to retire.

The army remained in position until night, in order to gain time to destroy the 18-pounder battery we had constructed the preceding night in advance. I then gave orders for the troops resuming the ground they occupied previous to the attack.

Our loss has been very severe, but I trust it will not be considered, notwithstanding the failure, that this army has suffered the military character to be tarnished. I am satisfied, had I thought it right to renew the attack, that the troops would have advanced with cheerfulness. The services of both army and navy, since their landing on this coast, have been arduous beyond any thing I have ever witnessed, and difficulties have been got over with an assiduity and perseverance beyond all example by all ranks, and the most hearty co-operation has existed between the two services.

It is not necessary for me to expatiate to you upon the loss the army has sustained in major-general the honorable sir E. Pakenham, commander-in-chief of this force, nor could I in adequate terms. His services and merits are so well known, that I have only, in common with the whole army, to express my sincere regret, and which may be supposed at this moment to come particularly home to me.

Major-general Gibbs, who died of his wounds the following day, and major-general Keane, who were both carried off the field within 20 yards of the glacis, at the head of their brigades, sufficiently speak at such a moment how they were conducting themselves. I am happy to say major-general Keane is doing well.

Captain Wylly, of the fusileers, military secretary to the late commander of the forces, will have the honor of delivering to your lordship these despatches. Knowing how much he enjoyed his esteem, and was in his confidence from a long experience of his talents, I feel I cannot do less than pay this tribute to what I conceive would be the wishes of his late general, and to recommend him strongly to your lordship's protection.

I have, &c.

JOHN LAMBERT,

Major-general, commanding.

No. 97.

From colonel Thornton to major-general the honorable sir Edward Pakenham.

Redoubt, on the right bank of the Mississippi, Jan. 8, 1815.

SIR,

I lose no time in reporting to you the success of the troop which you were yesterday pleased to place under my orders, with the view of attacking the enemy's redoubt and position on this side of the river.

It is within your own knowledge, that the difficulty had been found so extremely great of dragging the boats through the canal which had been lately cut with so much labor to the Mississippi, that, notwithstanding every possible exertion for the purpose, we were unable to proceed across the river until eight hours after the time appointed, and even then, with only a third part of the force which you had allotted for the service.

The current was so strong, and the difficulty, in consequence, of keeping the boats together, so great, that we only reached this side of the river at day-break, and, by the time the troops were disembarked, which was effected without any molestation from the enemy, I perceived by the flashes of the guns, that your attack had already commenced.

This circumstance made me extremely anxious to move forward, to prevent the destructive enfilading fire, which would, of course, be opened on your columns from the enemy's batteries on this side; and I proceeded with the greatest possible expedition, strengthened and secured on my right flank by three gun-boats, under captain Roberts of the navy, whose zeal and exertions on this occasion were as unremitted as his arrangements in embarking the troops, and in keeping the boats together in crossing the river, were excellent.

The enemy made no opposition to our advance, until we reached a piquet, posted behind a bridge, at about 500 paces from the house in the Orange grove, and secured by a small work, apparently just thrown up.

This piquet was very soon forced and driven in by a division of the 85th regiment, under captain Schaw, of that regiment, forming the advanced guard, and whose mode of attack for the purpose was prompt and judicious to a degree.

Upon my arrival at the Orange Grove, I had an opportunity of reconnoitring, at about 700 yards, the enemy's position, which I found to be a very formidable redoubt on the bank of the river, with the right flank secured by an entrenchment extending back to a thick wood, and its line protected by an incessant fire of grape. Under such circumstances it seemed to me to afford the best prospect of success, to endeavour to turn his right at the wood; and I accordingly detached two divisions of the 85th, under brevet lieutenant-colonel Gubbins, to effect that object, which he accomplished with his usual zeal and judgment, whilst 100 sailors, under captain Money, of the royal navy, who, I am sorry to say, was severely wounded, but whose conduct was particularly distinguished on the occasion, threatened the enemy's left, supported by the division of the 85th regiment, under captain Schaw.

When these divisions had gained their proper position, I deployed the column composed of two divisions of the 85th regiment, under major Deshon, whose conduct I cannot sufficiently commend, and about 100 men of the royal marines, under major Adair, also deserving of much commendation, and moved forward in line, to the attack of the centre of the intrenchment.

At first, the enemy, confident in his own security, shewed a good countenance, and kept up a heavy fire, but the determination of the troops which I had the honour to command, to overcome all difficulties, compelled him to a rapid and disorderly flight, leaving in our possession his redoubts, batteries, and position, with 16 pieces of ordnance, and the colors of the New Orleans regiment of militia.

Of the ordnance taken, I enclose the specific return of major Mitchell, of the royal artillery, who accompanied and afforded me much assistance, by his able directions of the firing of some rockets, it not having been found practicable, in the first instance, to bring over the artillery attached to his command.

I shall have the honor of sending you a return of the casualties that have occurred, as soon as it is possible to collect them, but I am happy to say they are extremely inconsiderable when the strength of the position and the number of the enemy are considered, which our prisoners, (about 30 in number) agree in stating from 1500 to 2000 men, commanded by general Morgan.

I should be extremely wanting both in justice and in gratitude, were I not to request your particular notice of the officers whose names I have mentioned, as well as of major Blanchard, of the royal engineers, and lieutenant Peddie, of the 27th regiment, deputy-assistant-quarter-master-general, whose zeal and intelligence I found of the greatest service.

The wounded men are meeting with every degree of attention and humanity by the medical arrangements of staff-surgeon Baxter.

The enemy's camp is supplied with a great abandance of provisions, and a very large store of all sorts of ammunition.

On moving to the attack, I received a wound, which shortly after my reaching the redoubt, occasioned me such pain and stiffness, that I have been obliged to give over the command of the troops on this side to lieutenant-colonel Gubbins, of the 85th light infantry; but, as he has obtained some reinforcement, since the attack, of sailors and marines, and has taken the best precautions to cover and secure his position, I will be answerable, from my knowledge of his judgment and experience, that he will retain it, until your pleasure and further orders shall be communicated to him.

I have the honor to be, &c.

W. THORNTON, colonel,
lieut.-col. 85th reg.

To major-gen. the hon. sir E. M. Pakenham, K.B. &c.

No. 98.

Return of the ordnance taken from the enemy by a detachment of the army acting on the Right Bank of the Mississippi, under the command of colonel Thornton.

Redoubt, Right Bank of the Mississippi,
January 8, 1815.

I brass 10-inch howitzer, 2 brass 4-pounder field pieces, 3 24-pounders, 3 12-pounders, 6 9-pounders, 1 12-pounder carronade, not mounted.

On the howitzer is inscribed, "Taken at the surrender of York Town, 1781."

J. MITCHELL, maj. capt. royal-artil.

No. 99.

From vice-admiral Cochrane to Mr. Croker.

Sir, Armide, off Isle au Chat, January 18, 1815.

An unsuccessful attempt to gain possession of the enemy's lines near New Orleans, on the 8th instant, having left me to deplore the fall of major-general the honorable sir Edward Pakenham, and major-general Gibbs; and deprived the service of the present assistance of major-general Keane, who is severely wounded, I send the Plantagenet to England, to convey a despatch from major-general Lambert, upon whom the command of the army has devolved, and to inform my lords commissioners of the Admiralty of the operations of the combined forces since my arrival upon this coast.

The accompanying letters, Nos. 163 and 169, of the 7th and 16th ultimo, will acquaint their lordships of the proceedings of the squadron to the 15th of December.

The great distance from the anchorage of the frigates and troop ships to the bayou Catalan, which, from the best information we could gain, appeared to offer the most secure, and was, indeed, the only unprotected spot whereat to effect a disembarkation, and our means, even with the addition of the captured enemy's gun-vessels, only affording us transport for half the army, exclusive of the supplies that were required, it became necessary, in order to have support for the division that would first land, to assemble the whole at some intermediate position, from whence the second division could be re-embarked in vessels brought light into the lake, as near the bayou as might be practicable, and remain there until the boats could land the first division and return.

Upon the 16th, therefore, the advance, commanded by colonel Thornton, of the 85th regiment, was put into the gun-vessels and boats, and captain Gordon, of the Seahorse, proceeded with them, and took post upon the Isle aux Poix, a small swampy spot at the mouth of the Pearl river, about 30 miles from the anchorage, and nearly the same distance from the bayou, where major-general Keane, rear-admiral Codrington, and myself joined them on the following day; meeting the gun-vessels and boats returning to the shipping for troops, and supplies of stores and provisions.

The honorable captain Spencer, of the Carron, and lieutenant Peddy, of the quarter-master-general's department, who were sent to reconnoitre the bayou Catalan, now returned with a favorable report of its position for disembarking the army; having, with their guide, pulled up in a canoe to the head of the bayou, a distance of eight miles, and landed within a mile and a half of the high road to, and about six miles below New Orleans, where they crossed the road without meeting with any interruption, or perceiving the least preparation on the part of the enemy.

The severe changes of the weather, from rain to fresh gales and hard frost, retarding the boats in their repeated passages to and from the shipping, it was not until the 21st that (leaving on board the greater part of the two black regiments, and the dragoons) we could assemble troops and supplies sufficient to admit of our proceeding; and, on that day, we commenced the embarkation of the second division in the gun-vessels, such of the hired craft as could be brought into the lakes, and the Anaconda, which, by the greatest exertions, had been got over the shoal passages.

On the 22d, these vessels being filled with about 2400 men, the advance, consisting of about 1600 men, got into the boats, and, at eleven o'clock, the whole started, with a fair wind, to cross Lac Borgne. We had not, however, proceeded above two miles when the Anaconda grounded, and the hired craft and gun-vessels taking the ground in succession before they had got within ten miles of the bayou; the advance pushed on, and at about midnight reached the entrance.

A piquet, which the enemy had taken the precaution to place there, being surprised and cut off, major-general Keane, with rear-admiral Malcolm and the advance, moved up the bayou, and having effected a landing at day-break, in the course of the day was enabled to take up a position across the main road to New Orleans, between the river Mississippi and the bayou.

In this situation, about an hour after sun-set, and before the boats could return with the second division, an enemy's schooner of 14 guns, and an armed ship of 16-guns, having dropped down the Mississippi, the former commenced a brisk cannonading, which was followed up by an attack of the whole of the American army. Their troops were, however, beaten back, and obliged to retire with considerable loss, and major-general Keane advanced somewhat beyond his former position. As soon as the second division was brought up, the gun-vessels and boats returned for the remainder of the troops, the small-armed seamen and marines of the squadron, and such supplies as were required.

On the 25th, major-general sir E. Pakenham and major-general Gibbs arrived at head-quarters, when the former took command of the army.

The schooner which had continued at intervals to annoy the troops having been burnt, on the 27th, by hot shot from our artillery, and the ship having warped farther up the river, the following day the general moved forward to within gun-shot of an entrenchment which the enemy had newly thrown up, extending across the cultivated ground from the Mississippi to an impassable swampy wood on his left, a distance of about 1000 yards.

It being thought necessary to bring heavy artillery against this work, and also against the ship which had cannonaded the army when advancing, guns were brought up from the shipping, and on the 1st instant batteries were opened; but our fire not having the desired effect, the attack was defered until the arrival of the troops under major-general Lambert, which were daily expected.

Major-general Lambert, in the Vengeur, with a convoy of transports, having on board the 7th and 43d regiments, reached the outer anchorage on the 1st, and this reinforcement was all brought up to the advance on the 6th instant, while preparations were making for a second attack, in the proposed plan for which, it was decided to throw a body of men across the river to gain possession of the enemy's guns on the right bank. For this purpose the canal by which we were enabled to conduct provisions and stores towards the camp, was widened and extended to the river, and about 50 barges, pinnaces, and cutters, having, in the day-time of the 7th, been tracked under cover and unperceived, close up to the bank, at night the whole were dragged into the Mississippi, and placed under the command of captain Roberts of the Meteor.

The boats having grounded in the canal, a distance of 350 yards from the river, and the bank being composed of wet clay thrown out of the canal, it was not until nearly day-light that with the utmost possible exertions, this service was completed.

The 85th regiment, with a division of seamen under captain Money, and a division of marines under major Adair, the whole amounting to about 600 men, commanded by colonel Thornton, of the 85th regiment, were embarked and landed on the right bank of the river without opposition, just after day-light; and the armed boats moving up the river as the troops advanced, this part of the operations succeeded perfectly; the enemy having been driven from every position, leaving behind him 17 pieces of cannon.

The great loss, however, sustained by the principal attack having induced general Lambert to send orders to colonel Thornton to retire, after spiking the guns and destroying the carriages, the whole were re-embarked and brought back, and the boats by a similar process of hard labor were again dragged into the canal, and from thence to the bayou, conveying at the same time such of the wounded as it was thought requisite to send off to the ships.

Major-general Lambert having determined to withdraw the army, measures were taken to re-embark the whole of the sick and wounded, that it was possible to move, and the stores, ammunition, ordnance, &c. with such detachments of the army, seamen, and marines, as were not immediately wanted; in order that the remainder of the army may retire unincumbered, and the last division be furnished with sufficient means of transport.

This arrangement being in a forward state of execution, I quitted head-quarters on the 14th instant, leaving rear-admiral Malcolm to conduct the naval part of the operations in that quarter, and I arrived at this anchorage on the 16th, where I am arranging for the reception of the army, and preparing the fleet for further operations.

I must, in common with the nation, lament the loss which the service has sustained by the death of major-general the honorable sir Edward Pakenham, and major-general Gibbs. Their great military qualities were justly estimated while living, and their zealous devotion to our country's welfare, will be cherished as an example to future generations.

In justice to the officers and men of the squadron under my command, who have been employed upon this expedition, I cannot omit to call the attention of my lords commissioners of the Admiralty to the laborious exertions and great privations which have been willingly and cheerfully borne, by every class, for a period of nearly six weeks.

From the 12th of December, when the boats proceeded to the attack of the enemy's gun-vessels, to the present time, but very few of the officers or men have ever slept one night on board their ships.

The whole of the army, with the principal part of its provisions, its stores, artillery, ammunition, and the numerous necessary appendages, have been all transported from the shipping to the head of the bayou, a distance of 70 miles, chiefly in open boats, and are now re-embarking by the same process. The hardships, therefore, which the boats' crews have undergone, from their being kept day and night continually passing and repassing in the most changeable and severe weather, have rarely been equalled; and it has been highly honorable to both services, and most gratifying to myself, to observe the emulation and unanimity which has pervaded the whole.

Rear-admiral Malcolm superintended the disembarkation of the army, and the various services performed by the boats; and it is a duty that I fulfil with much pleasure, assuring their lordships that his zeal and exertions upon every occasion could not be surpassed by any one. I beg leave also to offer my testimony to the unwearied and cheerful assistance afforded to the rear-admiral by captains sir Thomas M. Hardy, Dashwood, and Gordon, and the several captains and other officers. Rear-admiral Codrington accompanied me throughout this service; and I feel much indebted for his able advice and assistance.

Captain sir Thomas Troubridge, and the officers and seamen attached under his command to the army, have conducted themselves much to the satisfaction of the generals commanding. Sir Thomas Troubridge speaks in the highest terms of the captains and other officers employed under him, as named in his letter, (a copy of which is enclosed,) reporting their services. He particularly mentions captain Money, of the Trave, who, I am much concerned to say, had both bones of his leg broken by a musket-shot, advancing under a heavy fire to the attack of a battery that was afterwards carried. The conduct of captain Money at Washington, and near Baltimore, where he was employed with the army, having before occasioned my noticing him to their lordships, I beg leave now to recommend him most strongly to their protection. The wound that he has received not affording him any probability of his being able to return to his duty for a considerable time, I have given him leave of absence to go to England; and shall intrust to him my despatches.

I have not yet received any official report from the captain of the Nymphe, which ship, with the vessels named in the margin,* were sent into the Mississippi, to create a diversion in that quarter.

The bombs have been for some days past throwing shells into fort Placquemain, but I fear without much effect.—I have sent to recall such of them as are not required for the blockade of the river. I have the honor to be, &c.

ALEXANDER COCHRANE,
vice-admiral, and commander in chief.

J. Wilson Croker, esq. &c.

No. 100.

Return of casualties on the 8th of January, 1815.

General staff;—1 major-general, 1 captain, killed; 2 major-generals, 1 captain, 1 lieutenant, wounded.

Royal artillery;—5 rank and file, killed; 10 rank and file, wounded.

Royal engineers, sappers, and miners;—3 rank and file, wounded.

* Nymphe, Herald, Ætna, Meteor, Thistle, Pigmy.

4th foot;—1 ensign, 2 serjeants, 39 rank and file, killed; 1 lieutenant-colonel, 1 major, 5 captains, 11 lieutenants, 4 ensigns, 1 staff, 9 serjeants, 222 rank and file, wounded; 1 lieutenant, 1 serjeant, 53 rank and file, missing.

7th foot;—1 major, 1 captain, 1 serjeant, 38 rank and file, killed; 2 captains, 2 lieutenants, 2 serjeants, 47 rank and and file, wounded.

21st foot;—1 major, 1 captain, 1 lieutenant, 2 serjeants, 65 rank and file, killed; 1 lieutenant-colonel, 1 major, 2 lieutenants, 6 serjeants, 1 drummer, 144 rank and file, wounded; 2 captains, 7 lieutenants, 8 serjeants, 2 drummers, 217 rank and file, missing.

43d foot;—2 serjeants, 1 drummer, 8 rank and file, killed; 2 lieutenants, 3 serjeants, 3 drummers, 34 rank and file, wounded; 1 captain, 5 rank and file, missing.

44th foot;—1 lieutenant, 1 ensign, 1 serjeant, 32 rank and file, killed; 1 captain, 5 lieutenants, 3 ensigns, 5 serjeants, 149 rank and file, wounded; 1 lieutenant, 2 serjeants, 1 drummer, 76 rank and file, missing.

85th foot;—2 rank and file, killed; 1 lieutenant-colonel, 1 lieutenant, 3 serjeants, 2 drummers, 34 rank and file, wounded; 1 rank and file, missing.

93d foot;—1 lieutenant-colonel, 2 captains, 2 serjeants, 58 rank and file, killed; 4 captains, 5 lieutenants, 17 serjeants, 3 drummers, 348 rank and file, wounded; 3 lieutenants, 2 serjeants, 1 drummer, 99 rank and file, missing.

95th foot;—1 serjeant, 10 rank and file, killed; 2 captains, 5 lieutenants, 5 serjeants, 89 rank and file, wounded.

Royal marines;—2 rank and file, killed; 1 captain, 2 lieutenants, 1 serjeant, 12 rank and file, wounded.

Royal navy;—2 seamen, killed; 1 captain, 18 seamen, wounded.

1st West India regiment;—5 rank and file, killed; 1 captain, 2 lieutenants, 2 ensigns, 2 serjeants, 16 rank and file, wounded; 1 rank and file, missing.

5th West India regiment;—1 serjeant, wounded.

Total loss—1 major-general, 1 lieutenant-colonel, 2 majors, 5 captains, 2 lieutenants, 2 ensigns, 11 serjeants, 1 drummer, 266 rank and file, killed; 2 major-generals, 3 lieutenant-colonels, 2 majors, 18 captains, 38 lieutenants, 9 ensigns, 1 staff, 5 4serjeants, 9 drummers, 1126 rank and file, wounded; 3 captains, 12 lieutenants, 13 serjeants, 4 drummers, 452 rank and file, missing.

Names of the officers killed, wounded, and missing.

Killed.

General staff;—Major-general the honorable sir Edward Pakenham, K. B. commander of the forces; captain Thomas Wilkinson, 85th regiment, major of brigade.

4th foot;—Ensign William Crowe.

7th foot;—Major George King; captain George Henry.

21st foot;—Major John Anthony Whittaker; captain Robert Renny; (lieutenant-colonel;) and lieutenant Donald M'Donald.

44th foot;—Lieutenant Rowland Davies, ensign M. M'Loskey.

93d foot;—Lieutenant-colonel Robert Dale; captain Thomas Hickins, and captain Alexander Muirhead.

Wounded.

General staff;—Major-general Gibbs, severely; (since dead;) major-general Keane, severely; captain Henry Thomas Shaw, (4th foot, brigade-major,) slightly; lieutenant Delacy Evans, (3d dragoons, deputy assistant-quarter-master-general,) severely.

4th foot;—Lieutenant-colonel Francis Brooke, slightly; major A. D. Faunce, (lieutenant-colonel,) severely; captain John Williamson, (major,) severely; captain Timothy Jones, (lieutenant-colonel,) severely; (since dead;) captain John Wynn Fletcher, severely; captain Robert Erskine, severely; captain David S. Craig, slightly; lieutenants Ellis, Parnal Hopkins, and Jeffery Salvin, slightly; lieutenants William Henry Brooke, Benjamin Martin, and George Richardson, severely; lieutenants Peter Boulby, and G. H. Hearne, slightly; lieutenants William Squire, Charles Henry Farrington, James Marshall, and Henry Andrews, severely; ensign Arthur Gerrard, slightly; ensign Thomas Benwell, severely; ensigns John S. Fernandez, and Edward Newton, slightly; lieutenant and adjutant William Richardson, slightly.

7th foot;—Captain J. J. A Mullins, slightly; captain W. Edward Page, severely; lieutenant Mathew Higgins, severely; lieutenant Charles Lorentz, slightly.

21st foot;—Lieutenant-colonel William Patterson, (colonel,) severely; (not dangerously;) Major Alexander James Ross, severely; lieutenant John Waters, severely; second lieutenant Alexander Geddes, severely.

43d foot;—Lieutenant John Myricke, severely; (left leg amputated;) lieutenant Duncan Campbell, severely.

44th foot;—Captain Henry Debbeig, (lieutenant-colonel,) slightly; lieutenant William Maclean, slightly; lieutenants Robert Smith, Henry Brush, Richard Phelan, and William Jones, severely; ensigns James White, B. L. Hayden, and John Donaldson, severely.

85th foot;—Lieutenant-colonel William Thornton, (colonel,) severely (not dangerously).

93d foot;—Captains Richard Ryan, P. O. K. Boulger, Alexander M'Kenzie, and Henry Ellis, severely; lieutenants H. H. M'Lean, Richard Sparke, and David M'Pherson, slightly; lieutenants Charles Gordon, and John Hay, severely.

95th foot;—Captain James Travers, severely; captain Nicholas Travers, slightly; lieutenants John Reynolds, sir John Ribton, John Gossett, W. Blackhouse, and Robert Barker, severely.

Royal marines;—Captain Gilbert Elliott, slightly; lieutenants Henry Elliott, and Charles Morgan, slightly.

1st West India regiment; —Captain Isles, severely; lieutenants M'Donald and Morgan, severely; ensign Millar, slightly; ensign Pilkington, severely.

Royal navy;—Captain Money, of his majesty's ship Trave, severely; midshipman Mr. Woolcombe, Tonnant, severely.

93d foot;—Volunteer John Wilson, slightly.

Missing.

4th foot;—Lieutenant Edmund Field, severely, wounded and taken prisoner.

21st foot;—Captain James M'Haffie; (major;) captain Archibald Kidd; lieutenants James Stewart, and Alexander Armstrong, taken prisoners; lieutenant James Brady, wounded, and taken prisoner;

lieutenant John Leavock, taken prisoner; lieutenant Ralph Carr, wounded, and taken prisoner; lieutenant J. S. M. Fonblanque, taken prisoner; second lieutenant Peter Quin, wounded, and taken prisoner.

43d foot;—Captain Robert Simpson, severaly, wounded, and taken prisoner.

44th foot;—Lieutenant William Knight.

93d foot;—Lieutenants George Munro, John M'Donald, and Benjamin Graves, severely wounded; volunteer B. Johnston.

FRED STOVIN, lieut.-col. dep.-adj.-gen.

No. 101.

From major-gen. Jackson to the American secretary at war.

Camp, four miles below Orleans,
January 9, 1815.

Sir,

During the days of the 6th and 7th, the enemy had been actively employed in making preparations for an attack upon my lines. With infinite labour they had succeeded on the night of the 7th in getting their boats across from the lake to the river, by widening and deepening the canal on which they had effected their disembarkation. It had not been in my power to impede these operations by a general attack—added to other reasons, the nature of the troops under my command, mostly militia, rendered it too hazardous to attempt extensive offensive movements in an open country, against a numerous and well-disciplined army. Although my forces, as to number, had been increased by the arrival of the Kentucky division, my strength had received very little addition: a small portion only of that detachment being provided with arms. Compelled thus to wait the attack of the enemy, I took every measure to repel it when it should be made, and to defeat the object he had in viw. General Morgan, with the Orleans contingent, the Louisiana militia, and a strong detachment of the Kentucky troops, occupied an intrenched camp on the opposite side of the river, protected by strong batteries on the bank, erected and superintended by commodore Patterson.

In *my* encampment every thing was ready for action, when early on the morning of the 8th the enemy, after throwing a heavy shower of bombs and Congreve rockets, advanced their columns on my right and left, to storm my intrenchments. I cannot speak sufficiently in praise of the firmness and deliberation with which my whole line received their approach. More could not have been expected from veterans inured to war.—For an hour the fire of the small arms was as incessant and severe as can be imagined. The artillery, too, directed by officers who displayed equal skill and courage, did great execution. Yet the columns of the enemy continued to advance with a firmness which reflects upon them the greatest credit. Twice the column which approached me on my left was repulsed by the troops of general Carroll, those of general Coffee and a division of the Kentucky militia, and twice they formed again, and renewed the assault. At length, however, cut to pieces, they fled in confusion from the field, leaving it covered with their dead and wounded. The loss which the enemy sustained on this occasion cannot be estimated at less than 1500 in killed, wounded, and prisoners. Upwards of 300 have already been delivered over for burial; and my men are still engaged in picking them up within my lines, and carrying them to the point where the enemy are to receive them. This is in addition to the dead and wounded whom the enemy have been enabled to carry from the field during and since the action, and to those who have since died of the wounds they received. We have taken about 500 prisoners, upwards of 300 of whom are wounded, and a great part of them mortally. My loss has not exceeded, and I believe has not amounted, to 10 killed, and as many wounded. The entire destruction of the enemy's army was now inevitable, had it not been for an unfortunate occurrence, which at this moment took place on the other side of the river. Simultaneously with his advance upon my lines, he had thrown over in his boats a considerable force to the other side of the river. These having landed, were hardy enough to advance against the works of general Morgan; and, what is strange and difficult to account for, at the very moment when their entire discomfiture was looked for with a confidence approaching to certainty, the Kentucky reinforcements, in whom so much reliance had been placed, ingloriously fled, drawing after them, by their example, the remainder of the forces; and thus yielding to the enemy that most formidable position. The batteries which had rendered me, for many days, the most important service, though bravely defended, were, of course, now abandoned; not, however, until the guns had been spiked.

This unfortunate rout had totally changed the aspect of affairs. The enemy now occupied a position from which they might annoy us without hazard, and by means of which they might have been able to defeat, in a great measure, the effects of our success on this side the river. It became therefore an object of the first consequence to dislodge him as soon as possible. For this object, all the means in my power, which I could with any safety use, were immediately put in preparation. Perhaps, however, it was owing somewhat to another cause that I succeeded even beyond my expectations. In negociating the terms of a temporary suspension of hostilities, to enable the enemy to bury their dead, and provide for their wounded, I had required certain propositions to be acceded to as a basis, among which this was one—that, although hostilities should cease on *this* side the river until 12 o'clock of this day, yet it was not to be understood that they should cease on the *other* side; but that no reinforcements should be sent across by *either* army until the expiration of that day. His excellency major-general Lambert begged time to consider of those propositions until ten o'clock of to-day, and in the mean time re-crossed his troops. I need not tell you with how much eagerness I immediately regained possession of the position he had thus happily quitted.

The enemy having concentrated his forces, may again attempt to drive me from my position by storm. Whenever he does, I have no doubt my men will act with their usual firmness, and sustain a character now become dear to them.

I have the honor to be, &c.

ANDREW JACKSON.

No. 102.

From commodore Patterson to the American secretary of the navy.

Marine battery, five miles below New Orleans,
January 13, 1815.

SIR,

I have the honor to inform you, that during the 2d and 3d instant, I landed from the ship and mounted, as the former ones, on the banks of the river, four more 12-pounders, and erected a furnace for heating shot, to destroy a number of buildings which intervened between general Jackson's lines and the camp of the enemy, and occupied by him. On the evening of the 4th I succeeded in firing a number of them, and some rice stacks, by my hot shot, which the enemy attempted to extinguish, notwithstanding the heavy fire I kept up, but which at length compelled them to desist. On the 6th and 7th I erected another furnace, and mounted on the banks of the river two more 24-pounders, which had been brought up from the English Turn, by the exertions of colonel Caldwell, of the drafted militia of this state, and brought within, and mounted on the intrenchments on this side the river, one 12-pounder; in addition to which general Morgan, commanding the militia on this side, planted two brass 6-pound field-pieces in his lines, which were incomplete, having been commenced only on the 4th. These three pieces were the only cannon on the lines, all the others being mounted on the bank of the river, with a view to aid the right of general Jackson's lines on the opposite shore, and to flank the enemy, should they attempt to march up the road leading along the levee, or erect batteries on the same, of course could render no aid in defence of general Morgan's lines. My battery was manned in part from the crew of the ship, and in part by militia detailed for that service by general Morgan, as I had not seamen enough to fully man them.

During the greater part of the 7th, reconnoitred the enemy at Villeré's plantation, whose canal, I was informed, they were deepening and opening to the river, for the purpose of getting their launches in, which, upon examination with my glass, I found to be true, and informed general Jackson of my observations by letters, copies of which I enclose herewith; a reinforcement to general Morgan's militia was made in consequence, consisting of about 400 militia from Kentucky, very badly armed or equipped, the general not having arms to furnish them, who arrived on this side on the morning of the 8th, much fatigued. At 1 A. M. finding that the enemy had succeeded in launching their barges into the river, I despatched my aide de camp, Mr. R. D. Shepherd, to inform general Jackson of the circumstance, and that a very uncommon stir was observed in the enemy's camp and batteries on the banks of the river, and stating again the extreme weakness of this side the river, and urging a reinforcement. I would have immediately dropped down with the Louisiana upon their barges; but to do so I must have withdrawn all the men from the battery on shore, which I deemed of the greatest importance, and exposed the vessel to fire by hot shot from the enemy's batteries, mounting six long 18 pounders, which protected their barges; and at this time she had on board a large quantity of powder, for the supply of her own guns, and those on shore, most of which was above the surface of the water, consequently exposed to their hot shot.

General Morgan despatched the Kentuckians immediately on their arrival, about 5 A. M. to reinforce a party which had been sent out early on the night of the 7th, to watch and oppose the landing of the enemy, but who retreated after a few shot from the enemy within the lines, where they were immediately posted in their station on the extreme right. At daylight the enemy opened a heavy connonade upon general Jackson's lines and my battery, leading their troops under cover of their cannon to the assault of the lines, which they attempted on the right and left, but principally on the latter wing; they were met by a most tremendous and incessant fire of artillery and musketry, which compelled them to retreat with precipitation; leaving the ditch filled, and the field strewed with their dead and wounded. My battery was opened upon them, simultaneously with those from our lines, flanking the enemy both in his advance and retreat with round, grape, and canister, which must have proved extremely destructive, as in their haste and confusion to retreat they crowded the top of the levee, affording us a most advantageous opportunity for the use of grape and canister, which I used to the greatest advantage. While thus engaged with the enemy on the opposite shore, I was informed that they had effected their landing on this side, and were advancing to general Morgan's breast-work. I immediately ordered the officers in command of my guns to turn them in their embrazures, and point them to protect general Morgan's right wing, whose lines not extending to the swamp, and those weakly manned, I apprehended the enemy's outflanking him on that wing; which order was promptly executed by captain Henley and the officers stationed at the battery, under a heavy and well directed fire of shot and shells from the enemy on the opposite bank of the river. At this time the enemy's force had approached general Morgan's lines, under the cover of a shower of rockets, and charged in despite of the fire from the 12-pounder and field-pieces mounted on the lines as before stated; when in a few minutes I had the extreme mortification and chagrin to observe general Morgan's right wing, composed, as herein mentioned, of the Kentucky militia, commanded by major Davis, abandon their breast-work, and flying in a most shameful and dastardly manner, almost without a shot; which disgraceful example, after firing a few rounds, was soon followed by the whole of general Morgan's command, notwithstanding every exertion was made by him, his staff, and several officers of the city militia, to keep them to their posts. By the great exertions of those officers, a short stand was effected on the field, when a discharge of rockets from the enemy caused them again to retreat in such a manner that no efforts could stop them.

Finding myself thus abandoned by the force I relied upon to protect my battery, I was most reluctantly, and with inexpressible pain, after destroying my powder, and spiking my cannon, compelled to abandon them, having only 30 officers and seamen with me. A part of the militia were rallied at a saw-mill canal, about two miles above the lines from which they had fled, and there encamped. I ordered the Louisiana to be warped up for the purpose of procuring a supply of ammunition, and mounting other cannon, remaining myself to aid general Morgan. A large reinforcement of militia having been immediately despatched by general Jackson to this side, every arrangement was made by general Morgan to dislodge the enemy from his position, when he precipitately retreated, carrying with him the two field-pieces and a brass howitz, after having first set fire to the platforms and gun-carriages on my battery, two saw-mills, and the bridges between him and general Morgan's troops, and re-crossed the river, and secured his boats, by hauling them into his canal. On the 9th we re-occupied our former ground, and recovered all the cannon in my battery, which I immediately commenced drilling and re-mounting; and on the evening of the 10th had two 24-pounders mounted and ready for service, on the left flank of a new and more advantageous position. From the 10th to the present date I have been much engaged in mounting my 12-pounders along the breast-work erected by general Morgan on this new position, having three 24-pounders (with a furnace) to front the river, and flank general Jackson's lines on the opposite bank, from which we fired upon the enemy wherever he appeard. Our present position is now so strong that there is nothing to apprehend, should the enemy make another attempt on this side.

To captain Henley, who has been with me since the destruction of his schooner, and who was wounded on the 8th, I am much indebted for his aid on every occasion, and to the officers commanding the different guns in my battery, for their great exertions at all times, but particularly on the trying event of the 8th. The exertions of general Morgan, his staff, and several of the officers of the city militia, excited my highest respect, and I deem it my duty to say, that had the drafted and city militia been alone on that day, that I believe they would have done much better; but the flight of the Kentuckians paralized their exertions, and produced a retreat, which could not be checked. The two brass field-pieces, manned entirely by militia of the city, were admirably served, nor were they abandoned till deserted by their comrades, one of which was commanded by Mr. Hosmer, of captain Simpson's company, the other by a Frenchman, whose name I know not. The 12-pounder, under the direction of acting midshipman Philibert, was served till the last moment, did great execution, and is highly extolled by general Morgan. The force of the enemy on this side amounted to 1000 men, and, from the best authority I can obtain, their loss on this side, I have since learned, was 97 killed and wounded; among the latter is colonel Thornton, who commanded; of the former, five or six have been discovered buried, and lying upon the field; our loss was one man killed, and several wounded.

I have the honor to be, &c.

DANIEL T. PATTERSON.

No. 103.

Report of the killed, wounded, and missing, of the army under the command of major-general Andrew Jackson, in the action of the 8th of January, 1815.

Killed;—Artillery, navy, and volunteers at batteries, 3 privates; 7th United States' infantry, 1 serjeant, 1 corporal; general Coffee's brigade, 1 private; Carroll's division, 1 serjeant, 3 privates; Kentucky militia, 1 private; majors Lacoste's and Dacquin's volunteers of colour, 1 private; general Morgan's militia, 1 private.

Total killed—13.

Wounded;—Artillery, &c. 1 private; 7th United States' infantry, 1 private; general Carroll's division, 1 ensign, 1 serjeant, 6 privates; Kentucky militia, 1 adjutant, 1 corporal, and 10 privates; volunteers of colour, 1 ensign, 3 serjeants, 1 corporal, 3 privates; general Morgan's militia, 2 serjeants, 2 privates.

Total wounded—39.

Missing:—Kentucky militia, 4 privates; Mogan's militia, 15 privates.

Total—19.

Total killed, wounded, and missing, this day—71.

Note—Of the killed, wounded, and missing, on this day, but 6 killed, and 7 wounded, in the action on the east bank of the river, the residue in a sortie after the action, and in the action on the west bank.

Recapitulation.

Total killed, 55; wounded, 185; missing, 93: grand total, 333.

Truly reported from those on file in this office.

ROBERT BUTLER.

No. 104.

From major-general Jackson to the American secretary at war.

Camp, four miles below New Orleans,
January 19, 1815.

SIR,

Last night, at 12 o'clock, the enemy precipitately decamped and returned to his boats, leaving behind him, under medical attendance, 80 of his wounded, including two officers, 14 pieces of his heavy artillery, and a quantity of shot, having destroyed much of his powder. Such was the situation of the ground which he abandoned, and of that through which he retired, protected by canals, redoubts, entrenchments, and swamps on his right, and the river on his left, that I could not, without encountering a risk, which true policy did not seem to require or to authorize, attempt to annoy him much on his retreat. We took only eight prisoners.

Whether it is the purpose of the enemy to abandon the expedition altogether, or renew his efforts at some other point, I do not pretend to determine with positiveness. In my own mind, however, there is but little doubt that his last exertions have been made in this quarter, at any rate for the present season, and by the next I hope we shall be fully prepared for him. In this belief I am strengthened not only by the prodigious loss he has sustained at the position he has just quitted, but by the failure of his fleet to pass fort St. Philip.

His loss on this ground, since the debarkation of his troops, as stated by the last prisoners and deserters, and as confirmed by many additional circumstances, must have exceeded 4000; and was greater in the action of the 8th than was estimated, from the most correct data then in his possession, by the inspector-general, whose report has been forwarded to you. We succeeded, on the 8th, in getting from the enemy about 1000 stand of arms of various descriptions.

Since the action of the 8th, the enemy have been allowed very little respite—my artillery from both sides of the river being constantly employed till the night, and indeed until the hour of their retreat, in annoying them. No doubt they thought it quite time to quit a position in which so little rest could be found.

I am advised by major Overton, who commands at fort St. Philip, in a letter of the 18th, that the enemy having bombarded his fort for eight or nine days, from 13-inch mortars without effect, had on the morning of that day retired. I have little doubt that he would have been able to have sunk their vessels, had they attempted to run by.

Giving the proper weight to all these considerations, I believe you will not think me too sanguine in the belief that Louisiana is now clear of its enemy. I hope, however, I need not assure you, that wherever I command, such a belief shall never occasion any relaxation in the measures for resistance. I am but too sensible that the moment when the enemy is opposing us, is not the most proper to provide for them.

I have the honor to be, &c.

ANDREW JACKSON.

P. S. On the 10th our prisoners on shore were delivered to us, an exchange having been previously agreed to. Those who are on board the fleet will be delivered at Petit Coquille—after which I shall still have in my hands an excess of several hundred.

20th—Mr. Shields, purser in the navy, has to-day taken 54 prisoners; among them are four officers. A. J.

No. 105.

From Major-general Lambert to earl Bathurst.

His majesty's ship Tonnant, off Chandeleur's Island, January 28, 1815.

My Lord,

After maturely deliberating on the situation of this army, after the command had unfortunately devolved upon me, on the 8th instant, and duly considering what probability now remained of carrying on with success, on the same plan, an attack against New Orleans, it appeared to me that it ought not to be persisted in. I immediately communicated to vice-admiral sir A. Cochrane that I did not think it would be prudent to make any further attempt at present, and that I recommended re-embarking the army as soon as possible, with a view to carry into effect the other objects of the force employed upon this coast; from the 9th instant it was determined that the army should retreat, and I have the satisfaction of informing your lordship that it was effected on the night of the 18th instant, and ground was taken up on the morning of the 19th, on both sides of the bayou, or creek, which the troops had entered on their disembarkation, 14 miles from their position before the enemy's line, covering New Orleans, on the left bank of the Mississippi, and one mile from the entrance into Lac Borgue: the army remained in bivouac until the 27th instant, when the whole were re-embarked.

In stating the circumstances of this retreat to your lordship, I shall confidently trust that you will see that good order and discipline ever existed in this army, and that zeal for the service, and attention was ever conspicuous in officers of all ranks. Your lordship is already acquainted with the position the army occupied, its advanced post close up to the enemy's line, and the greater part of the army were exposed to the fire of his batteries, which was unremitting day and night since the 1st of January, when the position in advance was taken up; the retreat was effected without being harassed in any degree by the enemy; all the sick and wounded, (with the exception of 80 whom it was considered dangerous to remove,) field artillery, ammunition, hospital and other stores of every description, which had been landed on a very large scale, were brought away; and nothing fell into the enemy's hands, excepting six iron 18-pounders, mounted on sea-carriages, and two carronades which were in position on the left bank of the Mississippi; to bring them off at the moment the army was retiring was impossible, and to have done it previously would have exposed the whole force to any fire the enemy might have sent down the river.

These batteries were of course destroyed, and the guns rendered perfectly unserviceable; only four men were reported absent next morning, and these, I suppose, must have been left behind, and have fallen into the hands of the enemy; but when it is considered the troops were in perfect ignorance of the movement until a fixed hour during the night, that the battalions were drawn off in succession, and that the piquets did not move off till half past three o'clock in the morning, and that the whole had to retire through the most difficult new made road, cut in marshy ground, impassable for a horse, and where, in many places, the men could only go in single files, and that the absence of men might be accounted for in so many ways, it would be rather a matter of surprise the number was so few.

An exchange of prisoners has been effected with the enemy upon very fair terms, and their attention to the brave prisoners and wounded that have fallen into their hands has been kind and humane, I have every reason to believe.

However unsuccessful the termination of the late service the army and navy have been employed upon, has turned out, it would be injustice not to point out how much praise is due to their exertions, ever since the 13th of December, when the army began to move from the ships, the fatigue of disembarking and bringing up artillery and supplies from such a distance has been incessant, and I must add, that owing to the exertions of the navy, the army has never wanted provisions. The labor and fatigue of the seamen and soldiers were particularly conspicuous on the night of the 7th instant, when 50 boats were dragged through a canal into the Missis ippi, in which there were only 18 inches of water, and I am confident that vice-admiral sir Alexander Cochrane, who suggested the possibility of this operation, will be equally ready to admit this, as well as the hearty co-operation of the troops on all occasions.

From what has come under my own observation since I joined this army, and from official reports that have been made to me, I beg to call your lordship's attention to individuals, who from their station have rendered themselves peculiarly conspicuous: major Forrest, at the head of the quarter-master-general's department, I cannot say too much of; lieutenants Evans and Peddie, of the same, have been remarkable for their exertions and indefatigability: sir John Tylden, who has acted in the field as assistant adjutant-general with me, (lieutenant-colonel Stovin having been wounded on the 23d ult. though doing well, not as yet being permitted to take active service,) has been very useful; on the night of the 7th, previous to the attack, rear-admiral Malcolm reports the great assistance he received from him, in forwarding the boats into the

Mississippi. Captain Wood, of the 4th regiment, deputy assistant adjutant-general, has filled that situtation since the first disembarkation of the troops with zeal and attention.

During the action of the 8th instant the command of the 2d brigade devolved upon lieutenant-colonel Brooke, 4th regiment; that of the 3d upon colonel Hamilton, 5th West India regiment; and the reserve upon colonel Blakeney, royal fusileers; to all these officers I feel much indebted for their services. Lieutenant-colonel Dickson, royal artillery, has displayed his usual abilities and assiduity; he reports to me his general satisfaction of all the officers under his command, especially major Munro, senior officer of the royal artillery, previous to his arrival, and of the officers commanding companies.

Lieutenant-colonel Burgoyne, royal engineers, afforded me every assistance that could be expected from his known talents and experience; that service lost a very valuable and much esteemed officer in lieutenant Wright, who was killed when reconnoitring on the evening of the 31st ultimo.

Lieutenant-colonel Mein, of the 43d, and lieutenant-colonel Gubbins, 85th regiments, field-officers of the piquets on the 18th, have great credit for the manner in which they withdrew the out-posts on the morning of the 19th, under the direction of colonel Blakeney, royal fusileers.

I request, in a particular manner, to express how much this army is indebted to the attention and diligence of Mr. Robb, deputy inspector of hospitals; he met the embarrassments of crowded hospitals, and their immediate removal, with such excellent arrangements, that the wounded was all brought off with every favorable circumstance, except such cases as would have rendered their removal dangerous.

Captain sir Thomas Troubridge, royal navy, who commanded a battalion of seamen, and who was attached to act with the troops, rendered the greatest service by his exertions in whatever way they were required; colonel Dickson, royal artillery, particularly mentions how much he was indebted to him.

The conduct of the two squadrons of the 14th light dragoons, latterly under the command of lieutenant-colonel Baker, previously of major Mills, has been the admiration of every one, by the cheerfulness with which they have performed all descriptions of service. I must also mention the exertions of the royal staff corps under major Todd, so reported by the deputy quarter-master-general.

Permit me to add the obligations I am under to my personal staff, lieutenant the honorable Edward Curzon, of the royal navy, who was selected as naval aide de camp to the commanding officer of the troops on their first disembarkation, each of whom have expressed the satisfaction they had in his appointment, to which I confidently add my own.

Major Smith, of the 95th regiment, now as acting military secretary, is so well known for his zeal and talents, that I can with great truth say that I think he possesses every qualification to render him hereafter one of the brightest ornaments of his profession.

I cannot conclude without expressing how much indebted the army is to rear-admiral Malcolm, who had the immediate charge of landing and re-embarking the troops; he remained on shore to the last, and by his abilities and activity smoothed every difficulty. I have the honor to be, &c.

JOHN LAMBERT,

Right hon. earl Bathurst, &c. major-general command.

P. S. I regret to have to report, that during the night of the 25th, in very bad weather, a boat containing two officers, viz. lieutenant Brydges and cornet Hammond, with 37 of the 14th light dragoons, unfortunately fell into the hands of the enemy, off the mouth of the Regolets: I have not been able to ascertain correctly the particular circumstances.

No. 106.

Return of casualties between the 9th and 26th January, 1815.

43*d foot*:—1 rank and file, killed; 1 lieutenant, 1 serjeant, 2 rank and file, wounded.

85*th foot*:—1 rank and file, wounded.

Total—1 rank and file, killed; 1 lieutenant, 1 serjeant, 3 rank and file, wounded.

Officer wounded.

43*d foot*;—Lieutenant D'Arcy, severely (both legs amputated).

FRED. STOVIN,

lieut.-col. dep. adj.-gen.

No. 107.

From major Overton to major-general Jackson.

SIR, Fort St. Philip, January 19, 1815.

On the 1st of the present month, I received information that the enemy intended passing this fort, to co-operate with their land forces, in the subjugation of Louisiana, and the destruction of the city of New Orleans. To effect this with more facility, they were first with their heavy bomb-vessels to bombard this place into compliance. On the grounds of this information, I turned my attention to the security of my command: I erected small magazines in different parts of the garrison, that if one blew up I could resort to another; built covers for my men, to secure them from the explosion of the shells, and removed the combustible matter without the work. Early in the day of the 8th instant, I was advised of their approach, and on the 9th, at a quarter past 10 A. M. hove in sight two bomb-vessels, one sloop, one brig, and one schooner, they anchored two and a quarter miles below. At half past 11, and at half past 12, they advanced two barges, apparently for the purpose of sounding within one and a half mile of the fort; at this moment I ordered my water battery, under the command of lieutenant Cunningham, of the navy, to open upon them. Its well-directed shot caused a precipitate retreat. At half past three o'clock P. M. the enemy's bomb-vessels opened their fire from four sea-mortars, two of 13 inches, two of 10, and to my great mortification I found they were without the effective range of my shot, as many subsequent experiments proved; they continued their fire with little intermission during the 10th, 11th, 12th, 13th, 14th, 15th, 16th, and 17th. I occasionally opened my batteries on them with great vivacity, particularly when they showed a disposition to change their position. On the 17th in the evening, our heavy mortar was said to be in readiness. I ordered that excellent officer captain Wolstonecroft, of the artillerists, who previously had charge of it, to open a fire, which was done with great effect, as the enemy from that moment became disordered, and at day-light on the 18th commenced their retreat, after having thrown upwards of 1000 heavy shells, besides small shells, from howitzers, round shot, and grape, which he discharged from boats under cover of the night.

Our loss in this affair has been uncommonly small, owing entirely to the great pains that was taken by the different officers to keep their men under cover; as the enemy left scarcely 10 feet of this garrison untouched.

The officers and soldiers through this whole affair, although nine days and nights under arms in the different batteries, the consequent fatigue and loss of sleep, have manifested the greatest firmness and the most zealous warmth to be at the enemy. To distinguish individuals would be a delicate task, as merit was conspicuous every where. Lieutenant Cunningham, of the navy, who commanded my water battery, with his brave crew, evinced the most determined bravery and uncommon activity throughout; and, in fact, sir, the only thing to be regretted is, that the enemy was too timid to give us an opportunity of dstroying him.

I herewith enclose you a list of the killed and wounded.

I am, sir, very respectfully,

W. H. OVERTON.

No. 108.

A list of the killed and wounded during the bombardment of fort St. Philip, commencing on the 9th, and ending on the 18th of Janury, 1815.

Captain Woolstonecroft's artillery—Wounded, 3.
Captain Murry's artillery—Killed, 2; wounded, 1.
Captain Bronten's infantry—Wounded, 1.
Captain Wade's infantry—Wounded, 2.
Total killed, 2; wounded, 7.

No. 109.

From major-general Lambert to earl Bathurst.

Head-quarters, Isle Dauphine, Feb. 14, 1815.

MY LORD,

My despatch, dated January 29th, will have informed your lordship of the re-embarkation of this force, which was completed on the 30th; the weather came on so bad on that night, and continued so until the 5th of February, that no communication could be held with the ships at the inner anchorage, a distance of about 17 miles.

It being agreed between vice-admiral sir Alexander Cochrane and myself that operations should be carried towards Mobile, it was decided that a force should be sent against Fort-Bowyer, situated on the eastern point of the entrance of the bay, and from every information that could be obtained, it was considered a brigade would be sufficient for this object, with a respectable force of artillery. I ordered the 2d brigade, composed of the 4th, 21st, and 44th regiments, for this service, together with such means in the engineer and artillery departments as the chief and commanding officer of the royal artillery might think expedient. The remainder of the force had orders to disembark on Isle Dauphine, and encamp; and major-general Keane, whom I am truly happy to say has returned to his duty, superintended their arrangement.

The weather being favorable on the 7th for the landing to the eastward of Mobile point, the ships destined to move on that service sailed under the command of captain Ricketts, of the Vengeur, but did not arrive in sufficient time that evening to do more than determine the place of disembarkation, which was about three miles from Fort-Bowyer.

At day-light the next morning the troops got into the boats, and 600 men were landed under lieutenant-colonel Debbeig, of the 44th, without opposition, who immediately threw out the light companies under lieutenant Bennett, of the 4th regiment, to cover the landing of the brigade. Upon the whole being disembarked, a disposition was made to move on towards the fort, covered by the light companies. The enemy was not seen until about 1000 yards in front of their works; they gradually fell back, and no firing took place until the whole had retired into the fort, and our advance had pushed on nearly to within 300 yards. Having reconnoitred the forts with lieutenant-colonels Burgoyne and Dickson, we were decidedly of opinion, that the work was formidable only against an assault; that batteries being once established, it must speedily fall. Every exertion was made by the navy to land provisions, and the necessary equipment of the battering train and engineer stores. We broke ground on the night of the 8th, and advanced a firing party to within 100 yards of the fort during the night. The position of the batteries being decided upon the next day, they were ready to receive their guns on the night of the 10th, and on the morning of the 11th the fire of a battery of four 18-pounders on the left, and two 8-inch howitzers on the right, each about 100 yards distance, two 6-pounders, at about 300 yards, and eight small cohorns advantageously placed on the right, with intervals between of 100 and 200 yards, all furnished to keep up an incessant fire for two days, were prepared to open. Preparatory to commencing, I summoned the fort, allowing the commanding officer half an hour for dcision upon such terms as were proposed. Finding he was inclined to consider them, I prolonged the period, at his request, and at three o'clock the fort was given up to a British guard, and British colours hoisted; the terms being signed by major Smith, military secretary, and captain Ricketts, R. N. and finally approved of by the vice-admiral and myself, which I have the honor to enclose. I am happy to say our loss was not very great; and we are indebted for this, in a great measure, to the efficient means attached to this force. Had we been obliged to resort to any other mode of attack, the fall could not have been looked for under such favorable circumstances.

We have certain information of a force having been sent from Mobile, and disembarked about 12 miles off, in the night of the 10th, to attempt its relief; two schooners with provisions, and an intercepted letter, fell into our hands, taken by captain Price, R. N. stationed in the bay.

I cannot close this despatch without naming to your lordship again, lieutenant-colonel Dickson, royal artillery, and Burgoyne, royal engineers, who displayed their usual zeal and abilities; and lieutenant Bennett, of the 4th, who commanded the light companies, and pushed up close to the enemy's works.

Captain the honorable R. Spencer, R. N. who had been placed with a detachment of seamen under my orders, greatly facilitated the service in every way by his exertions.

From captain Ricketts, of the R. N. who was charged with the landing and the disposition of the naval force, I received every assistance. I have the honor to be, &c.

JOHN LAMBERT,

Right hon. earl Bathurst, &c. Major-general command.

No. 110.

Return of ordnance, ammunition, and stores, captured from the enemy in this place, on the 12th instant.

Fort-Bowyer, Feb. 14, 1815.

Guns.

1 24-pounder, 2 9-pounders, outside the fort.
Iron—3 32-pounders, 8 24-pounders, 6 12-pounders, 5 9-pounders.
Brass—1 4-pounder.
Mortar—1 8-inch.
Howitzer—1 5½ inch.

Shot.

32-pounder—856 round, 64 grape, 11 case.
24-pounder—851 round, 176 bar, 286 grape, 84 case.
12-pounder—535 round, 74 grape, 139 case.
9-pounder—781 round, 203 grape, 429 case.
6-pounder—15 round, 75 bar, 13 case.
4-pounder—251 round, 38 grape, 147 case.
Shells—25 8-inch 74 5½ inch.
183 hand-grenades.
5,519 pounds powder.
1 triangle gin, complete.
16,976 musket ball-cartridges.
500 flints.
551 muskets, complete, with accoutrements.

JAS. PERCIVAL, ass.-com. royal artil.
A. DICKSON, lieut.col. com. royal artil.

No. 111.

Return of casualties in the army under the command of major-general Lambert, employed before Fort-Bowyer, between the 8th and 12th of February, 1815.

Royal sappers, and miners;—1 rank and file, wounded.

4th foot;—8 rank and file, killed; 2 serjeants, 13 rank and file, wounded.

21st foot;—2 serjeants, 2 rank and file, killed; 1 rank and file, wounded.

40th foot;—1 rank and file, killed; 1 rank and file, wounded.

Total—13 killed; 18 wounded.

F. STOVEN, D. A. G,

No. 112.

Return of the American garrison of Fort-Boyer, which surrendered to the force under major-general Lambert, 11*th of February*, 1815.

1 field-officer, 3 captains, 10 subalterns, 2 staff, 16 serjeants, 16 drummers, 327 rank and file, 20 women, 16 children, 3 servants not soldiers.

F. STOVEN, D. A. G.

No. 113.

Articles of capitulation agreed upon between lieutenant-colonel Lawrence and major-general Lambert for the surrender of Fort-Bowyer, on the Mobile point, 11*th February*, 1815.

Art. I. That the fort shall be surrendered to the arms of his Britannic majesty in its existing state as to the works, ordnance, ammunition, and every species of military stores.

II. That the garrison shall be considered as prisoners of war, the troops marching out with their colours flying and drums beating, and ground their arms on the glacis—the officers retaining their swords, and the whole to be embarked in such ships as the British naval commander-in-chief shall appoint.

III. All private property to be respected.

IV. That a communication shall be made immediately of the same to the commanding officer of the 7th military district of the United States, and every endeavour made to effect an early exchange of prisoners.

V. That the garrison of the United States remain in the fort until twelve o'clock to-morrow, a British guard being put in possession of the inner gate at three o'clock to-day, the body of the guard remaining on the glacis, and that the British flag be hoisted at the same time—an officer of each service remaining at the head quarters of each commander until the fufilment of these articles.

H. C. SMITH, maj. and mil. sec.

Agreed on the part of the royal navy,

T. H. RICKETTS, capt. H.M.S. Vengeur.
R. CHAMBERLAIN, 2d reg. U. S. infantry.
WM. LAWRENCE, lt.-col. 2d inf'y com'g.

Approved,

A. COCHRANE, com.-in-chief H.M. shipp.
JOHN LAMBERT, major-gen. commanding.

Test,

JOHN REID, aide-de-camp.

No. 114.

Letter from lieutenant-colonel Lawrence to general Jackson.

Sir, Fort Bowyer, February 12, 1815.

Imperious necessity has compelled me to enter into articles of capitulation with major-general John Lambert, commanding his Britannic majesty's forces in front of Fort Bowyer, a copy of which I forward you for the purpose of effecting an immediate exchange of prisoners. Nothing but the want of provisions, and finding myself completely surrounded by thousands—batteries erected on the sand-mounds, which completely commanded the fort—and the enemy having advanced, by regular approaches, within 30 yards of the ditches, and the utter impossibility of getting any assistance or supplies, would have induced me to adopt this measure. Feeling confident, and it being the unanimous opinion of the officers, that we could not retain the post, and that the lives of many valuable officers and soldiers would have been uselessly sacrificed, I thought it most desirable to adopt this plan. A full and correct statement will be furnished you as early as possible.

Captain Chamberlin, who bears this to E. Livingston, Esq. will relate to him every particular, which will, I hope, be satisfactory. I am, with respect, &c.

W. LAWRENCE, lieut.-col. com.

No. 115.

From general Jackson to the American secretary at war, Head-quarters, 7th military district.

Sir, New Orleans, 24th February, 1815.

The flag-vessel which I sent to the enemy's fleet returned a few days ago, with assurances from admiral Cochrane, that the American prisoners taken in the gun-boats and sent to Jamaica, shall be returned as soon as practicable. The Nymphe has been despatched for them.

Through the same channel I received the sad intelligence of the surrender of Fort-Bowyer: this is an event which I little expected to happen, but after the most gallant resistance; that it should have taken place, without even a fire from the enemy's batteries, is as astonishing as it is mortifying.

In consequence of this unfortunate affair, an addition of 366 has been made to the list of American prisoners; to redeem these and the seamen, I have, in conformity with propositions held out by admiral Cochrane, forwarded to the mouth of the Mississippi upwards of 400 British prisoners; others will be sent, to complete the exchange, as soon as they arrive from Natchez, to which place I had found it expedient to order them.

Major Blue, who had been ordered by general Winchester to the relief of Fort-Bowyer, succeeded in carrying one of the enemy's piquets, consisting of 17, but was too late to effect the whole purpose for which he had been detached—the fort having capitulated twenty-four hours before his arrival. I learn from the bearer of my last despatches to the enemy's fleet, who was detained during the operations against Fort-Bowyer, that his loss on that occasion, by the fire from the garrison was between 20 and 40. I have the honor to be, &c.

A. JACKSON.

No. 116.

Treaty of Peace and Amity between his Britannic Majesty and the United States of America.

His Britannic Majesty and the United States of America, desirous of terminating the war which has unhappily subsisted between the two countries, and of restoring, upon principles of perfect reciprocity, peace, friendship, and good understanding between them, have, for that purpose, appointed their respective plenipotentiaries, that is to say: his Britannic majesty, on his part, has appointed the right honorable James lord Gambier, late admiral of the white, now admiral of the red squadron of his majesty's fleet, Henry Goulbourn, esq. member of the imperial parliament, and under secretary of state, and William Adams, esq. doctor of civil laws:—and the president of the United States, by and with the advice and consent of the senate thereof, has appointed John Quincy Adams, James A. Bayard, Henry Clay, Jonathan Russell, and Albert Gallatin, citizens of the United States, who, after a reciprocal communication of their respective full powers, have agreed upon the following articles:

Art. I.—There shall be a firm and universal peace between his Britannic majesty and the United States, and between their respective countries, territories, cities, towns, and people, of every degree, without exception of places or persons. All hostilities, both by sea and land, shall cease as soon as this treaty has been ratified by both parties, as hereinafter mentioned. All territories, places, and possessions whatsoever, taken from either party by the other, during the war, or which may be taken after the signing of this treaty, excepting only the islands hereinafter mentioned, shall be restored without delay, and without causing any destruction, or carrying away any of the artillery or other public property originally captured in the said forts or places, and which shall remain therein, upon the exchange of the ratifications of this treaty, or any slaves, or other private property. and all archives, records, deeds, and papers, either of a public nature, or belonging to private persons. which. in the course of the war, may have fallen into the hands of the officers of either party, shall be, as far as may be practicable, forthwith restored and delivered to the proper authorities and persons to whom they respectively belong. Such of the islands in the bay of Passamaquoddy as are claimed by both parties, shall remain in the possession of the party in whose occupation they may be at the time of the exchange of the ratifications of this treaty, until the decision respecting the title to the said islands shall have been made, in conformity with the fourth article of this treaty. No disposition made by this treaty, as to such possession of the islands and territories claimed by both parties, shall, in any manner whatever, be construed to affect the right of either.

Art. II.—Immediately after the ratification of this treaty by both parties, as hereinafter mentioned, orders shall be sent to the armies, squadrons, officers, subjects, and citizens of the two powers to cease from all hostilities: and to prevent all causes of complaint which might arise on account of the prizes which may be taken at sea after the ratifications of this treaty, it is reciprocally agreed, that all vessels and effects which may be taken after the space of twelve days from the said ratifications, upon all parts of the coast of North America, from the latitude of twenty-three degrees north, to the latitude of fifty degrees north, as far eastward in the Atlantic Ocean as the thirty-sixth degree of west longitude from the meridian of Greenwich, shall be restored on each side: that the time shall be thirty days in all other parts of the Atlantic ocean, north of the equinoxial line or equator, and the same time for the British and Irish channels, for the gulf of Mexico, and all parts of the West Indies: forty days for the North Seas, for the Baltic, and for all parts of the Mediterranean. Sixty days for the Atlantic ocean south of the equator as far as the latitude of the Cape of Good Hope: ninety days for every part of the world south of the equator: and one hundred and twenty days for all other parts of the world, without exception.

Art. III.—All prisoners of war taken on either side, as well by land as sea, shall be restored as soon as practicable after the ratification of this treaty, as hereinafter mentioned, on their paying the debts which they may have contracted during their captivity. The two contracting parties respectively engage to discharge, in specie, the advances which may have been made by the other, for the sustenance and maintenance of such prisoners.

Art. IV.—Whereas it was stipulated by the second article in the treaty of peace of one thousand seven hundred and eighty three, between his Britannic majesty and the United States of America, that the boundary of the United States should comprehend all islands within twenty leagues of any part of the shores of the United States, and lying between lines to be drawn due east from the points where the aforesaid boundaries between Nova-Scotia, on the one part, and East Florida on the other, shall respectively touch the bay of Fundy, and the Atlantic ocean, excepting such islands as now are, or heretofore have been within the limits of Nova-Scotia: and whereas the several islands in the bay of Passamaquoddy, which is part of the bay of Fundy, and the island of Grand Menan, in the said bay of Fundy, are claimed by the United States as being comprehended within their aforesaid boundaries, which said islands are claimed as belonging to his Britannic majesty, as having been at the time of, and previous to, the aforesaid treaty of one thousand seven hundred and eighty-three, within the limits of the province of Nova Scotia: in order, therefore, finally to decide upon these claims, it is agreed that they shall be referred to two commissioners, to be appointed in the following manner; viz. One commissioner shall be appointed by his Britannic majesty, and one by the president of the United States, by and with the advice and consent of the senate thereof, and the said two commissioners so appointed shall be sworn impartially to examine and decide upon the said claims, according to such evidence as shall be laid before them, on the part of his Britannic majesty and of the United States respectively. The said commissioners shall meet at St. Andrews, in the province of New Brunswick, and shall have power to adjourn to such other place or places as they shall think fit. The said commissioners shall, by a declaration or report under their hands and seals, decide to which of the two contracting parties the several islands aforesaid do respectively belong, in conformity with the true intent of the said treaty of peace of one thousand seven hundred and eighty-three. And if the said commissioners shall agree in their decision, both parties shall consider such decision as final and conclusive. It is further agreed, that in the event of the two commissioners differing upon all or any of the matters so referred to them, or in the event of both or either of the said commissioners refusing or declining, or wilfully omitting, to act as such, they shall make, jointly or separately, a report or reports, as well to the government of his Britannic majesty, as to that of the United States, stating in detail the points on which they differ, and the grounds upon which their respective opinions have been formed, or the grounds upon which they, or either of them, have so refused, declined, or omitted to act. And his Britannic majesty, and the government of the United States, hereby agree to refer the report or reports of the said commissioners, to some friendly sovereign or state, to be then named for that purpose, and who shall be requested to decide on the differences which may be stated in the said report or reports, or upon the report of one commissioner, together with the grounds upon which the other commissioner shall have refused, declined, or omitted to act, as the case may be. And if the commissioner so refusing, declining, or omitting to act, shall also wilfully omit to state the grounds upon which he has so done, in such manner that the said statement may be referred to such friendly sovereign or state, together with the report of such other commissioner, then such sovereign or state shall decide exparte upon the said report alone. And his Britannic majesty and the government of the United States engage to consider the decision of some friendly sovereign or state to be final and conclusive, on all the matters so referred,

Art. V.—Whereas neither that point of the high lands lying due north from the source of the river St. Croix, and designated in the former treaty of peace between the two powers as the north-west angle of Nova Scotia, nor the north-westernmost head of Connecticut river, has yet been ascertained; and whereas that part of the boundary line between the dominion of the two powers which extends from the source of the river St. Croix directly north to the above mentioned north-west angle of Nova Scotia, thence along the said high lands which divide those rivers that empty themselves into the river St. Lawrence from those which fall into the Atlantic ocean, to the north-westernmost head of Connecticut river, thence down along the middle of that river to the forty-fifth degree of north latitude: thence by a line due west on said latitude until it strikes the river Iroquois or Cataraguy, has not yet been surveyed: it is agreed, that for these several purposes, two commissioners shall be appointed, sworn, and authorized, to act exactly in the manner directed with respect to those mentioned in the next preceding article, unless otherwise specified in the present article. The said commissioners shall meet at St. Andrews, in the province of New Brunswick, and shall have power to adjourn to such other place or places as they shall think fit. The said commissioners shall have power to ascertain and determine the points above mentioned, in conformity with the provisions of the said treaty of peace of one thousand seven hundred and eighty-three, and shall cause the boundary aforesaid, from the source of the river St. Croix, to the river Iroquois or Cataraguy, to be surveyed and marked according to the said provisions. The said commissioners shall make a map of the said boundary, and annex it to a declaration under their hands and seals, certifying it to be the true map of the said boundary, and particularizing the latitude and longitude of the north-west angle of Nova Scotia, of the north-westernmost head of Connecticut river, and of such other points of the said boundary as they may deem proper. And both parties agree to consider such map and declaration as finally and conclusively fixing the said boundary. And in the event of the said two commissioners differing. or both, or either of them, refusing or declining, or wilfully omitting to act, such reports, declarations, or statements, shall be made by them, or either of them, and such reference to a friendly sovereign or state, shall be made, in all respects as in the latter part of the fourth article is contained, and in as full a manner as if the same was herein repeated.

Art. VI.—Whereas by the former treaty of peace, that portion of the boundary of the United States from the point where the forty-fifth degree of north latitude strikes the river Iroquois or Cataraguy to the lake Superior, was declared to be "along the middle of said river into lake Ontario, through the middle of said lake until it strikes the communication by water between that lake and lake Erie, thence along the middle of said communication into lake Erie, through the middle of said lake until it arrives at the water communication into the lake Huron, thence through the middle of said lake to the water communication between that lake and lake Superior." And whereas doubts have arisen what was the middle of said river, lakes, and water communications, and whether certain islands lying in the same were within the dominions of his Britannic majesty or of the United States: in order, therefore, finally to decide these doubts, they shall be referred to two commisioners, to be appointed, sworn, and authorized to act exactly in the manner directed with respect to those mentioned in the next preceding article, unless otherwise specified in this present article. The said commissioners shall meet, in the first instance, at Albany, in the state of New York, and shall have power to adjourn to such other place or places as they shall think fit. The said commissioners shall, by a report or declaration, under their hands and seals, designate the boundary through the said river, lakes, or water communications, and decide to which of the two contracting parties the several islands lying within the said river, lakes, and water communications, do respectively belong, in conformity with the true intent of the said treaty of one thousand seven hundred and eighty-three. And both parties agree to consider such designation and decision as final and conclusive. And in the event of the said two commissioners differing, or both, or either of them, refusing, declining, or wilfully omitting to act, such reports, declarations, or statements, shall be made by them, or either of them; and such reference to a friendly sovereign or state shall be made in all respects as in the lattter part of the fourth article is contained, and in as full a manner as if the same was herein repeated.

Art. VII.—It is further agreed that the said two last mentioned commissioners, after they shall have executed the duties assigned to them in the preceeding article, shall be, and they are hereby authorized, upon their oaths, impartially to fix and determine, according to the true intent of the said treaty of peace of one thousand seven hundred and eighty-three, that part of the boundary between the dominions of the two powers, which extends from the water communication between lake Huron and lake Superior, to the most north-western point of the lake of the Woods, to decide to which of the two parties the several islands lying in the lakes, water communications and rivers, forming the said boundary, do respectively belong, in conformity with the true intent of the said treaty of peace of one thousand seven hundred and eighty-three; and to cause such parts of the said boundary, as require it, to be surveyed and marked. The said commissioners shall, by a report or declaration under their hands and seals, designate the boundary line aforesaid, state their decisions on the points thus referred to them, and particularize the latitude and longitude of the most north-western point of the lake of the Woods, and of such other parts of the said boundary, as they may deem proper. And both parties agree to consider such designation and decision as final and conclusive. And, in the event of the said two commissioners differing, or both, or either of them, refusing, declining, or wilfully omitting to act, such reports, declarations, or statements, shall be made by them, or either of them, and such reference to a friendly sovereign or state, shall be made in all respects, as in the latter part of the fourth article is contained, and in as full a manner as if the same was herein repeated.

Art. VIII.—The several boards of two commissioners mentioned in the four preceding articles, shall respectively have power to appoint a secretary, and to employ such surveyors or other persons as they shall judge necessary. Duplicates of all their respective reports, declarations, statements, and decisions, and of their accounts, and of the journal of their proceedings, shall be delivered by them to the agents of his Britannic majesty, and to the agents of the United States, who may be respectively appointed and authorized to manage the business on behalf of their respective governments. The said commissioners shall be respectively paid in such manner as shall be agreed between the two contracting parties, such agreement being to be settled at the time of the exchange of the ratifications of this treaty; and all other expenses attending said commissioners shall be defrayed equally by the two parties. And, in case of death, sickness, resignation, or necessary absence, the place of every such commissioner respectively shall be supplied in the same manner as such commisssoner was first appointed, and the new commissioner shall take the same oath or affirmation, and do the same duties. It is further agreed between the two contracting parties, that in case any of the islands mentioned in any of the preceding articles, which were in the possession of one of the parties prior to the commencement of the present war between the countries, should, by the decision of any of the boards of commissioners aforesaid, or of the sovereign or state so referred to, as in the four next preceding articles contained, fall within the dominions of the other party, all grants of land made previous to the commencement of the war, by the party having had such possession, shall be as valid as if such island or islands had, by such decision or decisions, been adjudged to be within the dominions of the party having such possession.

Art. IX.—The United States of America engage to put an end, immediately after the ratification of the present treaty, to hostilities with all the tribes or nations of Indians, with whom they may be at war at the time of such ratification; and forthwith to restore to such tribes or nations, respectively, all the possessions, rights, and privileges, which they may have enjoyed or been entitled to in one thousand eight hundred and eleven, previous to such hostilities: Provided always, that such tribes or nations shall agree to desist from all hostilities against the United States of America, their citizens and subjects, upon the ratification of the present treaty being notified to such tribes or nations, and shall so desist accordingly. And his Britannic majesty engages, on his part, to put an end immediately after the ratification of the present treaty, to hostilities with all the tribes or nations of Indians with whom he may be at war at the time of such ratification, and forthwith to restore to such tribes or nations respectively, all the possessions, rights, and privileges, which they may have enjoyed, or been entitled to, in one thousand eight hundred and eleven, previous to such hostilities: Provided always, that such tribes or nations shall agree to desist from all hostilities against his Britannic majesty, and his subjects, upon the ratification of the present treaty being notified to such tribes or nations, and shall so desist accordingly.

Art. X.—Whereas the traffic in slaves is irreconcilable with the principles of humanity and justice, and whereas both his Britannic majesty and the United States are desirous of continuing their efforts to promote its entire abolition, it is hereby agreed that both the contracting parties shall use their best endeavors to accomplish so desirable an object.

Art. XI.—This treaty, when the same shall have been ratified on both sides, without alteration by either of the contracting parties and the ratifications mutually exchanged, shall be binding on both parties, and the ratifications shall be exchanged at Washington, in the space of four months from this day, or sooner, if practicable.

In faith whereof, we the respective plenipotentiaries, have signed this treaty, and have thereunto affixed our seals.

Done, in triplicate, at Ghent, the twenty-fourth day of December, one thousand eight hundred and fourteen.

GAMBIER,
HENRY GOULBOURN,
WILLIAM ADAMS,
JOHN QUINCY ADAMS,
J. A. BAYARD,
H. CLAY,
JONATHAN RUSSELL,
ALBERT GALLATIN.

Now, therefore, to the end that the said treaty of peace and amity may be observed with good faith, on the part of the United States, I, James Madison, president as aforesaid, have caused the premises to be made public: and I do hereby enjoin all persons bearing office, civil or military, within the United States, and all others, citizens or inhabitants thereof, or being within the same, faithfully to observe and fulfil the said treaty, and every clause and article thereof.

In testimony whereof I have caused the seal of the United States to be affixed to these presents, and signed the same with my hand.

Done at the city of Washington, this eighteenth day of February, in the year of our Lord one thousand eight hundred and fifteen, and of the sovereignty and independence of the United States the thirty-ninth.

JAMES MADISON.

By the president,
JAMES MONROE.

INDEX.

A.

B.

INDEX.

C.

INDEX.

D.

INDEX.

E.

F.

INDEX.

G.

H.

INDEX.

I.

INDEX.

K.

L.

INDEX.

M.

N.

O.

P.

INDEX.

Q.

R.

S.

INDEX.

T.

Y.

FINIS.

ERRATA.

Vol. I. p. 54,		last line, *after* II. *read* III. and IV.
———	303,	last line, *dele* and III.
———	344,	last 2 from bottom, *for* 175 *read* 304.
Vol. II.	292,	last line, *for* 4 *read* 5.
———	293,	line 1, *for* less *read* not many more.
———	347,	—— 2, *for* Lefourche *read* Lafourche.

Printed and bound by Antony Rowe Ltd, Eastboure

www.ingramcontent.com/pod-product-compliance
Ingram Content Group UK Ltd.
Pitfield, Milton Keynes, MK11 3LW, UK
UKHW032045260826
14628UKWH00008B/3192

9 781843 423508